Understanding International Relations

ALSO BY CHRIS BROWN

International Relations Theory: New Normative Approaches

Political Restructuring in Europe: Ethical Perspectives (ed.)

Texts in International Relations
(ed. with Terry Nardin and N. J. Rengger)

Understanding
International Relations

Second Edition

Chris Brown

palgrave

First edition 1997
Reprinted five times
Second edition 2001

Published 2001 by
PALGRAVE
Houndmills, Basingstoke, Hampshire RG21 6XS and
175 Fifth Avenue, New York, N. Y. 10010
Companies and representatives throughout the world

PALGRAVE is the new global academic imprint of
St. Martin's Press LLC Scholarly and Reference Division and
Palgrave Publishers Ltd (formerly Macmillan Press Ltd).

ISBN 0–333–94850–5 hardback
ISBN 0–333–94849–1 paperback

This book is printed on paper suitable for recycling and
made from fully managed and sustained forest sources.

A catalogue record for this book is available
from the British Library.

Library of Congress Cataloging-in-Publication Data
Brown, Chris, 1945–
    Understanding international relations / Chris Brown.—2nd ed.
        p. cm.
    Includes bibliographical references and index.
    ISBN 0–333–94850–5 (cloth) — ISBN 0–333–94849–1 (paper)
    1. International relations. I. Title.

    JZ1305 .B76 2001
    327—dc21
                                                    00–069907

10   9   8   7   6   5   4   3
10   09   08   07   06   05   04   03   02

Printed in Great Britain by
Creative Print & Design, Ebbw Vale

Contents

Preface to the Second Edition

For this second edition of *Understanding International Relations* I have preserved the basic order of presentation and structure of the book – although I have eliminated the rather unnecessary division into 'Parts'. All chapters have been revised and updated, and some more substantial changes have been made. The two chapters on general theory (2 and 3) have been reorganized and, in the case of 3, substantially rewritten; Chapter 2 is now a short history of international relations theory in the twentieth century, while Chapter 3 provides an overview of contemporary theory, giving due weight to 'constructivism' and other post-positivist movements. Chapter 9 has been substantially recast to acknowledge the importance of Gramscian international political economy.

The biggest changes come in the final two chapters, for two reasons. The first edition of this book was written in the mid-1990s, and was still influenced by a 'post-Cold War' mindset. This must now be abandoned; teachers of IR may still do a double-take when they see 'St Petersburg' on the Departures Board at Heathrow, but for our students the Cold War really is history. We need to stop thinking about the future of world politics in terms drawn from the ideological and strategic conflicts of the second half of the twentieth century. The second major change concerns the 'G' word – globalization. The first edition of *Understanding International Relations* treated the notion in passing and with scant respect; this was a mistake. It is important not to accept the more extreme claims made on behalf of globalization, but it requires a particular insensitivity to the way of the world to deny that there are changes going on in the world economy and in global society of such magnitude that we are required to rethink most of the categories with which we have been wont to interpret international relations. The final two chapters now reflect these two re-orientations – perhaps insufficiently, but a fuller account of the impact of globalization will have to wait for the third edition, if such there be.

I am grateful to all those who have suggested ways in which the first edition could be improved, and to the many scholars who pointed out errors therein – there were so many of the latter that I am inclined to think that any errors that remain are their fault. Steven Kennedy has been, as always, an exemplary and enthusiastic publisher. Tim Dunne has commented helpfully on early drafts of several chapters. Since writing the first edition, I have moved from the University of Southampton to the London School of Economics. Once again I have had the pleasure of teaching an introductory International Relations course, this time to what must be one of the keenest and best-prepared group of students in the country; my thanks to them, and I add IR100 (LSE) to the list of courses acknowledged in the Preface to the first edition.

London, 2000   CHRIS BROWN

Preface to the First Edition

This is a textbook, an introduction to the discipline of International Relations. The aim is to present within a relatively small compass an overview of the current state of International Relations theory. This book could be used as a text for undergraduate-level introductory courses, but it could also serve as a general introduction to theory for the increasing number of postgraduate students of the subject. It is sometimes assumed that postgraduates need a different literature from undergraduates; this seems to me not to be the case – good students at all levels need to have their minds engaged and stimulated, and this book is written on the assumption that all of its readers will have enquiring minds and be willing to put in the effort required to understand ideas that are sometimes quite complex.

There is sometimes an assumption that 'theory' is something that is suitable only for 'advanced' students, and that an introductory text ought not to be theoretically oriented. The fear is that students are not interested in theory, that they study International Relations with a practical orientation and become alienated if asked to think conceptually and abstractly, and, most damagingly, that students want to be told the 'right' answers and not to be exposed to the scandalous fact that authorities differ even on quite basic issues. These positions must be resisted. All understandings of International Relations and of the other social sciences are necessarily theoretical, the only issue is whether this is made explicit or not and most good students are well aware that this is so. The real danger is that by presenting International Relations Lite as a kind of a-theoretical discourse, 'current-affairs-with-a-twist', an adjunct to 'higher journalism', we alienate the brighter theorists amongst our students, and attract only those with a more empirical cast of mind. This is particularly galling because International Relations today is a theoretically sophisticated and challenging social science, the location of important debates on, for example, agency-structure, gender, identity, and the further reaches of postmodern and

post-structural thought. Fortunately, this is reflected in the large number of theoretically sophisticated, high quality research students in the
subject – what is interesting, and depressing, is how many of these
students have discovered the importance of International Relations
theory for themselves, and how few have come to the subject via an
undergraduate education in IR.

When theory is taught, it is often as an adjunct to practice; its
'relevance' is repeatedly stressed on the apparent principle that inviting
students to think abstractly is to place so onerous a burden on them
that they must be promised an immediate and tangible reward in
exchange for their efforts. On the contrary, I think the theory of
International Relations is a fascinating subject worthy of study in its
own right – fortunately it happens also to have considerable practical
relevance, but anyone who pursues the subject solely on that basis is
going to miss a lot of the story, and, incidentally, much of the fun.

The following chapters fall into four sections, of unequal size. In the
first part, Chapters 1 to 3, after an introductory chapter on the nature
of theory, the evolution of International Relations theory is presented;
post-1914–18 liberal internationalism, the contest between liberalism
and realism in the 1930s, the post-1945 realist synthesis, the debate on
method in the 1960s, pluralism and structuralism, and the current
orthodoxies of neorealism and neoliberalism along with their critics.
This history is necessary if we are to understand current thinking on
International Relations; it provides the student with a basic vocabulary
and grammar of the discipline, without which reading the current
literature will be impossible. For most of the history of the discipline,
the state has been the central focus for concern, and realism the most
important theory, and Chapters 4 to 6 examine the characteristic topics
of realist, 'state-centric' international relations: theories of the state,
foreign policy decision-making, agency-structure problems, power,
security, war and the balance of power. In the third part, Chapters 7
to 10, less state-centric accounts of the world are investigated: the
notion of 'global governance', the workings of the world economy
and its characteristic institutions, and North–South relations. Finally,
in Chapters 11 and 12, the impact of the ending of the Cold War on
International Relations theory is examined.

Although this may seem to offer a kind of progression of ideas, I
have tried to avoid presenting this material in such a way as to
suggest that the newer ideas are better because they are newer, or,
for that matter, to suggest that any body of theory is self-evidently
true or false. I have views on most of the subjects covered in this

book, and usually it will not be too difficult to work out what they are, but I assume that the role of the textbook author is not primarily to condemn or praise, My aim is to present as fairly as possible the arguments in question. Thus, for example, I would not seek to hide the fact that I am out of sympathy with neorealist theorizing in International Relations, and the conclusion I draw in a number of chapters would, indeed, make this impossible to hide, but I would be disappointed if neorealists were to feel that my presentation of their work was loaded against them. Neorealism is an intellectually rigorous and challenging set of ideas – as are the notions of 'rational choice' upon which nowadays it is based. It deserves to be treated very seriously indeed and I hope I have done so in what follows.

At various points in the text I have made reference to 'post-positivist' International Relations, in particular to work on postmodernism, gender, and critical theory. However, this is a book about theory, not about methodology or the philosophy of science, and, for the most part, the coverage of post-positivism will be limited to areas where post-positivists have actually contributed theory, as opposed to presenting promissory notes on what post-positivist theory might look like when it actually arrives. This means coverage of these topics is rather more patchy, and less enthusiastic than their adherents would approve of. However, compromises have to be made, and my own area of international political theory is also represented only at a few points. My aim is to give a critical account of the current 'state-of-the-art' of the discipline rather than to anticipate its shape in the next millennium – although, naturally, a few markers for the future will be laid down, especially in the final chapter. To deploy in defence of this project an analogy close to my heart, some of the masterpieces of twentieth-century music are certainly atonal, or serial, but it is impossible to develop any real appreciation of, say, Schoenberg's Op. 31 *Orchestral Variations*, or Berg's *Lulu*, without grasping the principles of *tonality* these great works defy. This book is about the International Relations equivalent of these latter principles, with some pointers as to how they might be overcome. In any event, there are many modern composers who persist with tonality to good effect ... but I digress.

References have been kept to a minimum to improve the readability of the text; however, a short guide to further reading is attached to each chapter. I have tried to provide a mixture of readings – old and new, books and articles; given the constraints on library budgets, a reference to an old, but still useful work may be more helpful than one to an up-to-date but unobtainable text. I have tried to provide both. A full bibliography is provided at the end of the book.

All textbooks are, one way or another, multi-authored. I have been studying International Relations for 31 years, and teaching the subject for 26; this has involved exchanging ideas with so many teachers, colleagues and students that I find it difficult to say where my own thinking begins and theirs ends. Listing all the people who have influenced my views on International Relations theory over the years would be impossible; if I single out the rather diverse group of Michael Banks, James Mayall, John Groom, Susan Strange and Steve Smith for special mention, it is in no spirit of disrespect to many others. I have had very helpful comments on this text from a number of anonymous readers for the publishers. Graham Smith has helped me to avoid making silly mistakes about the environment, but still disagrees with my position on that subject. Susan Stephenson assisted in the preparation of the index. Most of all, I have had the advantage of extensive commentaries from two of the best of the younger generation of International Relations theorists in Britain today; Molly Cochran of Bristol University read Parts I and II, and was particularly helpful in clarifying a number of presentational points; and Tim Dunne of the University of Wales, Aberystwyth, read the whole text, improved the argument throughout, and, in particular, forced me to rewrite Chapter 12. With the usual disclaimer that remaining errors of fact and interpretation are all mine, thanks to the above, to colleagues at the Universities of Kent and Southampton, to Steven Kennedy, and to the around 1500 students on S314 (Kent) and PO 105 (Southampton) who, over the years, have attended my lectures (or not) and, variously, nodded in agreement, stared out of the window, looked confused, or laughed – sometimes even in appropriate places – all the while keeping me entertained and in gainful employment.

Southampton, 1997   CHRIS BROWN

1
Introduction

Defining International Relations

This book is an introduction to the discipline of International Relations; 'International Relations' (upper case – here frequently shortened to IR) is the study of 'international relations' (lower case) – the use of upper and lower case in this way has become conventional and will be employed throughout this book – but what are 'international relations'? A survey of the field suggests that a number of different definitions are employed. For some, international relations means the *diplomatic–strategic* relations of *states*, and the characteristic focus of IR is on issues of war and peace, conflict and cooperation. Others see international relations as about *cross-border transactions* of all kinds, political, economic and social, and IR is as likely to study trade negotiations or the operation of non-state institutions such as Amnesty International as it is conventional peace talks or the workings of the United Nations. Again, and with increasing frequency in the twenty-first century, some focus on *globalization*, studying, for example, world communication, transport and financial systems, global business corporations and the putative emergence of a global society. These conceptions obviously bear some family resemblances, but, nonetheless, each has quite distinct features. Which definition we adopt will have real consequences for the rest of our study, and thus will be more than simply a matter of convenience.

The reason definitions matter in this way is because 'international relations' do not have some kind of essential existence in the real world of the sort that could define an academic discipline. Instead there is a continual interplay between the 'real world' and the world of knowledge. The latter is, of course, shaped by the former, but this is not simply a one-way relationship. How we understand and interpret the

1

world is partly dependent on how we define the world we are trying to understand and interpret. Since it is always likely to be the case that any definition we adopt will be controversial, this presents a problem that cannot be glossed over. Some of the difficulties we face here are shared by the social sciences as a whole, while others are specific to International Relations. The arguments are often not easy to grasp, but the student who understands what the problem is here will have gone a long way towards comprehending how the social sciences function and why IR theory is a such complex and difficult, but ultimately very rewarding, subject for study.

It is generally true of the social sciences that their subject-matter is not self-defining in the way that is often the case in the natural sciences. An example may help to make this clear. Consider a textbook entitled *Introductory Myrmecology*. This will, on page 1, define its terms by explaining that Myrmecology is the study of ants, which is unproblematic because we know what an 'ant' is. The classificatory scheme that produces the category 'ant' is well understood and more or less universally accepted by the relevant scientific community; anyone who tried to broaden that category in a dramatic way would not be taken seriously. There is a scientific consensus on the matter. Ants do not label themselves as such; the description 'ant' is given to them by scientists, but since everyone whose opinion counts is of one mind in this matter, we need have no worries about forgetting that this is so. We can, in effect, treat ants as though they did, indeed, define themselves as such. By contrast, there are virtually no areas of the social sciences where this kind of universal consensus can be relied upon to define a field. Perhaps the nearest equivalent is found in Economics, where the majority of economists do agree on the basics of what an 'economy' is and therefore what their discipline actually studies – however, it is noteworthy that even here in the social science which most forcefully asserts its claim to be a 'real' science, there are a number of dissidents who want to define their subject-matter in a different way from that approved of by the majority. These dissidents – 'political economists' for example, or 'Marxist economists' – are successfully marginalized by the majority, but they survive and continue to press their case in a way that somebody who tried to contest the definition of an ant would not.

In the case of most of the other social sciences, even the incomplete level of consensus achieved by the economists does not exist. Thus, for example, in Political Science the very nature of *politics* is heavily contested: is 'politics' something associated solely with government and the state? We often talk about university politics or student politics – is this a legitimate extension of the idea of politics? What of the politics of the family? Much Western political thinking rests on a distinction between the public realm and private life – but feminists and others have argued that 'the personal is the political'. This latter point illustrates a general feature of definitional problems in the social sciences – they are not politically innocent. The feminist critique of traditional definitions of politics is that their emphasis on public life hid from view the oppressions that took place (and still take place) behind closed doors in patriarchal institutions such as the traditional family, with its inequalities of power and a division of labour which disadvantages women. Such critiques make a more general point; conventional definitions in most of the social sciences tend to privilege an account of the world that reflects the interests of those who are dominant within a particular area. There are no politically neutral ways of describing 'politics' or 'economics' – although this does not mean that we cannot agree amongst ourselves to use a particular definition for the sake of convenience.

What does this tell us about how to go about defining international relations/International Relations? Two things. First, we have to accept that if we can find a definition it will be a matter of convention; there is no equivalent to an actual ant here – 'international relations' does not define the field of 'International Relations', rather scholars and practitioners of the subject provide the definition. Second, while it may make sense for us to start with the conventional, traditional definition of the subject, we should be aware that this definition is sure to embody a particular account of the field – and that the way it does this is unlikely to be politically neutral. Instead, what we can expect is a definition of the field which, while purporting to be objective – simply reflecting 'the way things are' – is actually going to be, perhaps unconsciously, partisan and contentious. It follows that having started with the conventional account, we will have to examine its hidden agenda before moving to alternative definitions, which, of course, will in turn have their own hidden agendas.

There can be little doubt that the conventional definition of the field is that given first in the opening paragraph of this chapter, namely that IR is the study of the relations of states, and that those relations are understood primarily in *diplomatic, military* and *strategic* terms – this is certainly the way in which diplomats, historians and most scholars of IR have defined the subject. The relevant unit is the *state* not the *nation*; most states may nowadays actually aspire to be nation-states, but it is the possession of statehood rather than nationhood that is central – indeed the term 'interstate' would be more accurate than 'international' were it not for the fact that this is the term used in the United States to describe relations between, say, California and Arizona. Thus the United Kingdom fits more easily into the conventional account of international relations than Scotland, or Canada than Quebec, even though Scotland and Quebec are more unambiguously 'nations' than either the United Kingdom or Canada. The distinguishing feature of the state is *sovereignty*. This is a difficult term, but at its root is the idea of legal autonomy. Sovereign states are sovereign because no higher body has the *right* to issue orders to them. In practice some states may have the *ability* to influence the behaviour of other states, but this influence is a matter of power not authority (see Chapter 5 below).

To put the matter differently, the conventional account of international relations stresses the fact that the relationship between states is one of *anarchy*. Anarchy in this context does not necessarily mean lawlessness and chaos; rather it means the absence of a formal system of government. There is in international relations no formal centre of authoritative decision-making such as exists, in principle at least, within the state. This is why a stress is placed traditionally on diplomacy and strategy; although the term 'international politics' is often used loosely in this context, international relations are not really political, because, again on the traditional account, politics is about authority and government and there is no international authority in the conventional sense of the term. Instead of looking to influence government to act on their behalf, the participants in international relations are obliged to look after their own interests and pursue them employing their own resources – we live in, as the jargon has it, a *self-help* system. Because it is a self-help system, *security*, is the overriding concern of states and *diplomacy*, the exercise of influence, exists in a context where force is, at the very least, a possibility. The possibility that force might be exercised is what makes the state – which actually possesses and disposes of armed force – the key international actor. Other bodies are secondary to the state, and the myriad of other activities that take place across state boundaries, economic, social, cultural and so on, are equally secondary to the diplomatic–strategic relations of states.

What is wrong with this *state-centric* (an ugly but useful piece of jargon) definition of the subject? Placed in context, nothing very much. There is indeed a world that works like this, in which diplomats and soldiers are the key actors, and there are parts of the world where it would be very unwise of any state not to be continually conscious of security issues – in the Middle Eastern 'Arc of Conflict', for example. Moreover, it is striking that even those states that feel most secure can find themselves suddenly engaged in military conflict for reasons that could not have been predicted in advance. Few predicted in January 1982 that Britain and Argentina would go to war over the Falklands/ Malvinas later that year, or, in January 1990, that an Iraqi invasion of Kuwait would lead to a major war in the Gulf in 1990–1, but it is the nature of the international system that it throws up this kind of surprise.

For all that, physical violence and overt conflict are nowhere near as central to international relations as the traditional description of the subject would suggest. Most countries, most of the time, live at peace with their neighbours and the world at large. Transactions take place across borders – movements of people, goods, money, information and ideas – in a peaceful, routine way. We take it for granted that a letter posted in Britain or Australia to Brazil, the United States or South Africa will be delivered. Using e-mail or fax, we can order a book or a CD from another country, confident that our credit cards will be honoured. A cursory examination of the nearest kitchen, wardrobe or hi-fi rack will reveal goods from all around the world. We plan our holidays abroad without more than a passing thought about the form-alities of border crossing. What is truly remarkable is that we no longer find all this remarkable – at least not within the countries of the advanced industrial world. These developments seem, at least on the surface, to be very positive, but there are other things that happen across borders nowadays that are less welcome, such as problems of pollution and environmental degradation, the drugs and arms trade and other forms of international crime – these factors pose threats to our security, although not in quite the same way as war and violent conflict.

What implication does this have for a description of the discipline of International Relations? There are several possibilities here. We might well decide to remain committed to a state-centric view of the discip-line, but abandon, or weaken, the assumption that the external policy of the state is dominated by questions of (physical) security. On this account, states remain the central actors in international relations. They control, or at least try to control, the borders over which transac-tions take place, and they claim, sometimes successfully, to regulate the international activities of their citizens. They issue passports and visas, make treaties with each other with the intention of managing trade flows and matters of copyright and crime, and set up international institutions in the hope of controlling world finance or preventing environmental disasters. In short, national diplomacy goes on much as in the traditional model but without the assumption that force and violence are its central concerns. Most of the time 'economic statecraft' is just as important as the traditional concerns of foreign-policy management – even if it tends to be conducted by the ministry responsible for Trade or Finance rather than External Affairs.

A problem with this account of the world of international relations is hinted at by the number of qualifications in the above paragraph. States do indeed try to do all these things but often they do not succeed. Too many of these cross-border activities are in the hands of private organizations such as international firms, or take place on terrains where it is notoriously difficult for states to act effectively, such as international capital markets. Often the resources possessed by non-state actors – non-governmental organizations (NGOs) – are greater than those of at least some of the states which are attempting to regulate them. Moreover, the institutions that states set up to help them manage this world of *complex interdependence* tend to develop a life of their own, so that bodies such as the International Monetary Fund (IMF) or the World Trade Organization (WTO) end up out of the control of even the strongest of the states that originally made them. Frequently, states are obliged to engage in a form of diplomacy with these actors, recognizing them as real players in the game rather than simply as instruments or as part of the stakes for which the game is played. For this reason, some think the focus of the discipline should be on cross-border transactions in general, and the ways in which states and non-state actors relate to each other. States may still be, much of the time, the dominant actors, but this is a pragmatic judgement rather than a matter of principle and, in any event, they must always acknowledge that on many issues other players are in the game. International relations is a complex, issue-sensitive affair in which the interdependence of states and societies is as striking a feature as their independence.

For a diplomat of the 1890s this would have seemed a very radical view of the world, but in fact it stands squarely on the shoulders of the older, traditional conception of the discipline; the underlying premise is that separate national societies are relating to each other just as they always have done, but on a wider range of issues. Other conceptions of international relations are genuinely more radical in their implications.

Theorists of *globalization* while still for the most part conscious of the continued importance of states, refuse to place them at the centre of things. Instead their focus is on global political, social and, especially, economic transactions and on the new technologies that have created the Internet, the twenty-four-hour stock market and an increasingly tightly integrated global system. Rather than beginning with national states and working towards the global, these writers start with the global and bring the state into play only when it is appropriate to do so.

In 1996 when the first edition of this book was written this seemed a touch premature, but such is the pace of change in the modern world that the central role of the state in both international relations and International Relations must certainly now be questioned. The more extreme advocates of globalization clearly overstate their case – the idea that we live in a 'borderless world' (Ohmae 1990) could hardly survive an acquaintance with, say, the Tijuana/San Diego border – but more careful analysts can no longer be dismissed by traditional scholars of IR. The more interesting issues nowadays revolve around the *politics* of globalization; are these new global trends reinforcing or undermining the existing divide in the world between rich and poor? Is globalization another name for global capitalism, or, perhaps, in the cultural realm, Americanization? One radical approach to International Relations – sometimes called *structuralism* or *centre–periphery analysis* – has always stressed the existence of global forces, a world structure in which dominant interests/classes largely – but not entirely – located in the advanced industrial world, dominate and exploit the rest of the world, using economic, political and military means to this end. From this neo-Marxist viewpoint, rather than a world of states and national societies we have a stratified global system in which class dominates class on the world stage and the conventional division of the world into national societies is the product of a kind of false consciousness which leads individuals who make up these allegedly-separate societies to think of themselves as having common interests thereby, as opposed to their real interests which reflect their class positions. Clearly this vision of the world has much in common with that of globalization, although many advocates of the latter have a more positive view of the process, but 'structuralist' ideas have also fed into the somewhat confused ideology of many of the new radical opponents of globalization who have made their presence felt at recent WTO meetings.

It ought by now to be clear why defining International Relations is a tricky business, and why no simple definition is, or could be, widely adopted. Each of the positions discussed above has a particular take on the world, each reflects a partial understanding of the world, and if any one of these positions were to be allowed to generate a definition of the field it would be placed in a privileged position which it had not earned. If, for example, a traditional definition of International Relations as the study of states, security and war is adopted then issues of complex interdependence and globalization are marginalized, and those who wish to focus on these approaches are made to seem unwilling to address the real agenda. And yet it is precisely the question of what *is* the real agenda that has not been addressed. On the principle that there must be some kind of limiting principle if we are to study anything at all, we might agree that International Relations is the study of cross-border transactions in general, and thus leave open the nature of these transactions, but even this will not really do, since it presumes the importance of political boundaries, which some radical theorists of globalization deny. Definition simply is not possible yet – in a sense, the whole of the rest of this book is an extended definition of international relations. However, before we can approach these matters of substance we must first address another contentious issue, namely the nature of 'theory' in International Relations.

Perspectives and Theories

This is a 'theoretical' introduction to International Relations; we have already seen the difficulty involved in defining the latter term – can we do any better with 'theory'? As always, there are simple and complicated definitions of theory, but on this occasion simple is best – unlike defining 'international relations' where simplicity is misleading. Theory, at its simplest, is reflective thought. We engage in theorizing when we think in depth and abstractly about something. Why should we do this? Simply because we sometimes find ourselves asking questions which we are not able to answer without reflection, without abstract thought. Sometimes the question we are posing is about how things work, or *why things happen*. Sometimes the question is about *what we should do*, either in the sense of what action is instrumental to bringing about a particular kind of result or in the sense of what action is morally right. Sometimes the question is about *what something or other means*, how it is to be interpreted. Different kinds of theory are engaged here, but the root idea is the same – we turn to theory when the answer to a question that is, for one reason or another, important to us is not clear; of course, sometimes when the answer is apparently clear it may be wrong, but we will not be aware of this until something happens to draw our attention to the possibility that a mistake has been made.

Most of the time things *are* clear – or at least it is convenient for us to live as though they were. There are many questions which we do not try to answer theoretically – although in principle we could – because we regard the answer as obvious, and life is too short to spend a great deal of time thinking in depth and abstractly about things that are obvious. Instead, very sensibly, we concentrate on questions where the answer is not obvious, or, better, seems to be actually counter-intuitive. To extend an example used in a brief discussion of the role of theory by the late Susan Strange, we tend not to waste too much time asking ourselves why people characteristically run out of a burning building (Strange 1988: 11). If we wanted to theorize this, we could; a theoretical explanation would refer to phenomena such as the effect of fire on human tissue and smoke on human lungs, the desire of humans to avoid pain and death, and so on. The point is that this is all pretty obvious and there is no need to make a meal of it. On the other hand, if we wish to explain why people might run *into* a burning building, some kind of theorizing may be necessary. Again the answer might be readily to hand – they may be members of a firefighting service who have contracted to do this sort of thing under certain circumstances – or it might not. It might be the case, for example, that the person running into the building was a private individual attempting a rescue. In such circumstances we might well wish to think in some depth about the circumstances under which one person would risk his or her life for another – asking ourselves how common this kind of altruism is, whether it is usually kin-related and so on. It is interesting that even this simple example is capable of generating a number of different kinds of theory – examples might include explanatory theory, normative theory, interpretative theory. However, rather than follow up this artificial example, it would be better to move to an example central to the discipline; an example of a difficult question which, Strange suggests, only slightly overstating her case, is the formative question for our discipline, namely: Why do states go to war with one another?

In the nineteenth century there was not a great deal of theorizing on the causes of war in general – as opposed to commentaries on particular wars – because most people thought that the causes of war, at least in the international system of that era, were obvious. States went to war for gain, or in self-defence because they were attacked by some other state acting for gain. A premise of the system was that wars were initiated by states that hoped to be the victors, and hoped to reap benefits in excess of potential losses. War was sometimes a rational choice for states, and a legitimate choice too, because a majority of international lawyers believed that the right to declare war without any external approval was inherent in the nature of sovereignty. Wars were what states did, sometimes successfully, sometimes not. The self-evidence of this interpretation seemed supported by the historical record of nineteenth-century wars – successful diplomatists such as Bismarck, and imperialists such as Rhodes, fought wars of conquest which did, indeed, seem to bring results.

Now, if war is initiated on the basis of a simple cost-benefit analysis, it follows that if potential costs rise disproportionately to potential benefits, then there should be fewer wars – indeed, there should be none at all if costs were to rise very steeply while benefits stayed steady or actually fell. In the early years of the twentieth century, it seemed that just such a transformation was taking place. For modern indus-trial societies the benefits from conquest seem trivial by comparison with the costs that war would bring – large-scale death and destruction made possible by new weapons, the collapse of an interdependent world economy, political instability and turmoil. This was a common-place of the early years of the century, well caught by a best-seller of the day, Norman Angell's *The Great Illusion* (Angell 1909). It seemed obvious that war would no longer be a profitable enterprise. More-over, these economic realities were reinforced by increasing moral disquiet over the idea that states had a right to go to war whenever they wanted to.

Then came 1914, and the greatest war the European system had seen for three hundred years inaugurated a century of warfare. Of course, Angell had been absolutely correct. War was indeed disastrous to its initiators and many others too. Millions died pointlessly, regimes fell, economic chaos prevailed, and the seeds of a new war were sown. How could something so obviously and predictably counter-productive hap-pen? Twentieth-century theorizing about international relations begins here. Something seemed to be wrong with the 'obvious' answer and early students of international relations felt the need to think more deeply about the causes of war in order to answer a question which previously was thought not to demand a great deal of theoretical consideration. Over this century a number of theories of the causes of war have been elaborated, ranging from the role of special interests, to the psychological profile of particular countries or leaders. At the end of the day it may be the case that such work actually vindicates the 'common sense' of the 1900s by showing, for example, that both sides believed themselves to be acting defensively rather than deliberately initiating a war – indeed, the dominance of rational choice theory in, especially American, political science today means that cost-benefit accounts of war are as privileged today as they were in the nineteenth century – but the point is that this is a conclusion based on theory (a version of the 'security dilemma' – see Chapter 5 below) rather than commonsense, even though it confirms the latter.

Remaining with this example, we can see that there are various kinds of theory, various different circumstances in which abstract reflection is required. There are *explanatory* theories which attempt to explain why, under what circumstances, wars happen, and *normative* or *prescriptive* theories, which try to tell us what our attitude to war ought to be – whether, for example, we should volunteer to participate in a conflict or conscientiously object to it; to this pairing we can add theories which *interpret* events, which attempt to give meaning to them – something that the carnage of the First World War seemed especially to require. In principle, these kinds of theory are interrelated – we cannot explain an occurrence without simultaneously interpreting it and orienting ourselves towards it – although, in practice, it may often be convenient for us to adopt the working practice of taking them in isolation.

As well as there being different kinds of theory, it is also the case that each kind of theory comes in a plurality of versions – there always seem to be different, competing accounts of why something happened, or what we should do or what it means. There is rarely one single answer. Authorities differ; each offers apparently compelling reasons why their account is right, but each offers a *different* set of compelling reasons. Some students of International Relations find this rather scandalous, largely because it contradicts what our society regards as the most important exemplar of theory, the model of the natural sciences. In subjects such as Physics and Biology, students have 'proper' textbooks which tell you what is right and what is wrong in no uncertain terms. Obviously, there are major debates within these subjects but these debates are conducted at a rarefied level – textbooks generally convey the consensus prevalent amongst those who are qualified to have an opinion. Out-of-date theories are simply not taught, and advanced controversies are reserved for the professionals. As we have seen even in as basic a matter as the definition of the subject, this is not true in International Relations. Authoritative figures dispute with one another in public in what seems to be a very undignified way, and no idea ever really dies – although some get close to the point where resuscitation is difficult.

Is this a matter for concern? Partly this will depend on why we have so many theories. It might be the case that we have many competing theories because none of them is actually very satisfactory. In the case, for example, of the causes of war, there are theories that lay stress on the personality characteristics of leaders, or on the political character-istics of regimes, or on the anarchical character of the international system. Each seems to explain some aspects of war but not others. We might well feel that we do not really want to have so many theories in this case, but that we cannot afford to discard any of them because we are not sure which (if any) is right. Since any reduction in the number of theories might actually eliminate the correct answer (assuming that there is one correct theory), we have to keep them all in play. We cannot simply kill off the wrong answer, because we do not know which *is* the wrong answer.

If this were the only way of looking at the multiplicity of theories and perspectives in International Relations, then the discipline would be in rather poor shape. However, it should be noted that even from this pessimistic account of the discipline it does not follow that there are no rules of discourse or that any argument is as good as any other. The various competing theories of the causes of war each have their own account of what a good argument looks like and the number of perspectives available although multiple is not infinite. There are some bad arguments and a plurality of theories does not cover all possib-ilities, or validate all positions.

However, and in any event, it is possible to put another, rather less depressing, colouring on the existence of a plurality of theories. It may simply be the case that International Relations is not the sort of academic discipline where we should expect or welcome consensus and the absence of competing accounts of the world. In the first place, in International Relations, as in other branches of Political Science, we are dealing with ideas and concepts which are 'essentially contestable' because they have political implications. As we have seen above, in the natural sciences it is often possible to 'stipulate' a defini-tion, that is, to employ a definition of a concept which will be accepted because it is clearly set out in advance. In politics this is much more difficult – some would say actually impossible. As we have seen, even the attempt to stipulate a definition of the subject-matter of the dis-cipline, international relations itself, runs into difficulties. If we attempt to stipulate a definition of a key concept such as *power* we run into even greater problems. We might describe power in operation along the lines of the popular formulation that 'A has power over B to the extent that A can get B to do what A wants B to do' and for certain purposes this might work, but we would be open to the objection that this does not cover, for example, structural power – the ability to shape issues in such a way that outcomes are restricted before they actually come to the point of decision. What is crucial here is that this is not simply an intellectual objection to this stipulated definition. It is also a political objection. The people, groups or classes who hold structural power in a society may well be different from the people, groups or classes who hold the kind of relational power envisaged in our definition, and by defining power in this way the power of the former group will be overlooked (to their considerable advantage).

This is a case in favour of pluralism in theory that applies to Political Science in general, but there is a further point that applies with particular force to the study of International Relations. One of the reasons why International Relations is an interesting field of study is because it attempts to produce theory on the widest canvas available to us – not simply a theory of politics in one country or continent, but a theory of global relations. This means any worthwhile theory of international relations is going to have to be able to work with a multiplicity of cultures, with the aim of providing an account of the world that is not ethnocentric. What this involves in practice is the ability to keep in play a number of competing conceptions of how things are. We have to understand that politics often seems very different in the Middle East to the way it seems in Western Europe or Latin America. Even within these broad cultures there are significant differences that block understanding.

It may be helpful to illustrate this point with a couple of examples; first, as we will see in Chapter 2, one of the formative diplomatic experiences of the century was the sequence of disasters that befell the international order in the run up to the Second World War. In fact, so formative were these calamities that, 60-odd years later, 'appeasement' is still a term of abuse, and new dictators are routinely compared to Hitler and Mussolini. How do we account for these disasters? Incompetence played a role, but it is also clear that a major factor was that the leaders of Britain and France thought that their view of the world was shared by all leaders, including Hitler, when in fact it was not. The most striking example of this phenomena is actually supplied by the Soviet Union under Stalin, because, as is often forgotten, in this case appeasement of Hitler continued long after the outbreak of war had demonstrated the failure of this strategy in the West. Why did Stalin think that appeasement would work for him when it had failed for Chamberlain?

The answer seems to be that Stalin believed National Socialist Germany to be a capitalist state, and, as a good Leninist, he believed that the behaviour of capitalist states was driven by material needs, in particular, at this time, the need for raw materials to pursue the war. Between mid-1939 and mid-1941 Stalin acted upon this belief, appeasing Hitler by helping him to pursue his war against Britain and France. He believed this would prevent Hitler from attacking the Soviet Union; since Hitler was getting what he really wanted from the USSR without war, to engage in war would be irrational, especially in the context of an unfinished war in the West. As perhaps 20 million Soviet citizens discovered, this perception was a mistake. Stalin's logic had been impeccable, but Hitler was marching to a different drum. Hitler's vision of the future was of the vast Eurasian plains populated by 'Aryans', which meant that the Slavs, Jews, and other alleged undesirables who currently lived there simply had to be 'eliminated' – killed or driven into Asia. Moreover, Hitler wished to achieve this himself, and since it seems he believed (correctly as it happens) that he was destined to die relatively young, he was not prepared to wait until the end of the war with Britain before undertaking the conquest of Russia. Stalin seems genuinely to have been unable to grasp that this bizarre and evil concoction of ideas could have been seriously held by Hitler; even after the start of Operation Barbarossa – the German invasion of the Soviet Union – Stalin initially instructed his troops not to resist, on the principle that this could not be a real invasion, but must be a 'provocation' (Weinberg 1994: 186–205). We should be wary of drawing too many conclusions from such an extreme example of miscalculation, but the basic point is that Stalin's theoretical account of the world led him badly astray because it was monolithic rather than pluralist. He was wedded to the idea that there was always *one* right answer, *one* right strategy; what let him down was his unwillingness to grasp that alternative conceptions of the world might be equally powerful in the minds of other decision-makers.

Rather less dramatic instances of the same basic problem can be found in contemporary international politics. Note, for example, the difficulties the United States experiences when dealing with third world nationalisms and what is misleadingly called 'Islamic fundamentalism'. Although the US has its own fundamentalist politics – visible, for example, in debates on abortion and capital punishment in America

– the dominant tendency in American political science is to approach policy issues via a utilitarian calculation of costs and benefits, and a great deal of American politics is about the trading of favours. This reflects the high level of at least elite consensus in the US: politics is about the distribution of benefits within a generally agreed framework ('who gets what, where and when' in one famous definition), and political values and mind-sets are shaped by this fact. The point is that such mind-sets are of little use when it comes to interpreting the politics of regions of the world where no such framework exists, where political conflicts are tied into competing accounts of the meaning of human existence, and where the stakes are, literally, life and death.

Thus, American decision-makers seem to find it difficult to understand why their attempts to be helpful in the world are so often misunderstood. From a rational point of view what they were trying to do in Somalia in 1993 by way of establishing the rule of law and undermining the power of the warlords was so obviously in the interests of the Somali people that the fact that the latter turned against US troops so comprehensively in October of that year seemed the height of irrationality. Again, back in the 1970s, the Shah of Persia was bringing 'development' to his people, pushing up living standards and resisting 'Godless' communism, albeit while running a somewhat repressive regime; the decision of the Iranian people to support the Islamic Revolution, a less economically successful and a more repressive and violent regime which, for all its religious fervour, was actually much closer to Moscow than to its co-religionists in the Middle East, seems incomprehensible on a cost-benefit basis. In each case, a basic lack of understanding for the other person's point of view leads to policy mistakes – the underlying and very misleading assumption is that everyone, everywhere – with the exception of a few 'extremists' – thinks about politics in the way that Americans do. And, interestingly, when this expectation is disappointed American policy itself can turn to irrationalism, as in the CIA's ludicrous attempt to undermine Fidel Castro's authority by causing his beard to fall out, or the equally bizarre attempt in the 1980s to establish good relations with the leaders of Iran by presents of Bibles and cakes – the assumption in these cases seems to be that if people don't think like middle Americans their powers of reasoning must be so limited that they will be impressed by such inappropriate symbols.

This is, of course, exaggerated, and rather unfairly because the argument holds with equal force in the other direction – the inability of apparently informed opinion in much of the rest of the world to

understand how the US works, an inability that leads to the characteristic picture of the US as the Great Satan of contemporary world
politics, is every bit as much based on inappropriate mind-sets as the
example quoted above. In any event, the general point holds – students
of International Relations would be well advised to try to avoid sub-
scribing to theories which close down debates and attempt to impose a
single view on the world. If we are to be successful theorists of IR, we
must resist the tendency to define success in terms of simple models;
instead we must be prepared to live with quite high levels of ambiguity.

On the face of it, this may seem to suggest that the study of International Relations is likely to be a frustrating business. On the contrary, the need for this kind of openness to ambiguity is a reflection of
both the importance and the intrinsic interest of the subject. As students of international relations we have a grandstand seat for some of
the most exciting developments of our age, both in the 'real world' and
in the social sciences. We are well placed to observe and comprehend
what is sure to be one of the key themes of the twenty-first century, the
working out of the clash between global social and economic forces on
the one hand, and local cultures and political jurisdictions on the other.
International Relations could be more than just an academic discourse; it could provide one of the most important languages for the
peoples of the world to use in order to come to some understanding of
what is happening to them. The danger is that this language will be
impoverished by too ready a willingness to close down debates and
reach premature conclusions, by too firm a commitment to one
particular way of looking at the world – especially since that way is
likely to be that of the advanced industrial countries, the rich and
powerful West.

Conclusion

The aim of this chapter has been to discourage the notion that the
theory of International Relations can be studied via an initial stipulat-
ive definition, the implications of which are then teased out and
examined at length. Instead, the process is, or should be, almost
exactly the other way around. What is required is that we explore the
world of international relations from a number of different perspectives, taking each one seriously while we are examining it, but refusing
to allow any one account to structure the whole, denying a privileged
position to any one theory or set of theories. If, at the end of the day,

we are still interested in definitions, we will then be in a position to construct one, and in so doing identify ourselves with a particular theory or paradigm. Perhaps instead, we will find that this kind of identification does not help, and we will resist the tendency to enrol in any particular theoretical army. Either way, this is a decision that ought to come at the end, rather than the beginning, of a course of intellectual study.

Still, it is necessary to start somewhere – and just as there are no innocent definitions, so there are no innocent starting-points. The approach adopted here will be to begin with the recent, twentieth-century history of theorizing of international relations and with the theories which have underpinned this history. This starting-point could be said to privilege a rather conventional conception of the field, but in order to introduce new ideas it is necessary to have some grasp of the tradition against which the new defines itself. In any event, the approach here will be to begin with traditional, 'common-sense' perspectives on international relations.

Further Reading

Full bibliographical details of works cited are contained in the main Bibliography after Chapter 12 (p. 266)

Readings for the different conceptions of international relations described above will be provided in detail in the separate chapters devoted to them in the rest of this book. For the moment, it may be helpful to identify a small number of texts which set out the relevant differences quite clearly. Robert Jackson and Georg Sorenson's recent *Introduction to International Relations* (1999) is excellent. Richard Little and Michael Smith (eds), *Perspectives on World Politics: A Reader* (1991) is still a good collection of essays organized around state-centric, transnationalist and structuralist approaches. Paul Viotti and Mark Kauppi, *International Relations Theory* (1993) is organized on similar lines, providing brief extracts from important authors as well as a very extensive commentary. Scott Burchill and Andrew Linklater (eds), *Theories of International Relations* (1996) is an excellent collection of original essays on each of the major theories. Michael Doyle, *Ways of War and Peace* (1997) is an outstanding general study. Of the big US textbooks, Charles Kegley and Eugene Wittkopf, *World Politics: Trend and Transformation* (1999) is the most sensitive to theoretical pluralism.

Books on globalization open to alternative conceptions of IR are led by David Held *et al.*, *Global Transformations* (1999) and Jan Aart Scholte, *Globalization* (2000). William C. Olson and A. J. R. Groom, *International Relations Then and Now*, (1992) gives an overview of the history of the discipline. In contrast, Steve Smith, Ken Booth and Marysia Zalewski (eds), *International Theory: Post-Positivist Perspectives* (1996) is a very rewarding but more difficult collection of essays celebrating the range of approaches current in the field, and particularly interesting on methodological and epistemological issues, as is Booth and Smith, *International Relations Theory Today* (1994). John MacMillan and Andrew Linklater (eds), *Boundaries in Question* (1995) is an accessible collection on similar lines. A. J. R. Groom and Margot Light (eds), *Contemporary International Relations: A Guide to Theory* (1994) is a collection of bibliographical essays on different approaches and sub-fields, invaluable for anyone wishing to get a sense of the scope of the discipline today. Although, like the latter, beginning to date, Llewellyn D. Howell (ed.), 'International Studies: The State of the Discipline' (1991/92) is another good survey of the field.

A basic introduction to the philosophy of the natural sciences is A. F. Chalmers, *What Is This Thing Called Science?* (1982). More advanced debates over 'paradigms' and 'research programmes' – of considerable relevance to the social sciences – can be followed in the essays collected in Imre Lakatos and Alan Musgrave (eds), *Criticism and the Growth of Knowledge* (1970). Martin Hollis, *The Philosophy of the Social Sciences* (1995) is a good introduction to its subject, but students of International Relations have the benefit of his *Explaining and Understanding in International Relations* (1991) co-authored with Steve Smith, which is, without doubt, the best survey of methodological and philosophical issues in the field.

The view that the social sciences can be studied in the same way as the natural sciences is often termed 'positivism', and positivists draw a sharp distinction between 'positive' and 'normative' theory – a classic statement of this position is by the economist Milton Friedman in his book *Essays in Positive Economics* (1966). A firm rebuttal of this distinction is offered by Mervyn Frost, *Ethics in International Relations* (1996), especially Chapter 2, while the more general position that most key concepts in politics are 'essentially contested' is put by William Connolly, *The Terms of Political Discourse* (1983). The essays in Smith, Booth and Zalewski (1996) and Booth and Smith (1994) (see above) are mostly anti-positivist in orientation, in stark contrast with the current, rational choice-oriented orthodoxy examined in Chapter 3 below; Michael Nicholson, *Causes and Consequences in International Relations: A Conceptual Survey* (1996) demonstrates that not all sophisticated positivists are realists. Chris Brown, *International Relations Theory: New Normative Approaches* (1992a) is a survey of normative theories of international relations; more up to date is Molly Cochran's *Normative Theory in International Relations* (2000); Mark Neufeld, *The Restructuring of International Relations Theory* (1995) is a good brief introduction to 'critical' international theory and Richard Wyn Jones's excellent *Security, Strategy and Critical Theory* (1999) has a wider range than its title would suggest. Jim George, *Discourses of Global Politics: A Critical (Re) Introduction to International Relations* (1994) covers so-called 'postmodern' approaches to the field: Jenny Edkins, *Poststructuralism and International Relations* (1999) is equally good, and more recent. A relatively accessible introduction to constructivism is Alexander Wendt, *Social Theory of International Politics* (1999).

Finally, for an interesting debate on the relationship between theory and practice, William Wallace, 'Truth and Power, Monks and Technocrats: Theory and Practice in International Relations' (1996), Ken Booth, 'A reply to Wallace' (1997) and Steve Smith, 'Power and Truth: A Reply to William Wallace' (1997).

2

The Development of International Relations Theory in the Twentieth Century

Introduction

Wherever different territorially-based political orders coexist in the same social world some form of international relations is to be found – even though the term itself was not coined until the end of the eighteenth century (Bentham 1789/1960: 426). The academic study of International Relations, on the other hand, existed only in embryo before the First World War. In the second half of the nineteenth century when the social sciences as we know them today began to be differentiated, when 'Economics' emerged out of Political Economy as an allegedly scientific field of study, and when 'Sociology' and 'Politics' and 'Social Theory' came to be seen as addressing different agendas – a position that would have surprised Jean-Jacques Rousseau, Adam Smith or Immanuel Kant – 'International Relations' remained unidentified as a discrete focus for study. Instead, what we nowadays think of as International Relations was for the most part seen as simply one facet of a number of other disciplines (History, International Law, Economics, Political Theory) – although, as Brian Schmidt has demonstrated, political scientists addressed the field rather more systematically than had previously been thought to be the case (Schmidt 1998).

Pace Schmidt, it was not until the slaughter of 1914–18 persuaded a number of influential thinkers and philanthropists that new ways of thinking about international relations were required that the field of IR emerged. These philanthropists saw it as essential to *theorize* international relations, to move our level of understanding of the subject above that provided by an education in 'current affairs', and in setting this goal they established a concern with theory that has dominated the new discipline – perhaps to its disadvantage – ever since. Certainly, IR has always been a theoretically conscious social science, although this is often denied by the purveyors of new learning, which is, it might well be argued, a little too concerned with its own history, a little too self-referential. It has become customary to write of the history of IR theory in terms of a series of rather grandly titled 'Great Debates' between meta-theoretical positions such as *realism* and *idealism*, or *positivism* and *constructivism*, but it is by no means clear that this is a helpful way of characterizing the past of the discipline – rather it may encourage a tendency to navel-gazing.

There is a broader issue here, which concerns the origins of IR theory. To simplify matters, has theory developed in response to events/changes in the real world (as has been the conventional belief), or is the process of theory development internal to the discourse, a product of the dynamics within a particular community, as revisionist disciplinary historians such as Schmidt suggest? Common sense suggests that both processes are involved. It is certainly the case that theories are never abandoned until a replacement is available, but, equally, it would go against the record to suggest that the international history of the twentieth century was not implicated in theory development – perhaps more to the point, the separation between a real world and a world of theory is, as Chapter 1 argued, a little artificial. In any event, in this and the next chapter the story of attempts to understand IR will be told with only a minimal number of references to the great debates, and the question of the origins of theory will be left open, with references made to both the above positions where appropriate; instead, in this chapter, an historical sketch of the conceptual development of the subject will be offered, while in the next the currently dominant approach and its main critics will be examined.

Liberal Internationalism and the Origins of the Discipline

The destruction on the battlefields of 1914–18 produced a sequence of reactions. The first response of many was to assign personal responsibility for the carnage – in Britain and France the Kaiser was widely blamed and 'Hang the Kaiser' became a popular cry, although after the war no serious attempt was made to reclaim him from his exile in the Netherlands. Even during the conflict, more thoughtful people quickly came to the conclusion that this was an inadequate response to the causes of war. While Germany might bear a greater responsibility than some other countries, there was something about the system of international relations that was culpable, and a variety of different thinkers, politicians and philanthropists gave thought as to how to change the system to prevent a recurrence. Most of these individuals were American or British (and, in fact, the discipline of International Relations remains to this day largely a product of the English-speaking world, although, happily, this may not be the case for much longer). The dominant mood in France was for revenge against Germany, while in Russia the Bolshevik Revolution of 1917 posed a challenge to the very idea of international relations – a challenge that will be reviewed later in this book. In Germany the ideas of British and American thinkers were eagerly adopted at the hour of her defeat, which led to widespread disillusion when these ideas were only imperfectly realized at the Versailles Peace Conference in 1919. Britain and America were the homes of the new thought, partly because these two countries were less devastated by the war than others, and thereby, perhaps, more willing to look beyond the immediate issues, but also because the anarchic nature of world politics seemed particularly unfortunate to those nurtured by the liberal traditions of the two English-speaking powers. Given this latter point, the new thinking that was produced in Britain and America is conveniently summarized as 'liberal internationalism' – the adaptation of broadly liberal political principles to the management of the international system.

In Britain, liberal internationalist ideas were developed by Fabians and radical liberals through bodies such as the Union for Democratic Control; although there was some sympathy for these ideas in the government of the day, the general Foreign Office line was a more traditionalist one. Their account of what went wrong in 1914 stressed the failure of diplomacy, and in particular the slowness of the great powers in mobilizing an international conference on the problems of the Balkans, rather than any systemic failure. However, if British liberal internationalism was largely unofficial, in the United States these ideas were espoused by the President himself, Woodrow Wilson, and set out in the Fourteen Points speech of January 1918, in which America's war aims were specified. Liberal internationalism offered a two-part diagnosis of what went wrong in 1914 and a corresponding two-part prescription for avoiding similar disasters in the future.

The first element of this diagnosis and prescription concerned *domestic politics*. A firm liberal belief was that the 'people' do not want war; war comes about because the people are led into it by militarists or autocrats, or because their legitimate aspirations to nationhood are blocked by undemocratic, multinational, imperial systems. An obvious answer here is to promote *democratic political systems*, that is, liberal-democratic, constitutional regimes, and the principle of *national self-determination*. The rationale here is that if all regimes were national and liberal-democratic, there would be no war.

This belief links to the second component of liberal internationalism, its critique of pre-1914 *international institutional structures*. The basic thesis here was that the anarchic pre-1914 system of international relations undermined the prospects for peace. Secret diplomacy led to an alliance system that committed nations to courses of action that had not been sanctioned by Parliaments or Assemblies (hence the title of the Union for Democratic Control). There was no mechanism in 1914 to prevent war, except for the 'balance of power' – a notion which was associated with unprincipled power-politics. What was deemed necessary was the establishment of new principles of international relations, such as 'open covenants openly arrived at', but, most of all, a new institutional structure for international relations – a *League of Nations*.

The aim of a League of Nations would be to provide the security that nations attempted, unsuccessfully, to find under the old, balance of power, system. The balance of power was based on private commitments of assistance made by specific parties; the League would provide public assurances of security backed by the collective will of all nations – hence the term 'collective security'. The basic principle would be 'one for all and all for one'. Each country would guarantee the security of every other country, and thus there would be no need for nations to resort to expedients such as military alliances or the balance of power. Law would replace war as the underlying principle of the system.

These two packages of reforms – to domestic and institutional structures – were liberal in two senses of the word. In political terms, they were liberal in so far as they embodied the belief that *constitutional government and the rule of law* were principles of universal applicability both to all domestic regimes and to the international system as such. But they were also liberal in a more philosophical sense, in so far as they relied quite heavily on the assumption of an underlying *harmony of real interests*. The basic premise of virtually all this thought was that although it might sometimes appear that there were circumstances where interests clashed, in fact, once the real interests of the people were made manifest it would be clear that such circumstances were the product of distortions introduced either by the malice of special interests, or by simple ignorance. Thus, although liberal internationalists could hardly deny that in 1914 war was popular with the people, they could, and did, deny that this popularity was based on a rational appraisal of the situation. On the liberal view, international politics are no more based on a 'zero-sum' game than are international economics; national interests are always reconcilable.

The liberal belief in a natural harmony of interests led as a matter of course to a belief in the value of education. Education was seen as a means of combating the ignorance that is the main cause of a failure to see interests as harmonious, and thereby can be found one of the origins of International Relations as an academic discipline. Thus, in Britain, philanthropists such as David Davies, founder of the Woodrow Wilson Chair of International Politics at University College Wales, Aberystwyth – the first such chair to be established in the world – and Montague Burton, whose eponymous chairs of International Relations are to be found at Oxford and the London School of Economics, believed that by promoting the study of international relations they would also be promoting the cause of peace. Systematic study of international relations would lead to increased support for international law and the League of Nations. Thus it was that liberal internationalism became the first orthodoxy of the new discipline – although, even then, by no means all scholars of International Relations subscribed to it – international historians, for example, were particularly sceptical.

The peace settlement of 1919 represented a partial embodiment of liberal internationalist thinking. The principle of national self-determination was promoted, but only in Europe – and even there it was rather too frequently abused when it was the rights of Germans or Hungarians that were in question. The Versailles Treaty was dictated to the Germans, rather than negotiated with them, even though the Kaiser had been overthrown at the end of the war and a liberal-democratic republic established in Germany. Germany was held responsible for the war and deemed liable to meet its costs; the allies very sensibly did not put a figure on this notional sum, hoping to decide the matter in a calmer atmosphere later, but the issue of German reparations was to be a running sore of the inter-war years. A League of Nations was established, incorporating the principle of collective security, but it was tied to the Versailles Treaty and thus associated with what the Germans regarded as an unjust status quo – a judgement soon shared by much liberal opinion after the publication of John Maynard Keynes's *The Economic Consequences of The Peace* which attacked the motives of the allies and portrayed the new Germany as the victim of outmoded thinking (Keynes 1919). The United States Senate refused to join the League as constituted by the Treaty, and, initially, neither Germany nor Russia were allowed to join. The unfortunate truth was that liberal internationalist ideas were not dominant in the minds of any statesmen other than Wilson, and Wilson – by then a sick man – was unable to sell these ideas to his fellow-countrymen, partly because he had allowed opposition leaders of the Senate no part in the negotiation of the peace. This was a mistake that Franklin Roosevelt learnt from and did not repeat a generation later.

For all that, the 1919 peace settlement was by no means as harsh as might have been expected, and in the 1920s it seemed quite plausible that the undoubted defects of Versailles would be corrected by the harmonious actions of the major powers. The Locarno Treaties of 1926 symbolically confirmed the western borders of Germany, and, more importantly, re-established more-or-less amicable relationships between the leading powers, a process helped by changes of personnel at the top. Gustav Stresemann in Germany, Aristide Briand in France, and Austen Chamberlain (followed by Arthur Henderson) in Britain seemed committed to peaceful solutions to Europe's problems. A symbolic high tide was reached at the Treaty of Paris in 1928 – the so-called Kellogg–Briand Pact, in which a proposal to mark 150 years of US–French friendship by the signature of a non-aggression pact somehow became transformed into a general treaty to abolish war, thereby closing the legal loopholes that the sharp-eyed found in the Covenant of the League of Nations. Virtually all countries signed this Treaty – albeit usually with legal reservations – which, a cynic might remark, is one of the reasons why virtually all wars started since 1928 have been wars of 'self-defence'.

In short, as the 1930s dawned it seemed at least possible that a new and better system of international relations might be emerging. As no one needs to be told, this possibility did not materialize: the 1930s saw economic collapse, the rise of the dictators, a series of acts of aggression in Asia, Africa and Europe, an inability of the League powers led by Britain and France to develop a coherent policy in response to these events, and, finally, the global war that the peace settlement of 1919 had been designed to prevent. Clearly these events were catastrophic in the 'real world' but they were equally damaging in the world of ideas. Indeed, the two worlds, as always, were interwoven together – it was the inability of decision-makers and intellectuals to think sensibly about these events which, at least in part, explained their inability to produce effective policy. The apparent inability of liberal internationalists to cope with these events suggested the need for a new conceptual apparatus, or perhaps for the rediscovery of some older ideas.

The 'Realist' Critique of Liberal Internationalism

Returning to the root ideas of liberal internationalism, it is easy to identify the problems this approach faced in the 1930s. In 1919 liberal internationalists believed that 'the people' have a real interest in and desire for peace and that democratic regimes would, if given the chance, allow these interests and desires to dominate. The enemy of peace, on this account, was the kind of militarist, authoritarian, autocratic, anti-democratic regime which had, allegedly, dominated Germany, Austria–Hungary and Russia in 1914. Now, some of the crises of the 1930s were caused by this kind of regime – Japanese militarism in Manchuria and China and 'Francoism' in the Spanish Civil War fit the bill quite well – but most were not. Hitler's Germany and Mussolini's Italy were not traditional military autocracies; rather, they were regimes which had come to power by quasi-democratic means and remained in power by the mobilization of popular support. There were no elections in Germany after 1933, but what evidence exists suggests that the National Socialists had clear majority support well into the war, perhaps even to its very end.

Moreover, these regimes, although popularly supported, actually glorified war. The rhetoric of fascism and national socialism stressed the virtues of armed struggle and its importance in building the nation. And, of course, the stated ends of these regimes – turning the Mediterranean into an Italian lake, depopulating Eastern Europe of Slavs, Jews and other alleged inferiors and repopulating it with 'Aryans' – could not be achieved by any means other than war. Although Hitler still maintained in his public orations that he was forced to resort to force by the obstinate and malicious behaviour of the enemies of the *Volk*, it was quite clear that this was nonsense – unless a reluctance to commit suicide be deemed a sign of obstinacy. The fact that Nazism remained a popular force in spite of this posture – perhaps, in some cases, because of it – dealt a terrible blow to liberal thinking.

The consequences of this blow were felt in particular with respect to support for the League of Nations and the rule of law. The basic premise of liberal internationalism was that the force of world opinion would buttress the League of Nations and that no state would be able to act against this force. The point of collective security under the League was to prevent wars not to fight them. The League's cumbersome procedures would act as a brake to prevent a nation that had, as it were, temporarily taken leave of its senses from acting rashly – international disputes would be solved peacefully because that was what the people *really* wanted. The behaviour of Hitler and Mussolini made it clear that, in this context at least, these ideas were simply wrong. The liberal internationalist slogan was 'law not war' – but it became clear as the 1930s progressed, that the only way in which 'law' could be maintained was *by* 'war'.

An inability to understand this basic point bedevilled liberal thought in the 1930s. Well-meaning people simultaneously pledged full support for the League *and* never again to fight a war, without any apparent awareness that the second pledge undermined the first. When the British and French governments attempted to resolve the crisis caused by Italy's invasion of Ethiopia by the Hoare–Laval Pact which was seen as rewarding the aggressor, public opinion was outraged, Hoare was forced to resign, and the last real chance to prevent Mussolini from falling under Hitler's influence was lost. The public wanted the League to act, but the British government held, almost certainly correctly, that the public would not support a war, and therefore ensured that the sanctions that were introduced would not bring Italy to its knees. The 'appeasement' policy of Britain and France (and, as is often forgotten, of the United States and the USSR) posed a real dilemma for many liberal internationalists. They did not know whether to praise figures like Chamberlain for avoiding war, or condemn them for condoning breaches of international legality and betraying the weak. Usually they resolved this dilemma by doing both.

What this seemed to suggest to many was that there were flaws in the root ideas of liberal internationalism, its account of how the world worked, and, in particular, its account of the mainsprings of human conduct. Gradually, new ideas emerged – or, perhaps more accurately, re-emerged, since many of them would have been familiar to pre-1914 thinkers. Perhaps the deepest thinker on these matters in the 1930s was the radical American theologian and critic Reinhold Niebuhr. Niebuhr's message is conveyed in shorthand in the title of his 1932 book, *Moral Man and Immoral Society*; his point was that liberals wildly exaggerated the capacity of collectivities of humans to behave in ways that were truly moral (Niebuhr 1932). Niebuhr held that 'men' had the capacity to be good, but that this capacity was always in conflict with the sinful acquisitive and aggressive drives that are also present in human nature. These drives are given full scope in society and it is unrealistic to think that they can be harnessed to the goal of international peace and understanding in bodies such as the League of Nations.

These are powerful ideas which resonate later, but the intense Christian spirit with which they are infused – and the pacifism to which, initially at least, they gave rise in Niebuhr – limited their influence in the 1930s. Instead, the most influential critique of liberal internationalism came from a very different source, E. H. Carr, the quasi-Marxist historian, journalist and, in the late 1930s, Woodrow Wilson Professor of International Politics. Carr produced a number of studies in the 1930s, the most famous of which was published in 1939 – *The Twenty Years Crisis* (Carr 1939). This book performed the crucial task of providing a new vocabulary for International Relations theory. Liberal internationalism is renamed 'utopianism' (later writers sometimes use 'idealism') and contrasted with Carr's approach which is termed 'realism'. Carr's central point is that the liberal doctrine of the harmony of interests glosses over the real conflict that is to be found in international relations, which is between the 'haves' and the 'have-nots'. A central feature of the world is scarcity – there are not enough of the good things of life to go around. Those who have them want to keep them, and therefore promote 'law and order' policies, attempting to outlaw the use of violence. The 'have-nots', on the other hand, have no such respect for the law, nor is it reasonable that they should, because it is the law that keeps them where they are, which is under the thumb of the 'haves'.

Politics has to be based on an understanding of this situation. It is utopian to suggest that the have-nots can be brought to realize that they ought to behave legally and morally. It is realistic to recognize that the essential conflict between haves and have-nots must be managed rather than wished away. It is utopian to imagine that international bodies such as the League of Nations can have real power. Realists work with the world as it really is, utopians as they wish it to be. In fact, as Ken Booth has demonstrated, Carr wished to preserve some element of utopian thought, but, nonetheless, realism was his dominant mode (Booth 1991b). The power of words here is very great – the way in which 'realism', a political doctrine which might be right or wrong, becomes associated with 'realistic', which is a quality of judgement most people want to possess, is critically important in its success.

Carr's position reveals its quasi-Marxist origins, and its debt to Mannheim's sociology of knowledge, in its stress on material scarcity and its insistence that law and morality serve the interests of dominant groups (Mannheim 1936/1960). On the other hand, the fact that the 'have-nots' of the 1930s were, on his account, Hitler's Germany and Mussolini's Italy suggests that Carr's Marxism was laced with a degree of power-worship – an impression also conveyed by his monumental *History of the USSR*, which is often regarded as being rather too generous in its judgement of Stalin. The first edition of *The Twenty Years Crisis* contained favourable judgements of appeasement that Carr thought prudent to tone down in the second edition (Fox 1985). Nonetheless, Carr made a number of effective points. It was indeed the case that the League of Nations and the idea of collective security was tied up with the peace settlement of 1919 and therefore could be seen as defending the status quo. Equally, the leading status-quo nations, Britain and France, had not built up their position in the world by strict adherence to the rule of law, however much the British might wish to tell themselves that they had acquired their empire in a fit of absentmindedness. But, above all, it was the policy failure of liberal internationalism as outlined above which gave Carr's ideas such salience and credence. As is often the way, a new theory is called into being by the failure of an old theory.

In any event, realism seemed to offer a more coherent and accurate account of the world than the liberal ideas it critiqued, and it formed the basis for the 'post-war synthesis' which is the subject of the next section of this chapter. However, before leaving the original version of liberal internationalism behind, there are a few general points that can be made. First, it is becoming clear that the liberal account of the origins of the First World War was faulty at a number of points, two of which still have considerable significance. The modern historiography of the origins of the war suggests that the gut feeling of Allied public opinion at the time (that Germany started the war as a deliberate act of policy) was rather more to the point than the more refined view of liberal intellectuals to the effect that no one was to blame. Of greater significance is the second point, which is that Germany in 1914 was not the militarist autocracy that some liberals took it to be. In reality, it was a constitutional state, governed by the rule of law, and with a government which was responsible to parliament as well as to the Emperor. Certainly, it was not a 'democracy' – but then no country was in 1914; even the widest franchises (in the United States and France) excluded women from the vote. What this suggested was that the liberal view that constitutional, liberal-democratic regimes are less likely to engage in war than other types of regime required a great deal of refinement.

A second point that is worth making here is that some of the criticisms of liberal internationalism – including some made above – take too little notice of the unique quality of the threat posed to international order in the 1930s. To put the matter bluntly, we must hope that it was rather unusual for the leaders of two of the most powerful countries in the world – Germany and the USSR – to be certifiable madmen. The lunatic nature of Hitler's plans to replant the world with true Aryans makes him an exceptional character to be a leader of any kind of state, let alone a Great Power – it is this latter point which makes comparison with figures such as Saddam Hussein misleading. The Munich analogy has been applied repeatedly since 1945, and 'appeaser' is still one of the worst insults that can be thrown at a diplomat, but all the dictators the world has thrown up since then – Nasser, Castro, Hussein – have been mere shadows of the real thing, not so much because of their personalities but because of their lack of access to the sinews of world power. Judging a set of ideas by their capacity to cope with a Hitler or a Stalin seems to set far too high a standard.

In a similar vein, it is striking how much of liberal internationalism has survived its defeat at the hands of realism. The 'settled norms' of the contemporary international order are still essentially those of 1919 – national self-determination, non-aggression and respect for international law combined with support for the principles of sovereignty. The United Nations is, in effect, a revision of the League of Nations, even if it was convenient to gloss over this in 1945. Liberal internationalism is, without doubt, an incoherent and flawed doctrine and we are still attempting to cope with its contradictions – in particular its belief that nationalism and democracy are compatible notions – but it is, nonetheless, a remarkably resilient doctrine, possibly because the values it represents seem to be widely shared by the peoples of the world.

The Post-War Synthesis

After 1945, realism became the dominant theory of International Relations, offering a conception of the world which seemed to define the 'common sense' of the subject. Most practising diplomats had always held views on international relations which were more or less realist; they were now joined by academics, as the discipline of International Relations expanded on broadly realist lines, and by opinion-makers more generally, as the leader writers and columnists of influential newspapers and journals came increasingly to work from the same general perspective. To a striking extent, realism remains to this day the dominant theory of International Relations. Most of the rest of this book will be an account of the struggles between realism and its critics, and if the latter have been increasingly effective over the years, it is difficult to deny the fact that realism still, in one form or another, provides the dominant mode of discourse in the discipline. Paradoxically, this dominance explains why this section on the realist post-war synthesis can be quite brief, while there are interesting things to be said about this period, most of the substantive theories developed in these years remain current and will be discussed in later chapters.

Although Carr remained influential, the post-war dominance of realism owed more to the work of other writers – Carr himself was switching his attention at this time, from International Relations towards Soviet history. In Britain, Martin Wight was an important figure, although his Chatham House pamphlet on *Power Politics* (1946/1978) is, despite its title, only dubiously realist in inspiration. In the United States, Niebuhr remained influential, as did the geopolitician Nicholas Spykman (Spykman 1942) and the diplomat George Kennan (Kennan 1952). However, the key realist of the period was Hans J. Morgenthau, a German-Jewish émigré to the United States in the 1930s who published a series of books in the 1940s and 1950s, the most influential of which was *Politics Among Nations: The Struggle for Power and Peace*, a book which was to become the standard textbook on International Relations for a generation or more (Morgenthau 1948).

There were two major differences between Morgenthau and Carr. In the first place, Morgenthau, influenced partly by figures such as Niebuhr, partly by his own experiences in the 1930s, saw the mainspring of realism as lying not in scarcity, a product of the human *condition*, but in sin, a product of human *nature*. The aggressive, power-seeking nature of states stems from the imperfect human material of which they are constructed. It could well be argued that this shift was a mistake. Unless explicitly defended on theological grounds, it leads towards psycho–sociological explanations for social behaviour, which are rarely satisfactory, and which in any event tend not to support notions of inherent aggressiveness. Even amongst theologians there would be a reluctance to defend the version of original sin which seems to underlie much of Morgenthau's work – a strange foundation, since Morgenthau's Judaic heritage did not commit him to this stance.

Morgenthau's second difference from Carr was equally suspect on intellectual grounds, but, none the less, was the key to the success of *Politics Among Nations*. Morgenthau systematized realism. His book is full of lists – the six principles of political realism, the three foreign policy strategies open to states and so on. This made it a very successful textbook, but at the cost of a significant coarsening of the realist position. By contrast, Carr's *The Twenty Years Crisis* is a complex, nuanced book, open to a variety of different readings. The same is true of some of Morgenthau's other works, but most of the complexity in *Politics Among Nations* is provided by accident, as a result of some rather loose formulations, rather than by design. However, a simple guide to realism was what was required in 1948. Twenty years later, Hedley Bull commented that the United States had become the dominant power in the world without needing to develop a deep knowledge of the kind of statecraft practised in Europe; now they had this need, and American realism provided them with a 'crib to the European diplomatic tradition' (Bull in Porter 1969: 39). This is patronizing, but broadly true.

Morgenthau's account of realism can be boiled down to one basic proposition about international relations, which is that international relations is about *states* pursuing *interests* defined in terms of *power*. This simple formula opens up in all sorts of ways and the different component terms will be discussed at length below. A few comments to situate these later discussions may be helpful here. First, the *state* is the key actor in international relations. Other bodies such as international organizations (governmental and non-governmental), economic enterprises, pressure groups, even individuals, may, in certain circumstances, exercise influence and act independently of states, but the state is the key actor because the state is the institution through which all these other bodies operate, the institution which regulates these other bodies and decides the terms under which they can act. As we will see in later chapters, it is a moot point whether this position will hold for the twenty-first century, but, for the moment, it should simply be noted that the claim is *not* that the state is the *only* actor but that it is the *most significant* actor; it is important not to 'win' arguments against realism by burning straw people.

Stress on *interests* conveys two notions, first that states have interests, second that state interests dominate state behaviour. The idea that states (nations) have interests could be problematic – can an institution rather than a person have interests in any meaningful sense? The realist position is that states are like 'persons', capable of possessing interests, and thus that the 'national interest' is not simply a shorthand term for the interests of whatever group controls the administrative structure of the state. States behave in accordance with these interests and not in response to abstract principles (such as collective security) or a desire to act altruistically. States never sacrifice themselves; they are essentially egoists. This seems straightforward, but could actually easily become tautological. Suppose states define a system of collective security as in their interest and act to support such a system even when their own material interests are not directly threatened by an aggressor – would this be egoistic behaviour? Clearly pinning down the idea of the national interest and using it in the analysis of foreign policy poses real problems, as we will see below.

National interests may be complex and difficult to identify in concrete terms, but the realist proposition is that a degree of simplicity can be introduced by assuming that whatever else states seek, they seek *power* in order to achieve other goals. The need for power stems from the anarchical nature of the international system. There is no authoritative system of decision-making in international relations; states are obliged to look after themselves in what has become known as a 'self-help' system. Power is a complex notion; we can think of power as 'capability' – the physical force necessary to achieve a particular goal – but capability is always cashed out in a behavioural relationship. The actual possession of assets has political meaning only in relation to the assets possessed by others – although skill in deploying one's assets counts for something. One of the problems here is that while measuring assets is not too difficult, measuring power in a relationship can be very tricky indeed.

We will return to each of these points in the chapters that follow. For the moment, one further general point is worth making, namely that it is not always clear what *kind* of theory realism is. Morgenthau obviously thinks of it as *descriptive* and *explanatory* – describing how the world is, explaining how it works; but there are also clear *prescriptive* elements here – he is telling statesmen how they *should* behave, what they should do. Moreover, there is a critical edge to his doctrines. One of the points about the notion of the 'national interest' is that it can be employed to criticize the behaviour of a particular government. These different kinds of theory sit uneasily together. When Morgenthau attended 'teach-ins' at American universities in the early

1960s in order to protest that the Vietnam War was against the national interests of the United States, he was highly irritated by the tactics of State Department spokespersons who would quote back at him citations from his writings of the 1940s. Of course, he was right to think that they were missing the point – that the reasons why the national interest might call for engagement in European security in the 1940s had little bearing on the reasons why the national interest might call for disengagement in Vietnam in the 1960s. However, the young men and women from the State Department also had a point – *Politics Among Nations* is, at times, a very confusing text, purporting, inaccurately, to be simply an account of how things are, while actually, and inevitably, containing a very strong lead on how they should be.

International Relations and the Behavioural Sciences

Morgenthau's text contains a great many 'laws of politics', that is to say generalizations that are held to apply very widely, perhaps universally. This seems to imply endorsement of the 'covering law' model of explanation, whereby something is deemed to have been explained when its occurrence can be accounted for under some general law. Such theorizing is in keeping with the aspiration of realism to make a scientific study of international relations. However, there are features of Morgenthau's account which seem to undermine this aspiration. In the first place, it is clear that states and statespersons do not have to obey the laws of politics – otherwise, what would be the point of trying to persuade them that they should? Second, and perhaps more important, the ways in which Morgenthau generates and establishes his laws seem highly unscientific. A key text here is in the Preface to the second edition of *Politics Among Nations*, where Morgenthau quotes with approval a sentence of Montesquieu to the effect that the reader should not judge the product of a lifetime's reflection on the basis of a few hours' reading. This seems to run against the scientific ethos, which holds that seniority and breadth of experience must always take second place to the logic and quality of an argument. If a smart undergraduate spots a genuine flaw in the lifetime's work of a distinguished scholar this is (or, at least, is supposed to be) a matter for congratulation, not rebuke.

In short, the scientific claims of realism are seemingly belied by its apparently unscientific methods – a point that was seized on in the 1950s and 1960s by the comparatively large number of ex-natural scientists who were attracted to the field, especially in the United States. These people were either former physicists with a guilty conscience over nuclear weapons, or systems analysts employed by bodies such as the RAND Corporation to improve the quality of United States policy-making, especially in the area of defence. These figures were joined by imports from the behavioural sciences, who were attuned to a version of the social sciences that involved an attempt to study the actual behaviour of actors rather than the meanings they assigned to this behaviour.

The aim of the behaviouralists was to replace the 'wisdom literature' and 'anecdotal' use of history represented by Morgenthau and the traditional realists with rigorous, systematic, scientific concepts and reasoning. There were various dimensions to this. It might involve casting old theories in new, rigorous forms – as with Morton Kaplan's 'balance of power' models in *System and Process in International Politics* (Kaplan 1957). It might involve generating new historical data-bases and time-series to replace the anecdotalism of traditional diplomatic history – as in J. D. Singer and associates' 'Correlates of War' Project at Ann Arbor, Michigan (Singer *et al.* 1979). It might involve the use of mathematical models for the study of decisions – as in game theoretic work and early rational choice theory in the hands of people such as Thomas Schelling at Harvard (Schelling 1960). Less conventionally, it might involve the creation of new concepts that undermined state-centric International Relations altogether – as in the work of social theorists such as John Burton (1972), Kenneth Boulding (1962) and Johann Galtung (1971).

In the mid-1960s, this work generated a fierce counter-attack on behalf of traditional, or, as they called it, classical International Relations, led by British scholars, in particular Hedley Bull (Bull in Knorr and Rosenau (eds) 1969); however, unlike the contest between utopianism and realism, this debate only engaged the interests of a minority of scholars, except, perhaps, in the United Kingdom, where an educational system still divided into two cultures meant that the majority of International Relations scholars were more amenable to attacks on 'scientism' than their North American cousins. In practice, by the 1960s the majority of US graduate students in International Relations (which means the majority of the future members of the profession) were receiving training in the methods of the behavioural sciences, and a methodology which essentially reflected this training took hold and has not yet weakened its grip. Moreover, the traditionalists/classicists had little to offer by way of alternative to the behavioural revolution, largely because their own ideas of science and reliable knowledge were, in practice, very close to those of the scientists. The aspirations to science of Morgenthau and Carr have been noted, and any doctrine which claims to be based on how things really are is obviously open to those who claim to have a better grasp of this reality. Positivism – the belief that the facts are out there to be discovered and that there is only one way to do this, only one form of reliable knowledge, that generated by methods based on the natural sciences – reigned in both camps, and the differences were largely of style rather than substance. Indeed the most effective critiques of behaviouralism – until, that is, the post-positivist revolution of the late 1980s – came from the so-called 'post-behaviouralists', scholars who accepted the goal of science, but who were critical of the behaviouralists for their unwillingness to engage with the pressing political issues of the day.

The so-called 'behavioural revolution' did, however, generate a number of new ideas, and these, combined with changes in the real world, brought about quite striking changes to International Relations theory in the 1970s.

Challenges to the Realist Synthesis

For the most part, the behaviouralists were realists – their aim was to fulfil the realist claim to scientific status rather than to undermine it. However, in the 1960s and the early 1970s major challenges to realism did emerge, driven not by developments in the academy, but by events in the real world. Two sets of events were of particular significance, one set focusing on changes in the world of Great Power diplomacy ('high' politics), the other pointing to the significance of less dramatic socio–economic changes ('low' politics). Taken together these changes produced the dominant theories of the 1980s and 1990s – 'neorealism' and 'neoliberal institutionalism' (neoliberalism for short) – as well as fuelling challenges to this new orthodoxy such as 'structuralism' 'constructivism' and 'globalization' theory, and assisting in the revival of the English School theory of international society. The final section of this chapter will set the scene for these contemporary notions.

The first set of changes reflect the shift in the nature of 'high' politics in this period. Realism as a doctrine originated in the troubled years of the 1930s and was established as orthodoxy at the height of the Cold War, which is to say, in times when the reality of Great Power competition could not be denied, nor the dangers underestimated. By the beginning of the 1960s, and especially after the Cuban Missile Crisis of 1962, the Cold War took a new turn, and relations between the super-powers became markedly less fraught – having looked over the brink in 1962, both sides decided that nothing was worth fighting a nuclear war for. This new mood – which led eventually to the process of 'détente' – was accompanied by a new focus of attention in the United States, namely the developing disaster of the Vietnam War, the most striking feature of which, from the point of view of realist theory, was the inability of the US to turn its obvious advantages in terms of power into results on the ground or at the conference table. Perceptions and psychology are important here. In point of fact, it is not too difficult to explain either the lessening of tension in Great Power relations or the failure of US policy in Vietnam using sophisticated realist categories, but, in superficial terms, it did look as if power politics were becoming less important in this period. This dovetailed with the second, more significant set of changes that led to a reassessment of the post-war synthesis, the changes in the area of 'low' politics.

The post-war realist synthesis was based on the assumption that the state is the key actor in international relations (and a unitary actor at that) and that the diplomatic–strategic relations of states are the core of actual international relations. Gradually, through the 1960s and 1970s, both of these assumptions seemed less plausible. Studies of foreign policy decision-making revealed that the unitary nature of, at least Western pluralist, states was illusory. Whereas bodies such as the United Nations could plausibly be seen as no more than arenas wherein states acted, new international organizations such as the European Economic Community (the then title of the European Union) or the functional agencies of the United Nations seemed less obviously tools of the states who brought them into being. Business enterprises had always traded across state boundaries, but a new kind of firm (rather confusingly termed the 'multinational corporation' or MNC) emerged, engaging in production on a world scale, and, allegedly, qualitatively different from the old firms in its behaviour. International diplomatic strategic relations are of central importance when the stakes really are matters of life and death, but as the possibility of the Cold War turning into a 'Hot War' declined, so the significance of international social and, especially, economic relations increased. All told, the feel of international relations seemed to be changing quite rapidly,

The changes were nicely caught in the title of a book, *Transnational Relations and World Politics* (1971), edited by figures who would be almost as significant for the next generation of IR theory as

Morgenthau had been for the previous generation, Robert Keohane and Joseph Nye. This collection did not develop a theory as such, but its description of the world posed an interesting theoretical challenge. Conventional, realist, state-centric International Relations assumes that the significant relations between different societies are those which take place via the institutions of the state. Everyone acknowledges that there are a myriad of ways in which the peoples of one country might relate to the peoples of another, a great number of cross-border transactions, movements of money, people, goods and information, but the conventional assumption is, first, that the relations that really matter are inter-state relations and, second, that the state regulates, or could regulate if it wished, all these other relations. The model suggested by Keohane and Nye relaxes both parts of this assumption. First, it can no longer be assumed that inter-state relations are always the most important; in the modern world, the decisions and actions of non-state actors can affect our lives as much as, if not more than, the decisions and actions of states. Second, it can no longer be assumed that states have the power to regulate effectively these actors; in principle, some states may have this capacity but, in practice, they are loath to exercise it given the potential costs of so doing in economic, social and political terms. Much of the time states are obliged to negotiate with non-state actors. Conventional International Relations endure but they are now accompanied by many other '*Transnational Relations*' – relationships which involve transactions across state boundaries in which at least one party is not a state. To reiterate an important point, realists have never denied the existence of such relationships but they had downplayed their significance. The transnational relations model questioned this judgement.

Pluralism and Complex Interdependence

Keohane and Nye's transnational relations collection espoused no theory of the new IR; their *Power and Interdependence* (1977/1989) went some way towards meeting this need. In this classic work they proposed *complex interdependence* as a new account of international relations to run alongside realism, and set out three key differences between the two approaches. First, complex interdependence assumes that there are *multiple channels of access* between societies, including different branches of the state apparatus as well as non-state actors, as opposed to the unitary state assumption characteristic of realism.

Second, complex interdependence assumes that for most international relationships *force will be of low salience*, as opposed to the central role that force is given in realist accounts of the world. Finally, under complex interdependence there is no *hierarchy of issues;* any 'issue-area' might be at the top of the international agenda at any particular time – whereas realism assumes that security is everywhere and always the most important issue as between states (Keohane and Nye 1977/ 1989: 24). These latter two points are, of course, related; it is largely because of the low salience of force in these relationships that there is no hierarchy of issues. The complex interdependence model does not assume that these three features exist everywhere – there may be, indeed are, relations where realism still holds. The point is to challenge realism's claim to be the only theory of international relations, holding for all relationships.

States have always been interdependent; what is new about *pluralism* is that rather than seeing relationships as a whole, they are seen as disaggregated. Different *issue-areas* – such as security, trade or finance – display different modes of mutual dependence. The politics of complex interdependence stems from these differences. The *sensitivity* of actors varies according to circumstances, as does their *vulnerability*. By sensitivity is meant the degree to which actors are sensitive to changes in a given issue-area, by vulnerability is meant the extent to which they are able to control their responses to this sensitivity – thus, for example, all advanced industrial nations in the early 1970s were very sensitive to the price of oil, but they varied considerably in their vulnerability to price changes; some had options to deal with the situation (such as developing their own resources, or increasing industrial exports) which others did not. This opens up the possibility of actors employing strengths in one area to compensate for weaknesses in another. A favourite case study for this process was the 'Smithsonian Crisis' of 1971, which revolved around the decision of the US government to attempt to force a change in the rate at which dollars were changed into gold. Under the rules of the Bretton Woods system, finance was supposed to be kept separate from trade, and both were to be isolated from military–security concerns – but in 1971 the US employed trade sanctions as a means of forcing parity changes, and US diplomatic heavyweights such as Henry Kissinger were wheeled on to back up the American stance by making scarcely veiled threats about a re-evaluation of US security guarantees to Germany and Japan if these countries failed to respond positively. Since the US was not reliant on foreign trade, and was a clear provider of security, it was able to use its comparative invulnerability and insensitivity in these areas in order to compensate for its greater sensitivity and vulnerability in the realm of international finance (Gowa 1983).

Another feature of the world as seen by pluralists is that '*agenda-setting*' is a matter of some significance. In the realist world of power politics, the agenda sets itself – what is or is not significant is easy to determine in advance, because only the big issues of war and peace are truly significant. Not so for pluralism, where, in principle, any issue could be at the top of the international agenda – here the ways in which actors are able to promote issues in international organizations and elsewhere becomes a significant subject for study. In some issue areas there may actually be a quite clear-cut route for promoting items to the top of the agenda – such issue-areas may actually be characterized by quite a high degree of international order; they may constitute *regimes*. A regime is to be found where there are clearly understood principles, norms, rules and decision-making procedures around which decision-makers' expectations converge in a given area of international relations (Krasner (ed.) 1983: 2). The politics of regimes is an interesting feature of pluralist analysis which will be explored in greater detail in Chapter 9 below.

In the mid-1970s pluralism seemed to be in the process of establishing itself as the dominant approach to the theory of International Relations. Traditional realism looked decidedly passé. Pluralism had preserved some of the more convincing insights of realism, for example about the importance of power, while offering a far more complex and nuanced account of how these insights might be operationalized in international political analysis. Indeed, some of the most convincing critiques of pluralism came from the so-called 'structuralists' who stressed the extent to which the pluralists were modelling a rich man's world – their account stressed the dependence of one group of countries upon another rather than their interdependence, and argued that the poverty of the poor was directly caused by the wealth of the rich. The alleged chain of exploitation that linked rich and poor, the development of underdevelopment that had over the centuries created present-day inequalities, was the focus of these writers. However, pluralists were able to respond that on their account of the world 'mutual dependence' did not amount to equal dependence and the structuralists were simply describing a special case that could be subsumed under the complex interdependence model. All told, in the mid-to-late 1970s pluralism looked like a research programme that was in pretty good shape.

Further Reading

The history of theories of international relations from the Greeks to the present day is well surveyed in David Boucher, *Political Theories of International Relations* (1998); Brian Schmidt's *The Political Discourse of Anarchy: A Disciplinary History of International Relations* (1998) is a pioneering work of disciplinary historiography.

To fully understand the evolution of theory in the first half of the last century it is necessary to form a view about the causes of the two world wars and the crises of the 1930s. William Keylor, *The Twentieth Century World: An International History* (1992) is the best available overview. James Joll, *The Origins of the First World War* (1984) synthesizes the debate on the origin of the war; and H. Koch (ed.), *The Origins of the First World War* (1972) provides extracts from the key controversialists. A. J. P. Taylor's famous work, *The Origins of the Second World War* (1961), the thesis of which is that Hitler's diplomacy was not significantly different from that of previous German leaders is now widely regarded as unsatisfactory; current thinking is summarized in E. M. Robertson (ed.), *The Origins of the Second World War: Historical Interpretations* (1971) and G. Martel (ed.), *The Origins of the Second World War Reconsidered: The A. J. P. Taylor Debate after Twenty-Five Years* (1986). D. C. Watt's *How War Came* (1989) offers a measured account of the diplomacy of the last year of peace and is equally valuable on appeasement, as is Paul Kennedy, *The Realities behind Diplomacy* (1981). Christopher Hill, '1939: the Origins of Liberal Realism' (1989) is a fine combination of history and theory. Gerhard L. Weinberg, *A World at Arms: A Global History of World War II* (1994) is the best single-volume account of the history and diplomacy of the Second World War.

A collection of essays on the liberal internationalists of the inter-war period, David Long and Peter Wilson (eds), *Thinkers of the Twenty Years Crisis: Interwar Idealism Reassessed* (1995) provides for the first time a convenient, sympathetic and scholarly account of these writers. Apart from the works of classical realism by Niebuhr, Spykman, Kennan and Carr cited in the text, attention should be drawn to Herbert Butterfield, *Christianity, Diplomacy and War* (1953) and Martin Wight, *Power Politics* (1946/1978). Morgenthau's *Politics Among Nations* has been through a number of editions; it is still worth reading, but the most recent heavily-cut version is to be avoided. Of recent works by classical realists, by far the most distinguished is Henry Kissinger's monumental *Diplomacy* (1994).

These works are discussed in a number of valuable studies: book-length works include Michael J. Smith, *Realist Thought from Weber to Kissinger* (1986); Joel Rosenthal, *Righteous Realists* (1991); and A. J. Murray, *Reconstructing Realism* (1996). Less sympathetic but equally valuable is Justin Rosenberg, *The Empire of Civil Society* (1994). Martin Griffiths, *Realism, Idealism and International Politics: A Reinterpretation* (1992) argues that the so-called 'realists' are actually, in a philosophical sense, idealists. Chapters by Steven Forde and Jack Donnelly on classical and twentieth-century realism, respectively, are to be found in Terry Nardin and David Mapel (eds), *Traditions of International Ethics* (1992); Donnelly has followed this up by *Realism and International Relations* (2000). On Morgenthau, Peter Gellman, 'Hans Morgenthau and the Legacy of Political Realism' (1988) and A. J. Murray, 'The Moral Politics of Hans Morgenthau' (1996) are very valuable. On Carr, the essays by Booth and Fox cited in the text are crucial; see also Graham Evans, 'E. H. Carr and International Relations' (1975).

On the debate over methods, Klaus Knorr and James Rosenau (eds), *Contending Approaches to International Politics* (1969) collects the major papers, including Hedley Bull's 'International Theory: the Case for a Classical Approach' and Morton Kaplan's equally intemperate reply 'The New Great Debate: Traditionalism vs. Science in International Relations'. The best account of what was at stake in this debate is to be found in Martin Hollis and Steve Smith, *Explaining and Understanding International Relations* (1991). Bull's critique is probably best seen as part of a wider British reaction to American dominance of the social sciences in the 1950s and 1960s, but it has some affinities with more sophisticated critiques of positivism such as Charles Taylor, 'Interpretation and the Sciences of Man' (1971) or William E. Connolly, *The Terms of Political Discourse* (1983).

Many of the leading 'pluralist' writers of the 1970s became the 'neoliberal institutionalists' of the 1980s, and their work is discussed in the next chapter – the second edition of Keohane and Nye's *Power and Interdependence* (1977, 2nd ed. 1989) clarifies their relationship with realism.

3

International Relations Theory Today

Introduction: Rational Choice Theory and its Critics

Just as the post-war synthesis was dominated by Morgenthau's 1948 text, so contemporary IR is fixated on Kenneth Waltz's 1979 volume *Theory of International Politics*. Not only was realism revitalized by this book, but also anti-realists have felt obliged to respond to its arguments. In the 1960s it was said (by Kenneth Thompson) that IR theory constituted a debate between Morgenthau and his critics; in the 1980s, 1990s and 2000s the name of Waltz should be substituted for that of Morgenthau (although, in both cases, it is what the author is believed to have written rather than what was actually on the page that is crucial).

The merits of *Theory of International Politics* will be discussed below, but the success of the book does not simply rest on its own qualities, impressive though these are. The wider context is provided by the rise to dominance of *rational choice theory* in the Political Science community in the United States. The presupposition of rational choice thinking is that politics can be understood in terms of the goal-directed behaviour of individuals, who act rationally in the minimal sense that they make ends–means calculations designed to maximize the benefits they expect to accrue from particular situations (or, of course, minimize the losses). This overall perspective – sometimes termed 'neo-utilitarian' – draws much of its strength from the discipline of Economics, where rational choice assumptions are fundamental, and was widely applied in the study of domestic politics in the US from the 1960s onwards, with electoral, interest group and congressional politics in the forefront. It encourages the application of tools such as game theory to the study of politics, and opens up the possibility of quantitative studies employing regression analysis (and other statistical techniques largely developed by econometricians). Arguably, both the individualism of rational choice theory and its scientific aspirations are particularly congenial to the American psyche, which accounts for the dominance of this approach in the US, as opposed to its comparative unimportance in Britain and, until recently, much of the European continent.

Although Waltz's realism is sometimes described as *structural realism*, and structuralism is generally seen as the polar opposite of rational choice theory, it is the possibilities opened up by assimilating his approach to rational choice theory that account for the long-term significance of his work – and, contrariwise, the bitterest and most sustained critiques of Waltz have come from opponents of rational choice theory. In effect, Waltz made possible the integration of IR theory into the dominant mode of theorizing politics in the US – what remains to be seen is whether this constitutes a giant leap forward in our abilities to comprehend IR, or a major detour down a dead-end. The rest of this chapter sets out these alternatives.

From Realism to Neorealism

The very term *neorealism* is somewhat contentious, because many realists regard the ideas it conveys as containing nothing that would merit the prefix 'neo' – nonetheless most observers disagree, and feel that something did change with realism in response to the pluralist challenge and neorealism is one way of noting this change. In any event, there is general agreement that the most significant realist/ neorealist work is Kenneth Waltz's *Theory of International Politics* (1979). Waltz is a scholar with a classical realist background. His first major work, *Man, the State and War* (1959), is still a starting-point for modern thinking about the causes of war and, for the most part, is a work of international political theory in the traditional mould; in the 1950s Waltz had been the secretary of the American Rockefeller Committee for the Study of the Theory of International Relations which was founded in 1954, and was conventionally realist in orientation and traditionalist in method. *Theory of International Politics*, on the other hand, is anything but traditionalist in style and presentation, or conventional in its arguments.

Waltz's basic strategy for preserving realism in the face of the pluralist challenge is to restrict its scope. First, whereas for Morgenthau 'theory' is quite a loose term – despite his frequent references to laws of politics and the like – for Waltz, theory is defined quite precisely in his first chapter, and in terms drawn from the thinking on scientific method of Karl Popper as refracted through the lens of modern economic theory. Waltz is concerned to produce interrelated, linked, law-like propositions from which testable hypotheses can be drawn – although he does acknowledge that 'testing' is likely to be a more impressionistic process in International Relations than it is in the exact sciences. Waltz vehemently denies being a 'positivist' in any wider sense of the term, but his apparent belief that there are real-world regularities that it is the role of theory to explain would seem to put him in that camp, at least given the usual implications of the term positivism (Waltz 1997, 1998).

However, Waltz does not just restrict the kind of theory he is producing; crucially he also restricts its scope. His aim is to produce a theory of the *international system* and not a general account of all aspects of international relations. This enables him to gaze benignly on many of the changes described by the pluralists, because they do not address the nature of the international system as such, only aspects of its component units. One of the positions he advocates most forcefully is that it is only possible to understand the international system via *systemic* theories; to attempt to understand the system by theories which concentrate on attributes of the units that make up the system is to commit the ultimate sin of *reductionism*. We know reductionism is wrong because we know that there are patterns of the international systems that recur over time even when the units that make up the system change; these patterns must be the product of the system itself, and cannot be the product either of mutable features of its subsystems, or of human universals, such as an alleged tendency towards aggression, that, by definition, appear throughout history and not simply in international systems. Thus, to take one of his examples, Lenin must be wrong to explain imperialism in terms of the dynamics of monopoly capitalism, because imperialism has been around for ever, while monopoly capitalism is of recent origin (Waltz 1979: 19ff.). In fact, this is not a compelling critique of Lenin, because the latter recognizes this point and stresses that modern imperialism is different from its predecessors – nonetheless, Waltz's general point is clear.

Once we focus on the system we can see, he suggests, that there are only two kinds of system possible – a *hierarchical* or an *anarchical* system. In a hierarchical system, different kinds of units are organized under a clear line of authority. In an anarchical system, units which are similar in nature, even though they differ dramatically in capabilities, conduct relations with one another. The distinction between hierarchy and anarchy is crucial to Waltz; the present system, he argues, is clearly anarchical, and has been since its late medieval origins. None of the changes identified by the pluralists amounts to a change of system – this would only come if hierarchical institutions were established, that is, some kind of world government. Much of *Theory of International Politics* is given over to demonstrating that this is not taking place, and that the sort of developments identified by pluralists only scratch the surface of things; the underlying reality of the system remains the same.

The international system is a 'self-help' system; states (which for theoretical purposes are assumed to be unitary actors) are obliged to look after themselves, because there is no one else to look after them. Waltz does *not* assume that states are self-aggrandizing, necessarily aggressive bodies, but he does assume that they desire to preserve themselves. This means that they are obliged to be concerned with their security, and obliged to regard other states as potential threats. They must continually adjust their stance in the world in accordance with their reading of the power of others and of their own power. The result of these movements is the emergence of a *balance of power*. The balance of power is *the* theory of the international system. Balances of power can be defined in terms of the number of 'poles' in the balance – the metaphor gets a bit confused here – and the number of poles is defined by the number of states who can seriously threaten each other's basic survival; Waltz argues that this means the system (in 1979) is *bipolar*. Only the United States and the USSR have the ability to threaten each other's survival. As we will see, most writers on the balance of power see bipolar balances as inherently unstable, because changes in the capacity of one actor can only be met by similar changes in the other – and this process is always likely to get out of sync. Waltz disagrees; according to him, bipolar systems are easier to manage because there are fewer interested parties involved.

This is a theory of the structure of the international system, and a good question would be how structure relates to 'agency' – what does it mean to say that states *must* behave in certain kinds of ways? Again, how can it be assumed that a balance of power will always emerge or that states will be able to manage a bipolar system, given that they do not consciously wish to create balances – indeed, most states would prefer to eliminate potentially threatening states (that is, all states other than themselves). Waltz's answer to these questions is that there is no actual guarantee that balances will form or that power management will be successful; however, states that do not respond to the signals sent to them by the international system, that is to say states that ignore the distribution of power in the world, will find that they suffer harm as a result, indeed under some circumstances could face loss of independence. Since states do not want this to happen the likelihood is that they will take the necessary steps (Waltz 1979: 118). But they may not; some states, but not very many in the twentieth century, have actually lost their independence, while others because of a favourable geographical position, or some other natural advantage, have the luxury of being able to make quite a few misreadings of the state of the international system without suffering serious harm. Nonetheless, the tendency is for states to respond to their cues.

Here, and at other points throughout the work, Waltz employs analogies drawn from neoclassical economics, and especially the theory of markets and the theory of the firm. The pure competitive market is a classical example of a structure that comes into existence independent of the wishes of the buyers and sellers who, nonetheless, create it by their actions. Each individual actor must respond to the signals sent by the market – but must in this sense simply means that, say, farmers who attempt to sell at a price higher than the market will bear will be unable to unload their crops, while farmers who sell for less than they could get are passing up opportunities for gain which will be taken up by others who will drive them out of business. Similarly buyers will not want to pay more than is necessary and will not be able to pay less than the going rate. The market structure emerges out of these decisions, yet the decisions are shaped by the market structure. The analogy can be taken further. In an uncompetitive market, an oligopoly, a small number of firms are able to manage prices and output in such a way that by avoiding direct competition each is better off than they would otherwise be. These firms have no interest in each other's survival – Ford would like to see General Motors disappear and vice versa – but as profit-maximizers they realize that positive attempts to get rid of the competition would be far too dangerous to contemplate; a price war might bring down both firms. In the same way, the United States and the Soviet Union had a common interest in regulating their competition, even though each would have preferred the other to disappear had this been achievable in a riskless, costless way.

It is this economic analogy that might be said to justify the 'neo' in 'neorealism'. In effect, and crucially in terms of the influence of his work, Waltz is offering a 'rational choice' version of the balance of power in which states are assumed to be self-interested egoists who determine their strategies by choosing that which maximizes their welfare. This is a long way in spirit from the agonized reliance on the mainspring of the sinfulness of man characteristic of Morgenthau and the 'righteous realists' (Rosenthal 1991). In this respect, he is closer to Carr, whose quasi-Marxist emphasis on scarcity and the human condition seems to parallel Waltz's account of anarchy and the desire for self-preservation. Carr did not adopt a rational choice mode of theorizing, but even this style of reasoning is not unknown in the classical tradition. Rousseau's fable of the stag and the hare is similar in import to Waltz's account of the egoism of states: a band of hunters can collectively meet their needs by bringing down a stag, but at the crucial moment one leaves the hunt in order to catch a hare, satisfying his individual needs, but causing the stag to be lost – an excellent illustration of the problems involved in collective action. Nonetheless, in spite of these predecessors, there is something new here in the way in which Waltz puts together the argument. His theory is obviously controversial, but it remains not only the most convincing restatement of the realist position in recent times, but also a restatement that links IR theory to the mainstream of (American) political science. *Theory of International Politics* is, justly, the most influential book on International Relations theory of its generation.

From Neorealism to Neoliberalism

From the perspective of the late 1970s it might have been anticipated that the way International Theory would develop in the remaining decades of the twentieth century would be along the lines of a contrast between (neo)realism and pluralism, with, perhaps, a left-wing critique of both theories hovering in the background. To some extent this has happened, and a number of accounts of contemporary International Relations theory are presented in terms of three perspectives or 'paradigms' (Little and Smith 1991; Viotti and Kauppi 1993). However, in the United States, which is the effective home of the discipline, theory developed in a rather different way. The pluralists of the 1970s mostly became the 'neoliberal institutionalists' of the 1980s and 1990s, and in the process came rather closer to neorealism that might have been expected.

Scholars such as Robert Keohane and Robert Axelrod developed models which shared a lot with neorealism (Keohane 1984, 1989; Axelrod 1984: Axelrod and Keohane 1985). They accepted the two basic assumptions of international anarchy and the rational egoism of states; the aim of their analysis was to show that it was possible for rational egoists to cooperate even in an anarchical system. Drawing material from the same kind of sources as the neorealists – in particular game theory, public choice and rational choice theory – they recognized that cooperation under anarchy was always liable to be fragile. 'Free rider' states – who took the gains of cooperation without contributing to the costs – would always be a problem, and the 'prisoner's dilemma' game modelled very clearly the difficulty of relying on promises of cooperation made in circumstances where enforcement was impossible. However, if international regimes could be established within which information could be exchanged and commitments formalized, the possibilities for cooperation would be enhanced. Establishing regimes is a difficult process, and most of the existing regimes in, especially, the international political economy were established by a 'hegemonic' power, the United States, in the immediate post-war era – a 'hegemon' in this context being defined as a state that has the ability to establish rules of action and enforce them, and the willingness to act upon this ability. One of the key propositions of most of these writers is that US hegemony has declined dramatically in recent years, thus posing a problem – is it possible for cooperation to continue 'after hegemony'? The answer usually given is 'yes' – but at suboptimal levels, because what is happening is that the regime is living on the capital built up under hegemony; the details of this argument will be examined in Chapter 9 below.

The neoliberals are clearly saying something rather different about international cooperation than the neorealists, but a common commitment to rational choice theory makes them part of the same broad movement. The neorealist Joseph Grieco in an article 'Anarchy and the Limits of Cooperation' helpfully sets out the points of disagreement between the two camps (Grieco 1988).

Grieco suggests that a key issue concerns *absolute* as opposed to *relative* gains from cooperation. Neoliberals assume that states are essentially concerned with the absolute gains made from cooperation; as long as they are happy with their own situation, they will not be too worried about how well other states are doing. There is a clear parallel here with liberal trade theory, where the fact that parties will gain unequally from trade that reflects comparative advantage is deemed less important than the fact that they will all gain something. Neorealists, on the other hand, assume that each state will be concerned with relative gains from cooperation, that is with how well other states are doing as well as how well it is doing. This follows from the neorealist focus on the balance of power, which rests precisely upon the assumption that states will continually scan each other for signs that their relative power position is changing. This difference in orientation, Grieco suggests, means that neorealists and neoliberals focus on quite different problems when it comes to the limits of cooperation. For neoliberals, it is not at all difficult to see why states cooperate – it is in their (absolute) advantage to do so. The problem, rather, as we have seen, is that states have a tendency to cheat, to become 'free riders', and what is needed is some mechanism that prevents cheating. This would allow states to realize their true long-term interest in cooperation as opposed to falling prey to the temptation to settle for short-term gains – it is easy to see why this branch of theory is termed neoliberal. For neorealists on the other hand, 'cheating' is something of a non-problem. From their point of view, the difficulty is getting cooperation going in the first place, because states will only cooperate when they expect that the gains they will receive will be greater than, or at least equal to, the gains of all other relevant parties – quite a tough criterion to meet.

Grieco argues that the neorealist assumption that states concentrate on relative gains is backed up by observations as to how states actually behave in the international system, and also by public opinion data which he shows suggests that the US public at least is more concerned with relative gains than with absolute gains. On the other hand, neoliberals can point to the extensive network of international institutions which exists and, indeed, is continually added to, which rather undermines the proposition that states are chronically unwilling to cooperate. From the neorealist perspective, the neoliberals are engaging in a doomed enterprise. While accepting an essentially Hobbesian definition of the situation – that is, the two criteria of anarchy and rational egoism – neoliberals argue that cooperation can take place without the presence of an Hobbesian 'sovereign'; this cannot be. Neoliberals argue that although cooperation will be suboptimal it will still be possible.

However this debate is resolved, what is clear is that neoliberals and neorealists are much closer together than their non-neo forebears. Whereas the latter understood the world in fundamentally incompatible terms, stressing either harmony or disharmony of interests, and the importance or unimportance of domestic structures, the 'neos' both rest their position on what are taken to be the facts of anarchy and of the rational egoism of states. It may be going too far to write of a unified 'neo-neo' position (Waever 1996), but certainly the two positions are close enough to be seen as offering different understandings of what is essentially the same (rational choice) research programme. Moreover, this is a research programme within which the work of the majority of IR scholars can be located. As will be apparent in subsequent chapters, within this research programme there is room for a great deal of variation, and even basic notions such as the balance of power can be challenged – perhaps states 'bandwagon' rather than 'balance'?; nonetheless, implicitly or explicitly, the 'anarchy problematic' established by Waltz, sets the agenda for most contemporary IR research. But, especially in the last few years, opposition movements are growing, and the rest of this chapter provides an overview of these movements, although perhaps the most fundamental challenge over matters of substance, that of theorists of globalization, is covered in its own terms in later chapters.

Constructivism and the 'English School'

As we will see, theorists of globalization reject the 'state-centrism' involved in neorealist/neoliberal rational choice theory in favour of an approach that stresses global social, economic, cultural and political forces. Other critics of rational choice IR are less concerned by its focus on the state, more critical of the implicit assumptions that underlie that focus, in particular the assumption that the nature of the state is, in some sense, given and that the rules that govern state behaviour are simply part of the way things are, rather than the product of human invention. By definition, rational choice IR theories assume that states engage in goal directed behaviour, but within a context that that is given in advance; they study how states play the game of being rational egoists in an anarchic world, but they take for granted that states *are* rational egoists and that the identification of the world as anarchic is unproblematic, in other words that the game is pre-ordained. Critics challenge this set of assumptions.

These critics share a hostility to rational choice approaches, but relatively little else, and finding even a rudimentary classification schema here is difficult; for purposes of exposition they are here divided into two groups. First, the work of *constructivists* and their *English School* cousins will be examined, then, moving progressively further away from the mainstream of IR theory, *critical theorists, post-structuralists* and others misleadingly termed *post-modern* writers will come under scrutiny.

Constructivism is the fastest growing oppositional movement within IR theory, but a good part of this growth is a by-product of the lack of any clear definition of what this approach might involve. Unfortunately, constructivism has become a bumper-sticker term, a label appropriated by those who wish to assert a degree of independence from mainstream American IR theory while maintaining a certain level of respectability – it has come to be seen as a kind of acceptable 'middle way' (Adler 1997). In the late 1980s and early 1990s this was not the case. Then, the writings Friedrich Kratochwil (1989), Nicholas Onuf (1989) and Alexander Wendt (1987, 1992) established constructivist ideas as a genuinely radical alternative to conventional IR.

The central insight of constructivist thought can perhaps best be conveyed by the notion that there is a fundamental distinction to be made between 'brute facts' about the world, which remain true independent of human action, and 'social facts' which depend for their existence on socially established conventions (Searle 1995). There is snow on the top of Mount Everest whether anyone is there to observe it or not, but the white and purple piece of paper in my pocket with a picture of Edward Elgar on it is only a £20 note because it is recognized by people in Britain to be so. Mistaking a social fact for a brute fact is a cardinal error – and one constructivists believe is made with some frequency – because it leads to the ascription of a *natural* status to conditions that have been produced and may be, in principle, open to change. Thus, if we treat 'anarchy' as a given, something that conditions state action without itself being conditioned *by* state action, we will miss the point that 'anarchy is what states make of it' and does not, as such, dictate any particular course of action (Wendt 1992). We live in 'a world of our making' not a world whose contours are predetermined in advance by non-human forces (Onuf 1989).

So far so good, but how are these approaches to be developed? A variety of different possibilities emerge. First, unfortunately, there may be no development at all, and in the 1990s a number of essentially empirical IR scholars have proclaimed themselves to be 'constructivist' in so far as they accept the above points, but have not changed their working methods in any significant way, at least not in any way that outsiders can discern. This is constructivism as a label. More to the point, and second, it might be noted that because a structure is the product of human agency it by no means follows that it will be easy for human agents to change its nature once it has been established – *agent-structure* questions tease out the relationships between these two notions (Wendt 1987). Such questions are of particular importance in the study of foreign policy and will be discussed in Chapter 4 below. Third, once we recognize that the nature of the game of international politics is not simply to be taken for granted, the road is opened up for a Wittgensteinian analysis of the *rules of the game*, an account of the ways in the grammar of world politics is constituted – Kratochwil and Onuf have been particularly important in developing this side of the constructivist project; for a paradigm of this kind of analysis the reader is referred to Kratochwil's account of the place of the rule of non-intervention within the Westphalian game of 'sovereignty-as-*dominium*' (Kratochwil 1995).

However, perhaps the most popular line of development has been in another direction, towards using constructivist ideas to throw light on normative issues, in particular those that revolve around matters of identity, and, by extension, on issues of cooperation between states (Ruggie 1998; Wendt 1999). As noted above, 'neo-neo' IR theory assumes cooperation takes place between egoists under conditions of anarchy, if, that is, it takes place at all. The identities of the actors in question is a matter of no significance, and norms promoting cooperation will have no purchase on what is essentially a process of ends–means calculation, in which the end ('security') is given in advance, and the same for all actors and the context is provided by a notion of anarchy that is essentially incontestable and unchanging. Constructivists challenge each item in this formulation. Identity *does* matter: US relations with, e.g. Canada and France, are different from her relations with Egypt and the People's Republic of China not simply for reasons of security, but because the first two countries share with the US a common (broad) identity that the latter two do not – more dramatically, as Ruggie points out, it mattered enormously that the US became (briefly) hegemonic post-World War II rather than the USSR, in ways that cannot be captured by those who simply portray 'hegemony' as an abstract requirement for a particular kind of co-operative regime. Equally, the idea that there is only one 'anarchy problematic' will not do; anarchy means 'no-rule' but need not, though it may, mean chaos. The possibility exists that within an anarchical framework norms can emerge.

This latter thought is developed extensively in the second half of Alexander Wendt's ambitious *Social Theory of International Politics* (1999). As the title suggests, this book is a deliberate attempt to set up an opposition to Waltz's *Theory of International Politics*, although, as the title also suggests, it also pays a kind of homage to the earlier volume. The first part of *Social Theory* presents a clear, albeit at times somewhat anodyne, version of constructivist epistemology, while the second half develops notions of the importance of identity and norms, and the politics of different kinds of anarchy – including the possibility of the emergence of an 'anarchical society'. This latter possibility highlights the connections between this version of constructivism and the work of a group of theorists generally known as the 'English School'.

The 'English School' is so named, because its major figures, although often not English, worked in England (in particular at the London School of Economics, and at Oxford and Cambridge) during its formative years. It is best defined as a group of scholars – most notably Martin Wight, Hedley Bull, Adam Watson, R. J. Vincent, James Mayall, Robert Jackson, and more recently Tim Dunne and N. J. Wheeler – whose work focuses on the notion of a 'society of states' or 'international society': the history of the English School is well told in Dunne (1998). The term 'international society' conveys two points, both of which are examined at length in the masterwork of the School, Hedley Bull's *The Anarchical Society* (1977/1995); first, the focus of study should be primarily on the world of states and not on substate entities or universal categories such as 'humanity'; however, second, states when they interact do not simply form an international *system*, a non-normative pattern of regularities, rather they form a *society*, a norm-governed relationship whose members accept that they have at least limited responsibilities towards one another and to the society as a whole. These responsibilities are summarized in the traditional practices of international law and diplomacy. States are assumed to pursue their interests in the international arena, but not at all costs – or, rather, if they do pursue them at all costs international society will be in danger. The link between this kind of thinking and Wendt's constructivist thought is clear. International relations take place under conditions of anarchy, but in an 'anarchical society'; states act within a system of norms which, most of the time, they regard as constraining. Moreover these norms are created by the states themselves; Dunne explicitly makes the connection in an article entitled 'The Social Construction of International Society' (1995).

This is not the only direction in which English School thought can be taken; Barry Buzan, the inspiration for a recent attempt to re-vitalize the School as a research programme, draws connections with neo-liberal institutionalist thought on regimes (Buzan 1993, 1999). Perhaps more to the point, the notion of international society is quite closely connected to an older, pre-rational choice, kind of realism. One way of

looking at the concept is to see it as an occasionally idealized concep-
tualization of the norms of the old, pre-1914 European states-system.
This is the real version of European statecraft as opposed to the 'crib'
that Hans Morgenthau and others prepared for the American domestic
political elite in the 1940s. If this is right, a good question would be
whether 'international society' provides a satisfactory starting point
for understanding our contemporary world order, where the majority
of states are non-European. It is at least arguable that the old order
worked as well as it did because there was quite a high level of cultural
homogeneity in the system; Europeans shared a common history,
albeit one of frequently violent relationships, and common Greco–
Roman cultural origins. Even so the divide between (Greek) Orthodox
and (Roman) Catholic Europe was a source of some tension, as had
been, in the sixteenth and seventeenth centuries, the divide in the West
between Protestant and Catholic Europe. How much more problematic would be the normative basis for an international society composed, as today it must be, of states based in many cultures – Islamic,
Hindu, Confucian and African as well as 'Western'?

There are two possible answers here. One is that although the
modern world is incontestably multicultural in social terms, the Western invention of the nation-state has proved remarkably attractive to
a great many different cultures. Whether because they genuinely meet a
need, or because, given the existing order, territorial political units are
more or less unavoidable, nation-states seem to be desired everywhere.
The only part of the world where the institution is under serious threat
from an alternative form of political organization is at its place of
origin in Western Europe in the form of the European Union. A
second answer is less contingent and more complex. It is that the
very rationale of 'international society' is its ability to cope with
cultural diversity.

An important writer here is Terry Nardin, whose account of international society as a 'practical association' has been highly influential
in recent years (Nardin 1983). Nardin's point is that, unlike a 'purpos-
ive association' such as NATO or the World Trade Organization
(WTO) which is built around a concrete project (collective defence or
the expansion of trade) and assumes common purposes amongst its
members, all of whom have voluntarily joined the organization in
question, international society is an all-inclusive category whose practices are authoritative on every state precisely because they do *not*
involve common purposes or a concrete project. The only common
purpose is to live together in peace and with justice, and in this context

justice is a procedural rather than a substantive notion. It is clear that, if these distinctions hold, the origins of the practices of international society in the European states-system are irrelevant to their authority today. These practices are authoritative precisely because they do not privilege any one conception of the 'Good', and this means that they are ideally suited for a world in which many and various such practices are to be found. Whether these distinctions *do* hold is a moot question in a world of 'globalization', a matter that will be discussed below.

To summarize, some versions of constructivism, especially that associated with Wendt's recent writings, and the English School, offer not-dissimilar critiques of the current intellectual dominance of rational choice IR theory, and cognate accounts of how the world might be studied other than through the assumption that rational egoists maximize their security under the anarchy problematic. In opposition to positivism, they share the view that theory in part constitutes the world. However, on some accounts, the critical impulse of early constructivist writings has been lost by Wendt; it is noticeable that in the *Review of International Studies* Symposium on *Social Theory of International Politics*, mainstream IR theorists were rather more favourably disposed towards his arguments than more radical critics, and Friedrich Kratochwil has argued that Wendt is in the process of constructing a new orthodoxy (*Review of International Studies* 2000; Kratochwil 2000). Certainly, Wendt has cast himself as a 'loyal opposition', challenging the mainstream, but eager for dialogue with it; the title of Wendt's recent book conveys this very nicely, at once a challenge and a tribute to Waltz. In any event, in the final section of this chapter, the work of oppositionists who can by no stretch of the imagination be thought of as loyal will be examined.

Critical, Post-Structuralist and 'Postmodern' International Thought

All constructivists are, in some sense post-positivist, indeed *anti*-positivist in so far as they reject the rational choice, neo-utilitarian reasoning of mainstream IR theory, but the currently dominant trend of constructivist thought, represented by Wendt and Ruggie, remains closely in touch with the research agenda of the mainstream – that is, the relations of states, specifically problems of cooperation and conflict. The writers to be considered in this final section on contemporary IR theory are much less wedded to this conventional agenda; they take their inspiration from elsewhere, in fact from a variety of elsewheres since there is no one source of inspiration for this 'new learning'. We find here Frankfurt School Critical Theorists, feminist writers, writers inspired by the French masters of thought of the last half century – Foucault and Derrida in particular – and even, although the word is much misused, the occasional genuine 'postmodernist'. These thinkers do not have a great deal in common, save for two important intellectual commitments; all desire to understand International Relations not as a free-standing discourse with its own terms of reference, but rather as one manifestation of a much broader movement in social thought, and all hold that theory must unsettle established categories and disconcert the reader. On both counts, IR must be seen in the context of Enlightenment and post-Enlightenment thought. Just *how* it is to be seen in this context is what is contested, and to understand this contest a step back has to be taken, in the direction of the Enlightenment itself.

To answer the question 'What is Enlightenment?' in a study of this scope is not possible, but a rough-and-ready account of what it has become customary to call the 'Enlightenment Project' can be given, building on Kant's famous answer to this question – Enlightenment is 'humanity's emergence from self-imposed immaturity' (Reiss 1970: 54). In other words, the Enlightenment mandated the application of human reason to the project of human emancipation. Human beings were challenged by the great thinkers of the Enlightenment to know themselves and their world, and to apply that knowledge to free themselves both from superstition and the forces of ignorance, and, more directly, from political tyranny, and, perhaps, the tyranny of material necessity. Originally, the main carrier of the project of emancipation was 'liberalism' in one form or another, but one belief held by all the writers examined here, and by most constructivists, is that contemporary forms of liberalism, such as the neo-utilitarianism represented by rational choice theory and mainstream IR theory, no longer perform this function. To use the influential formulation of Robert Cox, contemporary liberal theory is 'problem-solving' theory – it accepts the prevailing definition of a particular situation and attempts to solve the problems this definition generates – while emancipatory theory must be 'critical' – challenging conventional understandings (Cox 1981). Thus, whereas neorealist/neoliberal thinking accepts the 'anarchy problematic' as given, and seeks devices to lessen the worst side-effects of anarchy, the new approaches wish either to explore and elucidate the ways in which this problematic serves particular kinds of interests, and closes down particular sorts of arguments, or to shift the argument on to an altogether different subject.

If it is generally agreed by these authors that contemporary liberalism can no longer be seen as an emancipatory discourse, there is no agreement as to whether the project of emancipation itself is recoverable. Here a quite sharp divide emerges between those who believe it is, although not on modern liberal lines, and those who believe that the failure of liberalism in this respect is symptomatic of a problem with the goal of emancipation itself. The former look back to, variously, Kant, Hegel and Marx to re-instate the Enlightenment Project: the latter, variously, to Nietzsche, Heidegger and Foucault to critique the underlying assumptions of emancipatory theory.

The former group – call them 'critical theorists' for the sake of convenience – are clearly related to the left-oriented, progressivist, international thought of the last century and a half, including radical liberalism before it became part of the official world-view of the dominant international powers. The single most influential critical theorist was, and remains, Karl Marx; Marx it was who set out most clearly the propositions that 'emancipation' could not be simply a political process leaving economic inequalities untouched (which has been the failing of liberalism), that capitalism, though its subversion of traditional forms of rule was to be welcomed, itself created oppression, and, most important in this context, that capitalism was, at least potentially in his day, a world-system, a force that had to be understood in global rather than local terms – which means that 'emancipation' must be a global project. Unfortunately these core insights, which most critical theorists would endorse, were embedded by Marx within a framework that contained much that contemporary history has shown to be decidedly un-emancipatory. The direct descendants of Marx – the Bolsheviks in the Soviet Union, Mao and the Chinese Communist Party, and various national communist regimes in Cambodia, Cuba, North Korea, and Vietnam – were, between them, responsible for more human misery in the twentieth century that the adherents of any other world-view, Nazism included. Moreover, the various directly-inspired Marxist theories of IR – Lenin's theory of imperialism, and numerous variants of centre-periphery and world-systems analysis – have proved equally unsatisfactory, although, as will be seen below, highly influential in the non-Western world. As a result of this record, contemporary critical theorists tend to work with Marx via intermediaries, the most important of whom have been, for international political economists, the Italian/ Sardinian Marxist and victim of fascism, Antonio Gramsci, and for international political theorists, the Frankfurt School and, in particular, its leading modern theorist, Jürgen Habermas.

Setting aside the Gramscian heritage for later consideration, the contribution of Habermas to critical theory has been to move Marx-influenced thought away from economic determinism and the class struggle, and towards an engagement with Kantian ethics and Hegelian notions of political community. Habermas shares Kant's universalist account of ethical obligation which he recasts for our age in terms of 'discourse ethics'; moral issues are to be understood as resolvable via dialogue under ideal conditions, that is with no voice excluded and without privileging any particular point of view or taking for granted that inequalities of wealth and power are legitimate. Politics is an ethical activity which takes place within communities – but communities must be understood to be as inclusive as possible; some level of exclusion may be inevitable if citizenship is to be meaningful, but the basis for inclusion and exclusion is subject to moral scrutiny.

Habermas has written on the theory and practice of international relations in books and articles on such diverse subjects as Kant's *Perpetual Peace*, the Gulf War of 1990–1 and the Kosovo Campaign of 1999, but his standard bearers in English-language International Relations have been scholars such as David Held and Andrew Linklater, with a rather more Marx-oriented, wider, Frankfurt School perspective represented by Mark Neufeld and Richard Wyn Jones (Habermas 1997, 1994, 1999: Held 1995; Linklater 1998; Neufeld 1995: Jones 1999). Linklater and Held have developed different aspects of the notion of cosmopolitan democracy. Held's work is oriented towards an explicitly normative account of the need to democratize contemporary international relations; the central thesis is that in an age of globalization (of which Held has been a major theorist) the desire for democratic self-government can no longer be met at a national level and so the project of democratizing the international order must be prioritized, however difficult a task this may be. Linklater is less concerned with institutional change, more with the transformation of notions of political community, and the evolution of an ever-more inclusive dialogue. These are themes that clearly relate to Habermas's thought, but many writers in critical international studies – especially in subfields such as 'Critical Security Studies' – take a broader view of the critical theory project. Both Neufeld and Jones remain closer to the Marxian roots of critical theory than Linklater and Held, and are rather more critical generally of the powers that be in contemporary world politics.

These few comments can only give a flavour of the work of critical theorists – readers are urged to follow up the suggested reading listed below – but enough has been said to make it clear that the account of International Relations they offer is radically different from that of mainstream IR. A valuable illustration of the chasm in question can be found in the 1999 *Review of International Studies* Symposium on Linklater's *The Transformation of Political Community* (1998); the blank incomprehension of Randall Schweller, representing the main-stream, results in an almost-comically hostile response. However, in the same Symposium, the equally critical comments of R. B. J. Walker point in another direction. Linklater's brand of critical theory is ulti-mately devoted to the rescuing of the emancipatory project of the Enlightenment – but can this project be rescued? Ought it to be? Perhaps it is not so much a case of work such as rational choice IR betraying the Enlightenment Project, but rather representing it all too faithfully.

This is the approach taken by writers characteristically referred to as post-structuralist or sometimes, usually inaccurately, postmodern, and if the above account of Habermas and critical theory is dangerously thin, any attempt to provide an equivalent background for these scholars within a study of this scope presents even more difficulties – once again readers are urged to follow up some of the references given below. A few themes only can be identified; first, following up the reference to Walker above is 'inside/outside'; then, closely related, a new approach to ethics and to pluralism; next, speed, simulation and virtual reality and finally, the contribution of feminist writing.

For the critical theorist Linklater, the community is necessarily to some degree exclusionary, but the aim is to be as inclusive as possible and to make the costs of exclusion as low as possible – this is, of course, an explicitly normative project, although Linklater insists that trends supportive of this end are immanent in our current world order. Walker may share some of these normative goals, but is more directly concerned with the way in which the very system of sovereign states is constituted by and rests upon a sharp inside/outside distinc-tion (Walker 1993). It was the emergence of this sharp distinction in the early modern era that created the Westphalia System and, more recently has created the discourse of International Relations itself; moreover, the emancipatory discourses of the Enlightenment rest upon a structurally similar distinction; the privileging of a particular voice by the Enlightenment – European, rationalist, male – is not something that is incidental and can be eliminated by a better dialogue, any more than the bounded community can be redesigned to avoid the privileging of the interests of its inhabitants.

It is not always clear where Walker wishes to take these points, but writers such as William Connolly and David Campbell offer some suggestions. Both focus on issues of 'difference' and 'otherness' and both propose strategies for dealing with otherness that reject the universalism of conventional emancipatory politics. Campbell, in studies of the Gulf War and the Bosnia conflict, attempts to show the emptiness of rule-oriented approaches to ethics, symbolized by such constructions as Just War theory in which the actions of parties to a conflict are tested against an allegedly impartial and objective ethical yardstick (Campbell 1993, 1998). Instead he proposes an ethics of encounter, a more personal, less general approach to the identities and interests of groups and individuals, in which those identities and interests are not taken as given but are seen to be constructed in the course of conflicts – a classic illustration being the way in which the various parties to the Bosnian conflict are created by that conflict rather than representing pre-existent monolithic identities such as 'Muslims' or 'Serbs'. Connolly's interests are less obviously international, his contribution more closely related to the 'Culture Wars' of the modern US, but his critique of American pluralism as a unifying and categorizing force as opposed to the kind of 'pluralization' that he would favour, in which no attempt is made to privilege particular kinds of interest and where the self-definition of actors is respected, draws on similar resources (Connolly 1995).

Campbell and Connolly are self-described 'late-modern' writers, who have by no means lost contact with the notion of emancipation – their worry, most explicit in Connolly, is that conventional notions of emancipation are likely to combine with contemporary technology to create a world in which 'difference' is abolished, in which human variety is 'normalized' and, as Nietzsche put it over a century ago, everyone thinks alike and those who do not voluntarily commit themselves to the madhouse (Connolly 1991). The theme that the speed of modern life, the capacity for simulation and the creation of 'virtual reality' will fundamentally shift the ways in which we are able to think of ourselves as free and emancipated has been taken up in the discourses of IR, most prominently by James Der Derian. His early and pioneering work on the genealogy of diplomacy pursued Foucauldian themes, but his later work on spies, speed and 'anti-diplomacy' has rested in particular on the work of Paul Virilio – one of the only writers referred to in this section who could accurately be described as postmodernist, in so far his oeuvre suggests that the pace of contemporary existence (in every sense of the term) is actually taking us beyond the modern into a new era (Der Derian 1987, 1992, 1998). Der Derian's work on 'virtual war' has interesting connections with other attempts to trace the changing nature of warfare, and will be discussed briefly below, in Chapters 6 and 11.

There is no particular reason why feminist writings should be associated with post-structuralism as opposed to the other positions outlined in this chapter – and, indeed, one of the most influential of feminist writers on IR, Jean Bethke Elshtain, whose work on war and the public/private divide is discussed in a later chapter, certainly could not be described in these terms (Elshtain 1987, 1998). Nonetheless, the majority of feminist writers in the field do fall naturally into this section rather than, say the constructivist or critical theoretical section. The central point here is that the voice of the European Enlightenment is seen as masculine, and feminist writers such as Christine Sylvester (1994), Ann Tickner (1992), Cynthia Enloe (1989, 1993) and Cynthia Weber (1999) are not prepared to see the association of 'European, rationalist and male' as contingent (in the way that, for example, a liberal feminist simply concerned with 'women's equality' might). These writers share with the other authors discussed above the view that the project of emancipation of the Enlightenment is not recoverable by, in this case, simply adding women to the equation. Instead they attempt, in various ways, to develop accounts of the social world that trace the influence of gender in all our categories, most particularly, of course, in this context, in our notions of the 'international'.

As with the other writers in this section, the goal is to dislocate our sense of what is 'normal', to cause us to re-think assumptions that we did not even know *were* assumptions. Tickner and Enloe engage in this project in ways which ultimately connect back to the wider goals of critical theory and an expanded, revised notion of human emancipation. Other writers have no such ambition. Perhaps the most striking and controversial piece of writing in the latter camp is Cynthia Weber's account of US policy towards the Caribbean and Central America over the last generation in terms of the projection of fears of castration created by the survival of Castro's regime in Cuba (1999). This particular example of feminist IR writing is by no means typical, but the forging of links with another substantial body of contemporary social theory – in this case, gender studies and so-called 'queer theory' – certainly illustrates the general ambition of post-positivist IR to break away from the statist assumptions characteristic of mainstream theory.

Conclusion

The aim of this chapter has been to provide an overview of contemporary International Relations theory. As with any other sketch-map, it may not be possible to find a particular location by employing it – the further readings provide the information needed for that task – but the reader ought now to have some sense of how the often bewildering variety of IR theories relate to each other. As the above discussion suggests, one answer is 'not very closely'. As suggested in the introduction to this chapter, IR theory since 1980 has involved a dialogue with the work of Kenneth Waltz – or at times 'running battle' would be more appropriate – and the authors discussed in the second half of the chapter agree in their rejection of neorealism, but they agree on little else. Perhaps the only features post-positivist writers have in common is their post-positivism – that is, their rejection of the epistemological stance of rational choice theory, and, more generally, their rejection of a 'foundationalist' account of the world, in which knowledge can be grounded by the correspondence of theory to a knowable reality. Contrary to the occasional slur of their opponents, post-positivists do not deny the existence of a 'real world' but they do deny our ability to grasp that world without the aid of theoretical categories which cannot themselves be validated by an untheorized reality. Beyond these epistemological commonalities, it is difficult to characterize the opponents of the 'neo-neo' consensus.

However, the hope is that when, in future chapters, a particular theoretical position is mentioned it will now to be possible for the reader to have a sense of what conceptual baggage is associated with that position, and where he or she needs to go to find a fuller account. With this in mind, it is now possible to turn away, for the time being at least, from an emphasis on theory and look to the actual picture of the world that these theories have created. First, the world of states will be examined, then the world of global forces – but before that world is reached, after another three chapters, a re-examination of theoretical issues specifically oriented towards globalization will be required.

Further Reading

Although the books referred to in the main body of this chapter obviously have been significant for the debate between pluralists, neorealists, and neoliberals, the most interesting contributions to this debate have been in the form of journal articles, generally in *International Organization, World Politics* and *International Security*. These articles are also available in a number of convenient collections, with some overlap in terms of contents.

Robert O. Keohane (ed.), *Neorealism and its Critics* (1986) contains extensive extracts from Waltz, *Theory of International Politics* (1979), as well as critiques by J. G. Ruggie, 'Continuity and Transformation in the World Polity: Towards a NeoRealist Synthesis' (1983), Robert Cox, 'Social Forces, States and World Orders: Beyond International Relations Theory' (1981) and an edited version of Richard K. Ashley, 'The Poverty of Neorealism' (1984) as well as papers by Keohane himself, Robert Gilpin's response to Ashley, 'The Richness of the Tradition of Political Realism' (1984) and a response to his critics by Kenneth Waltz. This is certainly the best collection on the early stages of the debate.

David A. Baldwin (ed.), *Neorealism and Neoliberalism: The Contemporary Debate* (1993) is the best recent collection; it is largely shaped around Joseph M. Grieco, 'Anarchy and the Limits of Cooperation: A Realist Critique of the Newest Liberal Institutionalism' (1988), and also contains, amongst other important papers, Robert Axelrod and Robert O. Keohane, 'Achieving Cooperation under Anarchy: Strategies and Institutions' (1985); Robert Powell, 'Absolute and Relative Gains in International Relations Theory' (1991); and Arthur Stein, 'Coordination and Collaboration: Regimes in an Anarchic World' (1982), as well as a valuable summary of the debate by Baldwin, and reflections on the reaction to his original article by Grieco.

Friedrich Kratochwil and Edward D. Mansfield (eds), *International Organization: A Reader* (1994) has a wider remit and contains a number of articles which are very valuable for the study of regimes (see Chapter 9 below). The general theory sections contain a number of classic articles which are critical of the neoliberal-neorealist way of setting things up. Cox (1981) is again reprinted, along with edited versions of Kratochwil and J. G. Ruggie, 'International Organization: A State of the Art on the Art of the State' (1986) and, especially important, Alexander Wendt, 'Anarchy is What States Make of It: The Social Construction of Power Politics' (1992). Also reprinted is Robert O. Keohane's classic 'International Institutions: Two Approaches' (1988).

Charles W. Kegley Jr (ed.), *Controversies in International Relations Theory: Realism and the Neoliberal Challenge* (1995) is somewhat less focused on the immediate debates than its competitors and contains a number of original pieces: it reprints Grieco (1988) and also Kenneth Waltz, 'Realist Thought and Neorealist Theory' (1990) as well as valuable, state-of-the-art summaries by Kegley and James Lee Ray.

Michael E. Brown, Scan M. Lynn-Jones and Steven Miller (eds), *The Perils of Anarchy: Contemporary Realism and International Security* (1995) is an *International Security* Reader, especially valuable on realist thought on the end of the Cold War (see Chapter 11 below). Of general theoretical interest are Kenneth Waltz, 'The Emerging Structure of International Politics' (1993); and, especially, John Mearsheimer, 'The False Promise of International Institutions' (1994/5) and Paul Schroeder's critique of neorealist accounts of the development of the international system 'Historical Reality vs. Neo-realist Theory' (1994).

Important articles and essays not collected above include Robert Powell, 'Anarchy in International Relations: The Neoliberal–Neorealist Debate' (1994), Joseph Nye, 'Neorealism and Neoliberalism' (1988), Ole Waever, 'The Rise and Fall of the Inter-paradigm Debate' (1996) and, particularly important, Robert Jervis, 'Realism, Neoliberalism and Co-operation: Understanding the Debate' (1999). Book-length studies in addition to those referred to in the text should include Robert Gilpin, *War and Change in World Politics* (1981) and Barry Buzan, Charles Jones and Richard Little, *The Logic of Anarchy: Neorealism to Structural Realism* (1993).

A Special Issue of *International Organization* 'International Organization at Fifty' edited by Peter Katzenstein, Robert O. Keohane and Stephen Krasner (1998) provides an overview of current mainstream theory, including constructivist voices such as that of J.G.Ruggie. New looks at both liberalism and realism, but still within a rational choice framework can be found in Andrew Moravcsik, 'Taking Preferences Seriously: The Liberal Theory of International Politics' (1997) and Jeffrey W. Legro and Andrew Moravcsik, 'Is Anybody Still a Realist?' (1999). A Forum in *American Political Science Review*, December 1997, on Waltzian neorealism contains a number of valuable contributions, including a reply to his critics from Kenneth Waltz himself.

The main constructivist writings by Kratochwil, Onuf, Ruggie and Wendt are referenced in the text. The *European Journal of International Relations* has become a major source for the journal literature in this area – see, for example, Emmanuel Adler, 'Seizing the Middle Ground' (1997), Richard Price and Christian Reus-Smit, 'Dangerous Liaisions: Critical International Theory and Constructivism' (1998) and Stefano Guzzini, 'A Reconstruction of Constructivism in International Relations' (2000). Vendulka Kubálkova *et al., International Relations in a*

Constructed World (1998) is a useful overview. Rodney Bruce Hall's *National Collective Identity: Social Constructs and International System* (1999) is a model of serious constructivist scholarship, as is the collection, Friedrich Kratochwil and Yosef Lapid (eds.), *The Return of Culture and Identity in International Relations Theory* (1996). Kratochwil's critique of Wendt's *Social Theory of International Politics*, 'Constructing a New Orthodoxy? Wendt's *Social Theory of International Politics* and the Constructivist Challenge' (2000) is itself a major statement.

For the 'English School', Hedley Bull, *The Anarchical Society* (1977/ 1995) remains crucial, and an earlier collection, Herbert Butterfield and Martin Wight (eds), *Diplomatic Investigations* (1966), is still the best general introduction to the approach. Tim Dunne, *Inventing International Society* (1998) is rapidly establishing itself as a the standard history of the School. The most interesting development in this mode is the attempt of two younger scholars to develop a 'critical' international society theory: N.J. Wheeler, 'Pluralist and Solidarist Conceptions of International Society: Bull and Vincent on Humanitarian Intervention' (1992); Tim Dunne, 'The Social Construction of International Society' (1995); and Dunne and Wheeler, 'Hedley Bull's Pluralism of the Intellect and Solidarism of the Will' (1996). Following an initiative by Barry Buzan, with Richard Little and Ole Waever, there is now a very useful website promoting the English School as a research programme – <http://www.ukc.ac.uk/politics/englishschool.

Hazel Smith, 'Marxism and International Relations Theory' (1994) is a valuable bibliographical survey. Anthony Brewer, *Marxist Theories of Imperialism: A Critical Survey* (1990) is the best survey of both older and newer theories of imperialism. Fred Halliday, *Rethinking International Relations* (1994) offers the most accessible and best overview of the field from a (somewhat) Marxist perspective. Works on dependency theory and centre–periphery analysis will be discussed in Chapter 10 below. Gramscian international political economy is discussed in Chapter 9; Stephen Gill (ed.), *Gramsci, Historical Materialism and International Relations* (1993) is a useful collection, and a good survey is Randall D. Germain and Michael Kenny, 'Engaging Gramsci: International Relations Theory and the New Gramscians' (1998).

Habermasian critical theory is well represented by Linklater's *The Transformation of Political Community* (1998): see also his *Beyond Realism and Marxism* (1990) and the programmatic 'The Question of the Next Stage in International Relations Theory: A Critical-Theoretic Approach' (1992). The collection, James Bohman and Matthias Lutz-

Bachmann (eds) *Perpetual Peace: Essays on Kant's Cosmopolitan Ideal* (1997), contains essays by a number of important critical theorists, including Jürgen Habermas himself. The latter's *The Past as Future* (1994) contains some of his explicitly 'international' writings on the Gulf War and German politics. German speakers are referred to his *Die Zeit* essay on the Kosovo Campaign of 1999, as fine an example of critical thinking in practice as one could hope for, which it is to be hoped will soon be translated; Jürgen Habermas, 'Bestialität und Humanität: Ein Krieg an der Grenze zwischen Recht und Moral' (1999).

Major post-structuralist collections include James Der Derian and Michael Shapiro (eds), *International/Intertextual: Postmodern Readings in World Politics* (1989); Richard Ashley and R. B. J. Walker (eds), 'Speaking the Language of Exile: Dissidence in International Studies' Special Issue, *International Studies Quarterly* (1990), Michael Shapiro and Hayward R. Alker (eds), *Challenging Boundaries: Global Flows, Territorial Identities* (1996) and Jenny Edkins, Nalini Persram and Veronique Pin-Fat, (eds) *Sovereignty and Subjectivity* (1999). Jenny Edkins, *Poststructuralism and International Relations: Bringing the Political Back In* (1999) is an excellent, albeit quite difficult guide to this literature; easier going guides include Richard Devetak, 'Critical Theory' (1996) and 'Postmodernism' (1996) and Chris Brown, 'Critical Theory and Postmodernism in International Relations' (1994a) and ' "Turtles All the Way Down": Antifoundationalism, Critical Theory, and International Relations' (1994b). Also very valuable is Yosef Lapid, 'The Third Debate: On the Prospects of International Theory in a Post-Positivist Era' (1989).

Apart from the feminist writers mentioned in the text, readers are referred to V.Spike Peterson (ed.) *Gendered States: Feminist (Re) Visions of International Relations Thery* (1992), Marysia Zalewski and Jane Papart (eds) *The 'Man' Question in International Relations* (1997) and, best of recent textbooks in the area, Jill Steans, *Gender and International Relations: An Introduction* (1998). The debate between Adam Jones and his critics in the *Review of International Studies* provides an interesting insight into the issue of feminism and emancipation – Jones, 'Gendering International Relations' (1996), Terrell Carver, Molly Cochran and Judith Squires, 'Gendering Jones', (1998) and Jones, 'Engendering Debate' (1998).

4

The State and Foreign Policy

Introduction

In this and the next two chapters, the realist agenda will be examined – which is to say that these chapters will be concerned with the state, foreign policy, power, security, conflict and war. This is the 'realist' agenda in the sense that these are the topics identified by realism and neorealism as the important topics for the study of international relations, but, of course, there is no reason to be limited to saying realist things about this agenda; on the contrary, some of the conclusions drawn here will not be those that realism would draw – the aim is a critical engagement with these topics. Whether this realist agenda ought still to be the primary focus for the study of IR is, of course, a controversial issue, but there are good reasons for at least starting with this agenda – it is, after all, how the subject has been defined for most of the last century and even if the aim is to develop a different agenda there is much to be said for starting with the familiar before moving to the unfamiliar.

The State and International Relations

Realism offers a *state-centric* account of the world, and, because realism takes the state to be central to international relations, topics such as the study of foreign policy decision-making or the analysis of the components of national power loom large; for the same reason interstate 'war' is taken to be *sui generis*, unlike any other form of social conflict. This state-centricity suggests that realism ought to have a clear theory of the state and that this should be the natural jumping-off point for the rest of its thinking. As it happens this is not the case;

the lack of such a theory is an important problem at the heart of realism, indeed of International Relations as an academic discourse. It is striking that there are so few good studies of 'the state and IR' – John M. Hobson's excellent recent volume is the first introduction to the subject to be published for many a year (Hobson 2000).

However, although *theory* is missing, realism offers quite an elaborate *description* of the state and of its emergence. The state is a *territorially-based political unit* characterized by a central decision-making and enforcement machinery (a government and an administration); the state is legally 'sovereign' in the sense that it recognizes neither an external superior, nor an internal equal; and the state exists in a world composed of other, similarly characterized, territorial, sovereign political units. These criteria can each best be established by reference to alternative modes of political organization, some of which were the points of origin of the modern state. Thus we can see what the state is, by contrasting it with what it is *not*.

The state is a territorial political unit, and there is clearly no necessity that politics should be arranged on a territorial basis. In classical Greece, the political referent was the inhabitants of a place rather than the place itself – hence in the writings of the day it is never 'Athens' that is referred to, always 'the Athenians'. Obviously, the Athenians lived in a territory, but they were the focal point not the territory as such, and although the walls of the city were well defined, the boundaries of the wider territory occupied by the Athenians were not. In the medieval European world out of which the modern state emerged, political authority was personal or group based rather than necessarily territorial. While a ruler might, in principle, claim some kind of authority over a territory there would always be other sources of authority (and indeed power) to contest such a claim. The universal church under the authority of the Pope operated everywhere and its members, lay and clergy, were obliged to deny the secular ruler's writ in a number of critical areas of policy. Guilds and corporations claimed 'liberties' against kings and princes, often with success. Many individuals owed allegiance to powerful local magnates, who might in turn owe allegiance to 'foreign' rulers rather than to the nominal king of a particular territory. All of these factors fed into issues such as 'political identity'; any particular individual was likely to have a number of different identities of which territorial identity might well be the least politically significant. For the average villager, being the bondsman or woman of a particular lord would be of far greater significance than being 'English' or 'French', as would one's identity as a Christian. Moreover this latter, wider identity was a reminder that once upon a time in Europe the political order as well as the religious order had been universal; the Roman Empire cast a long shadow, understandably since, at its peak, it had offered more effective rule than any of its medieval successors.

The emergence of a system of states is the product of the downfall of this world, usually dated to the fifteenth and sixteenth centuries; the Peace of Westphalia which ended the Thirty Years War in 1648 is often seen as a convenient starting-point for the new order. The new system emerged for a number of reasons. New military techniques and technologies – especially the professionalization of infantry and improvements of siege-craft – favoured larger political units and undermined the defensive viability of towns and castles. Economic growth, connected to, but also promoting, the conquest of the Americas and voyages of exploration to the East, also allowed for the development of larger political units. On the other hand, administrative techniques and the technology of communication did not favour continental-wide political organization, and the break-up of the universal church undermined the ideological basis of European unity. The result was the emergence of relatively strong territorially-based political units, capable of exerting control domestically, but obliged to accept the existence of similarly formed political units externally. This is the *Westphalia System*, and over the centuries it has reproduced itself successfully throughout the world to create the modern global system.

This is the story of the origins of the system that state-centric International Relations tells and a good story it is, with plenty of opportunities for variation in the re-telling. Thus Marxists (and political economists more generally) can tell the story from a materialist perspective, stressing changes in the world economy and the processes of production. Technological determinists and military historians can point to the impact of new weapons technology and improvements in ship design. Others look to the importance of ideas, in particular to the revival of classical learning (the Renaissance), including classical ideas on politics, and the emergence of the Protestant religion and the concomitant break-up of the universal church. Most likely, some combination of these factors led to the emergence of the Westphalia System.

In any event, whichever version is adopted, even if we can tell where states *come from*, it still remains for us to say what states actually *do*. The standard account of the origins of the system does not offer a theory of the state – and this is a crucial omission since if, for example, we wish to understand 'foreign policy' and 'statecraft' we will be seriously handicapped in this ambition if we do not have a clear sense of what it is that states are motivated by, what their function is, how they work. In practice, of course, state-centric International Relations does have something approaching a theory of the state – the problem is that because this theory is largely implicit and not clearly articulated it pulls together a number of contradictory elements which need to be sorted out if progress is to be made. What, then, is the state?

One answer to this question is that the state is purely and simply a *concentration of power*, of brute strength, of basic (military) force. This is the *Machtpolitik* conception of the German thinker Treitschke in the nineteenth century, and it does, indeed, correspond quite well to the realities of state-formation in sixteenth-century Europe – or, for that matter, in parts of the Third World today (Treitschke 1916/1963). As described by, for example, Charles Tilly, what states did in the sixteenth century was raise taxes and make war, activities which complemented each other (Tilly 1990, (ed.) 1975). States that made war successfully expanded their territory and hence their tax base; with the expanded tax base they could raise more money to expand their armies and thus conquer more territory and so on. The idea that the state is essentially a military entity has a certain plausibility, and has recently been reinforced by the work of historical sociologists such as Michael Mann and social theorists such as Anthony Giddens. Mann suggests that 'societies' are artificial constructs held together by force, and the story of the Westphalia System is the story of militarism and successful conquest, while for Giddens the role of the nation-state and violence has been an undertheorized topic, an omission he wishes to rectify (Mann 1986/1993; Giddens 1985).

Some realist writers have signed up to this militarist account of the state, with approval (more or less) in the case of Treitschke, resignedly in other cases. The pacifism practised by Christian realists such as Niebuhr and Wight stemmed partly from their sense that, once one understood the working of the state and the states-system, the only moral attitude that could be adopted towards international relations was one of detachment from the struggle. However, in both cases, things are not clear cut. Niebuhr did believe in the possibility that the state could be based on something other than force, while Wight's ambiguity on the matter allows us to see him as an intellectual leader of the English school as well as the leading British post-war realist (Bull 1976). More characteristic of realism than a simple military account of the state has been a Weberian notion of power coupled with responsibility. Weber stresses that, ideally, the state should possess a monopoly of violence, but what it actually possesses is a monopoly of *legitimate* violence. This opens up a second front with respect to the theory of the state – the idea that the state is an institution which is legitimated by its people, because it represents them, acting on their behalf at home and abroad.

Whereas the idea that the state is a pure expression of power fits comfortably with absolutism and the pretensions of the princes and kings of early modern Europe, the idea that the state has this *representative* function is resonant of contract theory and the ideas of the Enlightenment, but perhaps especially of the post-Enlightenment emphasis on 'community' and the 'nation'. German thought is crucial here; it is to Herder that we owe the idea that the proper basis for political authority is the nation, the pre-given identity of a 'people' expressed in their folkways and, especially, their language (Barnard (ed.) 1969). In Hegel we find the idea that the constitutional *Rechtstaat* is the forum within which the tensions and contradictions of social life are resolved (Hegel 1821/1991). Combined with the revival of Roman-style republican patriotism promoted by French revolutionaries after 1789, these German ideas feed into the nationalist movements of the nineteenth century, and out of this mix emerges the 'nation-state' – the idea that the only legitimate form of state is the state which embodies and represents the nation.

Clearly, this is an account of the state that can be filled out in at least two directions. On the one hand, the nation-state could become simply a new manifestation of the *Machtstaat*. Instead of collecting and employing power in the name of the Prince, the power of the state is wielded on behalf of the nation. National glory and national honour replace the personal glory and honour of the ruler. *Raison d'état*, the logic of *Realpolitik*, power politics, is replaced by the *national interest* as the driving motivation of state conduct – but little else changes. Although not given to ruminations on national glory, Carl Schmitt, with his notion that the concept of the political is about a division between friends and enemies and that the modern state is an entity which rests on the externalizing of this dichotomy, can also be seen in this light (Schmitt 1932/1996). On the other hand, once the idea that the state represents the nation is current, the possibility exists that the state will come to see the welfare of its people, rather than its power as such, as central. The warfare state comes to be superseded by the welfare state. National well-being rather than national honour or glory defines the national interest. Nor is this simply a theoretical possibility; it is striking that some of the contemporary European states who have the strongest reputation for being peaceful, non-threatening, cooperative, good neighbours are also states which have a very strong sense of identity as *nation-states* – the Scandinavian countries are obvious examples here of countries which seemed to have been able to harness the sentiments of nationalism away from the drive for power, towards a concern for the welfare of the people.

However the influence of the nation/community makes itself felt, it is clear that this conception of the state is different from that of the state as simply a concentration of power. There is, however, a third conception of the state that stands somewhere between both the idea that the state is simply an accumulation of power, and the idea that the state has a positive role in promoting the interests of the people. This is the notion that the state does play a positive role in social life, but a role which is *facilitatory* rather than constructive, enabling rather than creative. This is a conception of the state that could be termed 'liberal' – so long as one were prepared to accept Thomas Hobbes as a proto-liberal – and which is certainly characteristic of English social contract theory and the thinking of the Scottish (as opposed to the French or German) Enlightenment. The thinking here is that individuals have interests and desires that drive them to cooperate with others, but that this cooperation is either impossible (Hobbes) or likely to be achieved only at suboptimal levels (Locke) in the absence of some mechanism for ensuring that agreements are adhered to, that is, without the coercive power of the state.

This is a theory of the state which makes it of very great importance in social life, but which denies it a creative role in forming the national interest – indeed, it denies that the 'national interest' has much meaning beyond being a kind of catch-all description of the sum of the individual interests of citizens. It is a theory of the state which has been the dominant line of thought for several centuries in the English-speaking countries – a fact of some significance given that International Relations is an academic discipline that has always been predominantly British and American in inspiration – and which has obviously influenced liberal internationalist theory. Indeed, it could be argued that one of the weaknesses of liberal internationalism was its inability to grasp that within some political traditions the state is given a far more exalted role than it is in liberalism, while from other perspectives the state is simply a concentration of power. The Anglo–American liberal account of the state is actually closer to a theory of 'administration' than it is to a theory of the state in the continental European sense. Some of the Anglo–American realists, especially continentally trained Anglo–Americans such as Morgenthau, were conscious of this difference, but it is noticeable that the neorealists and neoliberals, possibly because of the debt they owe to the economics profession, largely operate within a liberal theory of the state. Robert Gilpin's remark that the role of the state is to solve the problem of 'free riders' is a perfect expression of this point (Gilpin 1981: 16).

Finally, one the most compelling modern alternatives to this liberal theory of the state is the Marxist conception of the state as the executive arm of the dominant class – under capitalism, the ruling committee of the bourgeoisie. Marxism shares with liberalism the notion that the state is a secondary formation but rather than seeing it perform a valuable function for society as a whole, Marxists argue that the state cannot be a neutral problem-solver, but will always represent some particular interests – radical liberals such as the earlier John Hobson would agree, as would the very influential modern anarchist, Noam Chomsky, whose critiques of US/Western foreign policy rest upon the notion that state power is exercised on behalf of an unrepresentative elite (Hobson 1902/1938: Chomsky 1994). Although Marxism is no longer the official ideology of one of the two superpowers, Marxist ideas remain influential, especially when filtered through figures such as Chomsky; in fact, since many Marxist theorists now stress the 'relative autonomy' of the state, Chomsky and his followers are the main contemporary group of theorists who adhere to a crude Marxist account of the role of the state. Finally in this connection, it should be noted that the practical result of this crude position is usually to align Marxist/Chomskyan ideas with the 'hard' realist notion of the state as simply a concentration of power – Chomsky shares with realism a total rejection of the idea that the state could represent the 'people' or a community, much less be some kind of ethical actor; Chomskyans, Marxists and realists all agree that such talk represents liberal obfuscation. More than anything else, it is perhaps the opportunity he offers to be a 'left-wing' realist that accounts for the extraordinary popularity of Chomsky's conspiracy theories. In Chomsky the saloon-bar, cynical, realist can find justification without having to abandon progressivist sympathies.

Foreign and Domestic Policy: The 'Decision' as Focus

These theories of the state are obviously very different, and it might be expected that they would generate different theories of foreign policy and statecraft. Yet on the whole this has not happened; as we will see most accounts of foreign policy do not relate back to an explicit theory of the state, somewhat to their disadvantage. Rather, a vaguely liberal account of the state as a problem solver exists in the background of a great deal of foreign policy analysis (FPA) but is rarely articulated.

The working assumption of most FPA is that the state as a social institution exists in two environments: on the one hand, there is the (internal) environment that is composed of all the other institutions located in the territory demarcated by the state and their interactions with it and each other; on the other, there is the (external) environment composed of all other states and their interactions with it and each other. Conventional International Relations theory assumes that the state is constantly involved in attempts to intervene in both environments, that is, engages in 'domestic' and 'foreign policy'. Realist theory, as distinct from, for example, pluralism, assumes that these two forms of policy are different; in the case of domestic policy, the state is, in principle, capable of getting its way having decided on a course of action, that is to say it possesses both the authority to act, and the means to do so. In foreign policy this is not so; outcomes are the product of interdependent decision-making. The state cannot expect that other states will respect its authority, because in an anarchical system no state possesses authority, and whether or not the state has the means to get its way is a contingent matter – whereas domestically the state, in principle, possesses a monopoly of the means of coercion, internationally no state is in this position. What this means is that we can distinguish two aspects of the study of foreign policy; the way in which foreign policy is formulated – which might be rather similar to the way in which domestic policy is formulated – and the way in which foreign policy is implemented – which is likely to be very different. The latter is largely treated in the next chapter, policy formulation in this.

On the traditional account of foreign policy formulation, what is involved is recognizing and articulating the 'national interest' in so far as it affects a particular issue. Thus, for example, in the years prior to 1914 the British foreign policy establishment had to formulate a policy with respect to the changing pattern of forces in Europe, in particular the perceived growth of German power and the attempt by Germany to project this power on a world stage. British diplomacy already had a longstanding view with respect to the pattern of forces in continental Europe – namely that it was against any concentration that might control the Channel ports and the North Sea and thus undermine the Royal Navy and oblige Britain to develop a large enough army to defend itself from invasion – and the policy-making process of the decade prior to 1914 can be seen as a matter of adapting this view to new circumstances by shifting the focus of concern away from the traditional enemy, France, towards the new challenger, Germany. How and why did this adaptation come about? Rather more dramatically, in a few years in the 1940s the United States abandoned its long-held policy of 'isolationism', and, for the first time, became committed to an extensive range of peace-time alliances. How and why did this reversal occur?

One way of answering these and similar questions is by employing the methods of the diplomatic historian. Assuming the relevant documents are available, this may give us a satisfactory account of particular changes, but it is not really what we want. As students of international relations we wish to possess a general account of how foreign policy is made and the national interest identified. We are looking to identify patterns of behaviour rather than to analyze individual instances. We may sometimes employ the methods of the historian in our 'case studies', but our aim is to generalize, whereas the historian particularizes. How do we achieve generalizations about foreign policy formulation? Foreign-policy analysis (FPA) for most of the last 50 years tells us that the best way to do this is to break down the processes of foreign-policy-making into a series of 'decisions', each of which can in turn be analyzed in order that we may see what factors were influential in which circumstances. Thus a general theory of foreign-policy-making may slowly emerge.

The originators of the foreign-policy decision-making approaches were American behavioural scientists working in the 1950s, who saw themselves as effectively 'operationalizing' the idea of the national interest, developing large-scale classificatory schemas in which a place was made for all the factors that might have gone into making any particular decision, from the influence of the mass media, to the personality of decision-makers, from institutional features of the policy-making body, to socio–psychological factors about threat perception. These schemata were impressive, but a classification is not the same as an explanation; a list of all factors that *might* be relevant is much less useful than a theory which predicts which factors *will* be relevant. Moreover, putting a schema in operation, filling all the boxes, was an horrendously complex task. What was required was not so much a classification scheme as a model which would simplify the myriad factors involved; this was provided in 1971 by *Essence of Decision*, Graham Allison's outstanding case study of the Cuban Missile Crisis of 1962, one of the few genuine classics of modern International Relations (Allison 1971).

In fact, Allison provides three models of decision, each of which is used to provide a different account of the decisions that characterized the crisis – which are simplified to first, the Soviet decision to deploy Intermediate Range Ballistic Missiles (IRBMs) on Cuba, second, the American decision to respond to this deployment with a blockade and third, the Soviet decision to withdraw the IRBMs. His point is that, contrary to his title, there is no 'Essence of Decision', only different ways of seeing the same events.

His first model is the *Rational Actor Model* (RAM). This corresponds to the kind of analysis favoured by traditional accounts of the national interest. Foreign-policy decisions are assumed to be rational responses to a particular situation, formulated by a single unitary state actor. Rationality is seen in ends/means terms; that is to say, it is assumed that states choose the course of action that maximizes their gains/minimizes their losses in the context of a given set of values. Decisions can be studied by a process of rational reconstruction, armchair analysis in which the analyst puts him or herself into the position of the decision-maker, and attempts to simulate the processes of reasoning which might have led the decision-maker to act as he or she did. Thus, in order to explain why the Soviet Union deployed missiles when and where it did, one must specify the goals the Soviets wished to attain and the chain of reasoning that led them to think that such a deployment would meet these goals – always bearing in mind that the goals may not be those that are actually explicitly stated; indeed, the best way of approaching the real goals may be to work back from the actions taken. Rational reconstruction is a difficult business; a full 'simulation' would require the analyst to have all the information available to the decision-maker, and *only* this information – which is a tall order. Nonetheless, we engage in this kind of reconstructive thinking all the time and can usually come up with a fairly plausible account of how decisions are taken.

Allison suggests there are two kinds of problem with this model. First, the notion that action is fully 'rational' poses problems. The requirements for rational action are never actually met. They involve a fully specified set of values to be maximized, an account of all the possible courses of action available to the decision-maker and a set of algorithms that allow us to predict the consequences of each action. Perfect information such as this simply is not available – not to the original decision-maker, nor to later analysts. Such information would be the equivalent to, say, a fully specified decision-tree for a game of chess; still a practical impossibility even for the fastest computer. In fact we make decisions in much the same way that we play chess – we have some rules of conduct which help us especially in the early stages of a game when we face known situations, and later, when faced with unknown situations, we explore what we take to be the most promising moves, and act when we are satisfied that we have found the best move we can given time constraints. This is a 'rational' way to play the game or make decisions – although the possibility always exists that the next option we might have examined will be better than our actual choice – but reconstructing a game played like this is extremely difficult. Intuition may be more use than purely rational processes of thought, and one of the things that will need to be simulated is time pressure. We cannot assume that a move is always the best move even if made by a grandmaster; even grandmasters make terrible mistakes when the clock is ticking. The RAM assumes that states always intend the consequences of their actions, but the real circumstances under which decisions are made may falsify this assumption.

A second problem with the RAM is more practical. Even when we come to a conclusion using rational reconstruction there are almost always anomalies left unexplained. Thus Allison suggests that the most plausible RAM explanation of the Soviet IRBM deployment is that it was designed to close what they perceived to be a widening gap in capabilities between themselves and the US, but this leaves unexplained some of the features of the actual deployment which seem to have been almost calculated to encourage early discovery by the US. The alternative view that they were indeed *designed* to be discovered covers the anomalies but explains less overall than the missile-gap explanation.

Possibly a better RAM explanation could be found, but Allison suggests instead that we shift to another model of decision. The rational actor model assumes that decisions are the product of calculation by a single actor; the *Organizational Process Model* assumes that decisions are made by multiple organizations each of whom have characteristic ways of doing things – organizational *routines* and *standard operating procedures* – and are resistant to being organized by any kind of central intelligence. Not by accident, this fits in with earlier comments about coping with the lack of perfect information. When faced with a problem, organizations such as the KGB, Soviet Rocket Forces, or the American Navy and Air Force do not attempt to solve it by starting from scratch; rather they delve into their institutional memories and try to remember how they dealt with similar problems before. Thus, when tasked with building a missile base in Cuba, Soviet Rocket Forces (SRF) use the same basic layout they use in the Soviet Union, because experience suggests that this is the best way of building a missile base; the fact that it is identifiable to US air re-connaissance as such is not something that occurs to them. Conversely the KGB transported the missiles in secret and the dead of night, because that is how the KGB does things. This looks anomalous in the light of the almost publicity-seeking methods of the SRF – but it is only an anomaly if one assumes that someone is directing both organizations to behave in this way. On the contrary, it is possible that if the overall directors of the Soviet effort had known what was going on, they would have been horrified.

It might be thought that this exaggerates the autonomy of organizations, but a US example reinforces the point. The US Air Force under General Curtis Le May actually wanted to bomb the missile sites, but the report of probable casualties they produced was horrendous and they could not guarantee 100 per cent success; as a result the attack was put on hold by President Kennedy. A later investigation revealed that the Air Force had simply taken an existing plan to attack Cuban installations and added the missile sites – hence the predicted high casualties. Moreover, they had assumed the missiles were mobile and that some would be missed; in fact, the missiles were only 'mobile' in the context of a time scale running into weeks, and an attack could indeed very likely have produced a 100 per cent success rate. This is an interesting example precisely because the US Air Force were actually in favour of the operation; usually when the military provide high casualty estimates it is because, for one reason or another, they wish to dissuade the politicians from using force, a point which leads to the next of Allison's models.

The organizational process model downplays the idea of rational central control of decisions. In his final *Bureaucratic Politics* model, Allison deconstructs rational decision-making from another direction stressing the extent to which political factors external to the overt international issue may affect decision-making. One aspect of this is the way in which bureaucracies see the world from the perspective of their own organization. As the slogan has it, 'Where you sit determines where you stand'. In the United States, the State Department usually favours negotiation, the UN Representative action by the UN, the US Navy action by the US Navy and so on. It is not to be expected that organizations will promote courses of action that do not involve enhancements to their own budgets. More important is the fact that leaders have their own political positions to protect and defend. During the Cuban Missile Crisis President Kennedy knew that his actions could have posed severe political problems to his chances of re-election, and, more immediately, the Democratic Party's prospects in the mid-term Congressional elections in November 1962 – although, interestingly, research now suggests that this was not a determining factor in his actions (Lebow and Stein 1994: 95). The assumption of the Rational Actor Model (and of realism in general) is that foreign-policy decisions will be taken on foreign-policy grounds. The bureaucratic politics model suggests that this often will not be the case.

The conceptual models Allison established in *Essence of Decision* have survived remarkably well, even though his case study has been superseded by later work drawing on Soviet and American sources available since the end of the Cold War. It is, however, clear that the models need to be supplemented. The biggest lack in Allison is a sufficient account of the *socio–psychological, cognitive* dimension of decision-making. Decision-makers interact with their *perceived* environment, and it may well be that their perceptions are incorrect (Jervis 1976; Cottam 1986). It might be thought that one way to correct misperceptions would be to hear as many voices as possible when making a decision, but Irving Janis in *Victims of Groupthink* demonstrates that collective bodies of decision-makers are just as likely to be vulnerable to misperceptions as individuals (Janis 1972). It is the lack of a good account of these issues that has caused Allison's case study to become outdated – later research emphasizes the extent to which the Soviet decision to act was based on fears created by US policy, ironically, in particular, by policies designed actually to deter the Soviets. US warnings of the consequences of deploying missiles on Cuba were interpreted as threats and signals of an intent to undermine Soviet positions (Lebow and Stein 1994). An emphasis on cognitive processes is also present in recent work on the role of ideas and ideologies in foreign-policy decision-making (Goldstein and Keohane (eds) 1993); again, the ending of the Cold War has provided much stimulus to this work: (Lebow and Risse-Kappen (eds) 1995).

There are other general problems with Allison's models. The emphasis on *crisis* decision-making is one such; crises – situations in which high-value stakes are played for under pressure of time – may produce patterns of behaviour that are very different from those in operation during 'normal' decision-making. Allison's elaborate models may only work in countries which have highly differentiated institutional structures; certainly, it is difficult to apply the organizational process model in those countries which do not have extensive bureaucracies. However, it would be surprising if a 30-year-old case study were not to be superseded in some respects, and Allison's models themselves are still employed. There are two ways in which one could read this. It may be that this demonstrates how well designed the models were; on this account, foreign-policy decision-making is one of the best established areas in International Relations and the lack of recent innovation in this field is a point in its favour. On the other hand, this longevity could be seen as a sign of weakness, an indicator that this is an area of International Relations theory where not much is happening – where a few basic points have been made and there is little else to say. Similar points could be made with respect to a number of other areas of foreign-policy analysis. For example, the study of public opinion and foreign policy, or pressure groups and foreign policy, also seem to be areas where there have been relatively few recent innovations. Most of the work being done takes the form of empirical case studies which shuffle and reshuffle a small number of ideas rather than create new theories – although Brian White offers a number of reasons why this judgement might be contested (White 1999).

Why is this? A key factor here may be the dominance in recent years of neorealist and neoliberal modes of thought. Both approaches emphasize analysis of the international system at the expense of for-eign-policy analysis. Although Waltzian neorealism pays lip service to the importance of the study of foreign policy, it offers a top-down account of international relations, an account in which the supreme skill of the foreign-policy decision-maker lies in recognizing the signals sent by the system. The decision-maker is a skilled craftsman rather than a creative artist. Neoliberalism also offers an account of interna-tional relations which works from the top down, albeit one that emphasizes the possibilities of cooperation. In each case the assump-tion that states are rational egoists operating under conditions of anarchy limits the space available for foreign policy as an autonomous area of enquiry. Effectively the rational actor model is being reinstated, albeit under new conditions One of the ironies of the dominance of rational *choice* in contemporary mainstream International Relations theorizing is that it appears to be antithetical to foreign-policy analysis. One might have thought that 'choice' and 'policy' would go together, but in practice the way in which rational choice thinking is expressed in neorealism and neoliberalism undermines this potential partnership. The system is the focus, and the behaviour of the units that make up the system is assumed to be determined by the system; as Waltz puts it, any theory to the contrary is 'reductionist' and patently false because the persistence of patterns over time in the system is unconnected with changes in the units (Waltz 1979). On this account, traditional components of foreign policy analysis such as 'public opinion', the influence of the media, pressure groups, organizational structure and so on can do little more than confuse the policy-maker, deflecting his or her attention from the real issue, which is the relationship between the state and the system.

A key battlefield for the contest between FPA as conventionally understood and neorealism concerns the relevance or irrelevance of 'regime-type'. From a neorealist perspective the nature of a domestic regime, whether liberal-democratic, authoritarian or totalitarian is of relatively little significance. A state is a state is an egoistic actor attempting to survive under the anarchy problematic. All else pales into insignificance in the face of this imperative. Consider, for example, a highly influential essay by the leading neorealist John Mearsheimer; in 'Back to the Future: Instability in Europe after the Cold War' (1990), Mearsheimer envisages a reappearance of the old pre-1914 patterns in Europe, and suggests that one way of controlling and stabilising this process would be to assist Germany to become a nuclear-weapons state. This is an interestingly counterintuitive suggestion, but what is striking in the present context is that the fact that virtually all sections of German public opinion, bar a neo-Nazi fringe, would be wholeheartedly opposed to this policy troubles Mearsheimer not at all. If this is the 'right' policy, then the assumption is that it will be adopted – 'right' in this context means appropriate to international conditions (i.e. the requirements of the balance of power) rather than domestic pressures. There is a problem of 'agency' here – more pro-saically put, a problem of finding a German government that could introduce this policy without being hounded from office – but this is a secondary matter. Foreign policy on this count becomes analogous to completing a crossword puzzle – we have the grid and the clues, the task is to get to the right answer; the policy-maker/solver cannot influence or determine this answer, only discover it, and implement it as effectively as possible.

From virtually every other perspective (with the possible exception of that of Chomsky) the idea that regime-type is of no significance is seen as plain silly. It seems intuitively implausible that the leaders thrown up by liberal-democratic political systems will react to external stimuli in the same way as the makers of military coups or the leaders of totalitarian mass parties. There may be pressures pointing them in the same direction, but, surely, their own values will have some impact on the decisions they actually take – as the example of modern Germany and nuclear weapons illustrates. Moreover, it seems inherently implausible that domestic social and economic structure is irrelevant to foreign policy – that the shape of a nation's society has no influence on its international behaviour. One, very controversial but interesting, investigation of these intuitions comes from the so called 'democratic peace' hypothesis – the proposition that constitutionally stable liberal-democratic states do not go to war with each other (although they are, in general, as war prone as other states when it come to relations with non-democracies). The reason this is particularly interesting is because, unlike some other challenges to the neorealist mode of thinking, it is an argument that employs the same kind of positivist methodology as the rational choice realists employ – it, as it were, challenges the neorealists on their own ground. Although the idea was first popularized as a somewhat unconventional extrapolation by Michael Doyle of the work of the political philosopher Kant to contemporary conditions, its main developers in the 1990s were empirical researchers employing the latest statistical techniques to refine the initial hypothesis and identify a robust version thereof (Doyle 1983: Russett 1993: Gleditch and Risse-Kappen (eds) 1995; Brown, *et al.* (eds) 1996).

If democratic peace thinking were to become established it would – and to some extent it already has – reinstate and relegitimize a quite traditional research programme with respect to foreign-policy analysis. Institutions, public opinion, norms, decision-making – these were the staple diet of foreign-policy studies before the dominance of structural accounts of international relations shifted them from centre-stage. The 'Democratic Peace' has brought this older agenda back as a potential central focus for contemporary International Relations and it is interesting that its main, and vociferous, opponents have been neorealists and Chomskyans, both of whom recognize how important it is for their position that the proposition be refuted or defeated (Layne 1994: Barkawi and Laffey 1999). Moreover, and returning to the starting-point of this chapter, it should be noted that here, more than with any other topic in foreign policy analysis, we have a theory of foreign-policy which grows out of an explicit theory of the state.

Although attempts to widen the scope of democratic peace thinking have been largely unsuccessful, the core proposition that constitutionally stable liberal democracies do not go to war with each other remains unrefuted – the worst that can be said about this proposition is that it may be that this highly specific kind of peacefulness is the product of some factor other than regime-type, or a statistical artefact produced by generalizing from too few cases. If this core proposition remains unrefuted, then we are left with a large anomaly in contemporary International Relations theory – because although the practical implications of neorealist thinking on these matters seem to be challenged by a successful argument that is clearly 'reductionist', the logic of neorealism remains untouched. The two bodies of thought seem to point in opposite directions. We have here, in effect, something quite similar to the discontinuity that exists in Economics between 'microeconomics' whose dominant theory of the firm does not seem to gel very well with the 'macroeconomic' theories concerning the economy as a whole. Whether or not we should regard this as a problem is a moot point; economists seem not to be too worried by their particular problem, and perhaps their strategy of moving on on all fronts and hoping that eventually some unifying notions will emerge is the sensible one to adopt.

Conclusion: From Foreign Policy to Power

The next stage in this investigation is to move from the making of foreign policy to its implementation – the realm of diplomacy or, to employ an old term that has made something of a comeback recently, 'statecraft'. In a larger-scale study, such an examination would involve a full-length exploration of the arts and crafts of diplomacy, the art of negotiation and so on. In later chapters on, for example, the establishment of international economic regimes, such matters will be touched upon, but in this part of the book, which is overtly concerned with state-centric International Relations, and shaped by the realist tradition, it makes more sense to shift to another aspect of implementation – the ways in which power is employed by states to get their way in the world. A focus on 'power', however, inevitably brings in considerations which go beyond foreign policy as such – hence the next chapter will examine power as a whole, and the problems it generates.

Further Reading

On pre-Westphalian 'international' systems, A. B. Bozeman, *Politics and Culture in International History* (1960) and Martin Wight, *Systems of States* (1977) offer contrasting views; close to Wight but more in the nature of a textbook is Adam Watson, *The Evolution of International Society: A Comparative Historical Analysis* (1992), which is the best short guide to the origins of the Westphalia System.

The work of historical sociologists on the origins of the system and the nature of the state has become important in recent years: for overviews, see Richard Little, 'International Relations and Large Scale Historical Change' (1994); and Anthony Jarvis, 'Societies, States and Geopolitics' (1989); apart from books by Giddens, Mann and Tilly cited in the main text above, important substantive works include Ernest Gellner, *Plough, Sword and Book: The Structure of Human History* (1988); George Modelski, *Long Cycles in World Politics* (1987); Paul Kennedy, *The Rise and Fall of the Great Powers* (1988); and Charles Tilly (ed.), *The Formation of National States in Western Europe* (1975).

On the state, P. Evans, D. Rueschemeyer and T. Skocpol (eds), *Bringing the State Back In* (1985) is, as the title suggests, a reaction to the absence of theorizing about the state. Friedrich Meinecke, *Machiavellism: The Doctrine of Raison d'Etat and its Place in Modern History* (1957) is a monumental, irreplaceable study. John M. Hobson, *The State and International Relations* (2000) is an excellent recent text on the subject.

Deborah J. Gerner, 'Foreign Policy Analysis: Exhilarating Eclecticism, Intriguing Enigmas' (1991) and Steve Smith, 'Theories of Foreign Policy: An Historical Overview' (1986) are good surveys of the field. Important general collections include Charles F. Hermann, Charles W. Kegley and James N. Rosenau (eds), *New Directions in the Study of Foreign Policy* (1987), Michael Clarke and Brian White (eds), *Understanding Foreign Policy: The Foreign Policy Systems Approach* (1989) and, on actual foreign policies, the classic Roy C. Macridis (ed.), *Foreign Policy in World Politics* (1992). Brian White, 'The European Challenge to Foreign Policy Analysis' (1999) is an interesting riposte to some disparaging remarks on FPA in the first edition of this volume. Christopher Hill, *The New Politics of Foreign Policy* (2001) will be a standard work in this area.

Recent critical works on Allison's classic study include Jonathan Bender and Thomas H. Hammond, 'Rethinking Allison's Models' (1992) and David A. Welch, 'The Organizational Process and Bureaucratic Politics Paradigm' (1992). The second, revised, edition of Allison's classic, (with Philip Zelikow 1999) is reviewed at length in Barton J. Bernstein, 'Understanding Decisionmaking, US Foreign Policy and the Cuban Missile Crisis' (2000). On the features of crisis diplomacy, see Michael Brecher, *Crises in World Politics: Theory and Reality* (1993); James L. Richardson, *Crisis Diplomacy* (1994); and Richard Ned Lebow, *Between Peace and War: The Nature of International Crisis* (1981). On cognitive processes and foreign policy see works by Jervis, Janis and Cottam cited in the main text.

Micro–macro problems in International Relations theory are discussed in Fareed Zakaria, 'Realism and Domestic Politics: A Review Essay' (1992), and the domestic–international interface in Peter B. Evans, Harold K. Jacobson and Robert D. Putnam (eds), *Double-Edged Diplomacy: International Diplomacy and Domestic Politics* (1993). Much older but still valuable is James N. Rosenau (ed.), *Domestic Sources of Foreign Policy* (1967). Alexander Wendt, 'The Agent/Structure Problem in International Relations Theory' (1987) is important here; see also Martin Hollis and Steve Smith, *Explaining and Understanding International Relations* (1991) – a debate between Wendt and Hollis and Smith has been underway in the *Review of International Studies* since 1992. On the older issue of the 'Levels-of-Analysis' problem, see Nicholas Onuf, 'Levels' (1995). Agent–structure issues feature in Alexander Wendt's important study *Social Theory of International Politics* (1999).

On the 'Democratic Peace' thesis, Bruce Russett, *Grasping the Democratic Peace: Principles for a Post-Cold War World* (1993) is crucial. For a Kantian perspective, see Michael Doyle, 'Liberalism and World Politics' (1986) and the articles cited in the text. Tarak Barkawi and Mark Laffey, 'The Imperial Peace: Democracy, Force and Globalization' (1999) challenge the thesis from a 'left' position, while realist opponents are well represented in the *International Security* Reader *Debating the Democratic Peace* (1996). Joanne Gowa, *Ballots and Bullets: The Elusive Democratic Peace* (1999) is an important study. A selection of additional articles might include: Chris Brown, '"Really-Existing Liberalism" and International Order' (1992b); Raymond Cohen, 'Pacific Unions: A Reappraisal of the Theory that "Democracies Do Not Go To War with Each Other"' (1994); Bruce Russett, J. L. Ray and Raymond Cohen, 'Raymond Cohen on Pacific Unions: A Response and a Reply' (1995); and John MacMillan, 'Democracies Don't Fight: A Case of the Wrong Research Agenda' (1996).

5

Power and Security

Introduction: Statecraft, Influence and Power

From a foreign-policy perspective, states attempt to change their environment in accordance with aims and objectives they have set for themselves. From a structural perspective, states attempt to adapt to their environment, making the best of the cards the system has dealt them. Either way, states act in the world. How? What is the nature of diplomacy or 'statecraft' – a slightly old-world term that has recently been given a new lease of life? The best discussion of this topic is that of David Baldwin, who produces a four-way taxonomy of the techniques of statecraft which provides a useful starting-point for this discussion. *Propaganda* he defines as 'influence attempts relying primarily on the deliberate manipulation of verbal symbols'; *diplomacy* refers to 'influence attempts relying primarily on negotiation'; *economic statecraft* covers 'influence attempts relying on resources which have a reasonable semblance of a market price in terms of money'; and *military statecraft* refers to 'influence attempts relying primarily on violence, weapons, or force' (Baldwin 1985: 13). The rest of this chapter examines the questions raised (or in some cases, avoided) by this classification.

A common feature of these techniques is that they are techniques of '*influence*'. The best way to think of influence is in terms of its two antonyms – authority and control – and then to ask whether influence is synonymous with power. States attempt to exert influence rather than *authority* because authority is something that can only emerge in legitimate relationships which do not exist between states. That is to say, it is an essential feature of the nature of authority that those over whom it is exercised acknowledge that those exercising it have a right to do so – that is to say, they are authorized to act. In international relations there is no authority in this sense of the term, or at least not with respect to issues of any real political significance. The contrast between influence and *control* works rather differently. When control is exercised, those who are controlled have lost all autonomy, they have no decision-making capacity. From a realist perspective, states would actually like to exercise control over their environment, but if any one state ever actually was in a position to control another, the latter would cease to be a 'state' in any meaningful sense of the term, and if any state were able to control all other states, then the current international system would be replaced by something else, namely an Empire.

Recasting these points, the exercise of influence is the characteristic way in which states relate to one another because we have neither a world government (a world-wide source of legitimate authority) nor a world empire (a world-wide source of effective control). In the absence of these two polar positions, only relationships of influence remain. Of course, in actual practice, there may be some relationships which approach the two poles. In an elaborate military alliance such as NATO, the governing council, the Supreme Allied Military Commander in Europe (SACEUR), and, in some circumstances, the president of the United States, could be said to exercise a degree of legitimate authority, having been authorized by the members of NATO to act on their behalf. However, this authority is tenuous and could be withdrawn at any time, albeit at some cost. Conversely, the degree of influence exercised by the former Soviet Union over some of its 'allies' in Eastern Europe at times came close to actual control, although even at the height of Stalinism the freedom of action of the weakest of the People's Republics was greater than that of the Baltic States which were incorporated into the Soviet Union in 1940. Sometimes freedom of action may only mean the freedom to give way to the inevitable, but even this can be meaningful; in the pre-war crises of 1938 and 1939, neither Czechoslovakia nor Poland had any real freedom, apart from that of determining the circumstances under which they would fall into Nazi control, but the way in which they exercised this final freedom had a real influence on the lives of their populations.

The relationship between influence and *power* is more complicated. Power is one of those terms in political discourse that are so widely used as to have become almost devoid of meaning; the suggestion that its use should be banned is impracticable, but understandable. Common-sense usage of the term power suggests that it is quite closely related to influence – a 'powerful person' is an influential person – but there are forms of influence that do not seem to rely on power as the term is usually understood, and there are forms of power that are only indirectly connected to influence. This is a particularly important relationship for a state-centric, especially a realist, view of the world, and, unlike the distinctions between influence and authority or control, this matter is too sensitive to be determined by definition. It is only by generating a quite sophisticated understanding of power that the realist view of the world can be comprehended – but, equally, such an understanding is required if realism is to be transcended.

Dimensions of Power

Power is a multi-faceted and complex notion, and it makes sense to think of the term under three headings, always bearing in mind that the three categories this will generate are closely interrelated. Power is an *attribute* – it is something that people or groups or states possess or have access to, have at hand to deploy in the world. Power is a *relationship* – it is the ability that people or groups or states have to exercise influence on others, to get their way in the world. These two dimensions of power are clearly not separable, and most realist accounts of international relations have a story to tell about them. A third dimension of power in which it is seen as a property of a *structure* is less easily incorporated into realist accounts of the world, at least in so far as these accounts rely on the notion that power can only be exercised by an actor or agent.

The idea that power is an *attribute* of states is a very familiar notion to traditional accounts of international relations. Most old textbooks, and many new ones, offer a list of the components of national power, the features of a country that entitle it to be regarded as a 'great' power, or a 'middle' power, or, more recently, a 'superpower'. These lists generally identify a number of different kinds of attributes that a state might possess in order to entitle it to claim its position in the world power rankings. These might include: the size and quality of its armed forces; its resource base, measured in terms of raw materials; its geographical position and extent; its productive base and infrastructure; the size and skills of its population; the efficiency of its governmental institutions, and the quality of its leadership. Some of these factors are immutable – geographical position and extent would be the obvious examples (although the significance of geographical features can change quite sharply over time). Others change only slowly (size of the population, rates of economic growth) while yet others can change quite rapidly (size of the armed forces). These points allow us to make a distinction between *actual* power and *potential* or *latent* power – the power that a state actually possesses at any one point of time as opposed to the power it could generate in a given time period.

The significance of any one of these factors as against the others will change over time. Population size and geographical extent can only add to the power of a state to the extent that the administrative, communication and transport infrastructure allows it to do so. For example, until the construction of the Trans-Siberian Railway in the 1890s, the quickest way to get from St Petersburg or Moscow to Vladivostok was by sea via the Baltic and North Seas and the Atlantic, Indian and Pacific Oceans, which meant that Russian land power in the East was at the mercy of British sea power, and in those circumstances the great size of Russia could rarely be translated into a genuine political asset. A relatively small country with a highly productive economy may be more powerful than a much larger country with a less productive economy – but there are limits. For example, no matter how economically successful Singapore is it will never be major military power in the absence of a sufficiently large population base. A culture that gives great respect to those who bear arms may be an important factor in developing effective armed forces, but the nature of modern mechanized warfare may mean that technically skilled civilians can be more effective than old-style warriors, always presuming, that is, that such civilians are prepared to risk their own lives and take those of others. Nuclear weapons may act as the great equalizers of military power, and yet it may be that only those states which possess a very large land mass and dispersed population are actually able to threaten to use them.

These sorts of propositions amount to the folk wisdom of power politics. As with most examples of folk wisdom there are alternative and contradictory versions of each proposition, and it is very difficult to think of ways of validating them short of the exchange of anecdotes. In any event, most of the time in international relations we are not actually interested in power as an attribute of states, but in power as a *relational* concept. Indeed, all of the attributes listed above only have meaning when placed in a relational context – thus, for an obvious example, whether a country has a 'large' or a 'small' population is a judgement that only makes sense in relation to some other country. Relational power also, of course, takes us back to the notion of influence.

The American political scientist Robert Dahl offered a classic formulation of relational power when he suggested that power is the ability to get another actor to do what it would not otherwise have done or not to do what it would otherwise have done (Dahl 1970); the first of these relationships we could call 'compellance', the second 'deterrence'. Either way, on this count, power is not something that can be measured in terms of the attributes of a state but only in action, in the effect one state has on another. There is a real distinction being made here, even if the contrast between power-as-attribute and power-as-influence-in-a-relationship is somewhat obscured by the ambiguity of ordinary language, at least of the English language, where 'power' can be synonymous with both 'strength' and 'influence' – unlike the French language, where *puissance* (power, might) and *pouvoir* (capability) are more clearly delineated.

Of course, it might be the case that what we have here are simply two different ways of looking at the same phenomenon. Some such argument lies behind the *basic force* model of power, which suggests that it is a reasonable assumption that the power an actor is able to exercise in a relationship is a direct reflection of the amount of power in the attribute sense possessed by that actor. In other words, we can, in effect, pass over the relational aspect of power fairly quickly, because it is the resources that are brought to the relationship that really count. The suggestion is that if we wish to know whether in any particular situation one actor will actually be able to exert power over another, the obvious method of answering this question is to compare the resources that the two actors bring to the relationship. As the folk wisdom has it, God is on the side of the big battalions.

The problem with this account of power is that it is self-evidently false – or rather can only be made true by the addition of so many qualifications that the clarity of the original idea is lost and the proposition simply becomes the tautology that the more powerful state is the state that gets its way in any relationship. To employ an oft-cited example, it is clear that by any attribute measure of power the United States was a stronger country than North Vietnam, and that even in terms of the resources devoted to the Vietnam War the United States had more men, tanks, planes and ships committed than had the North Vietnamese. If we want to explain why, nonetheless, the United States was effectively defeated by North Vietnam, we have to develop our analysis in various ways. In the first place, we have to introduce into our calculations factors such as the quality of the leadership of the two countries, and the effects of their domestic political and social structures on the conduct of the war – the role, for example, of the American media in undermining support for the war in the United

States, the skill of the Vietnamese army at irregular jungle warfare, and the inability of the United States to find local allies with sufficient support in the countryside of Vietnam. Each of these factors could be assimilated to a basic force model – after all, the skill of its army and political elite has always been identified as an element of the power of a state – but only at the cost of introducing highly subjective elements into the calculation. The merit of the basic force model is that it allows us to make more or less precise calculations – this is lost if we have to start assessing the relative skills of national leaderships.

However, there are two more fundamental objections to the basic force model; first, the context within which power is exercised is important, as is, second, the asymmetrical nature of many power relationships. As to *context*, very few relationships actually only involve two actors. Generally there are many other parties indirectly involved. In the Vietnam War numerous third parties influenced the outcome. We simply cannot say what would have happened had the United States been able to act without bearing in mind the reactions of, on the one hand, North Vietnam's potential allies, China and the Soviet Union, or, on the other, America's own allies in the Pacific and Europe. A pure two-actor power relationship is very unusual, and certainly was not present here.

If anything, *asymmetry* is even more important than context. The difference between compellance and deterrence, referred to above, is part of this. What exactly it was that the United States wanted in Vietnam was never clear (that was one of their problems), but it certainly involved a number of positive changes to the political architecture of Vietnam, such as the emergence of a government in the South capable of winning the allegiance of the people. The North Vietnamese, on the other hand, simply wanted the Americans to go away; they were confident that if they did go away they would be able to deal with any local opposition – as indeed proved to be the case. The North Vietnamese could wait; their aim was to win by surviving, rather than to bring about any positive change in their relationship with the United States.

This opens up a dimension of relational power that goes well beyond the basic force model of power. One definition of power is that power is the ability to resist change, to throw the costs of adaptation on others, and, characteristically, the ability to resist change requires fewer resources to be placed on the line than the ability to bring changes about. In international politics as in war, the assumption must be that there are tactical advantages to a defensive as opposed to an offensive posture.

What all this suggests is that it is not possible to assimilate attribute and relational power into one algorithm, or at least, that such an algorithm would have to be so complicated, and hedged around with so many provisos, that it would not be able to perform the role of simplifying the analysis of power. This is unfortunate, because there are a number of circumstances where we might actually want a *measure* of power, and measuring the influence of a state is, in every respect, more difficult than measuring its attributes. When, for example, we move on to consider the notion of the 'balance of power' we will want to ask ourselves what it is that is being balanced, and how we could tell whether a balance exists. In each case it would be helpful if we were able simply to assume that power is measurable in terms of attributes. Once we are obliged to accept that power-as-influence is not directly related to power-as-attribute we are bound to encounter problems.

The measurement of influence is bound to be difficult because what we are looking for are changes in the behaviour of an actor that are *caused* by the attempt of another to exert power, and, of course, in any practical situation there are always going to be a range of other possible reasons why an actor's behaviour might have changed which either could have been determining even in the absence of the actions of another, or, at the very least, which reinforced the effects of the latter. There may be some cases where it is possible to identify a moment in the course of negotiations, or in the process of making a particular decision, where it can be said that such-and-such a consideration was decisive, but the standard literature on decision-making suggests that this sort of 'essence of decision' is rare. Moreover, even when a particular decision can be pinned down in this way, the circumstances leading up to the decisive moment are always going to have been complex and involve a number of different factors. In effect, the attempt to isolate one factor, a particular influence-attempt, involves the construction of a counter-factual history – what would the world have been like had someone acted differently? Nonetheless, these difficulties should not be exaggerated; historians cope with this dilemma all the time – any historical narrative is obliged to confront the problem of assigning influence to particular factors and this seems to get done without too much hardship.

In any event, while power-as-influence is not directly based on the resources a state has at its disposal, indirectly these resources remain crucial. Influence rests on the ability to make threats in the event of non-compliance, and/or offer rewards for compliance – that is, on *positive and negative sanctions* or 'sticks and carrots' as the vernacular has it – and this ability is clearly related to the attributes of power possessed by a state. States that attempt to exert influence in the world, to alter the international environment in their favour, solely on the basis of reasoned argument or by relying on the skills of their representatives are likely to be disappointed. This does not mean that all influence-attempts rest on explicit threats or promises; the ability of a state to make effective threats/promises will generally be known and taken into account by interested parties without having to be made explicit. In fact, explicit threats – and even more so, action to back up threats – tend to be made when it is unclear that the message is getting across or when credibility is at stake. It should also be noted that threats and rewards need not relate directly to tangible factors – some states may have a degree of prestige such that other states wish to be associated with them.

These propositions can be illustrated by reference to a number of recent episodes in international relations. The negotiations in 1993 and 1994 which brought about real progress in relations between the Israeli government and the Palestine Liberation Organization and the creation of limited self-rule in some areas of the Gaza Strip and the West Bank were brokered by the good offices of a number of parties, ranging from the government of Egypt to private individuals in Norway. However, when an initial deal was struck the signing ceremony took place on the White House lawn, because it was deemed necessary by all parties that the power of the United States be associated with the outcome. Only the United States possesses the ability to reward progress and punish lack of progress – underwriting by Norway or Egypt would not do. As the peace process has unfolded, this fact has become if anything even more salient, as has the fact that the exercise of this influence is crucially related to domestic politics in the US; there is a limit to what any American politician seeking election or re-election can demand in the way of concessions from Israel. In any event the efficacy of threats and rewards offered by the US or anyone else will vary according to the issues at stake; as time has passed and a Palestinian Authority has been established, core values have come closer to the surface for both parties, and the ability of outsiders to persuade them to compromise has diminished.

In the peace process in Bosnia which led in 1995 to the Dayton Accords, the movement from implicit to explicit threats, and finally to overt action can be observed. In this case the United States had stayed in the background of the process during 1993–5, but with the implicit threat that it would become involved if the Bosnian Serbs refused to compromise. This had no effect; eventually the US became involved and the threat became explicit. This also had no effect, and it was not until a short bombing campaign by the US and NATO forces in response to the fall of the town of Srebrenica and the accompanying atrocities that the Bosnian Serb leadership finally, grudgingly, moved towards a degree of compliance. Action was necessary here perhaps because intentions had been misread – although it may also have been the case that the Bosnian Serb leadership found it easier to justify to their own people giving way to actual coercion than they would have yielding even to an explicit threat. Such at least was believed by some NATO analysts in 1999 when the campaign to end Serbian oppression of ethnic Albanians in Kosovo commenced, although in the event it turned out that a far more substantial military effort was necessary on this occasion before Yugoslav policy was reversed. In both instances, a continuing American presence is required – without the power of the United States at its disposal it seems unlikely that the international force in Bosnia charged with implementing the Dayton Accords could perform its mandate, even given the involvement of the major European NATO members, and, similarly, K-FOR in Kosovo can only act effectively because it is known that ultimately US military power backs up the local commanders.

Finally, it is worth noting the impact of a very different kind of power – that associated with the great prestige of a particular figure, such as Nelson Mandela of South Africa. Thus, the South African delegation played an important role in bringing about the relatively successful outcome of the Nuclear Non-Proliferation Treaty Review Conference of 1995, partly through skilful diplomacy, but also because they were able to exploit the unwillingness of other delegations to find themselves in opposition to South Africa, and, for another example, the willingness of the Libyan government to hand over for trial its nationals who were suspects in the Lockerbie bombing owed something to the good offices of by then ex-President Mandela. On both occasions the more conventional lobbying of the US government was rather less successful – partly no doubt, because the US did not have enough to offer on these particular issues. On the other hand, the limits of this sort of power are also apparent, for example in the unwillingness of the then-military rulers of Nigeria to respond favourably to South African pressure to grant a reprieve to condemned dissidents. The execution of Ken Saro-Wiwa while the 1995 Commonwealth Heads of Government Conference was under way suggests that the disapproval of Nelson Mandela took second place in the minds of these rulers to the need to preserve their power at home.

Before moving on to consider structural power there is one further feature of relational power that needs to be addressed. Dahl's definition of power, cited above, was formulated in the context of American debates on 'community power', and one of the strongest criticisms of his approach stressed the way in which his definition only allows us to see power in operation when a decision is to be made; there may be, it was argued, cases of '*non-decision-making*' where power is more effectively exercised than in the making of decisions (Bachrach and Baratz 1970). The ability to control what gets on to the agenda is more important than the ability to determine what happens when items are actually raised in discussion. This is widely regarded as a valid criticism of Dahl's definition of power in the context of a governmental system – does it apply to international relations? Whereas much of the earlier discussion of power could apply to many versions of pluralism as well as to realist notions, we now reach a point at which paths diverge. Clearly the power of non-decision-making is crucial to the analysis of agenda-setting within regimes, and thus of great significance to all versions of pluralism, including neoliberalism; however, for realists, neo- or otherwise, non-decision is a 'non-concept'. This is because, from a realist perspective, it is not possible for a state to be prevented from placing an item on the agenda, there being no agenda in any formal sense of the term. The key issues in international relations at any particular time are the issues that states with sufficient power to gain the attention of other states wish to be the key issues. No powerful state can be prevented from raising an issue; by definition, if an issue is not raised it is because the state that wished to raise it had insufficient power to do so. From a realist point of view there is no second meaning of power.

It might be that a similar point will emerge with respect to structural power – but this requires a more extensive examination. So far in this chapter, power has been treated as though it were something that is exercised by actors who realists presume to be states, but who might, in some circumstances, be other entities such as individuals or groups. This actor-oriented approach is a necessary feature of the way in which the consideration of power grew out of a consideration of foreign policy. We began with the state, moved on to consider how states formulate policy, took a short detour to examine the proposition that state action is determined by the international system, concluded that we had reason to doubt that this was entirely so, and then moved to the issue of foreign-policy implementation. Consideration of implementation raised the issue of techniques of statecraft and this led to a discussion of power, in which power has been seen as something that states either possess as an attribute or exercise in a relationship. This is a natural enough way to think of power if one's starting-point is the state – but there is another way of thinking of power which is not actor-oriented.

If we think of power as something in social life that brings about states of affairs, that instigates or prevents change, if, in other words, we take as our starting-point outcomes, it rapidly becomes clear that not all states of affairs come about because of the actions of individuals or groups or states – including as 'actions' in this case the legitimate exercise of authority as well as the exercise of influence. Some things happen without any apparent human agency. A society or a system is structured in such a way as to bring about certain kinds of outcomes independently of the will of any of its component parts. It makes sense to talk about power existing in these circumstances – powerful forces are at work, as it were – but it is *structural* power that is involved.

A good way of making sense of the idea of structural power can be found in the work of the Italian Marxian revolutionary, Antonio Gramsci. Gramsci's concern was to make the revolution and overthrow capitalism, but he came to realize in the 1920s that overthrowing capitalism in Italy, a relatively-developed bourgeois state, was a different, and certainly a more difficult, task than that which had faced Lenin in 1917. In Russia, which had been a very underdeveloped capitalist state, the power of capital was embodied in particular institutions which could be identified and engaged with in struggle – once defeated, capitalism was overthrown. In Italy, on the other hand, capitalism was so well established that it permeated all aspects of society; it controlled the 'common sense' of society, the ways in which ordinary people thought about politics, economics and social life in general. The effect of this capitalist 'hegemony' was that bringing about change becomes very difficult – checking and overthrowing capitalist/bourgeois institutions such as the firm or the liberal-democratic state is only a first step; the structural power of capitalism would remain as a more formidable obstacle to revolution than the resources of the overtly capitalist institutions.

How does this notion of structural power work in international relations? The direct application of notions of hegemony to international political economy will be discussed in Chapter 9; here the focus will remain on power understood more generally, and it will be noted that apparently similar ideas have been encountered above in the neorealist account of the international system; we now need to re-examine this account in the light of this new focus. What we find is that, somewhat contrary to first impressions, Waltz's version of systemic power is only partly structural in the sense outlined above. As we have seen, the international system allegedly sends messages to its members which, if correctly interpreted, will tell them what courses of action they should engage in – and Waltz assumes that since states wish to survive, they will become quite skilled interpreters of the state of the system. There is obviously an element of structural power in this. The rules of the game – the 'common-sense' understanding of how one should conduct international relations – stem from the imperatives of the system. It is clearly not the case that these rules, in general, reflect the power of any particular state; they are not understood as the product of the will of any state or group of states, even though they clearly do operate to the benefit of some states as opposed to others, by, for example, giving some more options than others possess.

However, Waltz's conception does not quite capture the full idea of structural power, because the states who make up the system have an existence that seems to be independent of it, and they possess the ability not only to exploit structural power in the manner that, say, capitalist enterprises exploit the structural logic of capitalism, but also to interact with, and even change the nature of, the rules of the game. Thus, in a bipolar system, according to Waltz, the two states concerned have the ability to regulate their competition and override the systemic imperative of 'self-help' which unless regulated might otherwise be expected to lock them into an highly destructive arms race. Even in a multipolar system where such regulation is more difficult, states have the ability to misread the signals sent by the system – whereas structural power which is really part of the common sense of a society does not need to be read at all. It just *is*. Waltz's system is a strange hybrid in which states are sometimes agents, sometimes automatons – too much of the latter for the foreign-policy analyst who looks for greater autonomy, too much of the former for a truly structural account of the system. Here we see, yet again, the impact of rational choice thinking on International Relations; states are rational egoists operating under conditions of anarchy and, however much Waltz wishes to deny it, his model cannot avoid being actor-oriented.

Better versions of structural power can be found elsewhere in the International Relations literature. From the realm of international political economy, Susan Strange makes a compelling case for the existence of four primary structures in world politics – the knowledge structure, the financial structure, the production structure and the political structure (Strange 1988). Each of these structures has a logic of its own, independent of its members, and structural power can be found in operation in each. The historical sociologist Michael Mann also identifies four key structures – in his case ideological, economic, military and political (Mann 1986/1993). His is a work of large-scale historical sociology and he is concerned not simply with the ways in which each of these structures determines outcomes, but also with changes in the relative importance of each structure over time.

What is interesting about these writers is that although both are, in some sense, providing realist accounts of the operation of international relations, neither accepts a state-centric view of the world, or a clear distinction between the domestic and the international – both of which are generally seen as key criteria for identifying realists. Neither of these two criteria is compatible with a truly structural account of the operation of power, and their determination to provide such an account takes them away from realism in the sense that the term has been used so far in this chapter and the previous one. In effect, as with the matter of non-decisional power, structural power in the full meaning of the term is a not a category which works from a realist state-centric perspective – which provides yet one more reason for going beyond this perspective. However, before taking this step there are still quite a few elements of the state-centric view of the world that need to be established and investigated.

Power, Fear and Insecurity

One of the defining features of realist accounts of international relations – of state-centric accounts in general – is an emphasis on the inherently *dangerous* nature of international relations. A level of watchfulness, if not fearfulness, which would be regarded as paranoid in other circumstances seems a necessary feature of international relations. A brief review of the story so far will clarify why this is so.

First, it is a premise of state-centric accounts of international relations that states determine their own aims and objectives in the international system, and that primary amongst these aims and objectives will be a concern for survival, both in the physical sense of a concern to preserve the territorial integrity of the state, and, more intangibly, in terms of a concern to preserve the capacity of the state to determine its own destiny, its way of life. This premise emerges from the notion that the state is *sovereign* and wishes to remain so, and the assumption holds independently of the nature of the state – thus, *Machtstaat* or *Rechtstaat*, absolutist monarchy or liberal democracy, it makes no difference; states wish to preserve their sovereignty, come what may. Second, it is a premise of state-centric views of international relations, that, given the absence of world government – that is, of a mechanism whereby interests can be pursued in the hope of achieving authoritative decision – the pursuit of interests is conducted by attempting to exercise power in the world, and power, in this sense, means the ability to make threats and offer rewards. Moreover, coercive means are part of the repertoire of positive and negative sanctions at the disposal of states in their conduct of foreign affairs, and the decision to use coercion is one that sovereign states reserve to themselves, with any commitment not to employ coercive means being contingent on circumstances.

Taken together, these two premises – each of which is no more than an elaboration of the implications of a system of *sovereign* states – ensure that insecurity and fear are permanent features of international relations. The very bare bones of the basic situation point to this conclusion, and the different ways in which flesh can be added to these bare bones may make the situation more or less dangerous but they do not and cannot produce the qualitative change that would be necessary to remove danger altogether.

The traditional realist account of state-centric international relations clearly makes life even more dangerous than the basic situation would suggest, because it adds to the pot the assumption that human beings have naturally aggressive tendencies that can only be constrained by the coercive force of government. The aims and objectives of states will include a desire to dominate not simply because this is a systemic imperative, but because human beings are like that. Domination is what they do. It may be that, as Carl Schmitt suggests, as between states the visceral hatreds of a 'friend–foe' relationship can be transformed into the political hostility of a friend–enemy relationship, and the impersonal quality of this relationship may mitigate some of the worst features of our primordial aggressiveness (Schmitt 1932/1996). As against this, the very impersonality of modern means of violence may undermine whatever natural restraints we have inherited as part of our animal nature. In any event, for a classical realist, aggression and violence are part of who we are, whether these features are perceived in theological terms or as having socio–psychological or socio–biological origins.

The neorealist emphasis on systemic imperatives as a source of conduct removes this notion of aggressiveness from the equation. It is the basic situation that is dangerous, not the nature of the human beings who are obliged to work within the international anarchy. Moreover, states are assumed to be rational in their decision-making, and not liable to be overcome by instinctual fears or hatreds. The neorealist state is a cold, impersonal entity, with no friends, but also no enemies. On the other hand, the neorealist account of the international system puts great stress on the dangers of the basic situation in which states find themselves. States are enjoined to pay constant attention to the relations of power that exist in the world; watchfulness is needed, because, in a Hobbesian sense, international relations is a state of war. For Hobbes, life in the state of nature – a clear analogy to the neorealist international system – is a state of war, not in the sense that fighting is continual, but in the sense that it is an ever-present possibility (Hobbes 1946).

The state-centric view of the English School theorists of *international society*, and of constructivists such as Alexander Wendt, looks at first sight to be offering a rather less fear-dominated account of the world. The assumption here is that although states are sovereign and the basic situation outlined above still holds, nonetheless they are in a social relationship with one another and there are some rules and practices that work to reduce the fear and tension that otherwise might exist. The rules of international law mandate non-aggression and non-intervention, and are taken seriously by states. There are certain kinds of 'settled norms' in international relations which regulate conduct. Such norms are settled not in the sense that every state always obeys them, but in the sense that even when breaking them states will pay allegiance to them, that is they will attempt to show that they are not really breaking them, or that they are doing so for wholly exceptional reasons (Frost 1996: 105). These rules are backed by diplomacy – an institution with a culture of its own oriented towards problem-solving and negotiation rather than violence and coercion. States are sovereign, but this does not stop them, most of the time, from obeying the rules; a degree of watchfulness is justified, but not the extent of fearfulness full-blown realist accounts suggest should be normal.

There are two problems with this, one fairly obvious, and one which may need more elaboration. In the first place, no theorist of international society ever suggested that all states all the time will play to the rules – the possibility that there will be dissatisfied customers in the international arena who will be prepared to use their power to damage others cannot be discounted. But there is a more serious problem here, which is that even with the best will in the world, even assuming that all states are abiding by the rules – and do not wish to employ violence and coercion in their relations with one another – there is still the possibility that this fact will not be recognized, and that insecurity will increase even if there is no 'objective' reason why it should.

This notion – the 'security dilemma' – is based on the complex relationship between 'intentions' and 'capabilities', and the ways in which the system of sovereign states encourages emphasis on the latter rather than the former, with the result that a spiral of insecurity may emerge on the basis of misperception. Thus, because there is a background level of possible insecurity even in an international order where the majority of states are unaggressive and broadly satisfied with life, states feel obliged to preserve the means of self-defence and to do so in a cost-efficient but also effective way, which sometimes involves enhancing this capacity. However, the capacity to defend oneself is also, most of the time, a capacity to act offensively. On the same chain of reasoning that leads the first, peaceful, state to preserve and occasionally enhance the effectiveness of its armed forces, a second state may see this as a potentially hostile act. The defensive intentions – which cannot easily be demonstrated, much less proven – will be less important than the offensive capabilities. If the second state reacts to these capabilities by expanding its own coercive capacity this is likely to be perceived as potentially hostile, and so the spiral sets in. The current (Summer 2000) US debate over National Missile Defence offers an interesting illustration of the reasoning here; a partial missile defence for the US would be purely defensive in intent, designed to deter attacks from 'rogue' states, but, if effective, such a system would render less credible Russian and Chinese deterrent forces and probably stimulate them to upgrade their systems, in turn increasing US anxiety, and so on.

This is a security *dilemma* rather than, for example, a simple mistake, because no one is behaving unreasonably or making unreasonable assumptions. It might, in fact, be a mistake to perceive hostility where there is none, but it is a reasonable mistake; better safe than sorry. There are too many historical examples of states not reacting in time, taking overt intentions as a reason for ignoring capability enhancements, and suffering as a result, for this possibility to be ignored. We do not have access to the intentions of states – we can only see their capabilities and work back from these. It is in the nature of the 'self-help' system in which states exist that they are likely to take a pessimistic view of the world, even in an international society. National leaders consider themselves to have a responsibility to their populations to be cautious and prudent and not to turn a blind eye to potential threats.

The idea of the security dilemma can be taken too far to imply that *all* international insecurity stems from some such process of reaction and overreaction. There seems no reason to hold to such a view. Sometimes states *do* have hostile intentions towards each other, in which case reacting to a build-up of capabilities is a sensible move. But the point is that even in a world largely composed of states who do not have any hostile intent, and who make rational, calculated decisions about their place in the world, insecurity is still endemic. Anarchy is anarchy even in an anarchical *society* – the existential situation of sovereign states coexisting in a world without government is inherently insecure and dangerous.

Conclusion: Managing Insecurity

And yet, the international system is not as anarchic in the usual, pejorative sense of the term, as these ruminations would imply. Much of the time there is a degree of order in the world and insecurity, while ever present, is kept at manageable levels. How? There are two institutions of international relations which, according to the state-centric tradition, preserve a degree of order and security in the international system. The first, predictably, is the *balance of power* – the idea that although force is the defining characteristic of the international system, some patterns of force may induce a degree of stability. The second institution for managing insecurity is, counter-intuitively, the institution of *inter-state war*. Whereas from a common-sense point of view war is a disaster and represents the breakdown of order, in the traditional state-centric view of the world, war, while still disastrous, nonetheless plays an important role in the actual preservation of the system. Quite plausibly, nowadays, neither of these institutions can work in the way the tradition wants them to, and this may be one more reason for abandoning the state-centric view of the world. However, before we can legitimately reach this conclusion, we must carry the argument through to the end, the task of the next chapter.

Further Reading

For this chapter the readings in Part 1 of Richard Little and Michael Smith, *Perspectives in World Politics: A Reader* (1991) are particularly valuable.

On diplomacy in general, see G. R. Berridge, *Diplomacy: Theory and Practice* (1995) and Adam Watson, *Diplomacy: The Dialogue of States* (1982); also Keith Hamilton and R. T. B. Langhorne, *The Practice of Diplomacy* (1995). For a wider notion of how states act, Steve Smith and Michael Clarke (eds), *Foreign Policy Implementation* (1985) and, for postmodern accounts of diplomacy, James Der Derian, *On Diplomacy: A Genealogy of Western Estrangement* (1987), Costas Constantinou, 'Diplomatic Representation or Who Framed the Ambassadors?' (1994) and *On the Way to Diplomacy* (1996).

David Baldwin. *Economic Statecraft* (1985) is a seminal study on the exercise of power/influence. On 'coercive diplomacy', see A. L. George, *The Limits of Coercive Diplomacy* (1971); Gordon C. Craig and A. L. George (eds), *Force and Statecraft* (1983); and Robert Art and Kenneth Waltz (eds), *The Use of Force: Military Power and International Politics* (1993). The Journal *International Security* is a major source of high quality material on the exercise of power – see for example the debate between Robert A. Pape, 'Why Economic Sanctions Do Not Work' (1997) and 'Why Economic Sanctions *Still* Do Not Work' (1998) and David A. Baldwin, 'Correspondence Evaluating Economic Sanctions' (1998) and 'The Sanctions Debate and the Logic of Choice' (1999/2000).

Most textbooks have extended discussions on power: particularly interesting are Hans J. Morgenthau, *Politics Among Nations: The Struggle for Power and Peace* (1948); and Raymond Aron, *Peace and War: A Theory of International Relations* (1967). George Liska, *The Ways of Power: Patterns and Meanings in World Politics* (1990); Robert Cox, *Production, Power and World Order: Social Forces in the Making of History* (1987); and David A. Baldwin, *Paradoxes of Power* (1989) are very different but stimulating discussions of different kinds of power. Geopolitics are currently becoming fashionable again – a good survey is Daniel Deudeny 'Geopolitics as Theory: Historical Security Materialism' (2000). For Gramscian notions of hegemonic power see Chapter 9.

Moving away from the international context, the standard work on community power is Robert Dahl, *Who Governs?* (1961). Classic critiques are in Paul Bachrach and Morton S. Baratz, *Power and Poverty* (1970); and Stephen Lukes, *Power: A Radical View* (1974). For a brief, but powerful, critique of Lukes, see Brian Barry, 'The Obscurities of Power' (1975).

Robert Jervis, *Perception and Misperception in World Politics* (1976) is the classic account of the 'security dilemma' and the 'spiral of insecurity'. Ken Booth (ed.), *New Thinking about Strategy and International Security* (1991) contains a number of articles critical of the notion. Further readings on new approaches to security are listed after Chapter 12; David Baldwin, 'The Concept of Security' (1997) is a useful survey that bridges old and new.

6

The Balance of Power and War

Introduction

The state-centric view of the world, especially in its realist variant, paints a picture of great insecurity and fear. Concerned for their own security, possibly desiring to dominate others, states are obliged to keep a watchful eye open for ways of enhancing their own power, and reducing that of others. Unrestrained and unprotected by any international government, states must look after their own security, even though they cannot but be aware that their attempts to do so may induce insecurity in others. Thus, the scene seems set for a wretched world, in which the idea of an international 'order' would be preposterous. Yet there is a degree of order in the world; international relations may be anarchic in the formal sense of lacking government, but they are not anarchic in the sense of lawless and disorderly – or at least not entirely so. How can this be?

According to realist International Relations theory, order of a kind and to a degree is preserved by two key institutions – the *balance of power* and *war*. The idea that the balance of power generates order is plausible enough, but to suggest that war is a source of order seems counter-intuitive, implausible and, indeed, somewhat distasteful. Nonetheless, this thought, however distasteful, must be borne with, because war, seen as a political instrument, does indeed play this role. It does so in two senses: first, as part of the balance of power, because, contrary to some accounts which suggest that the balance of power is designed to prevent war, war is an essential mechanism for preserving a balance, and, second, as a conflict-resolving mechanism that does something that the balance of power cannot do, namely bring about, as opposed to frustrate, change. In other words, war both complements and completes the balance of power. Without war, the balance

106

of power could not operate as a functioning institution of an international system or society. War and the balance of power stand together – or, perhaps, fall together, because it may well be that there are features of international relations in the early twenty-first century which mean that an account of the world in which war plays a central role is indefensible, not simply on moral grounds, but as a practical proposition. If this is so, yet more doubt will be cast on state-centric International Relations, to be added to the reservations already expressed in Chapters 4 and 5.

The first section of this chapter will examine the balance of power; after a cursory examination of the long tradition of balance of power thinking in the European states-system, two modern versions will be examined, or in one case re-examined – those of Kenneth Waltz and Hedley Bull. The next section will outline the political, Clausewitzian theory of war – in contrast to other accounts of war which stress its irrational, cataclysmic nature – and the role of war as a conflict-resolving mechanism in classical international relations. The final section will offer a number of reasons why this account of war, and the account of international relations upon which it rests, is, under current conditions, no longer plausible.

The Balance of Power

The balance of power is one notion that is virtually inescapable in the discourse of International Relations as it has developed over the last three or four centuries. The term goes back to at least the sixteenth century – although not to pre-modern times; according to Hume, the Greeks knew nothing of it (1987) – and was theorized in the eighteenth century and after. It appears in treaties (for example that of Utrecht 1713), in the memoirs of statesmen and diplomats and in the writings of historians and lawyers. To the diplomats of the *Ancien Régime*, it was the underlying principle that created stability. By contrast, to radical liberals such as Richard Cobden it was a mere chimera, a simple collection of sounds with no meaning (Cobden in Brown *et al.* (eds) 2001). In the twentieth century it has been invoked at one time or another by all the major international actors.

Unfortunately, no one can agree on what it means. Scholars such as Martin Wight and Herbert Butterfield have between them collected examples of at least eleven different meanings revealed in the writings or speeches of its adherents. Nor is there internal consistency in the way particular writers use the term – Inis Claude, for example, notes that Hans Morgenthau shifts back and forth between several different meanings in his chapter on the subject in *Politics Among Nations*, a chapter explicitly designed to clear up confusions (Claude 1962: 25). No doubt most every other writer could be exposed in the same way.

What is to be done about this confusion? Claude more or less gives up, and tries to restrict the term to a description of the system of states as a whole – thus, a balance of power system is simply the term we give to a system which is based on sovereignty and the absence of world government. However, this is a little too defeatist. There is a root idea of some importance here, and it would be a shame to lose this as a result of past confusions. This root idea is the notion that only force can counteract the effect of force, and that in an anarchical world, stability, predictability and regularity can only occur when the forces that states are able to exert to get their way in the world are in some kind of equilibrium. The notion of a 'balance' is rather a bad metaphor here, if it suggests the image of a pair of scales, because this implies only two forces are in equilibrium. Better, although less conventional, is the image of a chandelier. The chandelier remains level (stable) if the weights which are attached to it are distributed beneath it in such a way that the forces they exert (in this case the downward pull of gravity) are in equilibrium. There are two advantages to this metaphor; in the first place it makes more difficult some of the more perplexing usages associated with the idea – it would become clear, for example, that 'holding the balance' is rather difficult, while a balance 'moving in one's favour' is positively dangerous if standing under a chandelier.

More seriously, it conveys the idea that there are two ways in which equilibrium can be disturbed, and two ways in which it can be re-established. The chandelier moves away from the level if one of its weights becomes heavier, without this being compensated for – if, let us say, one state becomes more powerful than others for endogenous reasons, for example, as a result of faster economic growth than other states. It also becomes unstable if two weights are moved closer together without compensatory movement elsewhere – if, for example, two states form a closer relationship than heretofore. Restoring stability can also take two forms – another weight increasing, or two other weights moving closer together. Put differently, disruptions are both created and potentially rectified by *arms racing*, or by *alliance* policy, or by some combination of the two.

To illustrate these points in more concrete terms, consider a highly simplified account of the international system in Europe after 1871.

First, in 1871, the system is more or less in equilibrium, following Prussia's victories over Austria–Hungary (1866) and France (1870–1), and, crucially, following Bismarck's decision not to use these victories to create a Greater Germany by incorporating parts of the Dual Monarchy in the new German Empire. There were tensions in the system, and loose, temporary alliances between states, but, on the whole, the system was in equilibrium. However, on one reading, in the late nineteenth century, German power increased as a result of German industrialism and population growth, to the point that a German superpower began to emerge, contrary to Bismarck's intentions. This industrial strength transmitted itself into an active German foreign policy via such measures as a larger army, and the growth of a navy virtually from scratch. The response of the other European powers was first, to attempt to enhance their own power (by, for example, in France, extending periods of military training, in Britain, engaging in naval building) and, second, to re-align, creating new military alliances. France and Russia ignored ideological differences and signed a formal alliance in 1892, Britain disregarded imperial rivalries and set aside a long policy of peacetime non-entanglement to become effectively associated with these two countries in 1904 and 1907 respectively. In short, both the methods identified above to deal with incipient disequilibrium were attempted.

There are three interesting points about this story, two of which can be made here, the third being held over to the end of this section. The first is that the flexibility of the system decreases as alliances become firmly established, because then the system begins to look bipolar, and in a bipolar system, by definition, disturbances to stability can only be met by internal changes, and not by the construction of alliances. This is one of the reasons why classical balance of power theorists say that the ideal number of states in a balance is five – because this allows for three vs. two formations which can be adapted as becomes appropriate, as opposed to bipolar systems which are inherently inflexible. However, Kenneth Waltz argues that in a bipolar system power management is easier as two parties can negotiate their way to stability more easily than is the case with any larger number.

This first observation is somewhat arcane; more significant is the second point, the difficulty of thinking about the balance of power while using theoretically sophisticated notions of 'power'. Balance of power theorists tend to see power as an attribute of states – Claude, for example, defines power in military terms throughout his work – and thus tend to be committed to a 'basic force' model of influence.

However, as was shown in Chapter 5, basic force models are either wrong or tautological. If, on the other hand, we try to work with power-as-influence as our starting-point, the simple stories advocates of balance of power relate become incredibly complex narratives. For example, returning to the post-1871 narrative offered above, the idea that German power was the major disruptive influence rests on a basic force model of power; once we look at influence as revealed in outcomes, things look very difficult. We find that in most of the diplomatic crises of the period the German government was on the losing side, quite unable to convert its undoubted physical strength into favourable results at the conference table. This was why the German political elite in the years up to 1914 had such a strong sense that the rest of the world was against them; they were conscious of their *lack of influence*, others were conscious of their *superabundance of power*.

How do balances of power become established? Morgenthau argues that when states pursue their national interests and seek power in the world, a balance will emerge, 'of necessity' – but this is a very dubious argument, since he is well aware that sometimes balances of power do not emerge (Morgenthau 1948: 161). If he were not so aware, his advocacy of balance of power policies would be hard to explain; one does not need to proselytize on behalf of something that is really going to happen 'of necessity'. Moreover, the historical record gives little support to the idea that balances of power are in some way 'natural' phenomena – as Martin Wight remarks, the historical record shows a tendency towards the concentration of power rather than towards its balanced distribution (Wight in Butterfield and Wight (eds), 1966: 167). More generally, anyone who wishes to argue that balances of power always will emerge is obliged to provide some account of agency, some explanation of how this automatic process gets translated into state policy.

Two accounts of the balance of power which do meet, or successfully avoid, this criterion are given by Bull and Waltz. Waltz's theory as outlined in *Theory of International Politics* was discussed briefly in Chapter 3. On his account, the 'balance of power' is what will happen if states take notice of their surroundings, adjust their policies to changes in the configuration of power worldwide, and, a critical proviso, if the actual distribution of power is such that a balance *can* emerge. Waltz does *not* argue that balances of power will always emerge – for example, when discussing the bipolar nature of the current (1979) world he remarks that the most likely shift away from bipolarity would be towards unipolarity – that is an end to the anarchical system – if the Soviet Union were unable to remain in competition with the United States (Waltz 1979: 179). His point is, rather, that other states would not want this to happen, and would do everything they could in terms of realignment and enhancing their own capabilities to stop it from happening – a point neorealists have repeated since the end of the Cold War.

On Waltz's account, the system influences agents via the imperatives of rational choice. To act in such a way that balances of power emerge is to act as a rational egoist in the face of a particular set of circumstances, namely in response to changes in the distribution of power that might affect adversely a state's capacity for self-preservation. It should be stressed that states do not wish to create balances of power, at least not as a first preference. This is even true, perhaps especially true, of bipolar balances. Each party would actually like the other to disappear, and would be prepared to take steps to bring this about if it could do so without risk. But, of course, this is not possible, and the 'second best' solution is to jointly manage a bipolar balance. Again, generalizing the point, no state really wants to see a balance of power emerge; balances of power are accepted because there is no better game in town, no alternative source of security anywhere near as effective.

Waltz is clear that the balance of power *is* the theory of international politics, but it should be stressed that other writers employing the same general line of argument have come to different conclusions. One alternative to balancing is 'bandwagoning' – that is to say, lining up behind a state that is rising in power – and it has been argued quite cogently both that this is sometimes a rational strategy to follow and that the historical record suggests that states are actually every bit as likely to bandwagon as to balance (Walt 1987). However one judges the argument here, the central point is that it is not quite as obvious that states will engage in balancing behaviour as Waltz assumes; there are other rational responses they might have to the security dilemmas that face them.

Hedley Bull, in his *The Anarchical Society*, briefly considers the idea that a balance of power might emerge, as he puts it, 'fortuitously', simply as an unintended consequence of the actions of states (Bull 1977/1995: 100). However, having considered this possibility he rejects it on the grounds that such fortuitous circumstances could not be expected to provide the basis for any kind of medium- to long-term stability. States motivated only by rational egoism would take the first chance to upset a balance. Instead, the burden of his argument is that the balance of power is a necessary adjunct to any kind of international order, that only when power is balanced have states any real freedom in the world, and that balances of power will only emerge and be sustained when states are aware that this is so and willing to act accordingly. In other words, the balance of power is a kind of artefact, something that states, or a significant proportion of states, are willing to see as a desirable end. If a balance of power is to work, states must *want* it to work, must be committed to the idea that the preservation of the system of states is desirable. As always with theorists of international society, it is the normative basis of the relationship that is crucial. To return to the European example outlined above, the balance of power was established initially in 1871 because Bismarck was committed to at least a version of these norms; he wanted Germany to be the most powerful state in Europe, but he did not want the system to be replaced with a German Empire – thus he was willing to assist in the birth of a new balance of power, in contrast to at least one of his successors, Hitler, and possibly also to the Emperor William II.

On this account the balance of power is an *artefact*, something made by human beings; is it a *cultural* artefact? It might be thought that the motivation Bull seems to think is necessary could only come from a society which is, to some degree, culturally homogeneous, and it might be doubted whether the normative basis for the balance of power could work in the modern, post-European world. Bull was clearly concerned about this as evidenced by his last work on *Justice in International Relations*, and on the expansion of the international system (Bull 1984; Bull and Watson (eds) 1984). On the other hand, Frost has argued that the 'settled norms' of the modern system, norms which have been tacitly accepted by almost all states, include a commitment to the continuation of the system and that this entails the need to preserve a balance of power – there is no need to assume that this is a specifically European attitude (Frost 1996).

On Bull's account we aim to preserve a balance of power in order to preserve international 'order'. Does this mean 'peace'? Not necessarily. Here, the third point raised by discussion of the post-1871 system can be made. Post-1871 was also pre-1914; what does the outbreak of war in 1914 tell us about the balance of power system that preceded it? It might be thought that it tells us that this system failed in 1914 – but it could equally well be argued that in terms of the preservation of international order, the 1914–18 war and subsequent events, amount to a *vindication* of the balance of power. At a human level, this is a terrible conclusion, but one that is difficult to avoid if one accepts that preventing the dominance of the system by any one power is a good, and if one acknowledges that, in some circumstances, this can only be achieved by violence and war. It may well be that, generally, international order equates to peace, but this cannot be guaranteed; sometimes the price of peace will be too high. This is a view sanctioned by the history of the last four centuries, which can easily be told in terms of a series of bids for hegemony that were successfully resisted by a balance of power politics that relied upon war as a possible tactic.

War plays an important role in maintaining a balance of power system, as a concomitant to alliance politics and arms races – that is to say, these latter are ways of maintaining a balance without war, but if they fail war may be necessary. However, there is a further role for war in this kind of international system. The balance of power is about stability, equilibrium, the prevention of change, but, sometimes, the resolution of conflict requires change, change that can only come via war. In this sense, war does not indicate the failure of conflict resolution – rather, war is a *means* of conflict mechanism. This is a point that needs to be explored in some depth.

The Political Conception of War

In the twentieth century, the common-sense view of war came to be that it is a pathological phenomenon, that war represents a breakdown, a malfunctioning, of the international system, or, perhaps, a sign of the immaturity of a people or a civilization – this latter was the view of, for example, Freud (Freud 1985). However, to understand the role of war in a balance of power system, it is necessary to realize that this is mistaken. War is a *normal* feature of international relations, a normal part of the functioning of the international system, in no sense pathological, although it may be regrettable. To see how this could be so, we need to examine briefly some alternative accounts of the causes of war, before outlining the view of war that makes sense of this position – the Clausewitzian or political conception of war.

The causes of war is a subject dominated by one study, and it is extraordinary that Kenneth Waltz, the author of *Theory of International Politics*, the book that raised the level of theoretical discourse in the discipline so dramatically in 1979, should also have authored, in 1959. *Man, the State and War*, the standard work in question – although, from some perspectives, the later book could be regarded as an elaboration and re-working of the third section of the earlier study. In the 1959 volume, Waltz identifies three 'images' of the causes of war, the third of which formed the basis for his later study.

The first image stresses *human nature*. Wars occur because of some aspect of human nature, an argument that can be cast in theological, psychological, psychoanalytic, or, popular nowadays, socio–biological terms. We are fallen creatures, cast out of the Garden of Eden, preternaturally prone to violence. We are possessed by 'Thanatos', a death-wish. We are the only animal that kills intra-specifically, that does not possess an inhibitor to prevent us killing our own kind (it should be noted that this is not actually the case, although it is widely believed to be true). These are elaborate arguments, and they may contain some element of truth, but they do not explain war. War is not similar to murder or grievous bodily harm, individual acts of violence – war is a *social* institution, and as such requires a social explanation. To explain social phenomena by reference to the nature of individuals is 'reductionist' – a term Waltz would also employ to some effect in his later study.

The second image focuses on the nature of societies rather than of human beings. War is caused by a particular kind of *society* – the choice here is very wide, ranging from autocracies and monarchies (the liberal view) to democracies (the autocratic view), from capitalist societies (the Leninist view) to communist societies (the capitalist view). Once again, one can tell a good story in support of the war-proneness of each of these kinds of society, but each explanation misses a crucial point. As far as we can tell, all societies which have had any kind of regular contact with other societies seem to have experienced some kinds of war – even those democracies that do not fight other democracies fight non-democratic systems with some regularity. The only exceptions to the ubiquity of war are a few rare cases where extreme climatic conditions – as with the Inuit in the Arctic – make war effectively impossible. This suggests that the second image is no more capable of providing general explanations of war than the first.

This leaves the third image which, as will have been anticipated, points to the international *system* as the essential cause of war. The argument here has been rehearsed above enough times to make any lengthy restatement redundant. States have interests, which at times may clash; in an anarchical system there is no way of resolving such a clash of interests which is binding on the parties; most of the time the parties will not wish to resolve their difficulties by violence, but sometimes they will – war is the ultimate resort of states who can see no other way to have their interests met. It should be noted here that the third image explains why war is *possible* – in order to explain why any *actual* war takes place we will need to bring into play societal and individual factors. One final way of making the same point is to stress the difference between *civil* and *international* war. A civil war is a pathological condition, it does represent the breakdown of normality. In principle, states have methods of conflict resolution which forbid the use of force; sometimes a problem emerges which cannot be contained by these mechanisms, and violence – civil war, if on a large enough scale – ensues as a result. International war is *not* like this; as between states, war *is* the (ultimate) mechanism for the resolution of conflict.

This is a political account of war, and an account of war as the product of a rational choice, a weighing of the costs and benefits of the instrumental use of force. This sounds quite modern, but the writer who first set out this position and identified the key points in the argument did so nearly two centuries ago. This was the Prussian general and prototypical military intellectual, Carl Clausewitz, whose master work, *On War*, was published posthumously in 1831. Clausewitz was a moderately successful senior staff officer, with campaign experience in the service of the Czar and the King of Prussia in wars against Napoleon, and later an instructor at the Prussian Staff College, the most advanced centre for military thought of its day. In this latter capacity he produced the drafts for *On War*, and its origins are reflected in the fact that most of its contents examine the minutiae of tactics and strategy, and, given the changes in technology and society generally, are of little relevance today. However, Clausewitz was an intellectual soldier, a product of post-Enlightenment German thought, someone who was steeped in current thinking on the state and society. As a result, in addition to the technicalities, his book also includes some (quite short) reflections on the nature of war and its role in the international relations of the day – reflections which have been required reading ever since.

The gist of these reflections is that war is (or should be) a controlled, rational, political act. War is an act of violence to compel our opponent to submit to our will; in famous words, it is not a mere act of policy but 'a true political instrument, a continuation of political activity by other means' (Clausewitz 1976: 87). Here we see the continuity between war and peace. War is not the end of political activity, it is conducted for political purposes. Clausewitz was a soldier, but a soldier who stressed the importance of political control of the armed forces. On his account, war rests on a trilogy of factors – animosity directed against the enemy which is provided by 'the people', the management of contingency which is the role of the army, and the aims and objectives of the war which are determined by the political leadership. It is crucial that these three moments are not confused; the army are entitled to ask of the government that they be given resources appropriate to the tasks in hand, but they are not to set these tasks. The government sets objectives but should not interfere with the means chosen for their achievement. The people should support army and government, but not restrict their freedom of action.

In a few pages of Clausewitz we see, in condensed form, the essential features of the realist view of the world – and perhaps of any state-centric view of the world (although theorists of international society and Wendtian constructivists would resist this conclusion). The extent to which Clausewitzian ideas chime with neorealist thought is striking. Although the former does not use the terms 'costs' and 'benefits' it is clear that this is what he understands by the instrumentality of war. An interesting question is whether Clausewitz was an 'offensive' or a 'defensive' realist, to use the current terminology; defensive realists assume that states are essentially reactive, prepared to defend their position but not likely to pre-empt potential opponents, while offensive realists assume that states will attempt to solve their security dilemmas by striking first if they can get away with it. One suspects that Clausewitz would have sympathized with the latter position, but, at the very least, the prudent, calculating manner he advocates involves the rejection of crusades and vendettas. Moreover, for Clausewitz and his philosophical contemporaries, war is fought on behalf of the nation, and underwritten by national support, but it is not fought *by* the nation. As in the writings of his great contemporary Hegel, war is for armies and a clear distinction is to be drawn between combatants and non-combatants. Civilian, or, at least, political, control, is central – Clausewitz would have subscribed to Lloyd George's maxim that war was too important to be left to the generals, and would have had no sympathy for the bombast of some twentieth-century commanders, or the view – held, for example, by Eisenhower against Churchill in the Second World War – that war is a technical business and that politicians have no business interfering in strategic concerns. A Clausewitzian approach would have spared the twentieth century many disasters. The downside is also readily apparent – a willingness to use force that seems not to grasp the moral seriousness of the decision to employ violence for political ends, an acceptance of the notion that states must always be the judges in their own cases, an inability to see beyond the confines of the nation to a wider humanity. In the nineteenth century we might accept that a Clausewitzian view of war is an accurate description of how things were, and, on the whole, a more satisfactory view than the alternatives. In the twentieth century there were many reasons for doubting this.

War in the Twentieth Century

In the nineteenth century, the view that war was a legitimate act of state was broadly accepted by international lawyers as a concomitant to the doctrine of sovereignty. So long as the war-making body had the authority to act, and followed the correct legal procedures, a proper declaration of war for example, war could be waged lawfully, and without any legal interest in the reasons for this act of state. This is no longer the case. The Covenant of the League of Nations of 1919, the Pact of Paris of 1928, the United Nations Charter of 1945 and the London Charter of the same year – which established the War Crimes Tribunal that sat at Nuremberg – taken together have established a new legal regime in which war is only legitimate in two circumstances, as an act of self-defence, or as a an act of law enforcement to assist others in defending themselves. Not only is this the current legal position; it also seems to correspond to the ways in which most people thought about war in the twentieth century, namely as a disaster that should be avoided at almost all costs – indeed, the current law on war is more likely to be criticized for being too permissive than for restricting the activity too closely. Both morally and legally, a Clausewitzian view of war seems today to be unacceptable.

Of course, from a realist point of view, all this is by-the-by. If states still make war on Clausewitzian lines, then the fact that law and public opinion goes against them is neither here nor there. At best it explains some of the peculiarities of modern war, in particular the unwillingness to call a spade a spade – hence the British government always refers to the South Atlantic Conflict of 1982 rather than the Falklands War, the problems involved in fighting a declared war being too complicated to contemplate. But do states still make war as a rational act of policy? Some try to, sometimes – but on the whole, twentieth-century conditions worked against war being fought in terms of Clausewitzian calculations. There are two points here, one about the *actual* calculations, the other about the *role* of calculations in decisions for war.

The first point is simple; in the twentieth century the costs of war rose dramatically, while the benefits either remained the same or, more often, fell. As mentioned in Chapter 1 above, Norman Angell saw this in the years before 1914 and it has become even truer post-1945. The rise in destructiveness of war has been exponential – from the mayhem of machine guns, breechloading artillery and barbed wire in the First World War, to the strategic bombing of the Second to the threat of nuclear annihilation of a potential Third World War. The economic structures of society are destroyed by war, financial resources dissipated, political stability undermined. The benefits of success have not risen in the same way; in material terms the rewards for a successful war are now less significant than they once were. National wealth does not, on the whole, come from the conquest of territory or the cornering of raw materials – although, as the invasion of Kuwait in 1990 suggests, there may still be, in some circumstances, possibilities here. A successful war may remove an enemy or competitor, and there may be circumstances in which this is a very worthwhile result – but on the whole one would expect far fewer wars to emerge from rational calculation in the twentieth century than in the nineteenth. Yet the former was a century of warfare, by most statistical indices more war-prone than the latter, which suggests that war is no longer fought as a rational act, but for some other reason.

A clue to this other reason comes when we examine the fate of Clausewitz's trilogy under modern conditions. The people, the army and the government are supposed to have one function each which fits in with the other two – the raw feelings of the people are harnessed to political ends by the government which are then translated into action by the military. This can still work, but only rarely. Returning to an earlier example, the North Vietnamese were remarkably Clausewitzian in their approach to the Vietnam War – not altogether surprisingly since their ideological influences – Marx, Engels, Lenin and Mao – were all avid readers of Clausewitz. The North Vietnamese people were mobilized behind the war, but not allowed a say in its execution. The political leadership held tight control over the objectives of the war, and the army was given freedom of action only in its proper sphere of operation. By contrast, the US army was given no clear objectives in Vietnam. The US president interfered with military operations, to the point of actually choosing bombing targets from the White House briefing rooms. The US public was never mobilized behind the war effort, and, via the media and Congress, set political constraints on the war which were detailed, inconsistent and deeply harmful to the development of a coherent strategy.

The key point here is that this latter state of affairs is far more common than the Clausewitzian purity of the North Vietnamese. North Vietnam, the Prussia of South East Asia, recreated a Clausewitzian environment by having nationalism without democracy, and a state strong enough to control the army and not to be constrained by informal expressions of popular opinion. This is a very unusual combination. In the advanced industrial countries public opinion and democratic institutions mean that 'the people' are hard to mobilize, and, once mobilized, will refuse to play their designated role as cheerleaders of the government and army – they insist on playing a major role in determining goals and approving (or more likely disapproving) strategies and tactics. In the less developed countries, nationalism without democracy is quite common, but the state rarely has the capacity both to control its own armed forces and to ignore the disaffection of its people. Riots and civil unrest can be every bit as effective in influencing war aims as a democratic media and free elections.

In short, Clausewitzians face two problems when dealing with public opinion. In the first place, it may be very difficult to get the public 'on side' as the phrase goes. In the 1930s it took a long time for opinion in Britain and the United States to realize that war was probably necessary – in the 1960s the US was never able to persuade a large enough majority of Americans that Vietnam justified the effort they put into it. However, once public opinion is 'on side' it is very difficult to restrain it. Whatever the merits of the 'unconditional surrender' doctrine of the Allies in the Second World War, it is clear that any alternative approach – and especially any suggestion that in future the Soviet Union might prove more of a problem than post-war Germany – would have been ruled out by public opinion. Perhaps public opinion would have been right, and was right over Vietnam – but the point is that is not a very Clausewitzian way of doing business.

There is, however, an even more fundamental problem with the Clausewitzian account of war, which is that it may be *culturally specific*. Nineteenth-century European war was a very formal business, with uniformed armies occupying clearly delineated territory, a code of conduct which was usually (although not always) observed, a formal declaration and a formal end, the peace treaty. The 'decisive battle' was a feature of Napoleonic, Clausewitzian and Victorian accounts of war – Creasy's *Fifteen Decisive Battles* is a key text here, showing a clear progression from Marathon to Waterloo (Creasy 1902). States fight in a formal way and make peace in a formal way. Hanson calls this *The Western Way of War* (1989) and traces it back to the wars of the Classical Greek cities, in which citizen heavy-infantry would fight one, highly stylized, battle per campaigning season, with a clear-cut way of determining winners and losers based on possession of the battlefield. This, he suggests, gives modern Europe its governing idea of what a war is like. However, he argues that it is highly untypical of the warfare of most civilizations, which is much more informal, is not dominated by set-piece battles, and rarely leads to any kind of decisive moment, much less a peace treaty.

The West is, of course, aware of this kind of warfare, but regards it as the exception rather than the rule and gives it special labels – guerrilla war, low-intensity conflict, police actions, dirty wars, Kipling's 'savage wars of peace'. The point to make here is that the exception may be becoming the rule. As we have seen, constitutionally secure liberal democracies do not fight each other – but then *no one* fights each other in the old way any more, except on very rare occasions such as the Falklands/Malvinas War of 1982 or the Gulf War of 1990–1. Even in these two cases, the parties that were clearly defeated have refused to behave like nineteenth-century gentlemen and make treaties which acknowledge this fact. Instead, they hang on, hoping something will turn up. Again, the Israelis have repeatedly 'defeated' their enemies in set-piece battles but they have been unable to turn these victories into political results – indeed every 'successful' military action seems to have weakened their bargaining power. More characteristic of modern warfare was the imbroglio in former Yugoslavia in the 1990s, where quasi-regular armies vied with armed bands of 'volunteers', and local warlords owed only tenuous loyalty to their nominal superiors, where alliances shifted on a day-by-day basis and the 'frontline' was difficult to define, where territory changed hands without set-piece battles, and where formal armistices and peace treaties were signed and broken, signed again and broken again. This was the non-Western way of warfare encroaching on the West in a most painful way.

There is at least some evidence that can be read as suggesting that some Western military thinkers have understood this shift in the nature of warfare rather better than Western governments or public opinion. The US armed forces have been developing doctrines for the employment of coercive measures of a non-conventional kind for some time. The new American soldier ('land warrior') will be expected to display his or her prowess by employing the latest technologies not in set-piece battles against regular opponents, but in more informal situations where the political interests of the United States need to be supported by a show of violence. This capacity for 'virtual war' which, given the publicity surrounding it, may be intended to be 'virtual deterrence', has been mapped by postmodern enthusiasts such as the Tofflers (1993) and Der Derian (1992).

One of the reasons why the Western way of war is being rejected in the West itself is, perhaps, traceable to wider changes in late modern society, and in particular to the apparent ending of the 'warrior culture' in the West. Although Western public opinion has not abandoned the idea that it may sometimes be necessary to use force in international relations, the demand nowadays is to minimize casualties amongst ones own troops, and also amongst 'enemy' civilians. The US reliance on air-power, its refusal to commit its troops in battle until the ground has been thoroughly prepared by 'precision' bombardment has been noted by many writers, and is in part a reflection of this changing ethos (Coker 1994, 1998; Ignatief 2000). The Kosovo Campaign of 1999 represents the apotheosis of this approach – a 'zero casualty' war, for NATO at least, to most people's surprise apparently actually won by air power.

A central feature of this kind of warfare is that it *cannot* so easily be seen as a viable means of conflict resolution. In the 1860s there were conflicting views of the future shape of German politics. Prussia under Bismarck settled the matter by allowing Von Moltke to win him three Western, Clausewitzian wars in succession – decisive battles at Sadowa in 1866 and Sedan in 1870 determined the outcome. Defeat was reluctantly accepted, peace treaties were signed, the German Empire was formed under the aegis of Prussian military might. A problem was solved, although a new problem emerged, as is usually the way. It seems inconceivable that a sequence of events such as this could happen today. Wars are not formally declared, they do not formally end, they peter out or they fester on. Sometimes a stalemate emerges, sometimes imposed from outside – the 'non-war' in Cyprus in 1973 has been stifled by a UN peacekeeping force but the conflict remains unsolved, indeed the very stalemate removes the impetus for solution. In other circumstances, such as Somalia and Rwanda, the impact of informal war may be the collapse of a society and a descent into anarchy, a descent which outsiders are effectively powerless to halt because, in the absence of clear enemies, clear battle lines and regular armies, external intervention becomes almost impossible. Even in Kosovo, where the military outcome was decisive, it is by no means the case that the losers have accepted the verdict of the (air) battlefield – instead NATO is faced with the prospect of maintaining Kosovo as a protectorate for the foreseeable future. All this suggests that any account of war which tries to give the modern phenomenon its older, European function will miss the point in a very big way.

Conclusion: The End of State-Centric International Relations?

Over the last three chapters we have seen a number of cracks appear in the edifice of state-centric International Relations theory. We have seen that theorists of decision-making have undermined the idea that foreign policy is radically different from domestic politics; the notion that states follow the national interest is difficult to support from these studies. Structural theories of international relations shift the emphasis away from foreign policy, but in turn are unable to resolve the problem of agency – and their emphasis on the irrelevance of domestic factors is undermined somewhat by the phenomenon of the 'democratic peace'. Power is a notion that seems clear and easy to understand, but once the distinction between power-as-attribute and power-as-influence is introduced many of the usual certainties about the operation of power disappear. The balance of power, again, is an idea which has a degree of intuitive plausibility, but, again, which crumbles once the logic of the notion is exposed.

At one level, the weakness of the political conception of war is simply one additional reason for suspicion about state-centricity, yet one more example of a feature of international relations not behaving quite in the way it is supposed to. In reality, the malaise here goes much deeper. A Clausewitzian view of war is an essential requirement for the balance of power to operate; the two institutions stand together, and if, as suggested here, they fall together the whole state-centric edifice is in ruins – certainly this is so for any variant of realism. The point is that war and the balance of power are not simply additional extras that can be set aside if things do not work out. On the contrary, they are at the heart of both Waltz's anarchical system and Bull's anarchical society. They are the devices that permit the system or society to operate, and if they are in difficulties, it is in difficulties.

And yet, the logic of state-centricity remains compelling. If the initial premises hold, that is, we live in an anarchical world, in which states are the major actors, and if states are motivated by rational egoism, then a neorealist world seems inevitable – although if states are able to temper this egoism with a concern for norms some kind of international society might emerge. If, nonetheless, we live in a world which in

many respects is not characterized by this kind of international relations, which seems to be the case, then it seems likely there is something
wrong with these assumptions. We have already seen that one of these
assumptions, that of rational egoism, can only be sustained by some
quite heroic surgery. In the chapters to come, the other assumptions
will equally be put to the test. The most basic of these assumptions is
that of anarchy, and there are two ways in which the notion of anarchy
can be challenged.

In the first place, we need to take seriously some of the propositions
about the role of theory outlined in Chapter 1. In particular, we need
to pay serious attention to the implications of the view that knowledge
is constructed, not found, that it rests on social foundations and not
upon some bedrock of certainty. If we acknowledge the sense in which
'international anarchy' is a construction by states – 'Anarchy is What
States Make of It' – we will be less surprised by its illogicalities, and
more willing to ask whose interests it serves (Wendt 1992, 1999). Partly
this is a question of historicizing international anarchy, of grasping the
insubstantial nature of the timeless generalities of (neo)realism and
placing them in some kind of historical context. This task is undertaken very ably by Rosenberg, although, unfortunately, the historical
narrative he wishes to employ to replace realism's a-historicism is
based on a Marxism that seems equally problematic, given the political
and intellectual failings of that nineteenth-century doctrine (Rosenberg, 1994). However, there are also questions here about power and
knowledge that need to be raised.

The *anarchy problematic*, to anglicize Richard Ashley's phrase, does
not simply serve the interests of rich and powerful states by legitimiz-
ing certain ways of exercising power, it also sets in place a particular
conception of politics which privileges *all* states (Ashley 1989c). The
notion that states exist in order to protect their populations from
external dangers is legitimized in this way – even though it is quite
clear that most people most of the time are in far more danger from
their 'own' governments that they are from foreigners. The private–
public distinction which pervades Western conceptions of politics and
has characteristically supported the exclusion of women from public
life in the West rests on the same foundations as the Western way of
warfare – the original public figures were the soldiers who fought the
set-piece battles of the Greek cities (Elshtain 1987). In short, a state-
centric conception of *international* politics carries with it a quite extensive amount of political baggage from other areas of social life – the
notion that international relations is different from all other spheres of

social life, and thus that International Relations is a different kind of discipline from the other social sciences is one of the least compelling propositions of conventional realist international thought.

These are thoughts that will be pursued in the rest of this book, which begins with an attempt to cross-examine 'anarchy' in an essentially empirical way. Is it actually the case that we live in an ungoverned system? Clearly there is no 'government' in the conventional, Western sense of the term – a limited set of institutions that makes and enforces authoritative decisions – but is this the only available model of what a government is? Realists, neorealists, neoliberals and international society theorists all stress that in international relations, 'in the last instance' there is no 'ultimate' decision-making power. Thus sovereignty is a defining feature of the system, and nothing has really changed or ever will short of the emergence of a world-empire. But, how important is 'the last instance'? It might well be argued that we only very rarely and *in extremis* come close to reaching 'the last instance'. Can the network of quasi-governmental institutions within which the states-system is today embedded really be dismissed quite so readily? We may not have world government, but perhaps we do have 'global governance' and it is to this phenomenon that we now turn.

Further Reading

Classical texts on the balance of power by Brougham, Von Gentz and Cobden are collected in M. G. Forsyth, H. M. A. Keens-Soper and P. Savigear (eds), *The Theory of International Relations* (1970); a similar collection with a wider remit is Chris Brown, Terry Nardin and N.J. Rengger (eds), *Texts in International Relations* (2001). Hume's excellent essay 'The Balance of Power' is very much worth reading 250 years on, and is most conveniently found in David Hume, *Essays: Moral, Political and Literary* (1987).

Modern 'classics' on the balance of power include E. V. Gulick, *Europe's Classical Balance of Power* (1955); Chapters 2 and 3 of Inis L. Claude, *Power and International Relations* (1962); Ludwig Dehio, *The Precarious Balance* (1965); and essays by the editors both entitled 'The Balance of Power' in Herbert Butterfield and Martin Wight (eds), *Diplomatic Investigations* (1966) as well as discussions in Morgenthau and other standard texts. Morton Kaplan, *System and Process in International Politics* (1957) is a classic of a different kind from the behavioural movement of the 1950s, containing an attempt to pin down the rules of a balance system. J. N. Rosenau (ed.), *International Politics and Foreign Policy: A Reader* (1969) contains extracts from Kaplan, Waltz, Singer and others, still valuable over 30 years on. Contemporary debate on the balance of power is dominated by Kenneth Waltz, *Theory of International Politics* (1979) – see the articles from *International Security* in Michael E. Brown, Sean M. Lynn-Jones and Steven E. Miller (eds), *The Perils of Anarchy* (1995), especially Stephen M. Walt, 'Alliance Formation and the Balance of World Power' (1985); and Paul Schroeder, 'Historical Reality vs. Neo-realist Theory' (1994) for critiques and alternatives largely from within the neorealist camp. A non-neorealist alternative to Waltz is provided by Hedley Bull, *The Anarchical Society* (1977/1995). A good, fairly conventional collection on the balance of power is a Special Issue of *Review of International Studies*, Moorhead Wright (ed.), The Balance of Power' (1989).

Lawrence Freedman (ed.), *War* (1994) is a very useful reader which contains short extracts from a wide range of sources. The acknowledged classic on the subject is Carl von Clausewitz, *On War* (1976): this edition/translation by Michael Howard and Peter Paret contains extensive commentary and fine introductory essays, and is to be preferred to all the many alternatives available. Michael Howard, *Clausewitz* (1983) is the best short introduction. Paret (ed.), *Makers of Modern Strategy from Machiavelli to the Nuclear Age* (1986) is a reissue of a classic collection on the great strategists. Colin Gray, 'Clausewitz Rules, OK! The Future is the Past with GPS' (1999) is, in principle, a defence of Clausewitzian ideas, in practice, a somewhat intemperate attack on those authors unwise enough to think that one or two things might have changed since the beginning of the nineteenth century (including the present writer in the first edition of this book).

On the causes of war, two major studies stand out: Kenneth Waltz, *Man, the State and War* (1959); and its only equal, Hidemi Suganami, *On the Causes of War* (1996), an earlier, brief version of which is 'Bringing Order to the Causes of War Debate' (1990): Stephen Van Evera's *Causes of War: Power and the Roots of Conflict* (1999) is rightly highly regarded, but too much focused on the offensive/defensive realist debate for non-rational choice oriented readers – a short version is 'Offence, Defence and the Causes of War' (1998). Other useful works include Geoffrey Blainey, *The Causes of War* (1988) and John G. Stoessinger, *Why Nations go to War* (1990).

For more recent thinking on Just War and legal restraints on violence, see Adam Roberts and Richard Guelff (eds), *Documents on the*

Laws of War (2000); Geoffrey Best, *War and Law since 1945* (1994); Michael Walzer, *Just and Unjust Wars* (1992); and Terry Nardin (ed.), *The Ethics of War and Peace* (1996). Wider reflections on the changing nature of warfare are to be found from a number of sources, some 'academic', some not: a selection of recent books which raise serious questions about the nature of war and its shape in the future would include John Keegan, *The Face of Battle* (1978); Jean Bethke Elshtain, *Women and War* (1987); Victor Davis Hanson, *The Western Way of War: Infantry Battle in Classical Greece* (1989); James Der Derian, *Antidiplomacy: Spies, Terror, Speed and War* (1992); Alvin and Heidi Toffler, *War and Anti-War* (1993); Christopher Coker, *War in the Twentieth Century* (1994) and *War and the Illiberal Conscience* (1998); Michael Ignatief, *Virtual War* (2000). Ignatief focuses on the Kosovo campaign of 1999 – interesting military strategic analyses of that conflict are Daniel A. Byman and Matthew C. Waxman, 'Kosovo and the Great Air Power Debate' (2000) and Barry Posen, 'The War for Kosovo: Serbia's Political Military Strategy' (2000), both from *International Security*.

7

Global Governance

Introduction: Sovereignty, Anarchy and Global Governance

Anarchy is basic to state-centric International Relations because *sovereignty* is basic to state-centric International Relations. As Hinsley and others have demonstrated, 'sovereignty' emerged in the sixteenth and seventeenth centuries as a double-headed notion (Hinsley 1966). On the one hand, rulers were sovereign in so far as they accepted no internal, 'domestic' equals; on the other hand, they were sovereign in so far as they accepted no external, 'international' superiors. This notion came to gain normative acceptance in the second half of the seventeenth century – conventionally, following the Westphalia Peace Conference that ended the Thirty Years War – and remains the base upon which the structures of anarchy are constructed. The extent to which the norms of Westphalia have governed international practice is debatable; the Westphalia notion of sovereignty may indeed, as Krasner suggests, be a matter of 'organized hypocrisy' given the extent to which rulers have actually always intervened in each others affairs, but, at least in principle, the claim to be a sovereign entails acknowledgement of the sovereignty of others (Krasner 1999; Kratochwil 1995).

In any event, the absence of an external superior implies the absence of 'government', which is the definition of anarchy. Were a world government to emerge it would, by definition, undermine state sovereignty. Some international society theorists believe that this would be a bad thing because sovereignty allows for the flourishing of plural conceptions of the good; all international society theorists, and all realists, believe that it is unlikely to happen because states will do all they can to prevent it. This is a clear and logical argument, but it does involve glossing over another respect in which sovereignty is a double-sided notion, in addition to the internal–external dimension.

Sovereignty is both a *juridical status* and a *political concept*. On the one hand, to say of a state that it is sovereign is to make a judgement about its legal position in the world, namely that it recognizes no legal superior, that it is not, for example, a colony or part of a suzerain system, or subject to the kind of controls European states exercised over some non-European states in the nineteenth and early twentieth centuries. On the other hand, to say that a state is sovereign generally implies that it possesses certain sorts of capacities; the ability to act in certain kinds of ways, to perform certain tasks. Krasner suggests, helpfully, that this ability can be divided into a capacity to do things internally and a capacity to control cross-border transactions – this distinction will be important later, but can be disregarded for the time being. Now, one essential difference between these two meanings of sovereignty is that the first is unqualified – states either are, or are not, legally sovereign – while the second clearly involves matters of degree, that is to say, both the tasks themselves can be added to and subtracted from without losing the basic idea, and the manner in which they are performed can be more or less effective. On the one hand we have sovereignty as a *status* which states either possess or do not possess, on the other we have sovereignty as a *bundle of powers and capacities* which can grow larger or smaller.

   This distinction was of no great significance in the early years of the 'Westphalia System' because the kinds of powers that states exercised were limited in scope and range. Tax collection and 'pacification' – the establishment of law and order – were the main domestic activities of states, and warfare and imperialism the main external activities; here differential capabilities were most striking, but this in no sense under-mined the idea of anarchy – indeed, as Kenneth Waltz insists, a key feature of anarchy is that the units in an anarchical system try to perform the same functions with different capabilities (Waltz 1979). However, once it became accepted that amongst the functions of a sovereign state are the achievement of certain kinds of social goals – a welfare system, or at least a welfare safety net for example – and successful regulation, if not actual management, of the economy, the situation does change quite dramatically, because here it is clear that exercising these powers effectively might well, in some circumstances, be impossible without external cooperation and a degree of pooling of sovereignty. Thus, to take a very simple example, one of the 'powers' a state has is the power to set up a postal service – but such a service will be of limited value unless it is possible to send and receive letters across state boundaries, and to arrange this effectively states have actually had to give up certain powers to an international body, originally the Universal Postal Union of 1874. The bundle of powers that a state possesses as a 'sovereign' body is thereby simultaneously diminished *and* enhanced – the state now has the capacity to set up an effective postal system, but it buys this capacity by giving up part of its capacity to regulate this system, because there are now rules it must accept if it wishes to remain part of the wider body, that is, if it wishes to preserve its capacity to exercise its sovereign powers and run an effective postal service. The convoluted nature of this sentence is not accidental – it is symptomatic of a concept, sovereignty, being asked to do more work than it can handle; to be truly sovereign it may be necessary to surrender part of one's sovereignty.

Another way of putting the same point is that the 'fit' between state and society/economy has altered since the beginning of the Westphalia System. Initially social policy was minimal and economic activity was, for the most part agricultural, local and small scale. Even those countries most dependent on trade, England and the Netherlands, grew 90 per cent of their own food requirements in the sixteenth and seventeenth centuries, and only a little less in the eighteenth. However, with the coming of manufacturing and the factory system, and recognition that efficiency gains – economies of scale – could be achieved via production for a wider market, the range and scope of economic activity expanded, and with it the possibilities for social policy. The first consequence here was a step up in the optimum size of states; Britain and France created 'single-markets' by removing local obstacles to trade, while Germany moved from a Customs Union to a single state. However, the needs of the new societies went beyond these steps; gradually from the 1860s onwards, regulatory international bodies were established: the International Telegraphic Union of 1865; the establishment of an International Bureau of Weights and Measures in 1875; and the International Labour Office in 1901 (Murphy 1994). In the twentieth century, the League and UN systems accelerated the institutionalization of functional cooperation. Each of these new institutions reflected the functional needs of states, and taken together they cover most of the major activities in which states engage. Each grew out of the exercise of sovereign powers, but each constituted a diminution of sovereignty, in the sense that here we have powers which can only be exercised effectively by a degree of pooling of sovereignty.

Moreover, this process of institutionalized regulation does not simply involve the new social and economic forces of the last two centuries. It is also the case that the most basic external capacity of the state – the capacity to make war – is now regulated, albeit some-what ineffectively, in a way that would have been difficult to believe 150 years ago. The various Hague and Geneva Conventions, the legal restraints of the Pact of Paris and the United Nations Charter, and the emergence of customary restraints on the employment of force do seem to place some kinds of inhibitions on the exercise of state power. International law is more elaborate today than in the past, and in many respects more effective – even with respect to issues normally seen as central to the sovereign rights of states.

What these reflections suggest is that, although the world lacks government, because states have been unwilling to surrender their *juridical* status as sovereign, their attempts to rule effectively and exercise their *political* sovereignty have created extensive networks of global 'governance' – a somewhat archaic word which originally was synonymous with government, but which has been pressed into service as a convenient term for the collective impact of the various disparate quasi-governmental institutions which have proliferated (internally and externally) over the last century or more (Rosenau and Czempiel (eds) 1992). Much of the rest of this book will examine these networks. As indicated above, a great deal of the growth of global governance has taken place in the context of an expanding global economy and Chapters 8–10 will reflect this context, examining the growth of the world economy, its institutional framework, and a number of theories and perspectives which have been employed to chart the relationship between both state and economy, and the international system and the global economy. This will involve examining 'regime theory', 'the theory of hegemonic stability' and the Gramscian notion of hegemony as sometimes alternative, sometimes compatible, ways of conceptualizing cooperation in the global economy today.

However, before moving towards the study of global political economy, this chapter will examine some theories of international co-operation which, although encompassing international economic relations, have a wider compass and are not primarily focused on this sphere of international life. *Functionalism* as a theory offers an account of international functional cooperation which attempts to transcend the state, and create a new global order as does its offshoot, the *world society* approach. *Neofunctionalism* and *federalism* on the other hand, look to the creating of new larger states via the integration of existing states – a process that could lead to the creation of a world state. By way of contrast, the theory of *collective security* attempts to create an alternative method of power management to the balance of power without attempting to create a world government but by the self-limitation of sovereign states. Each of these ideas will be examined, in some cases rather briefly, and discussed in the context of the United Nations system, and, on occasion, the European Union – the latter as the site of the most significant derogations of sovereignty yet made by states in the modern system.

Before proceeding to this agenda, however, it may be worth stressing one important point about the notion of 'global governance', namely that its relevance varies quite dramatically from issue to issue and from one part of the world to another. It makes sense to talk of the global governance of, say, world trade, and institutions such as the regular meetings of the 'G7' and 'G8' – the leading industrial powers in the world sometimes (G8) including Russia – and of the world's political elite at Davos, suggest that attempts are frequently made to bring even 'high' political issues within the governance model. However, it would be a mistake to see the growth of global governance as a steady process encroaching on all areas of international life and all regions of the world. There are many parts of the world where a savage Hobbesian realism is the most accurate way of theorizing politics, domestic and international, and there are some aspects of international politics where no states have proved willing to give up their sovereign prerogatives. Further, to assert the existence of global governance is not to assert the absence of political conflict. In short, and to re-iterate an earlier point, global *governance* is not the same thing as global *government* – much less responsible and representative government – and the extent to which the world as a whole is orderly and norm-governed should never be exaggerated.

Functionalism

Federalist ideas can be dated back to the peace projects of the eighteenth century and to Kant's 'Perpetual Peace' – if not earlier, to the assumed unity of the medieval world – and thus, strictly speaking, are the earliest attempts to reach an understanding of the growth of international institutions; however, there are good reasons for beginning this survey with an examination of *functionalism*. Functionalism is the most elaborate, intellectually sophisticated and ambitious attempt yet made not just to understand the growth of international institutions, but also to plot the trajectory of this growth into the future, and to come to terms with its normative implications. It is an original set of ideas, parallel in scope to realism, but, unlike realism, it has little contact with past diplomatic tradition. While one figure, David Mitrany, could reasonably claim to be the originator of functionalism, his account of the world has been taken up and employed in case studies and theoretical work by scholars such as Joseph Nye, Ernst Haas, J. P. Sewell, Paul Taylor, A. J. R. Groom and, in a rather idiosyncratic way, by John Burton and theorists of *world society* such as Christopher Mitchell and Michael Banks. Functionalism is certainly the most important approach to international institutions to have emerged in the twentieth century – which is not to say that all of its ideas, or even most of them, stand up to critical scrutiny.

The key to an understanding of functionalism is that although it offers an explanation for the past growth and future prospects of international institutions it is not *primarily* a theory of institutional growth. Rather, it is an account of the conditions of peace. It emerged in the 1940s as a reaction to state-centric approaches to peace such as federalism and collective security. Mitrany's insight was that these approaches failed not because the demands they made on states were too radical – the common criticism – but because they were not radical enough. Collective security leaves untouched the sovereign power of states to determine whether or not to respond to its imperatives; legally states may be bound to act in certain kinds of ways but they retain the power to disregard legality when it suits them. Federalism on a world scale might create the conditions in which states are no longer capable of acting in this way, but, for precisely this reason, states are unwilling to federate. Both approaches fail because they attempt to work with the grain of sovereignty while producing results which go against the grain of sovereignty – a *frontal assault on juridical sovereignty which leaves political sovereignty intact is bound to fail*. Instead, Mitrany argued that a 'working peace system' could only be constructed from the bottom up, by encouraging forms of cooperation which bypassed the issue of formal sovereignty but instead gradually reduced the capacity of states to actually act as sovereigns (Mitrany 1966). Two formulae here summarize the argument – 'form follows function' and 'peace in parts' (Nye 1971).

'Form follows function' collapses a number of propositions. First, cooperation will only work if it is focused on particular and specific activities ('functions') which are currently performed by states but which would be performed more effectively in some wider context. Second, the form which such cooperation takes should be determined by the nature of the function in question; there is no common form which will appropriate to all examples of functional cooperation. Thus, for some functions a global institution will be appropriate – disease knows no frontiers, an effective postal system should be universal – while for others regional, or even local, institutions are all that is necessary. For some functions the exchange of information is all that is required – for example, global weather forecasting – in other cases power of decision may need to be vested with functional institutions. Workers' organizations and employers' groups should be concerned with labour standards, medical doctors and health administrators with the eradication of disease. Each functional organization should be set up in such a way that it is appropriately designed to cope with its particular function.

'Peace in parts' describes the hoped-for collective outcome of these individual cases of functional cooperation. The functionalist model of sovereignty stresses the primacy of the political dimension of sovereignty described above. Sovereignty is a bundle of powers. As these powers are gradually shifted away from the state to functional organizations, so, gradually, the capacity of the state to act as a sovereign will diminish. There is an element of political psychology involved here; the assumption is that the loyalty individuals give to states is a product of the things states do for them and as other institutions take over the performance of particular activities so loyalty will drain away. Moreover, the result of functional cooperation is not to create a new, larger, more effective state – instead the territorial basis of the system will, itself, be undermined by the precept that form follows function. Gradually the territorial state will come to exercise fewer and fewer functions – instead states will be anomalous institutions attempting to be multi-functional and territorial in a world in which most of the business of governing and administration will be carried out by bodies that are functionally specific and non-territorial.

Mitrany's basic ideas have inspired a number of later theoretical works, and some very famous case studies, in particular *Beyond the Nation State*, Ernst B. Haas's account of the International Labour Organization (ILO), and *Functionalism and World Politics*, J. P. Sewell's account of UNESCO (Haas 1964; Sewell 1966). Clearly the 'Functional Agencies' of the United Nations system provide a range of possible case studies – although, for the most part, they breach the injunction that 'form follows function', being all global bodies, and mostly dominated by states rather than the performers of functions. Functionalism has also influenced thinking on regional organizations, although, as the next section will suggest, only in a 'neo' form. The connection between functionalist ideas and Burton's notion of the *'cobweb'* model of world society (Burton 1972) is clear, and acknowledged by writers such as Mitchell and Groom, if not by Burton himself. Accounts of the world economy which stress *globalization* owe much to functionalist thinking, likewise recent work on the *debordering* of states. In short, we have here a model of global governance which has quite widespread influence even if the full version of Mitrany's vision is subscribed to by very few. What are the problems with functionalism – why has it not been even more influential?

In a comment on Haas's famous study, the English realist F. S. Northedge remarked that the ILO is 'beyond the nation-state' in the same way that Trafalgar Square is beyond Charing Cross Station. The meaning of this somewhat enigmatic remark is that while the ILO with its tripartite structure of state, trade unions and employers' representatives is undoubtedly in a different place from (cf. spatially beyond) the nation-state, it can in no sense be said to have *transcended* that institution. An extremely elaborate network of institutions has emerged in the world but, contrary to the expectations of functionalists, the Westphalia System remains in place and sovereignty is undiminished as a guiding principle. It seems that the sovereign state has been able to ringfence functional cooperation, and isolate itself from the supposedly corrosive effects of functionalism.

From a realist point of view it is clear what has gone wrong; the political psychology of functionalism is misconceived. Individuals do not give their loyalty to the state instrumentally, simply because the state performs a range of functions from weather forecasting to economic management and the justice system. Instead, loyalty rests on two pillars. First, loyalty to the state is an affective phenomenon rather than purely instrumental – for many, the state represents the nation, the nation is Burke's contract between generations past, present and future, and this contract rests on ties of birth, language, attachment to a territory, and a culture, none of which are factors which can be diminished by functional cooperation across state boundaries. But second, in so far as loyalty is instrumental, it is the ability of the state to provide basic physical security that is the key, the ability to protect the people from outsiders – and the performance of this function is, literally under Mitrany's model, the last thing that governments will surrender.

It could be argued that this realist position rests on as implausible a view of political psychology as does functionalism: very few states are actually nations, most people are more in danger from their own governments than from foreigners, much of the time 'loyalty' is coerced rather than freely given. However, behind the realist position lies a rather better general criticism of functionalism which rests on a less romantic view of the state. Mitrany – along with some at least of his successors – offered an essentially a-political account of functional cooperation. He approached problems with the soul of a technician. The underlying assumption is that the problems that functional co-operation is supposed to solve are essentially technical problems which admit to a technical solution. Administration can be divorced from politics – a very nineteenth-century, positivist view of the world, and one shared, for example, by John Burton whose notion of 'systemic' problem-solving, as opposed to the non-systemic approach of states, rests on a similar distrust and marginalization of the political (Burton 1968).

The difficulty, of course, is that even the most technical of solutions to the most technical of problems will always have political implications, will always have the potential to benefit one group and disadvantage another. The basic rule of the Universal Postal Union, which is that each state has an obligation to deliver international mail on its own territory, seems as purely technical a solution to the problem of an effective mail system as can be imagined, yet it has enormous political implications when it comes to issues such as the dissemination of political, religious or pornographic material through the mail. The gathering of information for effective weather forecasting seems innocuous but will be resisted by closed societies. At the other extreme, no one needs to be reminded of the political implications of such matters as labour standards or the regulation of trade or international capital markets. All of these examples of functional cooperation involve the distribution of gains and losses, a determination of who gets what, where and when. There are no technical problems, there are no technical solutions, and because of this, states are often very unwilling to allow problems to be dealt with 'functionally'. Thus it is that the state-centric nature of the functional agencies of the United Nations is not an accident. No major state has been willing to allow issues which it regards as political to be dealt with in an allegedly non-political way, and even if they were so willing it is moot whether their populations would be equally tolerant when the consequences became clear.

For this reason, the full-blown functionalist model of international cooperation has to be regarded as a failure – however, as will be apparent in what follows and in Chapters 8 and 9, functionalist arguments still play quite an important role in the way in which international institutions are conceptualized. No theory of similar range or scope has yet been produced, and some at least of the language of functionalism persists in other, less ambitious, but perhaps more successful theories. Moreover, the functionalist opposition to the principle of territoriality strikes a chord in the context of an era of globalization in which new notions of political space are emerging – although the drawbacks of functionalism's a-political approach should also be noted.

Integration Theory, Federalism and Neofunctionalism

Functionalism looks to the creation of a new world order in which the sovereign state takes a back seat. By way of contrast, integration theory looks to the creation of new states by the integration of existing states, generally on a regional basis and possibly, in the long run, to the creation of a single world state. Since 1945 the most important testing ground for ideas on integration has been Europe, thus the following discussion of *federalism* and *neofunctionalism* takes a European focus – however, it should be remembered that most of the godfathers of the European process saw this as a stepping stone towards, in perhaps the very long run, the integration of the world.

In the immediate post-war world, many of the leaders of Western Europe, concerned to avoid a third European war, looked to the creation of a United States of Europe, a federal, or perhaps confederal, arrangement in which the sovereignty of its members would be suppressed. Some early institutions – in particular the Council of Europe – represented this aspiration in embryonic form, but it became clear in the course of the 1940s that a direct assault on the sovereignty of European states would not succeed; a fact that was finally confirmed by the failure of plans for a European Defence Union (EDU), scuppered by the French National Assembly in 1954. Instead, the founding fathers of European integration – Monnet, De Gasperi and Schuman – drew on some functionalist ideas, and on the experience of American aid under the Marshall Plan, to chart a different route to European unity. Functionalists look to undermine state sovereignty from below, by stripping away the powers of the state piecemeal, salami-style: in the Committee for European Economic Cooperation – later to become the Organization for Economic Cooperation and Development (OECD) – which was set up to distribute Marshall Aid, the European recipients were obliged to produce common plans for this distribution. The result of combining this strategy with that experience was a route to European *political* unity which went via European *economic* unity – hence the formation of the European Coal and Steel Community (ECSC) in 1952, and of Euratom and the European Economic Community (EEC) in 1956. These three institutions were later solidified as the European Community (EC), now rebranded as the European Union (EU).

These were, and are, unique organizations. Although in formal terms much of the decision-making power in the EU rests with state representatives in the Council of Ministers, the European Commission, a body of appointed bureaucrats, has the capacity to initiate policy, the European Court is empowered to decide many intra-community disputes, and, more recently, a directly elected European Parliament has some significant powers it can employ independent of state control. These institutions taken together mean that the (current) fifteen member-states and 300 million citizens of the Union are taking part in a unique process of international institutional cooperation.

How is this process to be understood? It clearly differs from the functionalist notions of Mitrany and his collaborators in two key respects. In the first place, the intention was and is to create a new *state* via international institution-building, and *not* to create a new kind of world order. The end result has always been intended to be the (con)federal Europe that could not be created by direct action. Although politicians in some parts of the community, especially Britain and Scandinavia, may find it convenient to deny this aspiration and to cling to the letter of the obligations they have undertaken as set out in the Treaty of Rome of 1957 and subsequent amendments, the spirit of these documents has always been towards political unity and a European federal system – although what federalism actually means in this context is contentious and will be discussed below. In any event, the European institutions were not and are not designed on a 'form follows function' basis, hence the opposition of many integrationists to the quasi-functionalist principle of a 'two- (or '*n*'-) speed Europe' in which different parts of the Union integrate at different rates.

Perhaps even more important is the second difference with functionalism. As with functionalism, the aim was that institutional cooperation would expand, as states discovered that cooperation in one area naturally led to cooperation in another; the difference is that in the European system this expansion (or 'spillover') is, and was intended to be, an overtly *political* process. The abolition of internal tariffs between member countries creates a political demand to equalize as far as possible production and transport costs. The idea is that political parties and pressure groups will gradually come to put pressure on central institutions rather than 'local' governments. Whereas politics is the enemy of functionalism, it was meant to be the driving force of European integration.

These two departures from the functionalist model lead some writers to distil from the European experience an approach to integration they called *neofunctionalism*, which could provide a theoretical basis for other examples of integration in, for example, Africa, or Latin America. It is important to put the matter this way round because sometimes the impression is given that Europe has been some kind of test for the neofunctionalist model. Not so – the idea that integration between states could come as a result of a politically driven process of spillover, the heart of neofunctionalism, was *drawn from* European experience rather than *applied to* it. In any event, regarded as a model, how does neofunctionalism fare? Not very well has to be the basic answer. The European experience has not proved to be exportable; other examples of integration have generally not followed the European (neofunctional) model. Moreover, even within Europe, the model clearly has not worked in any consistent way. Sometimes spillover has taken place, sometimes it has not. Some pressure groups have operated at the European level, others have not – it is striking, for example, that despite the obvious importance of the Common Agricultural Policy (CAP) and the extent to which CAP rulings are made in Brussels, farmers' organizations throughout the Union remain largely oriented towards putting pressure on their home governments rather than the central institutions. 'Functional autonomy' is the watchword here. European integration has proceeded by stops and starts rather than as a smooth process of spillover – and the factors that have, at different times, restarted the process have not followed any obvious pattern. Integration has taken place in ways and at speeds determined by the course of events and not in accordance with any theoretical model. Later writers have stressed 'intergovernmentalism' – on this account, the process of integration is driven by interstate bargaining; particular problems emerge and are solved politically by state governments and not in accordance with any functional logic. However, intergovernmental bargaining could lead in some circumstances to a degree of 'pooling of sovereignty' and the emergence of 'policy networks' on a European scale may be responsible for some kinds of change. In any event, it seems clear that the European experience really is *sui generis* and it may not be sensible to look to find here any general lessons about the processes of cooperation and international institution building.

However, before turning to the United Nations system and the theory of collective security it may be worth briefly returning to the starting-point of the post-war European experience, the aspiration to create a 'Federal Europe'. A great deal of debate in Britain in the last quarter century, and especially since the creation of a single European currency in 1999 (the 'Euro'), has centred on whether a federal Europe is desirable – an important issue since the Maastricht Treaty of 1992 specifically refers to this ambition. Part of the problem here rests in the fact that 'federalism' has different connotations in Britain from much of the rest of Europe, especially Germany. In Britain, the experience of the United States is crucial, and this experience is read as a process of *centralization*, whereby the federal government has increasingly come to take over powers once held by the states; federalism in Europe is seen as something that would 'reduce' Britain to the status of a Massachusetts or a Colorado within the Union, and rejected accordingly by Britain's political class. In Germany, on the other hand, federalism is seen in the light of the movement from the Second and Third Reich to the Federal Republic of Germany – that is, as a process of *decentralization*.

There is, nonetheless, a more important point at stake here than this parochial difference, and that is that on some accounts the European Union is already a federal system. Murray Forsyth points out that the defining characteristic of a federal system is that the federal authority has some powers that it can exercise effectively without reference to the lower levels and this is certainly the case within the European Union (Forsyth in Brown 1994c: 56). The EU is a 'weak' federal system but a federal system nonetheless. There may be a wider point here. There are in the world today quite a number of organizations that have some powers of this kind, including, on some interpretations, the United Nations itself, and it may be that the general unwillingness of analysts to use older categories such as 'federalism' to describe this situation is a mistake.

Global Governance and (Collective) Security

As suggested at some length in previous chapters, issues of security and insecurity have always been at the heart of the anarchy problematic, and it might have been expected that a chapter on global governance would address these issues directly and at some length by means of an examination of those institutions which had primary responsibility for security and the preservation of peace – the central institutions of the United Nations and its predecessor the League of Nations. Such expectations would have been shared by the 'Peace Project' designers of the eighteenth century, and would have remained current in the 1920s and 1930s at which time most theorists of international organization regarded the design and re-design of these institutions as their primary task. Even after 1945, the 'world peace through world law' movement continued to think in terms of institutional reform – however, by then, the heart had gone out of the enterprise and the most creative thinking was directed elsewhere, towards functionalism and integration theory (Clark and Sohn 1966). These latter notions are, of course, concerned with peace and security, but they represent an indirect approach to the problem and were adopted because of the failure of frontal assaults on sovereignty and anarchy. The final section of this chapter examines the lack of success of this frontal assault – and in the process qualifies somewhat the verdict of failure.

The most important twentieth-century attempt to change directly the way the world handles security issues was the doctrine of 'collective security' – the attempt to replace the 'self-help' balance of power system that prevailed before 1914 with a system that involved a commitment by each state to the security of every other state. We have already seen the fate of this doctrine in the 1930s in the context of the theoretical debate between liberal internationalism and realism; a second 'take' on this failure, concentrating more on the institutional side, and carrying the story through to the post-1945 era is now called for.

The formation of the League of Nations in 1919 emerged out of the contingencies of the First World War, and the United Nations was formed from the wreckage of the League at the end of the Second World War, but the roots of these institutions go much further back in the history of the European states-system. 'Roots' in the plural is important here, because a central problem of these bodies has always been that they have attempted to institutionalize and fuse two quite separate traditions, with quite different normative approaches to the problem of international order and global governance – the tradition of the 'Peace Project' and the tradition of the 'Concert of Europe'.

The most famous 'Peace Project' was Kant's 'Perpetual Peace' of 1795, but while the phrase 'perpetual peace' was a commonplace amongst the creators of 'Peace Projects' in the seventeenth and eighteenth centuries, Kant's work was actually untypical of most others (Reiss (ed.) 1970). The basic idea of these projects was clear, even though they differed markedly as to detail (Hinsley 1963). In order to overcome the scourge of war, the states of Europe would form a kind of parliament or federal assembly wherein disputes would be solved. Projectors differed as to such matters as voting mechanisms and enforcement procedures, but collective decision was central – states would no longer have the power to act as judges in their own cases. Impartial rules would be impartially applied to all. International relations would become a realm of law and not a realm of power – although the 'projectors' were suspicious of the international lawyers of the day, regarding them as, in Kant's phrase, 'sorry comforters', that is, apologists for power politics and the rights of states.

The Concert of Europe was very different in approach. This notion emerged in the nineteenth century, initially via the medium of the formal congresses which dealt with the aftermath of the Napoleonic Wars, later on a more informal basis. The idea of the Concert was that the Great Powers would consult and, as far as possible, coordinate policy on issues of common concern. The root idea was that great power brought with it great responsibility; managing the system in the common interest was something that the powers should do if they could – but, crucially, it should be noted that the 'common interest' was weighted towards the interests of the great powers themselves. Sometimes 'managing the system' might involve preserving a balance of power amongst the great at the expense of lesser players – as with the wholesale re-organizations of boundaries that took place after 1815. Sometimes, if the great powers were in conflict, it could not work at all, and Bismarck for one was wont to regard the notion of a European interest with disfavour. In any event, the Concert of Europe was, in no sense an impartial body, dispensing impartial laws. If it worked at all, it worked partially, in the interests of order perhaps, of the Great Powers certainly.

Both of these traditions still existed at the end of the twentieth century. Movements for institutional reform of the UN and global 'democratization' clearly draw on the tradition of peace projects, but, on the other hand, the informal 'contact group' of the United States, Russia, Germany, France and Britain, which oversaw policy on former Yugoslavia during the Bosnian war of the early 1990s was clearly a (wider) reincarnation of the Concert of Europe, with a similar attitude to the rights of smaller countries, as the Bosnian government discovered to its cost. However, the actual institutions set up in the League and UN represent an uneasy and unsuccessful hybrid of both traditions.

Thus the doctrine of Collective Security draws on the universalism of the Peace Projects – one for all and all for one – but is meant to be

operated by states which retain the power of deciding when the obligations of collective security are binding, unlike the institutions envisaged
by most of the projectors. Moreover, collective security sets in stone
and defends a status quo, with only a passing nod in the direction of
mechanisms for peaceful change, while the peace projectors envisaged
that their deliberative bodies would be able to bring about such change
in a lawful manner. The Council of the League and the Security
Council of the UN clearly reflect the idea of a Concert of Great
Powers, but they also attempt to be representative of the rest of the
system, and the norms the Security Council is supposed to enforce are
norms which stress the equality of states, not their differentiation. As
with the Concert, it has been tacitly recognized that the Councils
would operate effectively only when there was consensus amongst the
Great Powers. In the League, unanimity in the Council was required,
with the exception of the interested parties, who, if they were unable to
find any friends, generally responded to a negative vote by walking
out, while in the UN the famous 'veto' for the five permanent members
of the Security Council made such a walkout unnecessary. However,
the universalism of the organizations has made it difficult for this
prerequisite to be explicitly defended, hence the persisting sense that
the veto was some kind of mistake made in 1945, rather than an
essential feature of the system. The (Security) Council has been
expected to enforce the norms of collective security and universalism,
while, in its very nature, it represents the alternative, Concert, tradition.

A great deal of the rather poor record of these global institutions
since 1919 can be explained in terms of the contradictory impulses of
these two traditions. In effect, the system works properly only when
they both point in the same direction, which does happen sometimes,
but obviously cannot be relied upon. The only clear-cut example of a
collective security enforcement action occurred in Korea in 1950 as a
result of the temporary absence of the Soviet Union (one of the Veto
powers) from the Security Council, Even in 1990 when universal
principles and the interests of most of the Great Powers pointed in
the same direction with respect to Iraq's invasion of Kuwait, the
Coalition that enforced the law acted outside of UN control, albeit
with the sanction of a Security Council resolution.

Nonetheless, it is possible to exaggerate the extent to which the UN
system has failed to address problems of security. As in the case of
European integration, the failure of grand theory has been accompanied by quite a high degree of institutional and conceptual innovation.

When in the 1950s the UN was stymied by the Cold War, the then Secretary General of the UN, Dag Hammarskjöld, invented the notion of 'preventive diplomacy' – proactive attempts to keep the Cold War out of particular areas – and, with others, pioneered the notion of 'peacekeeping' – the employment of troops in UN uniforms with a mandate to assist the sides to a conflict if they wish to be kept apart. The UN has also offered mediation services, truce observers, and a number of other 'good offices' that parties to a conflict could use. There can be little doubt that these innovations have been genuinely helpful in a number of cases – and in the 1990 there were an increasing number of occasions upon which the UN was called upon to provide such services.

What is striking about these innovations is the way in which they combine the pragmatism of the Concert tradition with a 'politics from below' element which is universalist in origin. As with Concert politics, peacekeeping is, in the jargon of social work, 'non-judgemental'; the UN is able to act to help preserve order because it does not take sides, does not concern itself with the rights and wrongs of the case. This refusal to judge is, of course, totally against the ethic of collective security, which rests crucially upon a willingness to identify the wrong-doer – and it is noticeable that the UN's attitude is often criticized by those who feel they can actually tell right from wrong. Witness, for example, the resentment of the Bosnian government at the apparent willingness of the UN to treat Bosnian Serbs on a par with the 'legitimate' authority, and the feeling of the Coalition in 1991 that the then Secretary General of the UN was a little too willing to strike a deal with Saddam Hussein. However, the non-judgemental quality of the UN is much appreciated by many smaller member-states, who fear that if judgement is to be the norm they are more likely to be in the dock than on the judges' bench.

Preventive diplomacy and peacekeeping are not substitutes for collective security; they do not answer the basic question which is whether it is possible for international institutions to take us beyond a realist, self-help system in matters of security. Functionalism tries to do this by undermining sovereignty directly, but has been no more successful than were the Peace Projects of the eighteenth century. The attraction of collective security was that it did not try to undermine state sovereignty as such, rather it attempted to get sovereign powers to support a wider interest than the national interest. In the formal sense it failed in that there have been very few cases which have been overtly collective security operations – however, in an informal sense, some elements of a collective security system do seem to have taken hold. The closest analogy to an informal collective security system may be the old English common law idea of a *posse comitatus* – men called out by the sheriff to assist in the enforcing of the law, a notion which encompasses both medieval England and the 'posse' of Western movie fame. Something like this seems to be the best way of looking at the Gulf War of 1990–1. A group of states acted together to expel Iraq from Kuwait – the Coalition as posse – and the lawfulness of this action was attested to not by the presence of a sheriff, but by a positive vote of the UN Security Council.

In 1995 the posse – this time in the guise of NATO – intervened in Bosnia to create a 'level killing-field' again with the approval, but not under the command, of the UN, while in 1999 the NATO posse operated in Kosovo without the approval of the UN Security Council (albeit without its opposition either). Perhaps the most important task global institutions can perform today is not to solve security problems, but to give their blessing to those who can and do act. The UN's role comes close to that of the medieval papacy, rewarding an enterprise with its blessing – not really something those in power actually need, but something that they feel the better for nonetheless. When they do not receive the blessings of UN approval, powerful states may act anyway, if they believe this to be the right thing to do, or if their interests are crucially involved – but, as the example of Kosovo illustrates, action without UN approval generates a degree of uneasiness. These issues will be investigated further in the final chapter of this book, when the notion of humanitarian intervention in defence of human rights will be examined.

Conclusion

This somewhat inconclusive, and certainly incomplete, survey of theories of international organization leaves one with the conclusion that although the volume of global political institutions has increased quite substantially, and such expansion must have *some* effect on the world system, nonetheless if global governance relies on such institutions to undermine anarchy it will not succeed. At the beginning of the twenty-first century, as throughout the twentieth, basic decisions about security are still taken by states on the basis of national priorities – even though these states may, with some frequency, combine with others in alliances and 'posses'. Fortunately for the prospects of global governance, the issue does not rest there. Some of the most important advances in scientific knowledge have come about not when a question is answered differently, but when a different question is posed. Thus it is with state-centric international relations; the realist question about security remains subject to a realist answer – but is this still the most basic question? Are there not other issues of security which for many people have greater significance than military matters? Perhaps the central questions for international order in the twenty-first century will concern the world economy rather than the global political system – or rather, perhaps, in the twenty-first century the global political system will be in many areas indistinguishable from the global economy. To these issues we now turn.

Further Reading

J. N. Rosenau and E-O. Czempial (eds), *Governance without Government: Order and Change in World Politics* (1992) is a useful collection providing an overview of the subject. An earlier collected volume by the same editors, Czempial and Rosenau (eds), *Global Changes and Theoretical Challenges* (1989) contains a number of articles prefiguring the approach, including a valuable critique by Richard Ashley, 'Imposing International Purpose: Notes on a Problematic of Government' (1989b). Craig Murphy, *International Organization and Industrial Change: Global Governance since 1850* (1994) gives an historical perspective. An official view from the UN is *Our Global Neighborhood: Report of the Commission on Global Governance* (1995). Readings on international political economy (Chapter 8) and globalization and regimes (Chapter 9) are generally relevant.

On 'functionalism', David Mitrany's writings are central: see *A Working Peace System* (1966) and *The Functional Theory of Politics* (1975). A. J. R. Groom and Paul Taylor (eds), *Functionalism: Theory and Practice in World Politics* (1975) is an excellent collection, and other collections by the same editors are highly relevant – Taylor and Groom (eds), *International Organization: A Conceptual Approach* (1978); Groom and Taylor (eds), *The Commonwealth in the 1980s* (1984); Groom and Taylor (eds), *Frameworks for International Co-operation* (1994). Peter Willetts (ed.), *Pressure Groups in the International System* (1983) is a pioneering collection.

On the functional agencies of the UN works by Haas and Sewell referred to in the chapter are crucial: see also Robert W. Cox and

Harold K. Jacobson (eds), *The Anatomy of Influence* (1973). More recent work on these bodies casts its theoretical net a little wider into the area of 'regime' analysis, for example Mark W. Zacher with Brent A. Sutton, *Governing Global Networks: International Regimes for Transport and Communication* (1996). For Burtonian adaptations of functionalism see, for example, J. W. Burton, *World Society* (1972). Paul Taylor, *International Organization in the Modern World* (1993) is a good overview of theory in the area of international organization in general including recent thinking about the UN.

On theories of integration, Michael Hodges (ed.), *European Integration* (1972) provides useful extracts from the early theorists. William Wallace, *Regional Integration: The West European Experience* (1994) is a good overview of European developments, likewise Robert O. Keohane and Stanley Hoffmann (eds), *The New European Community* (1991). Andrew Moravcsik, *The Choice for Europe: Social Purpose and State Power from Messina to Maastricht'* (1998) has become an instant classic. Thoughtful reflections on sovereignty and contemporary European developments are, William Wallace, 'The Sharing of Sovereignty: The European Paradox' (1999a) and 'Europe after the Cold-War: Interstate Order or Post-Sovereign Regional System' (1999b).

On antecedents to the UN, for the peace projects, see F. H. Hinsley, *Power and the Pursuit of Peace* (1963), and for the Concert of Europe, Carsten Holbraad, *Concert of Europe* (1970); for the UN today, Taylor and Groom (eds), *Global Issues in the United Nations Framework* (1989) is a useful collection, as is Adam Roberts and Benedict Kingsbury (eds), *United Nations, Divided World: The UN's Role in International Relations* (1993). On the history of the United Nations classics such as I. L. Claude, *Swords into Plowshares* (1971) and H. G. Nicholas, *The UN as a Political System* (1985) are still valuable. For recent UN interventions, James Mayall (ed.), *The New Interventionism: 1991–1994* (1996) is invaluable; Mats Berdal, 'The United Nations in International Relations' (1996) is a useful review of recent literature. On the UN and the Gulf War, see Paul Taylor and A. J. R. Groom, *The UN and the Gulf War, 1990–1991: Back to the Future* (1992). At the time of writing (Summer 2000) the Kosovo campaign of 1999 has generated a great deal of commentary in e.g. *Survival, International Affairs* and *Foreign Affairs*, but in-depth academic studies are still missing, apart from Lawrence Freedman, 'Victims and victors: reflections on the Kosovo war' (2000)

8

International Political Economy

Introduction: Political and Economic International Systems

One of the defining characteristics of state-centric international relations has been to draw a clear distinction between 'domestic' and 'international' politics. When the volume of transactions that crossed state boundaries grew ever larger in the 1960s and 1970s, a subsidiary distinction became common, that between 'high politics' – the traditional interstate agenda of war and peace – and 'low politics' – the projection of essentially domestic concerns onto the international agenda. The assumption of realist, especially neorealist, thinking was that whatever 'global governance' might emerge it would be in this latter sphere rather than the former, and the essentially anarchic nature of 'high' politics would remain unchanged. In one sense, this assumption has turned out to be accurate. As established in Chapter 7, attempts to introduce collective management of security problems have not been markedly successful, and the great increase in the number of international institutions has come about because of other kinds of needs, other kinds of problems. Where, however, the realist position falls is at the outset, in the distinction between 'high' and 'low' politics – a distinction that collapses in the face of the 'high political' importance of what was once seen as the characteristically 'low political' activity of international economic relations. The world economy and attempts to manage and regulate the world economy are now at the heart of international relations in a way that would have been difficult to accept a century ago, and, albeit for different reasons, very surprising even 30 years ago.

The changing salience of the world economy is obviously tied up with a number of factors, but for the moment a fairly basic account of the importance of the world economy will suffice. In the late twentieth century, most governments in the world which did not rely on direct physical coercion to stay in power (as well as some that did) found that their well-being and survival in office was more or less directly determined by their success at economic management, and this is a task that cannot be understood in isolation from the international economy. The basic formula here was established over 25 years ago by Susan Strange – domestic political success is a function of the performance of the domestic economy; the latter, nowadays, is largely determined by international economic factors, and therefore the state of the international economy becomes a key factor in domestic politics, which in turn makes it a central concern of international politics (Strange 1970). Nowadays this is largely taken for granted, but it is worth remembering that this is a relatively new state of affairs. A century ago most governments would have rejected the idea that they were responsible for the state of the economy, and their electorates, such as they were, tended to agree – although issues such as free trade and protectionism could on occasion be crucial. Even when economic management did become critical it was not automatically the case that politics drove governments towards attempts to collectively manage the world economy – sometimes isolation was the aim, at other times the world economy was seen as a self-regulating mechanism which did not need, or was positively averse to, political management. It is only recently, with the collapse of the so-called 'Bretton Woods' system, that the real political significance of this aspect of global governance has become apparent to almost everyone.

This chapter and the next are devoted to 'international political economy'. The next section of this chapter will briefly examine the growth of the world economy up to the first decades of the twentieth century. This will be followed by a more extended account of the problems this growth generates and of some characteristic attitudes to these problems – liberalism, mercantilism and the like. The final section will examine the institutional framework which was established after the Second World War in order to deal with these problems – the Bretton Woods System (BWS) – and the reasons for its failure. Chapter 9 will continue the discussion, examining a number of different theories and perspectives which have been developed to understand the more chaotic system that has emerged over the 30 years since the demise of Bretton Woods – regime theory, the 'theory of hegemonic stability', radical accounts of neoliberal hegemony, and the recent debate between theorists of 'globalization' and 'internationalization'.

The Growth of the World Economy

Along with war, trade has been a feature of 'international' relations for millennia – indeed, amongst the classical and pre-classical Greeks the distinction between war and trade was only loosely drawn. Flotillas of ships would cruise the coast, trading if they met strength, engaging in piracy if they found weakness – the Vikings seem to have adopted a similar practice. However, the mere existence of the exchange of goods does not create an economy, much less a world economy. Here it may be helpful to introduce some distinctions made by Immanuel Waller-stein in his monumental study of the origins of the modern world system (Wallerstein 1974/1980/1989). Wallerstein begins by defining a 'world' in social rather than geographical terms. A world consists of those who are in regular contact with each other and in some extended sense form a social system – the maximum size of a world being determined by the effectiveness of the technology of transportation currently available; it is only in the twentieth century that the social and the geographical world are effectively the same. He then identifies 'microsystems' as self-contained societies, small 'worlds' with only limited exchanges with other worlds, exchanges limited to luxuries and conducted, characteristically, by trade caravans. These systems are of little interest to him, or us.

Our interest is in worlds where the long-distance movement of essen-tial, bulk, goods takes place, and Wallerstein suggests there are two kinds of worlds in which this happens. On the one hand there are 'Empires', on the other, 'world-systems' – or, in the terminology adopted here, world economies. In Empires, exchanges take place within the same political structure, characteristically in the form of 'tribute'. Thus Rome conquered Sicily and then Egypt in order to extract from those territories the grain it needed to feed the enormous population of the imperial city. The grain so transferred was tribute paid by the conquered to their conquerors. Within a world economy, on the other hand, exchanges takes place between territories under different political control, and thus tribute cannot be extracted; instead exchanges take place on an economic basis as 'trade'. Wallerstein suggests that such world economies occur quite often but are usually short-lived; his account of the *Modern World System* traces the formation of such an economy in Europe in the 'long sixteenth century' (1492–1648) and its spread in the years since.

Wallerstein's account of the structure of this world economy as necessarily divided into cores, peripheries and semi-peripheries is over-mechanical and contentious – although quite influential in the 'South' as we will see below – but his account of the early formation of the system makes good sense. Initially two sets of transactions were underway; the large-scale movement of sugar and spices, largely in the form of tribute within the Spanish Empire, and the trading of craft products and early manufactures from the 'advanced' areas of Europe, the Low Countries, England and Northern France for grain from Eastern Europe, and sugar from the Spanish Empire. The strength of this description is that it makes the point that from the beginning the world economy and the world political system were closely intertwined. On the basis of a marginally higher productivity the 'core' in north-west Europe was able to develop comparatively effective and powerful states and to dominate politically and economically both the 'feudal' systems of Eastern Europe and the overextended Habsburg/ Spanish power to the South.

Over the next two centuries this economy expanded. The 'agricultural revolution' in England, in particular, increased productivity markedly, and the spread of Empire generated important new commodities, in particular tea and slaves. In the Atlantic, the 'Golden Triangle' brought together basic manufactures from Britain, slaves from West Africa and sugar from the Caribbean. In the East the demand for tea from China, the lack of a product desired by the Chinese and the inability (at that time) to directly coerce the Chinese Empire led to the development of another triangle, this time involving Indian opium. However, for all the importance of this activity, it remained the case that as late as the end of the eighteenth century virtually all states were still, in large measure, self-sufficient, and although foreign trade was important to some, in particular the Netherlands and Britain, this importance was still largely marginal. Even Britain, the most important trading country, largely fed itself – the Corn Laws would not have been effective in excluding foreign competition had not the highly productive local agriculture been able both to feed the country and release labour for the new manufacturing concerns.

All this changes with the emergence of industrial society in the nineteenth century; by the second half of the century, for the first time ever, a genuinely world-wide large-scale division of labour existed. To a great extent Britain was at the centre of this change – with the highest level of urbanization the world had ever seen, and the lowest numbers on the land, this was a society that could only exist as part of a complicated web of exchanges, in which textiles, machine tools and machinery were exchanged for cotton, and later grain, from the United

States, beef from Argentina and mutton and wool from the Antipodes. This was possible because of changes in the technology of communication and transport. The railroads, steamships and refrigeration made possible the transport of perishable goods over long distances, and the telegraph made the creation of a genuine market possible. Many of these innovations depended also on the export of capital – American and Argentinean railways were largely financed by British capital, and the British shipbuilding industry and British shipping fleets met the demand for sea transportation directly. As the twentieth century arrived, so did competitors to Britain in the form of the new industrial powers of Germany and the United States. However, although these newcomers dominated some industries, chemicals for example, until 1914 Britain remained at the centre of the system.

What is particularly striking about the emergence of this complicated structure of exchanges of money, goods, services and people across national boundaries, is the extent to which it emerged unplanned and unprepared for. Questions such as: How can a large-scale division of labour work in a world based on territorial states? What difference does crossing a political border make to economic activity? How has this world economy changed international relations? were not answered because they were not posed. The system seemed to regulate itself, indeed, was widely believed to have grown as fast as it did not in spite of, but because of the absence of planning. However, after 1914 and the outbreak of the First World War and subsequent failures to re-establish the old system, it becomes clear that these questions are, actually, unavoidable.

Problems and Perspectives

What difference *does* crossing a political border make to economic activity? Consider a very basic situation – so basic in fact that, as we will see in Chapter 9, it has now been superseded – wherein a firm in one country (A) produces goods bought by consumers in another (B). How is this different from production and consumption taking place in the same country?

The first issue concerns *money*. The producer wishes to be paid in the currency of A, while the consumer wishes to pay in currency B. Until 1914, there were relatively few technical problems here, because virtually all currencies were convertible into precious metals, mainly gold, but sometimes silver. The Victorian Londoner travelling to Paris could be confident that his gold sovereigns would be readily convertible into gold francs – literally convertible, since each coin was effectively a weight of a certain quality of gold. And since paper money issued by the Bank of England was equally convertible into gold ('I promise to pay the bearer the sum of....' is still, meaninglessly, reprinted on British paper money) it also met few obstacles abroad, although paper issued by lesser banks might be unacceptable. As far as large-scale trading was concerned, bills of exchange issued by the great merchant banking houses were widely accepted throughout Europe and in the rest of the world.

A gold-based system was readily comprehensible, and required no special mechanism to operate, but there was one feature of the system that potentially posed political problems. If one country had firms that were more successful at selling abroad than another, or consumers keener to buy foreign goods, this might lead to a flow of gold in or out of the country. Ought this to be a source of concern? In the seventeenth century, when for the first time it became possible to measure gold flows if not accurately then at least to degrees of magnitude, the new proponents of 'political arithmetic', the 'mercantilists', argued that a positive, inward, flow of gold was good, a negative, outward flow bad. In the eighteenth century David Hume, in a splendidly concise essay, demonstrated that negative and positive flows would be self-correcting – inward flows would raise price levels and make exports more expensive, imports cheaper, and thus reverse the flow, and vice versa with outward flows of gold – although his argument begs the question whether governments would allow this mechanism to work (Hume 1987).

In any event, since 1914 a different problem has emerged. Since that date, most currencies most of the time have not been directly convertible into gold, and thus domestic price levels are not directly affected by the flow of precious metals, but this simply allows *balance of payments* crises to emerge and persist more readily. Moreover, although international payments were still linked to the price of gold indirectly until some 30 years ago, since 1973 this has not been the case, and, in any event, an indirect link requires management in a way that the old, self-regulating system did not. Once gold is no longer the key, *exchange rate policy* is something that all states have to have, and the political problem of establishing a reliable medium of exchange for international transactions becomes unavoidable.

Assuming this problem can be solved, an international economy based on a large-scale division of labour can emerge. In a system of uncontrolled exchange, patterns of specialization will emerge, with some countries producing one range of goods, others another. Some countries may become specialists in agricultural products, others in industrial goods. Does this matter? Ought states to have positive policies to promote the production of certain kinds of goods, or is this something where market forces can be allowed to decide? *Trade policy* joins *balance of payments policy*, and *exchange rate policy* as areas where, like it or not, states must have a position – and, in this context not to have a position is itself a position, and one with very considerable implications.

It is possible to identify two quite distinct orientations towards these problems that states might adopt, which can be termed *liberal* and *nationalist* – although it should be noted that nationalist views can take different political and social form – positions which, as their names suggest, are linked to wider philosophies and to different kinds of state. Historically, the *nationalist* approach to international economic relations comes first. As suggested above, following Hume, the mercantilist idea that states should aim for a positive inflow of gold has been seen to be a self-defeating policy because the effect on the trade balance of the consequent changes in price level will reverse the trade flow, but the general idea that the way one judges economic matters is in terms of the effect they have on the nation's position in the world and not from some other, less partial perspective, has never lost its appeal. Economic nationalism is still part of the common rhetoric of the political life of most countries, as witnessed by the universal desire of states to have a balance of payments surplus – impossible for all to achieve, of course, since every surplus is someone else's deficit. However, before pursuing this point we need to outline the most influential alternative to economic nationalism.

If economic nationalism came first in history and still has its adherents, economic *liberalism* has been the intellectually dominant position for most of the last two centuries. The basic liberal proposition is that although in some areas a degree of regulation may be a necessary evil, in general free market solutions to economic problems maximize welfare in the system taken as a whole, and should be adopted. There were three essential steps along the way to this conclusion, spread over a century from the mid eighteenth to the early nineteenth centuries. The first was Hume's demolition of the mercantilist love affair with gold. The second was Adam Smith's demonstration of the gains to be had from an extended division of labour in *The Wealth of Nations*, gains which are a function of the size of the market and therefore can, in principle, be increased by foreign trade. But the third and crucial step deserves a more extended examination – David Ricardo's 'theory of comparative advantage' which, although published in 1817, remains in an amended form the basis of liberal trade theory and the liberal international economic order (Ricardo 1971).

Ricardo's achievement was to provide a logically sound, albeit counter-intuitive, answer to one of the fundamental problems posed by international trade. It is intuitively easy to see why trade takes place when two countries have different kinds of resources, and thus produce different kinds of products. Europe could produce bananas under glass, and the Windward Islands could set up mini-textile mills and small-scale craft audio-visual and 'white goods' workshops, but it is not to difficult to see why, in fact, this does not happen and the Windward Islands grow bananas and import clothing, TVs and refrigerators from the industrial world. More generally, it is easy to see why two similar countries that are efficient in the production of different products would trade (although how they became efficient in different areas if they are really similar is another issue). But what is very difficult to see is how trade could be desirable and profitable in the quite common situation where two countries produce the same products and one of them is more efficient at producing *everything* than the other. Ricardo provides the answer, which is that although one country may be more efficient at producing everything, it will almost always be the case that the *comparative* costs of producing different products will be different, and thus even the least efficient country will have a comparative advantage in some product.

Ricardo's demonstration of this proposition assumes a two-country, two-commodity economy in which the costs of production are measured in labour-time – in deference to England's oldest commercial partner he takes Portugal and England and cloth and wine as his exemplars, and assumes that Portugal is more efficient in the production of both commodities. Thus, if it takes 80 hours of labour to produce a barrel of wine in Portugal, 120 in England and it takes 90 hours to produce a length of cloth in Portugal, 100 in England, then Portugal is more efficient in the production of both products. However, Portugal has a clear *comparative advantage* in the production of wine. If Portugal were to specialize in wine production it could produce the two barrels currently produced in the two countries using only 160 hours of labour. If England were to specialize in cloth it could produce two lengths using 200 hours of labour. If the two countries then traded cloth for wine, they could reach their existing level of production at a saving of 30 hours of labour *in toto* – how this saving is distributed being a function of the prices of the two commodities:

1 Production of Wine and Cloth without Specialization		
	Hours of labour to produce barrel of wine	*Hours of labour to produce length of cloth*
England	120	100
Portugal	80	90

2 Production of Wine and Cloth with Specialization		
	Hours of labour to produce two barrels of wine	*Hours of labour to produce two lengths of cloth*
England	–	200
Portugal	160	–

All this is, of course, much too simple and the modern demonstration of Ricardo's principle takes a chapter or more in the average economics textbook – on the other hand, Ricardo's version is comprehensible without knowledge of a specialized technical language, which is more than can be said for most textbook versions of the law of comparative advantage. Anyway, the basic idea is of enormous significance and underlies liberal economic thought to this day, including the neoliberal ideas which will be discussed in Chapter 9. What Ricardo demonstrated was that under virtually all circumstances trade would be beneficial to both parties. This is very much in contrast to the eighteenth-century belief – present, for example, in Rousseau and even in Kant, as well, of course, as in the work of the mercantilists – that trade was necessarily an activity which generated winners and losers. After Ricardo, economic liberals were able to argue that the removal of restrictions on trade would be to the benefit of all, because the general welfare would be maximized by the lowering of barriers between regions and countries. Each country by specializing in the products in which it has a comparative advantage and engaging in trade is contributing to the general good as well as to its own welfare. Some such belief was still, in the late twentieth century, at the heart of the 'embedded liberalism' of the modern trade system, and the basic argument was deployed by international economists such as Paul

Krugman, one of the most effective modern defenders of the gains from trade (Krugman 1998).

Ricardo provided liberals with a powerful argument, but he did not silence all opponents. The key issue for opponents was (and, in a different form, still is) the pattern of specialization established by free trade. If one country has a comparative advantage in the production of industrial goods, and another in the production of agricultural goods then the welfare of the system as a whole is maximized if specialization takes place – but might there not be other considerations involved here? One issue which will feature largely in 'Third World' or 'Southern' accounts of international relations is the terms of trade at which products are exchanged, and whether or not there is a trend moving against primary products, and this will be discussed below. More important for the moment is the power-political objection to the view that any pattern of specialization is, in principle, as good as any other.

This argument was articulated by the American statesman Alexander Hamilton in the 1790s in his 'Report on Manufactures' to the US Congress, but the central figure here is the German political economist and liberal nationalist Friedrich List, whose 1841 work *The National System of Political Economy* (republished in 1966) is the most impressive attack on liberal international political economy to be mounted in the nineteenth century. List's basic position was that in the conditions of the 1840s free trade was a policy that would set in concrete Britain's industrial predominance as the workshop of the world, leaving the German states – and others – in a subordinate position as the hewers of wood and drawers of water for the more sophisticated producers across the Channel. Because Britain was first in the field it would have a comparative advantage in heavy industry. It would therefore be cheaper for a country such as Germany to buy machine tools and other advanced technology from the British – but the dependence that this would create would turn the German states into second-rate powers. Moreover, the British had not achieved their predominance by following the prescripts of free trade. On the contrary, British economic strength was fostered behind many protective devices: the Navigation Acts which obliged British trade to be carried in British ships; the Corn Laws which protected the profitability of British agriculture; and so on. The British, remarked List, were kicking away the ladder up which they had climbed to their present position – denying others the advantages which they had exploited.

His solution was to develop German industry behind a protective wall of tariffs: the so-called 'infant industry' argument that the early stages of industrial development can only take place if local industries are protected from international competition. Perhaps when these industries grow up they will no longer need protection – although List, along with many later neo-mercantilists, envisaged a continuation of protection even after maturity, because the industries in question would remain central to German power and could not be exposed to the risks of competition. List's wider point here is that free trade and economic liberalism are generally promoted as in the common interest by those who are satisfied with the existing pattern of specialization. Those who, for one reason or another are not so satisfied, will be sceptical.

List's argument assumes that patterns of specialization will not shift rapidly. However, another objection to economic liberalism is based on the opposite assumption, namely that open markets will lead to very rapid change. This seemed plausible in the late twentieth century, where competition from the 'newly industrializing countries' very quickly undermined many sectors of the old industrialized world. Liberal economic relations rely on a willingness to adapt to change whatever the cost – but sometimes the cost in terms of social disloca- tion can be very high. Consider, for example, the run down of the coal industry in Britain from the 1970s, with over 200,000 jobs lost to foreign competition in under 20 years – similar patterns could be observed throughout the developed industrial world. The social dis- location this has caused has been very high, and it is by no means clear that measures to slow down the rate of change ought not to have been taken. Allowing the market to determine results on the basis of an abstract calculation of the general welfare presents major political and social difficulties. Modern 'protectionists' are not necessarily motiv- ated by a desire to preserve the nation's power; they may, instead, desire to protect social and community values – although it should be said that any kind of protectionism throws the costs of adaptation on others and therefore cannot be innocent of nationalist implications. This is one of the reasons why, until comparatively recently, Marxist writers have been very suspicious of positions which were not based on free trade.

Marx himself appears not to have contested the basic logic of Ricardo's argument. His point was to stress the extent to which liberal economic relations were a recent construction and not part of the 'natural' way of doing things. He is bitterly critical of the 'Robinson Crusoe' style of argument in which liberal economic relations are assumed to emerge naturally on the basis of simple common sense –

they are, instead, the product of a particular way of life, a mode of production, which emerged out of class struggle and the victory of the bourgeoisie over feudalism. However, once this is acknowledged, Marx seems to be quite willing to recognize the achievements of the political economists, and held Ricardo in particularly high esteem. That there were gains from trade was not contested by him, although these gains were seen as accruing to the dominant class and not to the general welfare of all. Moreover, Marxist political economists of the early twentieth century observed that trade was very clearly no longer conducted on liberal terms. 'Finance capital' dominated the state, and had a clear foreign policy based on the use of tariffs to extend the national economic territory and thereby allow national conglomerates to make monopoly profits. One of the reasons why socialists should oppose this policy was because it went against the requirements of internationalism, which included free trade.

In the second half of the twentieth century the commitment to free trade remained firm amongst most of the small Trotskyite groups that survived in the West, but most other Marxists (and social democrats more generally) made their peace with nationalism. In the Third World, neo-Marxist theories of dependency were explicitly anti-liberal in trade matters. In the Northern industrial world 'labour' and 'social democratic' parties found that a precondition for survival was to advocate the adoption of political measures to put some limits on freedom of trade. The basic political point here is that the gains from protectionism are always concentrated, while the gains from free trade are dispersed; conversely, the costs of protectionism are dispersed among the general population, whereas the costs of free trade bear heavily on vulnerable groups rather than the population at large. Other things being equal – which, of course, much of the time they are not – protectionism will be more politically popular than free trade.

The essential point in this discussion has been well captured by Susan Strange in the entertaining Prologue to her *States and Markets* (1988). Strange sets out 'Some Desert Island Stories', telling of the fates of three separate lifeboat-loads of survivors of a shipwreck, each of which, for a variety of reasons, designs, or allows to emerge, a different kind of society. One group sets up an authoritarian society in which security comes first, wealth second and freedom to choose and social justice a poor third. Another, egalitarian, community is high on justice and freedom, lower on wealth and lower still on security. A third is market oriented, high on wealth, lower on freedom and security, lower still on justice. Strange uses these three models to make two important points. The first is that every society is obliged to choose which values it will stress, and that this choice of values will lead to a choice of emphasis as between the state and the market. Thus a prime concern for security will privilege authority structures and the state, a prime concern for wealth will privilege the market. Strange's second point is equally relevant. It is that when societies with different value preferences meet in a world economy, each will continue to try to privilege its particular value position by shaping the biases of the world economy to fit its own pattern. This is a process that was much in evidence in the twentieth century, and is the subject of the final section of this chapter.

The World Economy and the Rise and Fall of the 'Bretton Woods System'

In 1914 the 'self-regulating' world economy of the nineteenth century collapsed under the strain of war. Most of the participants in the war imposed physical controls on exports and imports; movements of commodities across political boundaries became subject to direct political decision on the basis of the contribution of particular transactions to the war effort. This amounted to an unprecedented interference with trade, of far greater significance than the tariffs that most countries had adopted prior to the war. Tariffs may make foreign goods more expensive but they leave importing and exporting decisions to individual firms and consumers and not to the state, unlike physical controls. At the same time, the major combatants also 'went off the gold standard', ending the direct link between their currencies and the price of gold. In effect, in Europe at least, all aspects of the foreign economic activity of the state were harnessed to the war effort.

The intention was that all this would be temporary and that the old liberal international economy would be re-established after the war was over. In the immediate post-war era things were too chaotic to think of restoration, but Britain reverted to free trade and, in 1926, returned to the Gold Standard at the old rate as a symbol of her determination to resume leadership of a revived liberal economy. This was a decision that probably had disastrous effects on the British economy and no appreciable impact on the world economy. The rise of new competitors in the key area of textiles, coal and shipbuilding meant that the effort of maintaining the old rate was certain to require high interest rates and lead to unemployment. The problem of reparations lingered and was only held at bay by the willingness of US banks to lend to Europe, a willingness that more or less ended after the Wall Street Crash of 1929. Bank failures in Europe then led to pressures on sterling and, after a crisis in 1931 which led to the formation of a national government, Britain leaving the Gold Standard. In 1932 Britain established a system of Imperial Preferences, at last abandoning free trade and following the lead of the highly protectionist Hawley–Smoot Tariff which the United States Congress had passed in 1929.

Between 1929 and 1933 trade crashed world-wide, declining by the latter year to less than one-quarter by value of its 1929 figure. The Great Depression of the 1930s was trade-led – unlike, for example, the recessions of the 1980s when trade actually increased year on year, even when overall output fell. When recovery began in the 1930s it was on the basis of trade blocs – the Dollar Area, the Sterling Area, the Gold Franc Area and so on – and with much resort to bartering, sometimes on a basis which reflected political power rather than economic advantage, as with some of the barters arranged by the Nazis in the late 1930s whereby, say, Romania, would be obliged to exchange their oil for cuckoo clocks and other inessentials. In the collective memory of the world capitalist system this whole period was a disaster, and it remains the case that the memory of the Great Depression is one of the factors that promotes cooperation in the world economy today.

On some accounts, to be examined in more detail in Chapter 9, it was a lack of leadership that produced the depression – Britain no longer had the ability to lead, the United States had not the will. In any event, by the mid-1930s the United States was already taking the initiative at international trade conferences, and with the coming of the war, the establishment of the United States as the arsenal of democracy and the world's leading financial power, American opinion on the future of the world economy became crucial. A key figure here was Cordell Hull, the US Secretary of State. Hull believed firmly that it was the failure of the old liberal order that led to war, and that it was absolutely essential to re-establish that order after the war ended – this involved a commitment to free trade (or at least the replacement of physical controls and trade blocs by tariffs) and the restoration of convertible currencies by the abolition of currency blocs and exchange controls.

Most of America's future partners were occupied, enemies or communists, the exception being Britain and the British Empire. The

British were no longer free-trade oriented, and were committed to the Sterling Area. John Maynard Keynes, the radical economist of the 1930s and a convinced protectionist, was now Lord Keynes and a Treasury insider with great influence on policy. He believed, as did the British government, that convertibility would be disastrous to the pound since everyone would seek to convert to dollars, and free trade would lead to the swamping of British markets with American goods and a major balance of payments crisis which would cut the value of the pound still further, and impoverish the nation. US economic power was simply too great – thus the arguments of Friedrich List triumphed in the birthplace of David Ricardo; once again, the greatest economic power espoused free trade while weaker powers resisted as best they could – only this time Britain was on the other side of the argument.

The British and Americans met at Bretton Woods, New Hampshire, in 1944 to negotiate the shape of the post-war economic order, which thus became known as the Bretton Woods System. On the whole American ideas dominated Bretton Woods – inevitably given the relative power of the two countries – although Keynes and the British delegation were able to make some impact on the new system. The system that was designed met American notions of economic liberalism in several ways.

In the first place, attempts were made to 'de-politicize' the international economy by dividing up the various international issues amongst separate institutions. Thus an International Trade Organization (ITO) would handle trade matters, a World Bank would handle capital movements, and an International Monetary Fund (IMF) would deal with international money and balance of payments crises. These separate institutions would be functional agencies of the UN but isolated as far as possible from the Security Council and other UN bodies dealing with 'political' affairs; indeed, in practice, the UN has had no effective control over these organs. Moreover, the new institutions were to be run by boards of directors, and managing directors who, although appointed by states (in proportion to their relative economic strength – no question of 'one state, one vote' here) would have fixed terms of office and would be expected to act as functionaries rather than as political representatives. The emphasis would be on technical solutions to technical problems.

In the second place, these organs were to be regulatory rather than managerial in their approach to the problems they were designed to deal with – working with the grain of the capitalist system rather than against it. Thus the World Bank would not have funds of its own beyond a small amount of working capital, but would raise money commercially that it would then lend on to states at commercial rates to supplement private loans and intergovernmental dealings. The IMF would not be a world-wide central bank with the capacity to create international money (as Keynes had proposed) but a regulatory body designed to police a set of rules which required convertibility and national action to defend exchange rates. The IMF would help states to deal with balance of payments crises, but it would also lay down conditions for its help, thereby policing the policies of its members. The ITO would police the trade policies of its members, ensuring that the rules limiting quotas and promoting tariff reductions were enforced, although in the event it would be nearly 50 years before the World Trade Organization (WTO) was finally established in 1995, and in the meantime a more limited General Agreement on Tariffs and Trade (GATT) performed this function.

All of this reflected the power of the United States: ironically, since the official US position was that political power should play no part in international economic relations. The British view was that the system could not be set up under these terms – that Britain, for example, required protected markets in the Empire and exchange rate controls if she was to recover in the post-war years. Keynes took the view that what was needed was management and not just regulation. His preferred solution was for the abolition of all private capital movements and the financing of post-war reconstruction by low interest loans from a genuine bank which would create a new international currency – he suggested it should be called 'bancor' – which would be used for inter-bloc trade. Whether the British government would actually have accepted such a scheme is a moot point – as far as the Americans, who would have to finance it, were concerned, this was socialism pure and simple, and no American government could have obtained Congressional agreement. In practice the best that the British could do was to write into the constitutions of the new bodies rules which allowed states not to comply with regulations of the institutions 'in exceptional circumstances' or some similar form of words.

That such qualifications were needed was readily apparent in the immediate post-war period. In 1946 the British were forced to make sterling convertible as part of the conditions for a large post-war loan from the Americans, and the result was a run on sterling and the re-establishment of controls. No country in the 1940s was able to compete with the United States, which was the home of over half the capitalist world's industrial production. In practice, what led to the reconstruction of the capitalist world economy and a generation of prosperity was the Cold War. Marshall Aid, the European Recovery Programme, transferred some $15 billion in grants to Europeans and the Japanese – far more capital and on easier terms than Keynes had envisaged in his schemes – but it operated explicitly as a response to the threat of communism. Without such a spur there was no possibility that Congress would have passed such a generous programme. Meanwhile, the United States government agreed to all sorts of waivers *vis-à-vis* trade regulations and convertibility in the interests of stimulating recovery of her allies against Russia – including promoting the growth of the European Economic Community (EEC), which would soon be a major trade rival of the United States. The attempt to de-politicize international economic relations stood revealed as a pious hope rather than a reality.

In any event, for two decades after the early 1950s the world economy experienced unprecedented growth and prosperity. This growth was concentrated heavily in Europe and Japan, but even Britain and the United States grew steadily, and growth rates in what was coming to be called the Third World were high, although they were largely undermined by rising populations. By the end of the 1950s most of the leading economies had re-established currency convertibility, and the GATT 'Rounds' of tariff negotiations were well under way. Going into the 1960s the system seemed to be working pretty well, albeit not quite as originally intended. However, in the 1960s, crisis followed crisis for the Bretton Woods System, and by 1973 – when the attempt to work with fixed currency rates was abandoned – it is widely regarded as having, to all intents and purposes, ceased to exist. What went wrong? There are two kinds of explanation for the fall of Bretton Woods, one of which – the rise of new economic forces – will be examined in Chapter 9; the other goes to the heart of the system and the difficulties with attempting to manage an essentially liberal system on de-politicized lines.

This latter line of argument concentrates on problems of international liquidity. States engaged in trade wish to hold reserves of some acceptable international asset to tide them over bad periods – usually at least enough money to pay for three months' imports. Under Bretton Woods the intention was that since all currencies were convertible at fixed rates into each other this would no longer be a problem. However, in practice state central banks decided, very wisely, that this was nonsense, and sought to hold gold or a 'reserve currency' – mainly the US dollar, but also, in the sterling area, the UK pound.

There were some advantages to possessing a reserve currency – in particular the ability to print an internationally acceptable medium of exchange – but it did impose restrictions on the policies available to the countries concerned. In particular, such countries could not even think of devaluation without stimulating a 'run' on the currency. However, for a while the system worked quite well, but with a worm in the bud. As trade expands, states will want to expand their reserve holdings – but where can these reserves come from? Only from a balance of payments deficit on the part of the country with a reserve currency. Only thus can, say, US dollars be made available to act as a reserve currency. The problem is that the acceptability of the US dollar rests on the perception that the US economy is strong – but a strong currency would not be running the massive deficit needed to produce a reserve currency. To be acceptable the currency must be strong, to be available it must be weak. This is the 'Triffin' paradox, named after Robert Triffin, the economist who first identified it.

In the early post-war years there was no real problem here. The US economy was fundamentally healthy, and the outflow of dollars came in the form of Marshall Aid, US military spending in NATO and elsewhere (on causes her allies approved of) and US foreign investment which was desperately sought. US trade balances were positive, and the outflow of dollars looked like a sign of strength. In the 1960s, however, things changed. Now US foreign investment looked like 'the American challenge', and, with the worst of the Cold War over, US military spending was on Vietnam to the disapproval of most of their European allies. Worse, in the 1960s the American trade balance worsened with the rise of competition from Europe and Japan, and by 1969 was negative. The US dollar was no longer automatically 'as good as gold' and US financial policy was threatened by the 'dollar overhang', as the amount of US currency held abroad far exceeded US domestic gold stocks.

The result was a series of crises through the 1960s – beginning with assaults on the pound that forced devaluation and the effective ending of sterling's role as a reserve currency in 1968, after which attention turned to the dollar. Some of these crises were politically generated, as in the French attempt to bring back gold as the reserve currency by presenting dollars for conversion at the US 'gold window', but most were caused by 'speculators' shifting currency from one market to another. These speculators were readily demonized, but in fact were usually acting defensively as, for example, treasurers of corporations who did not want to find their assets depreciated if a run on a reserve currency led to devaluation. A number of measures were put in place to try to stop these crises – of particular significance being the invention of Special Drawing Rights (SDRs) at the IMF in 1969, SDRs being a genuine international currency created by the Fund – but on too small a scale to have much impact.

In the end the system crashed spectacularly, with the United States in 1971 breaking all the rules it had been so keen to establish in 1944. President Nixon needed results on the currency front to strengthen his political position at home, and he forced a US devaluation by unilaterally closing the gold window, imposing a selective tariff on goods from the US's main competitors and engaging in overt political–military threats to support his position – in other words, by throwing aside the ideas of depoliticization and 'separate tracks' upon which the system had been built. Yet again the ghost of List triumphed over his liberal adversaries, as the United States' advocacy of liberal solutions declined with its relative power. At the Smithsonian Conference of December 1971, the system was patched up, but it collapsed again two years later, after which currencies floated against each other in a (managed) market. Although the Bretton Woods institutions continue to exist, the norms of the old system are gone, probably for ever, and the institutions themselves exist in a new context, the subject of Chapter 9.

Further Reading

International political economy is an area well served by textbooks. Robert Gilpin, *The Political Economy of International Relations* (1987) offers an orthodox, (neo)realist account; Stephen Gill and David Law, *The Global Economy: Prospects, Problems and Policies* (1988) is neo-Marxist, Gramscian, in inspiration; Susan Strange, *States and Markets* (1988) is *sui generis* and highly entertaining. Less characterful than these three offerings, but reliable, are Joan Spero, *The Politics of International Economic Relations* (1997), David H. Blake and Robert S. Walters, *The Politics of Global Economic Relations* (1991) and David Balaam and Michael Veseth, *Introduction to International Political Economy* (1995). There are also a number of very valuable edited collections. G. T. Crane and A. M. Amawi (eds), *The Theoretical Evolution of International Political Economy: A Reader* (1999) has good historical coverage; Jeffrey A. Frieden and David A Lake (eds), *International Political Economy: Perspectives on Global Power and*

Wealth (2000) – reprinted articles – and Richard Stubbs and Geoffrey Underhill (eds), *Political Economy and the Changing Global Order* (1999) – original essays – are best on recent approaches, with Craig Murphy and Roger Tooze (eds), *The New International Political Economy* (1991) reflecting an interest in critical theory and epistemological sophistication. Most of the above books appear in various editions – the most recent should always be sought out. Richard Higgott, 'International Political Economy' (1994) provides a useful short bibliographical overview of the field.

Classic texts by Ricardo, List and Rudolf Hilferding are collected, with extended commentaries, in Chris Brown, Terry Nardin and N.J. Rengger, *Texts in International Relations* (2001). On List, see also David Levi-Faur, 'Economic Nationalism: From Friedrich List to Robert Reich' (1997).

Paul Krugman and Maurice Obstfeld, *International Economics: Theory and Policy* (2000); or John Williamson and Chris Milner, *The World Economy* (1991) are standard textbooks specifically on international economics, but any introductory economics text will convey the basics of comparative advantage and the gains from trade. Paul Krugman is a vigorous, accessible and entertaining defender of liberal orthodoxy on trade; see his *Rethinking International Trade* (1994), *Pop Internationalism* (1996) and *The Accidental Theorist and Other Despatches from the Dismal Science* (1998). Susan Strange, 'Protectionism and World Politics' (1985) makes a case for protectionism in some circumstances; Benjamin Cohen's review article 'The Political Economy of International Trade' (1990) is also useful.

Karl Polanyi, *The Great Transformation* (1975) is a fine overview of the changes wrought by industrialization over the last 200 years, and a sustained account of the nature of the liberal society it has created. The volumes of the *Pelican History of the World Economy in the 20th Century* are generally valuable: Derek H. Aldcroft, *From Versailles to Wall Street 1919–1929* (1977), C. K. Kindleberger, *The World in Depression 1929–1939* (1973), and Herman Van der Wee, *Prosperity and Upheaval 1945–1980* (1986) are particularly useful.

Richard N. Gardner, *Sterling–Dollar Diplomacy in Current Perspective: The Origins and Prospects of our International Economic Order* (1980) is the expanded version of the author's classic *Sterling–Dollar Diplomacy* (1969), the standard account of the origins of the Bretton Woods System. Andrew Shonfield (ed.), *International Economic Relations of the Western World 1959–1971*, Vol. I, *Politics and Trade* (Shonfield *et al.*), Vol. II, *International Monetary Relations* (Susan Strange)

(1976) is the standard history of the system. Strange, *Sterling and British Policy* (1971) is an account of the crises of the 1960s from a London perspective. Fred Block, *The Origins of International Economic Disorder* (1977) and E. A. Brett, *The World Economy. since the War* (1985) look at things from a Marxian perspective. The standard texts cover the crisis of 1971 – also useful is Joanna Gowa, *Closing the Gold Window: Domestic Politics and the End of Bretton Woods* (1983).

9

Conflict and Cooperation in the Global Economy

Introduction

In the 1950s and 1960s, under the aegis of the Bretton Woods System (BWS), the world experienced two decades of sustained economic growth; the economies that were destroyed in the Second World War grew faster than those of the US and the UK, and some 'developing' countries experienced much faster growth than others, but, even taking these variations into account, the world as a whole experienced an unprecedented across-the-board rise in living standards. Since the early 1970s, things have been rather different. The stability of the BWS has disappeared. Periods of high growth rates have been followed by stagnation, and, in many countries in the 1980s, substantial falls in real living standards. Mass unemployment at pre-1939 levels returned to Europe in the 1980s and, to a lesser extent, the US and Japan. A global restructuring of industrial production has taken place with well-established industries simply disappearing in some parts of the world – for example, iron and steel and coal-mining in the UK – while other countries previously thought of as producers of raw materials have become major manufacturing centres. A whole new set of technologies have been developed around the microchip, revolutionizing communications and extending into all areas of the home and office. In short, over the last 25 years there has been a major shake-down – perhaps several shake-downs – in the world economy, with rapid changes of fortune for particular countries and for groups within countries; a whole new set of winners and losers have emerged.

From the perspective of a student of international relations, the most interesting feature of this shakedown is that it is taking place within the context of a thriving world economy. The last time changes of anything like this magnitude and rapidity took place was in the 1930s, and then the world trading system simply collapsed. Countries turned to economic nationalism, and then re-built international links on the basis of trading blocs; today such blocs exist – the European Union, the North American Free Trade Area (NAFTA) – but as part of a global system, not on the exclusionary basis that they did in the 1930s. Indeed it is striking that world trade has actually increased every year of the last three decades, even when domestic economies have been in recession in large parts of the world. Moreover, this growth in world trade has taken place in the context of serious instability in currency markets, which is usually regarded as an inhibitor of trade. What is more, in spite of the great instability in the world economy, the degree of regulation of international economic activity has actually increased somewhat – for example, the General Agreement on Tariffs and Trade (GATT), a body whose role was to reduce tariffs in manufacturing trade, has been replaced by the World Trade Organization (WTO) with a much wider remit covering services and agriculture as well as manufactures, and with enforcement mechanisms that are, in principle, more effective.

How is the maintenance of a world economy under such apparently adverse conditions to be explained? Here it makes sense to refer to three different stories that can be told of the events of the last 25 years. First, there is the story of *economic globalization*; on this account the preservation of a world economy is hardly surprising, because of the rise of global economic forces – the so-called multinational corporation (MNC) and global financial markets. Effectively, the reason states have not taken the route of economic nationalism is because they have not been able to; states no longer have the capacity to control the world economy. Second, there is the story of the growth of international *regimes*; on this account, the preservation of a functioning world economy is to be attributed to the willingness of states to cooperate to preserve the perceived gains of an open economy. Far from being disabled by global forces, on this account those global forces are only able to come into play because states have provided a framework for them to do so. Third, and taking things in another direction, is the story of the *hegemony of neoliberalism*; on this account it is dominance of a particular set of ideas, generated by class-interests, that accounts for the preservation of a world economy. States, MNCs and markets operate in a world where 'common sense' dictates certain kinds of economic relationships which are favourable to the preservation of a world-system.

The rest of this chapter will be devoted to an elaboration of these three stories, but before proceeding with this, two points deserve to be noted. First, and this relates back to some ideas outlined in Chapter 1, it is worth noting that although these three stories offer very different pictures of the world, it is only comparatively rarely that the storytellers differ on matters of fact; much commoner are differences of interpretation – thus, for example, the existence of MNCs is denied by no-one; what is at stake is their importance compared to other actors or forces, and there are no 'knock-down' 'killer facts' that give us the answer here. This does not mean that all stories are equally good, but it does mean that there is no substitute for reasoned judgement in the decision as to which story to believe. Second, although these three stories have been elaborated in the context of international political economy, each has a much wider, more general frame of reference to fall back on. Globalization is about much more than simply economic transactions, as Chapter 12 will demonstrate. Regime theory is about the conditions under which rational egoists cooperate and as such is part of the wider 'neoliberal institutionalist' account of the world outlined in Chapter 3 above. Gramscian notions of 'hegemony' form the basis for a neo-Marxist account of the world as a whole. In examining these three accounts of the world we are not simply engaging in trying to find a technical explanation for particular features of the world economy, rather we are examining three competing world views.

From an International to a Global Economy?

The Bretton Woods System was put together on the assumption that the pattern of international economic activity established before the First World War could be put back together again. The key features of that pattern were first, that international trade took place between national firms, and second, that the primary function of international financial transactions was to facilitate trade. The state was assumed to encompass a national economy, and international economic activity took place between such national economies. As a result of a series of changes which have their origins much earlier but which have gathered pace since 1975, each of these assumption must now be challenged.

The most important of these changes is the rise in significance of the international business enterprise, or, MNC ('multinational' is something of a misnomer because many of the firms in question are mono-national in ownership and management, but the use of MNC as a generic term here is so widespread that it would be pedantic to try to replace it). Since MNCs are regarded by many as the modern equivalent of the inter-war 'merchants of death' and the root of all international evil, it is important to keep a sense of proportion when examining their influence. The first step is to make it clear that there are many different kinds of business enterprise that are multinational; their common defining feature is that they all operate across national boundaries and are based on *direct* foreign investment – the ownership and control of assets located abroad – as opposed to *indirect* or *portfolio* investment in which assets are purchased for the financial return, rather than the control, they bring, and as opposed to simply trading across frontiers. These different kinds of corporation create different kinds of problems and opportunities, and stand in different relationships to the territorial state.

Some MNCs are engaged in the *extraction of raw materials*; this is an activity whose location is determined by the accidents of geography and geology. Copper companies go where the copper is, oil companies where the oil is and so on – which means that these corporations do not usually have relocation as an easy business strategy, which, in turn, means they have an incentive to try to preserve good relations with local political elites. Unsurprisingly some of the most egregious acts of political interference by MNCs have involved such corporations. Other corporations engage in *manufacturing*, generally in the markets for which they are producing, that is in the industrialized world. Here direct political influence is comparatively unusual, although indirect influence is very great. Some MNCs have world-wide integrated production strategies, although the extent of this phenomenon is contestable. A third important category of MNC is made up of those corporations who engage in the *global manipulation of symbols* – the great multi-media and entertainment corporations, but also international banks – whose activities are highly deterritorialized, although, for the time being at least, their chief executives are still unable to avoid locating in one state or another, thus retaining a territorial link. Finally, for the sake of completion, mention should be made of international *holding companies*, where different firms producing different products in different countries are owned by the same corporation but where there is no attempt to produce a common business strategy – such holding companies may have little political significance by comparison with the other types of MNC; the fact that the specialist ice cream manufacturers *Ben and Jerry's* are now owned by the multinational Unilever is unlikely to have much significance if, as seems likely, the latter are content to preserve the former's independence as a precondition for success in a niche market.

While there are sharply contrasting views of the significance of these corporations, there are a few points that are accepted by all. First, there are a great many more MNCs operating in the world today than there were in the 1960s and 1970s, and many of these new corporations are engaged in 'cutting edge' economic activities, in the production of high-technology manufactures, or in global finance or information and entertainment rather than in the extractive industries or old-style 'metal-bashing'. Second, and largely because of the nature of these activities, these newer corporations carry out most of their activities in the advanced industrial world and the 'Newly Industrializing Countries' (NICs) rather than in the less developed countries generally or the least developed countries in particular. Third, whereas up to the 1960s nearly all large MNCs were based on American capital held abroad, the situation today is rather different; the United States is still the country with the largest individual *stock* of overseas capital, but in recent years the net flow of capital has been to the United States from Europe and Japan, and the total stock of American capital held by foreigners is larger than that of foreign capital held by Americans.

To reiterate, the point about the emergence of the MNC is that many of the assumptions that have guided past thinking now have to be abandoned. Readers will recall that in Chapter 8 much was made of the difficulties involved in economic transactions crossing borders, on the assumption that the producer in one country would be unconnected to the consumer in another. Today, a high proportion of international trade is 'intra-firm' trade, that is between different branches of the same corporation, although just how high a proportion is difficult to say because of the weakness of official statistics; it is probably between a quarter and a third by value of the trade of the advanced industrial countries. The possibilities for manipulating markets opened up by this phenomenon are tremendous; in principle, via 'transfer pricing', firms can move profits and losses from one area of operation to another at will, with a devastating effect on the effectiveness of national tariff and taxation policies and on international attempts to regulate trade.

Transfer pricing is an activity open only to MNCs – and, in practice, more easily controlled by tax authorities than this summary would suggest – but in other respects too much emphasis on MNCs as such can be misleading. Effectively all large corporations today are behaviourally 'multi-national' – that is to say, to some extent they think and plan globally even if they do not possess foreign assets. The old distinction between multinationals and others relied on a national compartmentalization of economic activity to which MNCs were an exception, a situation that no longer applies. The new technologies upon which production today is based work against any such compartmentalization.

The same point can be made with respect to a change in some ways more radical in its implications than the rise of MNCs – the emergence of *global financial markets*. One of the reasons for the collapse of the IMF's exchange-rate regime in the 1960s and 1970s was the existence of the 'Eurodollar' market. Once it was determined at Bretton Woods that private movements of capital would be allowed, and once the City of London was allowed to return to its traditional role with the ending of controls in 1951, the emergence of new capital markets was inevitable. 'Eurodollars' were foreign currencies held in banks beyond the regulatory reach of the country that issued them – the generic title derives from the fact that these were originally US dollars held in European (mainly British) banks. A market in Eurodollars existed alongside domestic capital markets; originally on quite a small scale and initially established for political reasons, it grew very quickly, largely because various features of US banking regulations encouraged US MNCs to keep working balances abroad. By the mid-1960s the 'Eurodollar slop' of currencies being moved from one market to another was a major destabilizing factor in the management of exchange rates.

The Eurodollar market still exists, but under different conditions. Whereas in the 1960s this was a market that was separate from, albeit linked to, domestic capital markets, nowadays all currency holdings are potentially 'Euro' holdings; with the end of regulation in most countries, national capital markets and national stock exchanges are simply local manifestations of a world-wide market and the creation of credit is beyond the control of national authorities. Trading takes place on a 24-hour basis, following the sun from Tokyo to Hong Kong to Frankfurt and London to New York and back to Tokyo. Some transactions in this market are clearly 'international' – foreign currency loans, the purchase of Eurobonds, and so on – whereas others are 'local', but the compartmentalization that once kept such activities apart and made of the former a limited specialization no longer exists. Just as the distinction between multi-national and national corporations is no longer of great interest, so the distinction between international and national capital markets is now somewhat unreal. In the aftermath of the rush to create new financial instruments in the 1980s, virtually any economic or financial activity can be 'securitized' and traded internationally. Thus it is possible to buy assets whose value is calculated on the basis of the cash flow generated by the repayments of loans for the purchase of automobiles in the US, and foreign bankers can exchange dollar debts for shares in Brazilian soccer teams.

What do these changes amount to? On the most extreme account we are seeing the ending of the nation-state as an economic unit and the emergence of a 'borderless' world (Ohmae 1990). This 'hyper-globalist' position, to use the terminology of David Held and his colleagues, has to be seen as an exaggerated response to the new situation – one might call it the view from business class, since no airline traveller in 'tourist' would be likely to imagine that border controls are unimportant (Held *et al.* 1999). A more considered position would argue that even if the state has not disappeared, its role is changing quite dramatically, and it may be in some sense in retreat (Strange 1996). Certainly globalization has made some forms of state intervention ineffective, but the political challenge posed by globalization has encouraged states to develop new techniques, and, perhaps most of all, new attitudes.

What we may be seeing is the emergence of a new kind of diplomacy involving firms and states. As technology comes to dominate production processes, so firms in advanced sectors come to find that their long-run survival depends upon their ability to conduct the research and development (R & D) that will keep them in the forefront of their sector. Successful research and development is largely a function of the absolute size of the 'R & D' budget and this in turn is largely a function of firm size. This means access to markets is crucial, either directly or via arrangements with other firms. Since states can, at a pinch, control access to markets – and can sanction or forbid franchising arrangements or take-overs – the desire that firms have to expand gives states a degree of leverage over their activities. On the other hand, states want successful, technologically-advanced firms to be located on their territories – inward investment generates employment, supports regional policy, provides a tax base and contributes to the export capacity of a country. This means that firms have something to offer states, and thus a good bargaining position.

Put another way, both states and firms are concerned with 'market share'; firms want the largest market share they can get, and states want firms with the largest market share they can get on their territories. The new diplomacy is about the ways in which firms and states achieve their ends. It is a triangular diplomatic system. States negotiate and bargain with other states – about access to each other's markets and, within the European Union, for example, about the crucial rules governing what degree of 'local content' is required for, say, a Toyota Corolla constructed in Britain to count as a British as opposed to a Japanese car. States negotiate and bargain with firms – about the terms and conditions upon which the latter are allowed to operate on the territory of the former, the tax concessions that new investment will attract, the location of this investment, the employment it will provide, and, currently in the case of the UK, the impact of joining or not joining the single European currency. Firms negotiate and bargain with firms – about co-production, about pooling research and development, about franchising, sometimes about co-ownership. Each of the three sides of this diplomacy affects the other two. The attractiveness of one state over another as a location for new investment (state–firm diplomacy) will often depend on its ability to guarantee access to the markets of other states (state–state diplomacy) and the degree to which incoming firms are able to negotiate deals with at least some of those already in the market (firm–firm diplomacy).

One of the features of this new diplomacy is that some of the traditional questions asked of multi-national corporations become rather less significant in the new circumstances. In the 1960s and 1970s the national origins of MNCs were a real issue and they were seen by many as agents of a form of American imperialism. Nowadays many MNCs are not American – Japanese auto producers and banks are particularly significant – and ownership is widely seen as less important than what large firms can do for states in terms of improving their economic performance. Xenophobic reactions to Japanese investment can still be found, but largely miss the point. Taking the motorcar industry as an example, given the R & D costs of producing new models, no purely national volume car producer will be able to survive in the twenty-first century – one way or another, all mass-produced cars will be 'world cars' produced by 'world companies'. Much of the past literature on MNCs paid great attention to the repatriation of profits, the implication being that foreign corporations exploited the local economy for the benefit of *rentiers* back home – as opposed, one imagines, to local capitalists who were socially responsible philanthropists. Nowadays any corporation, local or global, that does not invest most of its profits in research and development will not be around very long to pay out dividends to its shareholders. Perhaps most of all, the notion of 'sovereignty at bay' is highly misleading (Vernon 1971). On the one hand, as we have seen, sovereignty in the old sense of complete control of a territory probably never existed, and, in any event, is now long gone; on the other hand, the ability to be effectively sovereign today – to meet the welfare needs of one's population, to promote economic growth – depends crucially on getting into a healthy relationship with international business. A strong state is a state that is able to use MNCs for its own ends, not one that excludes them or prevents them from making a profit.

But, of course, this way of looking at the matter involves accepting that the existing order is more or less unchangeable in any radical way, and that all one can do is go with the flow. As the final section of this chapter will make clear, this is a highly contestable position; neo-Marxist critics base their account of the hegemony of neoliberal ideas precisely on this acceptance of the logic of global capital. Rather more social-democratically oriented critics make a similar point, but their response is based on the proposition that the importance of the economic trends identified above has been much exaggerated. Perhaps the most important study representing this perspective has been that of Paul Hirst and Grahame Thompson (1999). They make a number of telling points against too enthusiastic an acceptance of the idea of economic globalization. Although modern communications technology is impressive, the key step in making possible the emergence of global capital markets came with the invention of the electric telegraph in the mid-nineteenth century, and before 1914 global markets were more closely integrated than today. As to production, they demonstrate that a high proportion of the investment of most so-called multinational firms takes place in the home market. They do not argue that things remain as they were – rather their point is that cross-border economic transactions are best seen as taking place in an *internationalized* as opposed to a *globalized* world. Large states, at least, retain a degree of freedom of action.

The nature of the changes in global capitalism is an issue that will be taken up below in the final section of this chapter, but the focus now shifts to an alternative way of looking at the preservation of the world economy, a story which focuses on the attempts of states to regulate and govern economic activity, and argues that they are rather more successful at this than might have been expected.

Regime Theory

Did the Bretton Woods System collapse in the early 1970s? Certainly the system of fixed exchange rates which had been at the heart of the BWS and its then key institution, the IMF, collapsed in 1973, but arguably, the system as a whole continued, albeit not quite on the lines intended in 1944. The IMF became a key institution for dealing with the debt crisis of the 1980s, making symbolic loans to debtors on conditions which were taken by the global financial community as indicative of 'sound' economic policy while the World Bank became a major repository of development expertise. The GATT not only survived but, after the relatively successful 'Uruguay Round' was transformed in 1995 into the World Trade Organization (WTO). The WTO, which unlike the GATT, is not restricted to manufactured trade, and which has, in principle, quite effective enforcement mechanisms for its rulings on trade disputes, has become one of the main symbols of globalization, its meetings the occasion for large-scale demonstrations.

But although a potent symbol of *globalization*, the WTO is an *international* organization, created by states, perhaps the best current example of the capacity of states to cooperate even on issues of considerable political importance. At least at a first approximation, trade is one area of IR governed by an *international regime*, and it is now time to examine the theory of international regimes, a theory developed out of the complex interdependence model of international relations of the 1970s, which became a prime focus of debate between neoliberals and neorealists in the 1980s. The generally-accepted (although slightly contentious) definition of a *regime* is that it is a set of 'implicit or explicit principles, norms, rules and decision-making procedures around which actors' expectations converge in a given area of international relations' (Krasner (ed.) 1983: 2). The best way to elaborate this definition is to briefly work through the current trade regime using Krasner's expansions of the key terms.

The *principles* ('beliefs of fact, causation and rectitude') upon which the trade regime is built are the liberal notions elaborated in Chapter 8. Trade is Good. Free trade is better than controlled trade. Free trade promotes peace. These principles constitute the 'embedded liberalism' of the trade regime, and they exist in the background even when contrary practices are sanctioned. The *norms* ('standards of behaviour defined in terms of rights and obligations') of the regime give these principles some practical content. Thus it is a norm that if it is not possible for trade to be free, tariffs are a better mechanism for restraint of trade than physical quotas because they cause less interference in the market and are less discriminatory in impact. 'Most-favoured-nation' (MFN) clauses whereby tariff concessions made to one country have to be made to all are sanctioned by the norm of non-discrimination. It is a norm that, over time, tariffs should be reduced by multilateral negotiation. The *rules* ('specific prescriptions or proscriptions for action') of the trade regime set out in detail what these norms imply, and set out the sanctioned exceptions to these norms; they are to be found in the WTO Charter, in the Multi-Fibre Arrangement (MFA) and in various other legal and quasi-legal documents. The *decision-making procedures* ('prevailing practices for making and implementing collective choice') in this case have in the past consisted of the GATT Rounds, now focus on meetings of the WTO, the conference diplomacy of bodies such as UNCTAD, and, at a different level, on the trade disputes procedures set out in the WTO Charter.

Principles, norms, rules and decision-making procedures may be *explicit* or *implicit*. Explicit rules are written down somewhere, implicit rules are understood without being written down. We can see the difference here when examining some of the 'sanctioned' breaches of the norms of the trade regime. Non-discriminatory trade is a norm of the trade regime; it is considered damaging to have different trade rules for dealing with different countries. Readers will recall that the trade blocs of the 1930s were widely regarded as contributing to the unrest of that decade, if not to the outbreak of war as such. However, under GATT/WTO rules, 'customs unions' and 'free trade areas' such as the European Union and the North American Free Trade Area are explicitly licensed even though clearly discriminatory. Equally, it is permissible for industrial states to discriminate in favour of products from the 'Third World'. These are explicit exceptions to the non-discrimination rule.

On the other hand, the most popular method of discrimination today is probably the 'voluntary export restraint' (VER). This is a state-to-state or industry-to-industry agreement whereby one party promises to limit exports to the other – as, for example, in the deals struck between European countries and the major Japanese car manufacturers to limit the import of Japanese cars into European markets. Such restraints are discriminatory and based on quotas, and are therefore quite clearly in breach of the norms and principles of the trade regime. They are acceptable because, technically, they are 'voluntary'. This is clearly a fiction – they are only accepted voluntarily because if they were not tighter restrictions would be imposed on an involuntary basis – but it is a fiction that everyone goes along with, for their own reasons. This is a case of an 'implicit' rule of the trade regime and it is every bit as important as the explicit rules set out in the various treaties which establish the regime.

'*Around which actors' expectations converge*' – here we come to the heart of the matter. The 'actors' in the world trade – firms, states and individual consumers – have expectations about the principles, norms, rules and decision-making procedures that will apply in this area, and if these expectations converge, there is a regime. And if not, not. 'Converge' is a word which was deliberately chosen to avoid the idea that expectations have to be exactly the same (which, much of the time, they clearly are not) or that rules will always be obeyed (which, equally clearly, will not always be the case). Instead 'expectations converge' suggests that most of the time the actors will have similar expectations and most of the time they will be fulfilled – there is a degree of predictability and regularity about trade matters that is appreciably greater than would be expected in the absence of a regime.

Regimes are clearly seen as part of the governance of the international system, but it should be noted that, *pace* the importance of the WTO in this case, they represent a clear break from the emphasis on institutions characteristic of the old Bretton Woods System. The WTO is important, but so are other institutions such as UNCTAD and the MFA, and informal 'institutions' based on implicit rules may be as important as, or more important than, the official bodies. Regime theory is a genuine attempt to come to terms with post-Bretton Woods changes in the world economy outlined above, albeit an attempt that is fraught with difficulty. One major source of difficulty concerns the possibility of achieving the degree of regularity and predictability required for a regime to exist in the first place.

It should be recalled at this point that regime theory emerges out of the neoliberal theory of International Relations; that is to say that its root assumption is that states – and, for that matter firms – are rational egoists operating in an anarchical system. How is cooperation possible amongst rational egoists under anarchy? From a neoliberal perspective it is not too difficult to see why states (and firms) would want to cooperate – there are absolute gains to be had from cooperation, that is from mutual adjustments, and on neoliberal assumptions, states are concerned to make absolute gains. The problem is that the temptation to cheat may be overwhelming. States will continually be placed in a situation where it is in their interests that cooperation take place, but even more in their interests that the cost of cooperation be carried by others. This is a classic collective action problem. In domestic societies, one of the roles of government is to solve problems of collective action by enforcing compliance with a system of rules which are, in principle, in the common interest. Individuals are forced to meet the cost of public goods through the tax system, whether or not they would prefer to make voluntary contributions and hang on to the option of cheating. By definition, no such solution is available internationally – so how do states set up regimes in the first place, and why do these regimes persist to the extent they do? The most influential explanation for this phenomenon is the theory of *hegemonic stability*.

It is not clear who first used the term or popularized the idea, but an important early statement of what came to be known as the theory of hegemonic stability is that of Charles Kindleberger in the final chapter of his economic history of the 1930s, *The World in Depression 1929–1939* (1973). In examining explanations for the Great Depression, he tells the basic story as follows: the international economic system before 1914 was not, as it was usually taken to be, self-regulating. Instead, the hegemonic financial power of Great Britain, exercised by the quasi-autonomous Bank of England, had been employed to smooth over problems of cooperation generated by the operation of the Gold Standard. Britain had had the capacity to do this, given its enormous holdings of overseas capital. It also had had the will to do this, because, as the largest financial power, it had the biggest stake in the preservation of the system and was willing to pay the price that a hegemon must pay in terms of its own freedom of action. Its role as the hegemon was widely, albeit tacitly, accepted by other members of the system, in this case by financial authorities elsewhere. On Kindleberger's analysis, things fell apart in the inter-war period because of the lack of a hegemonic leader in the system. Britain tried after 1926 to regain its place, but it no longer had the financial clout to act as the stabilizer of the system; possibly the American banks on Wall Street had the financial power but neither they nor the American government were prepared to use this power to underwrite the world financial system. In any event, the rise of the dictators made it unlikely that any assertion of leadership would be widely accepted. Hence the collapse of the international economy after 1929–33.

On the other hand (and here the story is taken up by other writers, such as Stephen Krasner and Robert Keohane), after 1945 a new hegemonic economic power emerged, the United States. The US was the strongest financial and productive power and had the capacity to provide hegemonic leadership. Because the US leadership of the time recognized that it was in their interest to promote a flourishing world economy, the US was prepared to use this power to promote cooperation. And because of the poverty of the rest of the capitalist world, and their fear of the Soviet Union, American leadership was widely accepted. Thus it was that the post-war institutional structure was underwritten by the power of the US. The GATT rounds of tariff reduction were driven by American leadership, and the willingness of the US to abide by the rules of the system, and to use its political power to encourage others to do likewise, was critical. Moreover, because of the strength of the United States it was able, if it wished, to turn a blind eye to infractions of the rules by other states, if by so doing it was able to preserve the system. Thus the hegemonic power of the United States was able to act as a kind of substitute for international government, but without violating the basic assumption of rational egoism; the US performs this role because it is in its interests to do so. As the country with the largest stake in the preservation of the system, it is willing to act in accordance with the rules and to bear most of the transaction costs of running the system not as an act of altruism, but on the basis of enlightened, medium-term, self-interest.

However, hegemonic leadership is a wasting asset which creates the conditions for its own downfall. The hegemon is required to play fair – in the case of the trade regime, to open its borders to imports and to eschew the sort of creative measures that can undermine the rules of the system. However, its rivals are not so hampered. They will use the regime set up by the hegemon to the full, taking advantage of access to the hegemon's market, but relying on the hegemon not to overreact to their own measures to prevent its access to their markets. Gradually, the material basis upon which hegemony rests will be eroded and the hegemon will cease to have the capacity to act as such – instead it will start to play fast and loose with the formal rules, and, as a result, will no longer have the legitimacy to act as hegemon. Instead it will be perceived by other members of the system as acting solely in its own interests rather than in the interests of all. This, it is suggested, is more or less what has happened to US hegemony over the last 50 years – gradually its trade rivals outproduced it, partly because it was hampered in its actions by its responsibilities, and America then became incapable of continuing to act in the interests of all, and liable to succumb to the temptation to act on short-term self-interest.

The good news is that regimes may well survive 'after hegemony' (Keohane 1984). The hard work of setting up regimes has been taken by the hegemon, and the task now is the easier one of keeping them ticking over. The very fact that rules are written down and thus institutionalized makes it more likely that states will abide by them, while the institutions can provide a great deal of useful information that will prevent states acting against their own interests. The hypothesis is that most of the time when states act as free riders it is either because they do not believe they will be found out, or because they do not appreciate the longer-term consequences of their actions. The existence of institutions make it unlikely that either position will hold, which creates an incentive to cooperate. Thus it is that within the institutions created by the United States cooperation can continue, but at 'suboptimal' levels by comparison with the cooperation that can be generated by a hegemon.

As will be apparent below, the account of America's role given here is highly contentious, but before moving to examine this controversy it is worth picking up one or two features of the theory of hegemonic stability that are worthy of attention irrespective of the actual history of the last 50 years. First, how powerful does a state have to be to be deemed 'hegemonic'? The view that Britain was a hegemonic economic power in the nineteenth century suggests the answer 'not very'. Britain was never militarily very powerful – except for her navy and the Indian Army in the Indian Ocean and the Far East – and her role as workshop of the world barely lasted a generation. Even her financial power was waning before 1914. To be hegemonic clearly does not mean the ability to be predominant over all other rivals on all issues, but it is not clear just how powerful a state has to be in order to qualify.

Rather more fundamental is a second point. Does leadership require hegemony? David Lake has demonstrated that the United States began to take on a leadership role in trade talks in the 1930s at a point where it would not normally have been thought of as hegemonic (Lake 1988). Jarrod Wiener has examined the role of the United States in the Uruguay Round of GATT talks, a round which extended the range of the GATT to agriculture, services and intellectual property and which led to the formation of the WTO in 1995. The United States clearly exerted leadership in these negotiations, and yet virtually no one would suggest that *in the area of trade* the US is still hegemonic in the face of the trading strength of Japan and the European Union (Wiener 1995). Perhaps regimes work as well as they do because some state is prepared to take the lead, but there is no necessity for that state to be hegemonic – although a substantial resource endowment would be required since states are unlikely to allow a small or weak state to exercise a leadership role.

In any event, with or without a hegemonic leader, part of the success or failure of a regime is likely to be a function of the kind of activities it engages in – in the case of trade, one of the features of the system for over 20 years has been the comparative unimportance of easily negotiated barriers such as tariffs, and the far greater importance of non-tariff barriers (NTBs) to trade, which are far more difficult to negotiate. If, for example, one is trying to create a level playing field as between Japanese and European firms, the significance of factors such as the common external tariff of the EU is as nothing compared to factors such as the shape and structure of capital markets in the two areas. The competitiveness of Japanese firms rests partly on their ability to raise capital on a large scale at favourable rates over quite long time periods. The uncompetitiveness of European firms is marked by their inability to do this – it is hard to see how international negotiations could do anything to alter this situation. In other words the relative lowering of levels of cooperation in recent years may be a function of the intractability of the problems the trade regime faces rather than the decline of a hegemon.

In any event, the issue of American hegemony now needs to be addressed, not simply in order to understand the course of events over the last 50 years, but also because debates over the nature and form of American power raise issues which are fundamental to the new international political economy that has arisen as a result of globalization. However, before engaging in this detour, it is worth noting that the issue of hegemonic stability arises as it does partly because the 'Krasner' definition of a regime is so closely connected to manistream American rational choice IR. Other notions of a 'regime', associated particularly with European scholars and the constructivist turn in IR theory place more emphasis on the ideational component of regimes, rather than the rational egoism of rational choice theory – thus cooperation may be sustained because states come to believe that it constitutes a good in itself rather than simply because it is in their immediate or even medium term interest to cooperate, and the need for some kind of mechanism to enforce cooperation may be less compelling (Rittberger 1993: Hasenclever *et al.* 1997, 2000).

Is America a Declining Hegemon?

The so-called 'declinist' case is easy to see. In the immediate post-war years the United States was in a unique position in the world economy. Over half the industrial production of the capitalist world was in America. America was the world's richest country, its citizens the world's richest. Its rivals were defeated or exhausted. The US dollar was the only major currency that was regarded as safe. The US balance of trade was overwhelmingly positive and only prevented from being larger by the restraints on US exports that every country was obliged to institute. America was the foremost military power of the capitalist world and the other major capitalist powers all required US protection if they were to survive in a world where the hostility of the Soviet Union was taken for granted. Only Great Britain had any real independent military capacity, and it was (fairly) happy to accept the role of junior partner in institutions such as NATO, and in the new economic institutions created by the United States. American power straddled the ('free') world.

By the 1990s much of this had changed. The US now has perhaps rather under one-fifth of world GDP, and its share is declining as its growth rate remains slow by comparison with its competitors, especially Germany, Japan, and the Newly Industrializing Countries (NICs) of Asia and Latin America. Its citizens are still, just about, in real terms the wealthiest in the world but they have seen little or no average growth in real income for nearly a generation. Productivity is rising faster elsewhere, and the US has had a deficit on overseas trade for over a generation. Whereas the US was once the world's greatest capital exporter it is now the largest importer of capital. US budget deficits are only met by large-scale borrowing from abroad, especially from Japan. The US is the world's largest debtor country. American military power remains strong, for the time being, but the ending of the Cold War has meant that other countries no longer feel the need for US protection and are less enthusiastic about the exercise of American military power. Truly the power of the US has declined and it can no longer be a hegemon in the old sense – so the declinist argument goes.

There are some, as it were, technical objections to this thesis. It is clear that the position the US had in 1945 was anomalous and contingent – there was bound to be a considerable decline in the US share of world production once other countries recovered from the war. Even so, nearly one-fifth of the world's productive capacity still looks pretty impressive. Moreover, values are depressed by employing exchange rates which may be artificial. The 'purchasing power parity' (PPP) rate suggests that the US is still the richest country in the world. However, these technical arguments do not really meet the point. The more serious objection to declinism is that it misunderstands the true nature of the modern world economy, and, in particular, the importance of *structural power*.

We have met structural power in Chapter 5 above; it now comes into its own. The thesis of those who reject the neoliberal account of declining American hegemony is that while the US may indeed be less significant in some relationships, its structural position remains very strong. The world economy is designed around the US economy, and this gives the United States enormous advantages in its dealings with the rest of the world. To take an illustration from the declinist litany set out above, consider the ability of the United States to finance its government debt by overseas borrowing. Is this a sign of weakness or of strength? Surely the ability of the US to run its own government on the back of a significant part of the savings of the world ought to be seen as a sign of strength not weakness? The US is the world's largest debtor, but it is the only debtor whose debts are denominated in its own currency. President Reagan once remarked that he saw no real difference between raising taxes and borrowing to meet a deficit; critics pointed out that governments do not have to pay back taxes – but, as was often the way, Reagan's political instincts were sound, even if his grasp of the detail left something to be desired. Given the power of the printing press, repaying debt does have a different meaning if you are working with your own currency.

These are ad hoc arguments. The strongest opponent of the declinist thesis, Susan Strange, offered a more general account of structural power. She identifies four basic sources of structural power in the world today, interrelated but separable – the security, production, financial and knowledge structures. The *security* structure is based on the power to give protection against perceived threat, a power that can translate into other kinds of activities such as the administration of justice. *Production* is about who can make what, where, when and how, and, as Marxists have consistently argued, the mode of production determines many other aspects of social and political life. *Finance*, the control of credit, is basic to any advanced industrialized economy; investment no longer depends on the accumulation of capital but on access to credit. *Knowledge* is now and always has been a source of power – access to the most advanced technology is critical. 'What is common to all kinds of structural power is that the possessor is able to change the range of choices open to others without apparently putting pressure directly on them to take one decision or to make one choice rather than others' (Strange 1988: 29).

There are various features of this account that are noteworthy. First, as with Marxist accounts, Strange assumes that all structures are in contact with one another and influence each other – but, unlike Marxists, she makes no assumption that production is always the most important structure. Second, she takes *trade* – along with *transport*, *energy* and *welfare* – as a secondary structure of power, of importance but less significant than the primary structures. One of the reasons why we think trade is more important than it actually is, is because we are overimpressed by the institutional frameworks within which trade takes place, as opposed, for example, to the lack of institutions that surround international production. This is misleading. The various principles, norms and rules incorporated in the trade 'regime' have comparatively limited impact on the actual conduct of trade relations. The giant corporations trade with each other and, especially, engage in intra-firm trade, without paying too much attention to the official rules of the game – although it should be said here that Strange was writing before the emergence of the WTO, and, arguably, the rules are rather more important now than they once were.

Re-examining American power in the light of these thoughts it is clear that a different picture emerges from that of the 'declinist' literature. The United States still dominates the security structure of the world – and even after the end of Cold War this is still an important source of power given the general instability that has accompanied the end of that conflict. The world's production structure is still largely dominated by American corporations, even though these corporations do less and less of their actual production in the United States. The world's financial structures still rest on the US dollar and on capital markets which, although world-wide, are still based on the sheer size of the American economy. The most advanced areas of information technology, computer software and the information and entertainment industries – the heart of the knowledge structure – remain American. In short, in so far as the American economy ever was hegemonic – and this may be a misleading term in any event – it still is.

This account shares with orthodox regime theory the notion that in the immediate post-war period the United States was central to the establishment of many of the features of the global economy, and, equally, the thought that over the last two decades the United States has ceased to play so constructive a role. However, whereas regime theorists stress the *inability* of the US to act as hegemon, Strange stresses the *unwillingness* of the US to take a leadership role – especially in respect of financial structures. America has allowed the emergence of 'casino capitalism' not because it has been unable to stop the process, but because it has been unwilling to pay the price of leading in a responsible way (Strange 1986, 1999). According to Strange, President Lyndon Johnson is a key figure here – his unwillingness to either increase taxes to pay for the Vietnam War, or to cut his Great

Society programme of domestic reforms forced him to resort to the printing press and create the inflation which was the underlying cause of the disruptions of the 1970s. A failure of American leadership, and the inability of the American political system to behave responsibly and think in anything other than the shortest of short terms is what has been at the heart of the turmoil of the last quarter-century. Moreover, this turmoil will continue since no other country has the ability to step into America's place in the world economy. Apart from the lack of sources of structural power, other possible contenders, such as Japan, lack any wider legitimacy. One of the advantages of the American 'Empire' is that it is remarkably accessible to those with a degree of power or knowledge, in the way that more traditional societies never can be.

Seen in the light of these ideas, the discussion of regimes set out above needs considerable modification. In the first place, the extent to which the terms of cooperation set out in regimes actually reflect bargains between states rather than rules which control the real economic actors needs to be underlined. States have only a limited capacity to control firms, and the bigger the firm the more limited the capacity. Second, the extent to which anarchy is actually overcome by regimes needs to be put in question. The vision of a world in which international economic relations are actually rather orderly and predictable seems not to be accurate. Instead the international political economy works on somewhat different lines in a far more power-political way, albeit a power politics adopted to the conditions of the day, in which, Strange would argue, firms take part along with states in the kind of triangular diplomacy described in the opening section of this chapter.

A Different Kind of Hegemony?

As noted above, the World Trade Organization has become a potent symbol of globalization, but symbol here is the appropriate word, because the WTO is a small organization with relatively few actual powers. Clearly as the subject of protest, the WTO is a place-holder for something else – but what is the nature of the real driving force behind those changes in the global economy that so many people wish to resist? For many, the answer here is 'America'; globalization equals Americanization and the WTO is America's agent. As the last section of this chapter argued, American power is real and worries about

American decline are, understandably, not shared by those who are truly powerless in the face of changing global conditions. Nonetheless, the American position on both the WTO and economic globalization more generally is more ambiguous than any simple minded equation of the two would suggest. Many forces in American society, well represented in Congress, are deeply sceptical about the impact on the US of globalization and, in any event, it is by no means clear that the WTO regularly acts in the interests of the US or even of American capital. Globalization may equate to Americanization in some cultural areas, but hardly in economic terms.

A more plausible candidate for the real force behind global economic change is the MNC. On the whole, very large business enterprises are indeed in favour of globalization, and are strongly supportive of the WTO; the desire of such large corporations to extend their intellectual property rights, and to protect their capital investments, on a global scale is well known and reflected in WTO policy. However, the fact that MNCs want something does not explain why they get it. Given the apparent levels of resistance to changes in the world economy, how is it that these giant corporations are able to get their way? The temptation at this point is to reach for conspiracy theories of one kind or another, but although there sometimes *are* conspiracies, and particular MNCs have indeed used improper influence on occasion, it is not sensible to build a general account of the world on such a basis.

Far more compelling is the case for the third candidate for this role as the force behind economic globalization – the *hegemonic role of neo-liberalism*. This is hegemony in a different sense from that discussed above in the context of 'hegemonic stability'. There hegemony meant a certain kind of domination exercised by a particular actor, albeit with the tacit consent of others. Here hegemony refers to the way in which certain kinds of ideas become seen as so much part of the common sense of a society that they cease to be seen as 'ideas' at all, but rather become part of 'how things really are'. This notion of hegemony was developed by Gramsci in the 1920s, building on Marx's notion of ideology, but it is not necessarily tied to Marxist – as opposed to radical – accounts of the world. Feminists, for example, may note the ways in which particular accounts assigning different gender roles to men and women were, until very recently, similarly seen as part of 'common sense' in Western societies.

In the context of the global economy, it is argued that the last two decades have seen the emergence of a a hegemonic account of how domestic ecomomies ought to be run and how they ought to relate to the rest of the world. In the immediate post-1945 era a variety of different models of the economy coexisted; setting aside the communist command model, even within capitalism there was great variation, with different levels of planning and welfare provision in different countries or groups of countries; Keynesian ideas of demand management were accepted with varying degrees of enthusiasm. The majority of developing countries adopted socialist models of one kind or another, but usually with a substantial role for the private sector. However, since the late 1970s, the range of possible economic systems seems to have narrowed substantially. Apart from the biggest single change – the complete collapse of the communist model post-1989 – in the English-speaking countries and in Scandinavia welfare states have been under extreme pressure, and demand-management has been almost completely abandoned as a strategy. The economics profession has come to be dominated by neoclassical economic liberalism, and the political expressions of the latter, Thatcherism and 'Reagonomics' to the fore, have established a similar hegemony. It is increasingly the case that it is accepted as part of the common sense of the age that markets should be as free as possible, that physical controls, price controls and planning will not work, and that economies should be as open to the rest of the world as possible. This 'neoliberal' position is now dominant within the major international organizations, and, in the form of the 'Washington Consensus' has provided the intellectual backbone for the programmes recommended by the IMF and the World Bank for developing countries requiring the assistance of those bodies – although it should be said that this position is not quite as dominant as it once was; in any event, the impact of these ideas on the developing world will be examined in Chapter 10.

In effect, the New Labour and New Democrat administrations in the UK and the US have accepted a great deal of the economic thought of their Conservative/Republican predecessors, as have social democrat governments in most of the rest of the world. Only in France, the Benelux countries and, to a much lesser extent, Germany, is the hegemony of neoliberalism seriously resisted at a Government level – and even there it is doubtful whether the costs of an extremely expensive welfare state will be politically bearable for much longer. Neoliberal ideas are hegemonic on a global scale in so far as they have genuinely captured the common sense of the age about economic matters. This hegemony is discernable in the behaviour of the opponents of neoliberalism; it is striking that although a great many groups have presented strong critiques of economic globalization, positive alternatives are fewer on the ground. The demonstrators on the streets in the 'Battle of Seattle' at the last major WTO conference in November 1999 agreed they were opposed to the WTO, but were much less clear about what they favoured – and when alternatives were mooted they tended to be mutually contradictory. The opponents included economic nationalists, socialists, 'deep-green' opponents of industrial society as well as more moderate environmentalists and human rights activists, and their inability to find even the elements of a common programme seriously hampers their effectiveness as pressure groups. This inability to present a coherent alternative to neoliberalism is as clear a demonstration as could be given of the latter's hegemony.

In the above discussion, neoliberalism has been treated as a set of ideas, but, of course, it is far more than that; it is not necessary to be any kind of Marxist to think that the triumph of neoliberalism represents the triumph of certain kinds of interests – although, clearly, Marxists will have a particular account of the kind of interests that will shape systems of thought. It is at this point that the third story of the emergence of a global economy starts to interact with the first two stories. One of the forces driving neoliberalism has been the emergence of giant corporations in whose interests many of the precepts of neoliberalism work, while the rise of the giant corporation is itself partly shaped by the rise of neoliberal ideas. There is a dialectic at work here which makes it dificult if not impossible to say that one of these forces created the other. The spread of neoliberal ideas has been hastened by the restructuring of the world production system that has taken place over the last 20 years, *and vice versa*. Again, while it may not make a great deal of sense to see an undifferentiated 'America' as the force behind globalization, it makes a great deal more sense to point to the class interests of the major representatives of American capital, perhaps allied nowadays with an international/transnational business class. This way of looking at things allows one to hold at the same time the proposition that American power is in decline (in the sense that the ability of the US political system to control the international agenda is lessening) and that it remains as strong as it was (in the sense that a predominantly American corporate class still exercises a great deal of effective control in the world). The idea of the hegemony of neoliberalism adds content to the notions of structural power discussed in the previous section of this chapter.

Gramscian international political economy offers a persuasive critique of mainstream theorists of globalization and regimes; at the same

time, and less persuasively, there is a tendency for this work to fall
back into either an undifferentiated anti-Americanism or into a conspiracy theory in which the hegemony of neoliberalism is activated via
backroom deals. Further, the hegemony of neoliberal ideas can be
exaggerated, and often is. At least two, and perhaps three, of the
major advanced industrial countries, the G7, are either opposed to or
have serious reservations about neoliberal precepts (France, Germany
and Japan), and it remains open to doubt whether the European Union
will evolve in a neoliberal direction. As hegemonies go, neoliberalism
rests on a rather thin base – it is only in the US, the UK and the other
Anglo-Saxon democracies that opposition to neoliberalism has been
thoroughly marginalized. Writers such as Giovanni Arrighi and his
colleagues describe 'anti-systemic movements' as guerrilla-style forces
on the edges of the world economy – but this hardly presents an
accurate description of the French Government, wish-fulfillment
aside (Arrighi *et al.*, 1989).

Conclusion

In this chapter three different accounts of the development of global
forces have been offered – as will be apparent, they sometimes agree on
particular facts, if not on interpretation; the reader will have to form
his or her own view as to the value of these positions, hopefully on the
basis of an examination of some of the reading set out below. In the
final chapters of this book issues of economic globalization will be
addressed again, this time in a wider context, but before that, Chapter
10 will examine one area where the contest between neoliberal ideas
and their critics has been particularly fierce – the area of North–South
relations, and the debates over the place of the non-Western world in
the modern international system.

Further Reading

General texts on international political economy specified in the
Further Reading for Chapter 8 are also relevant here. The 'heterodox'
Journal *Review of International Political Economy* is an excellent
source of material on the different perspectives set out in this chapter;
Volume 1, 1994, contains a number of state-of-the-art papers under
the heading 'The Nature of International Political Economy' which

provide a good entry into the issues involved. Particularly instructive/ entertaining is the 'debate' between Stephen Krasner, 'International Political Economy: Abiding Discord' and Susan Strange, 'Wake up Krasner! The World *Has* Changed' (1994). Robert Gilpin, *The Challenge of Global Capitalism: The World Economy in the 21st Century* (2000) presents a wide-ranging, more orthodox, but by no means uncritical, account of the forces and ideas discussed in this chapter and offers another way into this material.

David Held *et al.*, *Global Transformations* (1999) and *The Global Transformations Reader* (2000) are key texts on globalization, as is Jan Aart Scholte, *Globalization* (2000). Earlier valuable works from a variety of positions include; Anthony McGrew *et al.*, *Global Politics: Globalization and the Nation State* (1992): Christopher Chase-Dunn, *Global Formation: Structures of the World Economy* (1989); P. Dicken, *Global Shift: The Internationalization of Economic Activity* (1992); Paul Kennedy, *Preparing for the Twenty-first Century* (1993); Kenichi Ohmae, *The Borderless World* (1990) and Michael Veseth, *Selling Globalization: The Myth of the Global Economy* (1998). Paul Hirst and Grahame Thompson, *Globalization in Question: The International Economy and the Possibilities of Governance* (1999) is a thoroughly researched and compellingly argued rebuttal of, at least, extreme versions of the thesis. The relationship between liberalism and globalization is explored in the *Millennium* special issue, 'The Globalization of Liberalism' (1995). Finally on globalization in general two characteristic papers by the late Susan Strange cover a great deal of the debate – the Review Essay 'Globaloney' (1998a) expresses one point of view, but the posthumous 'The Westfailure System' (1999) shows the reverse of the medal.

Specifically on the multinational corporation, Ohmae, *The Borderless World* (1990) and Robert Reich, *The Work of Nations* (1992) promote globalist accounts of the MNC, as does Richard Barnet and John Cavanagh, *Global Dreams: Imperial Corporations and the New World Order* (1994). More conventional accounts of MNCs would include Raymond Vernon, *Sovereignty at Bay* (1971); see also the *Millennium* special issue 'Sovereignty at Bay, 20 Years After' (1991); and Robert Gilpin, *US Power and the Multinational Corporation* (1975). The approach adopted here relies heavily on John Stopford and Susan Strange, *Rival States, Rival Firms: Competition for World Market Shares* (1991) – see also Strange, 'States, Firms and Diplomacy' (1992); and Louis Turner and Michael Hodges, *Global Shakeout* (1992). A valuable study of the state in the age of multinational economic actors is Philip Cerny, *The Changing Architecture of Politics* (1990).

On regimes, two collections are very important: Stephen D. Krasner (ed.), *International Regimes* (1983); and Volker Rittberger (ed.), *Regime Theory and International Relations* (1993). Apart from being more recent, the Rittberger collection involves European as well as American scholars – but Krasner has many classic papers and is still relevant. Also very valuable is the survey article Marc A. Levy, Oran R. Young and Michael Zürn, 'The Study of International Regimes' (1995). The 'European' approach to regimes is well represented by Andreas Hasenclever, Peter Mayer and Volker Rittberger *Theories of International Regimes* (1997) and the same authors' 'Integrating Theories of International Regimes' (2000). On post-war regimes and 'hegemonic stability' theory, J. G. Ruggie, 'International Regimes, Transactions and Change: Embedded Liberalism in the Postwar Economic Order' (1982); Robert O. Keohane, *After Hegemony* (1984); and *idem*, 'The Theory of Hegemonic Stability and Changes in International Economic Regimes, 1967–1977' (1980, 1989) are crucial. Further on hegemonic stability see two valuable overviews of the debate, David Lake, 'Leadership, Hegemony and the International Economy: Naked Emperor or Tattered Monarch with Potential' (1993); and Jarrod Wiener, 'Hegemonic Leadership: Naked Emperor or the Worship of False Gods' (1995). Paul Kennedy, *The Rise and Fall of the Great Powers* (1988) is a classic of 'declinism', while a robust rebuttal of the thesis is offered by Joseph S. Nye, *Bound to Lead: The Changing Nature of American Power* (1990) and, predictably, Susan Strange, 'The Persistent Myth of Lost Hegemony' (1987); see also Strange's final book *Mad Money* (1998b). G John Ikenberry, 'Constitutional Politics in International Relations' (1998), 'Institutions, Strategic Restraint and the Persistence of American Post-War Order' (1998/ 1999), makes many of the same points as conventional US regime theorists, but without buying into some of intellectual baggage carried by the latter.

The neo-Gramscian approach to IPE is well represented in the *Review of International Political Economy*. Texts taking this broad approach include Gill and Law (1988). The leading neo-Gramscian theorist is Robert W. Cox; see his *Production power and World Order: Social Forces in the Making of History* (1987) and his collected papers (with Timothy Sinclair) *Approaches to World Order* (1996). Other important studies include Kees Van der Pijl, *Transnational Classes and International Relations* (1998): Ronen Palan and Jason Abbott, *State Strategies in the Global Political Economy* (1996).

10

The View from the South

Introduction

The idea that there are specifically 'developing' countries with different needs from others is one that has appeared a number of times in this book, raising again the question whether different kinds of states generate different kinds of international relations. Is International Relations theory to be seen as universal in its findings or as working differently for different parts of the world – could there be, a 'view from the South' (leaving aside for a moment questions of terminology)? International Relations has been described as an 'American social science' (Hoffmann 1977), and on a simple headcount it is certainly true that most scholars of International Relations are American or work in the United States. However, it would be more precise to broaden the point; characteristically, the dominant ideas about international relations have always tended to originate in the rich and powerful parts of the world rather than in poorer, weaker areas. Does this matter? There are some 180-plus states in the world today, and yet the vast majority of scholars in International Relations work in fewer than ten of them, all comparatively rich, and all, except Japan and Korea, with majority populations of European origin. Scholars from elsewhere are generally trained in – and use textbooks written in – these countries. Again, does this matter?

There are two ways of thinking it might. The 'weak' thesis simply suggests that because international thought tends to be produced in rich and powerful countries, it tends to concentrate on the problems and interests of rich and powerful countries, neglecting those of poor and weak countries. On this account, there is no suggestion that different *kinds* of ideas are required to understand the problems of poor and weak countries; rather, the thinking is that the same ideas will work for them, if suitably adapted. The alternative, 'strong', thesis is that different ideas *are* required; it is not simply that dominant discourses in International Relations are applied to the problems of the rich and powerful – rather these discourses directly reflect the interests of the latter group, and cannot simply be adapted for use by the poor and weak. The poor and weak require new ideas, a discourse of their own to counter the dominant discourse.

Both 'weak' and 'strong' theses will be elaborated below, but the strong thesis is obviously the more challenging of the two and requires a few more preliminary comments. The context in which it is characteristically employed is to suggest that one group of states in the world is *qualitatively* different from another. The terminology here is problematic. The basic contrast sets on the one side the group of advanced, industrial, relatively wealthy states (conventionally the members of the OECD), and on the other side the '*South*' or the '*Less Developed (or Underdeveloped) Countries*' or the '*Third World*'. Each of these terms poses problems.

The '*Third World*' is a term that originated in France, and by analogy with the Third Estate of the French Revolution. Then, the First Estate were the clergy, the Second Estate the nobility, and the Third Estate the people; the First and Second Worlds were usually taken to be West and East in the Cold War and the Third World the Non-Aligned Movement (NAM), ex-colonies who refused to take sides in that ideological struggle. This once had a sort of plausibility, but while the NAM still exists it is as a broader pressure group, and with the end of the Cold War there is a good case for thinking that the term 'Third World' has lost its resonance.

'Less Developed (or Underdeveloped) Country' (LDC) catches a certain feature of the group of states we are attempting here to describe, namely that, on the whole, they are the poorer members of the United Nations, the countries whose per capita GDPs are markedly lower than those of the advanced industrial, OECD world. However, a categorization based solely on wealth presents problems. On the one hand, the actual *circumstances* of 'LDCs' vary dramatically; thus, India is a poor country, but has a very large and strong industrial sector, whereas most sub-Saharan African countries are poor and dominated by subsistence farming, and some Latin American countries combine great poverty with much high-technology industry. On the other hand, an emphasis on development makes of the category a group of those states who are not making progress, a club for losers, to put the matter unkindly. Apart from being patronizing this is not how the states themselves see things – thus Newly Industrializing Countries (NICs) such as Singapore still identify somewhat with the group even though they are wealthy enough to join the OECD, and the same might be said of some very rich oil-exporting states.

All-in-all, the term '*South*' seems the most appropriate, because it carries the least ideological baggage. It happens to be the case that the majority of advanced industrial states are to be found in the temperate zones of the Northern hemisphere (Australia, New Zealand and the divided economy of South Africa being the obvious exceptions), which gives the term 'South' a certain geographical credibility as a description of the rest of the world. Of course, 'South' conveys nothing apart from location, but this is a positive advantage because it does not load the dice in advance. Thus we can say that most Southern states are ex-colonies who achieved independence in the post-1945 period, most are composed of populations of non-European origin and culture, and most are poor relative to the Northern industrial countries, and although each component of this definition can be contradicted in particular cases the fact that the word we are using – South – does not itself contain any part of the definition allows us a degree of latitude. If what we are looking for is a way of suggesting that, contrary to appearances, Christian Brazil, Muslim Tunisia, Hindu India, poor Bolivia, rich Singapore, European-settled Argentina, African Ghana and Asian China or Malaysia all have something in common for the purposes of International Relations theory, then their 'Southern-ness' seems the most plausible contender to fit the bill.

What then might a 'Southern' view of international relations look like? The most likely contender for such a view has been the 'structuralist' or 'centre-periphery' account of international relations. The next section of this chapter will examine this perspective. We will then turn to one of the spin-offs of structuralism, the demand for a New International Economic Order (NIEO) that was made in the 1970s – a demand which also drew on other apparently distinctive 'Southern' notions of politics. The final sections will examine the changes of the 1980s and 1990s – including the impact of neoliberalism on the South, the demand for 'good governance', and the emergence of 'anti-systemic' movements.

Structuralism

Although the term itself has many meanings in social theory, in International Relations *structuralism* is a convenient term to refer to a cluster of theories which emerged in the 1950s, 1960s and 1970s whose aim was to give an account of the political and economic subordination of the South to the North; these theories – dependency theory, centre–periphery/core–periphery analysis, world-systems analysis – share the idea that North and South are in a *structural relationship* one to another; that is that both areas are part of a structure that determines the pattern of relationships that emerges. Structuralism is a general theory of international relations in the sense that it purports to explain how the world as a whole works, but it is also a 'Southern' theory in two senses; uniquely among modern theories of International Relations it actually originated in the South, and it is explicitly oriented towards the problems and interests of the South, designed to solve those problems and serve those interests. It is because of this 'Southern-ness' that structuralism has maintained its appeal over past decades, in spite of serious intellectual shortcomings.

A key figure in the development of structuralist ideas was the Argentinean economist Raúl Prebisch, a guiding light of the UN's Economic Commission for Latin America (ECLA) in the 1950s, even though his own position was rather less radical than that of later structuralists. Prebisch was influenced by Marxist–Leninist ideas on political economy, but rejected the assumption, common to Marx, Lenin and orthodox Communist parties in Latin America, that the effects of imperialism would be to produce capitalist industrialization in the South; in this he was influenced by the revisionist Marxist political economist Paul Baran, who argued, in *The Political Economy of Growth*, that monopoly capitalism in the mid-twentieth century was no longer performing a progressive role – instead, the industrialization of the rest of the world was being held back in the interest of maintaining monopoly profits in the centres of capitalism (Baran 1957). Prebisch's innovation was to identify the mechanism by which the capitalist centres held back the periphery. On his account, it was via the pattern of specialization that so-called 'free trade' established in the world economy. This pattern involved the South in the production of primary products (food, raw materials) which are exchanged for the manufactured goods of the North. Why is this pattern undesirable? Because, Prebisch argues, there is a long-term, secular trend for the terms of trade to move against primary products – to put the point non-technically, over time, a given 'basket' of a typical primary product will buy fewer and fewer baskets of manufactured products. Where 'x' bushels of grain bought a tractor in 1950, in 2000 it will take '$x + y$' bushels to buy a tractor.

This is a fundamental challenge to liberal economic thinking, which assumes that all economies have a comparative advantage in the production of some product(s) and that for purposes of trade and the general welfare it does not matter what the product in question is – hence, in the example in Chapter 8, it makes good sense for the Windward Islands to specialize in bananas and import manufactured goods from abroad. Prebisch's point is that in order to continue to import the *same* value of manufactured goods the Windward Islands will have to continually *increase* the value of banana exports, which will be difficult because of competition from other banana-producing countries, and because the demand for bananas is limited in a way that the demand for manufactured goods is not. In manufacturing, new products are being developed all the time, new 'needs' are being produced via technological innovation and the power of marketing. In agriculture, productivity gains are likely to be less dramatic while there is a limit to the market for even so desirable a product as a banana. Countries that specialize in agricultural and other primary products will be continually running on the spot in order to preserve existing living standards, let alone improve upon them.

Before looking at the implications of this position, we might ask whether Prebisch's argument stands up to close analysis, or to the record over the last 50 years. The simple answer is that this is still hotly contested. Liberal economists on the whole deny that there is a trend of the sort that Prebisch identifies. Prices of commodities rise and fall in response to general and particular factors, and there is no clear trend; moreover, whereas a bushel of grain is much the same in 1950 as in 2000, a tractor may be a much better product at the later date, justifying a higher price. Keynesian and (some) Marxian economists tend to be more sympathetic to the general thesis. As we will see below, to some extent the argument has been overtaken by events, as industrial production has moved South – and, in any event, much primary production has always been 'Northern'. However, none of this really matters, because in political terms Prebisch has been wholly triumphant. Until very recently, virtually all Southern governments and informed Southern opinion has been convinced of the basic truth of his position – that the liberal international economic order is biased towards the interests of the North and that free trade is detrimental to Southern interests.

What are the policy implications of this position? In the 1950s ECLA thinking was statist and nationalist, and summed up by the policy of *Import Substitution Industrialization* (ISI). The thrust of this policy was to protect and develop local industries in order to allow local suppliers to meet local demand, importing capital goods and technology but as few manufactured products as possible. By the mid-1960s there was no sign that this policy was actually working, and a rather more radical approach emerged – key names here include André Gunder Frank, Fernando Cardoso, Thestonio dos Santos, and, later, drawing on African experiences to support the Latin Americans, Arghiri Emmanuel, Immanuel Wallerstein and Samir Amin.

The difference between these 'structuralist' writers and the proponents of ISI is the difference between reform and revolution. ISI was designed as a strategy to improve the standing of the South within the capitalist world economy; many supporters of ISI, including Prebisch, wanted to overthrow this system in the long run, but, as fairly orthodox Marxists, they believed this could not happen until the forces of production had been sufficiently developed, until, that is, 'the time was ripe'. Orthodox, Moscow-leaning communist parties in Latin America supported local capitalists – according to them, the bourgeois revolution had to take place before the socialist revolution could arrive. According to the structuralists, all parts of the world economy were already capitalist by virtue of producing for the world market, hence there was no need to wait for capitalism to develop before making the revolution. Consequently, they opposed official communism – except in Mao's China and Fidel Castro's Cuba – instead giving their allegiance to rural guerrilla movements. The aim was to break the chain of exploitation that bound together the metropolitan centres and peripheral satellites of the world-system; the world trading system works to transfer resources from the poor to the rich, from the South to the North, and there is no way this system can be reformed and made to work in the interests of the peoples of the South.

From a structuralist perspective the statism and nationalism of import substitution strategies works to conceal the true nature of the world political economy, which is not, ultimately, about states, but about *classes and relations of production*. Capitalists everywhere exploit workers everywhere. Southern capitalists are junior partners to their counterparts in the great Northern centre; in principle, the workers everywhere also have a common interest – although here things are muddied by the propensity for the Northern proletariat to enter into (junior) partnership with capital. Developing Lenin's rather limited idea of a labour aristocracy in the imperialist countries bought off by the profits of imperialism, and adopting the fashionable 1960s notion, associated in particular with Herbert Marcuse, of the 'one-dimensionality' of the Northern proletariat, structuralists tended to write off the Northern working class. In any event, the structuralist model of the world was, in principle, resolutely non-statist. Capitalists everywhere were the enemy.

The intellectual strength of the structuralist view lay for the most part in its account of the history of the system. Frank's classic *Capitalism and Underdevelopment in Latin America* (1971) was largely a set of case studies defending in detail the view that close contact with the world economy resulted in the 'underdevelopment' of Latin America, while temporary breakdowns of the system (for example, in the two world wars) provided the only examples of successful development. Wallerstein's thought-provoking essays and lectures rest on the monumental achievement of his multi-volume *The Modern World System* (1974/1980/1989), which provides an account of the emergence and development of the system since the sixteenth century. The strength of these studies lies in the way they outline in combination the 'political' and 'economic' dimension of the systems, unlike the more conventional historical accounts upon which International Relations and liberal political economy usually rely.

However, the political strength of structuralism rests on shakier foundations. As Warren has suggested, a mixture of 'romantic' anti-capitalism and nationalist mythology has been important here – although Warren was somewhat unfair in suggesting that the originators of the model shared these views (Warren 1980). The unorthodoxy of the Marxism of the structuralists is clear; structuralists place far too much emphasis on trade as opposed to production, and fail to grasp the achievement of capitalism in transforming the world by the development of the productive forces (hence the label 'romantic'). Moreover, although structuralism is in principle non-statist, it is easy to see how it could be turned into a defence of the interests of Southern states – after all, most of the dispossessed of the world live in the South, and, given the Northern worker's betrayal of the revolution, it is easy to see how an anti-capitalist struggle could turn into a North–South conflict. The anomalous figures here are the Southern capitalists and Southern elites more generally, and these groups have a clear interest in blaming outsiders for the failure of development in the South, skating over as quickly as possible the thought that they might be implicated in this failure. However, whether structuralism is supported for good or bad reasons tells us nothing about the *merits* of its account of the world. But before such an assessment is made, an account of the most important development of the structuralist position would be helpful.

The South and the New International Economic Order

In the early 1970s a coalition of Southern states presented to the United Nations a programme for the reform of international economic relations, a programme that became known as the New International Economic Order (NIEO). The NIEO was incorporated in resolutions of the UN General Assembly, passed by very large majorities, and became the basic programme of Southern politics in the 1970s and much of the 1980s. Part of the inspiration for the NIEO came from structuralist theory, but the programme cannot simply be understood in these terms. In order to do so, it is necessary to go back a decade or so and observe the growth of a Southern *political* coalition in the 1950s and the 1960s; the question then becomes, why did this coalition adopt an *economic* programme as its trademark in the 1970s?

Most of the economic argument in the South took place in Latin America in the 1950s for the simple reason that Latin American decolonization took place in the early 1800s and these societies therefore had ample experience of what it was like to be an independent but subordinate state in the international system. In the rest of the South in the 1950s decolonization was taking place there and then – or should have been. Moreover, in Latin America, most governments were effectively committed to the West in the Cold War, as members of the American-led Organization of American States; however, as independent states emerged elsewhere, many of them wished to avoid taking sides as between East and West. The result of these two factors was the emergence in the 1950s of the politically-oriented *Non-Aligned Movement* (NAM). A key date here is the Bandung Conference of 1955, at which the agenda for Southern politics for a decade and a half was established.

The Bandung agenda centred around two basic issues: decolonization and the Cold War. The aim of the first was to push the old imperial powers into an ever-faster granting of independence to their colonies. By the mid-1960s it was clear that this agenda had been largely achieved. South Africa and Rhodesia/Zimbabwe remained under *apartheid* or in 'settler' hands, while war continued in the Portuguese colonial empire, but in the rest of the old empires formal independence had largely been achieved. Membership of the UN had more than doubled as the new states took their places, and the politics of the UN General Assembly was thereby transformed, with the old, built-in Western majority gone for good. However, these newly independent countries remained weak and (mostly) poor and uninfluential. The Cold War was also less salient by the mid-1960s. US–Soviet relations were beginning to become less fraught. Neither superpower was quite as inclined to push to sign up new allies as both had been a decade before; in the United States in particular, the Vietnam War was markedly lowering enthusiasm for new adventures in the South. In any event, the Cold War had always been a difficult issue for the South to handle; the NAM was widely seen as pro-Soviet in this contest, in spite of its title and this made it difficult for friends of the West to take part, which inevitably weakened the movement by lowering its coverage of the South. Such potentially powerful Southern states as Brazil, Argentina, Pakistan, Iran (under the Shah) and Saudi Arabia would not wish to join an anti-Western coalition.

All these factors pointed to a reorientation of the South in the 1960s. Decolonization and anti-racism remained on the agenda, and as symbolic political issues were joined by the issue of Israel and the Palestinians, especially after 1967. (In the 1950s Israel had good relations with most African states except, as it happens, with the anti-semitic *apartheid* regime in South Africa, but log-rolling in the South required that these contacts ended in order to bring the Arab world into the coalition.) However, the most important new issues were economic, and, in particular, the South's collective resistance to the North's dominance of the world's trading system. A key date here is 1964, which saw the formation of both the United Nations Conference on Trade and Development (UNCTAD) and the Group of 77. UNCTAD was a body set up by the UN to hold regular conferences on trade issues as they affected the South. Unlike the GATT or the other Bretton Woods institutions, UNCTAD works on a one-state, one-vote basis, thereby maximizing the key advantage held by the South in international forums – their sheer weight of number. The Group of 77 was the group of 'less-developed countries' that pressed for UNCTAD in the UN – which, given the pace of decolonization, more or less immediately had more than 77 members but still retained the name. Out of UNCTAD and the Group of 77 came the pressure to initiate the NIEO in the 1970s, and it was the voting power of the South in the UN General Assembly that ensured the programme would be adopted.

The programme itself had a number of components. In the area of *trade* it called for the establishment of a Generalized System of Preferences (GSP) for industrial goods from the South to increase the Southern share of manufacturing production to 25 per cent of the total by the year 2000, and an Integrated Programme for Commodities

(IPC) to level out fluctuations in the prices of commodities. *Aid* targets should be increased to 1 per cent of the industrial world's GDP, two thirds in the form of official aid. *Debt* should be cancelled and soft loans made available from the World Bank and its subsidiaries. In the area of *production* there should be extensive transfers of technology and research and development to the South; investment should be increased, but multinational corporations should be subject to a strict code of conduct – indeed the control of MNCs was a major plank in all Southern programmes at this time.

It should be noted that these are *reforms* of the liberal international economic order (LIEO), albeit very radical reforms. Purer structuralists criticized the NIEO, and later manifestations of NIEO policy such as the two Brandt reports, as failing to grasp the nettle of world revolution. This is clearly true – NIEO is a statist programme which looks to the continuation of a capitalist world economy. However, the reforms it envisaged are very radical, and share some elements of the structuralist position. In particular, the underlying assumption is that the failure to develop on the part of the South is to be attributed to the operation of the system and not, for example, to failings in the South itself. The obstacles to development are structural and must be removed. Moreover, this cannot be done with a free-trade, non-discriminatory system; scepticism about trade runs through NIEO thinking. A key theme of the NIEO is management, the need to replace reactive regulation with proactive management. The best way to see this is as a response to vulnerability. Southern states are vulnerable states who find it difficult to cope with the swings and roundabouts of the market, hence the desire for regulation. Those writers, such as Deepak Lal (1983), who stressed the fact that genuinely free markets would bring great benefits to the South in many areas, especially agriculture, were missing the point; although they might not have wanted to admit it in public, most Southern states would have refused a higher growth rate if the price had been greater political and social instability – as is usually the case.

In the 1970s the prospects for the NIEO looked moderately good. Although the major industrial powers had abstained or voted against the programme, there was evidence that within the North many of its ideas were popular – the Brandt reports of the early 1980s showed the sympathies of both social democrats and (some) Christian Democrats for the NIEO. In forums such as the UN Conference on the Law of the Sea (UNCLOS), the South acted as an effective negotiating bloc, while the success of the Organization of Petroleum Exporting Countries

(OPEC) in using producer power to push up revenues seemed a harbinger of future success. Moreover the Southern coalition at the UN seemed to be putting the North on the defensive generally, and combining quite effectively with the Soviet bloc who, although critical of the NIEO programme, were happy to join in the critique of the West – the Soviet line was that Southern countries should pull themselves up by their own bootstraps as the USSR had in the 1930s (presumably avoiding the millions of famine deaths that accompanied the process in Russia).

What went wrong? Three factors seem critical. In the first place, the South clearly overplayed its hand in the 1970s, mistaking votes in the UNGA and UNCTAD for the reality of power. What the South had was a degree of influence which had to be cashed out in terms of policy changes in the North; the South at times made such changes less likely by its conduct in the UN General Assembly. Such symbolic victories as the branding of Zionism as a racist ideology may have played an important role in cementing the Arab countries into the coalition but they were at best pyrrhic victories, actually making it much less likely that the US and its allies would take the demands of the South seriously. Some Southern countries did gain real power in the 1970s but when they did so, they used it for their own ends. The paradigm case here is Saudi Arabia which now has permanent directorships in the IMF and World Bank which it most definitely does not put at the disposal of the South.

In any event, the spirit of the age was against the South. Mention has been made of the Brandt reports signed by such social democratic and progressive conservative names as Edward Heath, Olaf Palme and Willy Brandt himself – true representatives of the post-1945 pattern of politics in Europe, and, to a lesser extent, the United States. But what is significant about Brandt I and II is that they were published in the early 1980s at exactly the point at which neoliberal ideas were coming to dominate Western agendas; the dominant political figures in Europe and North America were now Ronald Reagan and Margaret Thatcher and Thatcherism and Reaganomics set the tone for the politics of this era. This had two consequences, one psychological and one more specific. In psychological terms, the North was no longer interested in the views of, much less the approval of, the South. Whereas in the 1970s, US and British leaders were reluctant to see their position as too much at odds with the UN majority, the new leaders of these countries were much less concerned. A key moment here was the World Summit of Northern and Southern leaders at Cancun in Mexico in 1982. At this meeting, supposedly to promote understanding, the gulf between Thatcher, Reagan and the likes of Indira Ghandi, the prime minister of India at the time, was so wide that the experiment of holding such summits has yet to be repeated.

Of more immediate significance was the impact of Reaganomics on the South. President Reagan came into office in 1981 committed to increasing military spending, cutting taxes and balancing the budget. Since Congress would not allow him to cut welfare programmes dramatically, but did allow him his first two objectives, the third went by the board, and since the Federal Reserve Bank refused to inflate the currency beyond what it was allowing already the result was a substantial increase in US government borrowing. This in turn pulled in savings from the rest of the world and pushed real interest rates to unprecedentedly high levels. This had a serious effect on the economies of the advanced industrial world, but a disastrous effect on the South.

In the 1970s Southern countries with a reasonable credit rating had taken to engaging in extensive borrowing of foreign currency from the Northern commercial bank sector. At the time this had seemed a good idea to all concerned. Southern countries needed capital; bank loans seemed less likely to have political strings attached than capital from MNCs and since real interest rates were very low, sometimes negative, the banks were offering what looked like very good deals. The banks, on the other hand, had large amounts of money to lend – because of persistent international imbalances, and the piling up of surpluses in the 1970s, initially by the OPEC countries, later by Germany and Japan – and were glad to lend to foreign countries on the mistaken understanding that sovereign states could not go bankrupt. This, allegedly, is because they can always raise money through the tax system; possibly so, but domestic taxation does not raise foreign currency, and sovereign borrowers could certainly default on their debts, indeed had done so in the 1930s and earlier.

What in retrospect made this arrangement less than ideal for all concerned was that interest rates, although low in the 1970s, were variable and were renegotiated every three months. When they began to rise in the 1980s, a number of borrowers encountered difficulties in meeting the payments. Large Pacific borrowers such as South Korea renegotiated loans with Japanese banks, who were, in any event, accustomed to thinking in the long term. Latin American borrowers such as Mexico, Brazil and Argentina borrowed to repay interest on earlier loans, and, because of the number of banks concerned, got away with this dubious tactic until the crisis broke in mid-1982 with the suspension of payment of interest by Mexico on its foreign debt. The debt crisis that followed was a severe shock to the Western banking system, but a disaster for the South. For most of the rest of the decade the energies of most of the leading Southern countries and of bodies such as the World Bank and the IMF were devoted to trying to 'solve' the crisis – although what would count as a solution was clearly a matter for dispute. The argument over the NIEO was lost in the process – but, in any event, there were other factors that made this debate seem redundant.

The End of the 'Third World'?

The nature of these latter factors have been described in Chapter 9 from another perspective as the impact of the globalization of the world economy. A few basic points will make clear the impact of these changes. In classic Southern thinking from Prebisch onwards, the South is seen as a source of primary products for the world economy, and this is deemed a source of problems; however, over the past 20 years the South, or at least *parts of the South*, have become major centres for manufacturing production, easily reaching the NIEO targets in this respect without much assistance from the Northern states – indeed, the expansion in the South has been to an extent at the expense of jobs in the North. The significance of this can be underlined by examining classic writings of structuralists on industrialization in the South, where the possibility of such shifts are simply ruled out. Some have attempted to undermine the significance of these moves by, for example, describing Southern industrialization as *dependent* development – but without explaining adequately what *independent* development would look like.

Again, 20 years ago the MNC was regarded as an enemy of Southern development, exploiting local raw materials or cheap labour and expatriating profits; thus, in order to to avoid allowing the giant oil companies to share in the profits from exploiting its newly-viable oilfields, Mexico borrowed from the banks to finance this development – forgetting that banks have to be paid whether the investments they finance are profitable or not, while MNCs actually share the risks associated with new ventures of this kind. In any event, while MNCs continue to exploit their strengths, advanced production techniques have limited the amounts of raw materials used in production processes, and cut the proportion of the value of products which represent labour costs to the bone. Nowadays, manufacturing MNCs are concerned to find political stability, trained workers and access to global markets before they will invest or franchise, and profits that are not invested in R & D will be wasted. Today, in other words, Southern countries have to engage in the same kind of triangular diplomacy that is characteristic of Northern countries – albeit with slightly, but not greatly, different bargaining power. *Some* Southern countries have done very well out of this; others have been altogether ignored by the giant corporations.

Clearly, one of the features of the last 20 years has been stratification *within* the South. Some countries have done very well, such as the NICs of the Pacific Rim, and, to a lesser extent, Latin America, while others have done very badly, particularly in sub-Saharan Africa. Still others have experienced some success, but from a very low base, and mixed with the continuation of extremes of poverty, as is the case in India and the Philippines. China is rapidly becoming one of the world's leading industrial powers, while Singapore is richer than many Northern industrial countries. Meanwhile, living standards are actually falling in Bangladesh and Pakistan. There is no longer a characteristic Southern economy – hence the rhetoric about the 'end of the Third World' alluded to in the heading of this section, which dates back to the 1980s (Harris 1986).

It should be apparent that what is being suggested here is not that all is well in the South and that oppression and injustice are coming to an end. This is obviously not the case; poverty, malnutrition and hunger remain real problems, perhaps of increasing significance, and, even in those areas where industrialization is taking off, exploitation is rife. There is no difficulty finding examples of workers (often young women) living on starvation wages while assembling luxury goods for consumers in the advanced industrial world. High-pollution industries abound and in many cases these industries have been deliberately exported from the advanced industrial world. The point is that this exploitation is rather different in kind from the exploitation described and anticipated by the structuralists 30 years ago. Then the assumption was that the South would be pushed down as a concomitant to the North continuing to rise – the world economy was described as a zero-sum game in which the 'winnings' of the North matched the 'losses' of the South. Now, things look rather different. Certainly the North has continued to grow (albeit unevenly) and develop new products and industries, but the South has also experienced (equally uneven) growth. Contrary to expectations capital has moved to (some) Southern

countries. Moreover, real living standards, measured by such indicators as life-expectancy at birth as well as by GDP growth have, in
general, improved; average life expectancy in the South increased by 17
years between 1960 and the mid-1990s, though remaining 10 years or
more below that of the North (Scholte 2000: 213).

There are a number of ways in which this could be read. On the one
hand, it could be seen as a vindication of the structuralist logic of, for
example, Immanuel Wallerstein's world-systems analysis. Wallerstein
has always argued that the system needs cores, peripheries and semi-
peripheries, the latter forming a kind of 'middle-class' status acting as a
safety valve to keep the system relatively stable. From this perspective,
the structure chose countries such as Singapore and the other Pacific
Rim NICs in order to preserve its stability, and these countries have
simply risen at the expense of the rest of the South. There has been no
progress over the last generation – indeed Wallerstein contends that
progress is a Victorian illusion which social scientists must eliminate
from their thinking if they wish to understand the way the system
works (Wallerstein 1991b). The problem with this approach is clear;
even if it is possible to get past the mechanistic way of thinking that
sees the structure *choosing* some countries to play particular roles, still,
at the end of the day, this is a *post hoc* argument. Structuralists did not
predict that current trends would take place before the event; instead
the nature of the argument, its holism, means that *any* set of events can
be incorporated one way or another, however implausible the incor-
poration may be.

One alternative reading would be to reinstate some thinking about
developing countries common to both liberal and orthodox Marxist
writings in the 1950s and earlier. On this account, there is a natural
tendency for the capitalist mode of production (or, if you prefer, 'free
enterprise') to spread throughout the world and the basic obstacle to
this spread is not to be found in the 'world-system' but rather in the
policies adopted locally. Capitalists wish to 'exploit' the world via
industrialization and development – although they do not express
their intentions in such a manner – if they are allowed to and they
will do so unless prevented by local circumstances. Thus, if we wish to
explain why Australia has experienced faster growth and higher levels
of industrialization than Argentina, we should look not to the structural position – the same for both through much of this century – but
rather to local politics and policies. In Argentina in the crucial years
early in the century, agricultural interests were able to prevent protection of local industry and keep markets open for cheap manufactures

from abroad in the interests of low wages for agricultural workers, while in Australia democratic elections produced governments that protected local industry from foreign competition.

On this account the key to understanding recent changes in the South is that policy matters. If we look at the history of the last quarter century in the South, it has been those countries who have adopted appropriate policies that have reaped the reward of foreign investment, and those who have been unable to develop a coherent policy who have suffered. The triangular diplomacy described in Chapter 9 works here as elsewhere, and produces winners and losers as it does in Europe and North America. However, getting the policy right in this context does *not* mean simply adopting free market, liberal economic policies, as some more simplistic commentators have suggested, and as the neo-liberal proponents of the 'Washington Consensus' for some time in the 1980s and early 1990s made part of the conditions for assistance laid down by the IMF and the World Bank. Instead it has usually involved quite extensive state intervention in free markets in order to shape development in the right direction, and it has often, as the Australian example mentioned above suggests, involved overtly protectionist, nationalist, policies. Virtually none of the existing advanced industrial countries industrialized without protection, and it is unlikely that any state is going to achieve this feat in the future.

If policy matters, then the ability to make policy effectively becomes crucial. Over the last two decades a great deal of thinking about development has focused on forms of government in the South. On the whole, post-colonial governments in the South have been authoritarian and not respectful of human rights, and this has now become an international issue, with the rise in significance of the notion of 'good governance' to which we now turn.

Good Governance, the 'Standards of Civilization' and Quasi-States

One of the features of 'North–South' politics over the last decade has been the rise of linkage between assistance to Southern states and the issue of 'good governance'. The IMF has routinely required of recipients of its (rather limited) largesse that they adopt not just particular economic policies, but also political reforms – this has been part of the Washington Consensus referred to above, the new received wisdom on development issues that the Fund and the Bank promoted in the 1980s and early 1990s. Similarly, the Commonwealth now makes it a condition of assistance that its members have 'democratic' forms of government and protect human rights. In some respects this is a remarkable development – for most of the post-1945 era such demands would have been thought of as unacceptably neo-imperialist in character. The fact that many Southern states nowadays routinely come under this kind of pressure is to be attributed to a number of factors. The end of the Cold War has meant that the West no longer needs to sign up corrupt Southern elites in the struggle against communism – and such elites have no alternative superpower to turn to if the West make unwelcome demands. More generally, the recovery of Western self-confidence that was partly a result of the end of the Cold War, partly a matter of wider changes in attitude early in the 1980s, and the distraction in Southern politics caused by the debt crisis, has led to a far more interventionist Western attitude to the South – with quite striking results. Throughout Latin America military regimes have been replaced by at least quasi-democratic systems – after the Mexican elections of 2000, Castro's Cuba is the last bastion of non-democratic rule in Latin America – and in Africa numerous one-party states have been overthrown, or have overthrown themselves under pressure from the outside. Many non-democratic states remain, of course, protected either by their importance to the West as markets, or by their lack of need for Western approval – as in China and the authoritarian capitalist regimes of the Pacific Rim.

This change is remarkable, but it is definitely not unprecedented – indeed, in some respects, it represents a return to past patterns of international relations, patterns thought long dead and buried. In the nineteenth century, when the European states-system was dominant, it promulgated a set of ideas about government which it applied to non-European states which wished to be part of the system, and called them the 'Standards of Civilization'. These standards involved features such as the rule of law and protection of property and individual life, and societies whose legal codes either did not exist or were deemed inadequate were forced to allow Europeans to be subject to their own jurisdiction and courts. Thus in Japan, where Samurai warriors had the 'right' to murder commoners more or less at will, the authorities were forced in blatantly unequal treaties ('Capitulations') to allow Europeans charged with offences, and Japanese charged with offences against Europeans, to be tried in special, European courts – similar arrangements pertained in China and other Asian countries.

These treaties were, of course regarded as blatantly unfair – as indeed they were, although what Japanese and Chinese beneficiaries of fair legal systems thought about the matter might be rather more nuanced than the views of elites – and as the countries concerned improved their procedures they were lifted, in the 1890s in the case of Japan, not until the 1930s in the case of China. However, until the post-1945 period it remained the case that potential members of the international system were expected to possess certain kinds of abilities, and the expectation was that colonies would not achieve independence until they did. Robert Jackson has described the situation well in his seminal *Quasi-States* (1990). Up until the 1940s the assumption was that sovereignty had two dimensions that had to be in place for a state to be recognized as a member in good standing of the international community – positive and negative sovereignty.

Negative sovereignty means simply the right to be left alone to govern one's own affairs. It is an international legal status recognized by, for example, membership of the United Nations, whose Charter expressly forbids interference in matters of domestic jurisdiction (Article 2(7)) – although this might be qualified by other articles concerning human rights, threats to international peace and so on. Jackson's point is that in the past, negatively sovereign states were assumed to possess *positive* sovereignty – the ability actually to govern one's territory in an orderly and lawful manner. Positive sovereignty is about the ability to exercise effective control over a territory and to conceive of and execute projects. It is not a matter of the external power of the state – it is quite possible for a state to have little real power in the world but to be positively sovereign – but of its internal power and the uses to which it can be put. Not only did negative sovereignty *assume* positive sovereignty, it was also *justified* by it – the reason states were deemed to have a right not to be interfered with was because they were deemed to have the capacity to govern themselves. States would not be recognized by the international community unless they were deemed to have this capacity.

Jackson's thesis is that since 1945 a great deal of this has gone by the board. Whereas the early beneficiaries of decolonization clearly were positively as well as negatively sovereign – India, for example, had, and still has, a reasonable effective civil administration – a head of steam built up to extend decolonization to political entities that could only be 'quasi-states' rather than the real thing. The norm of national self-determination came to override the requirement that the 'nation' in question had the actual capacity to govern itself. The process was particularly pernicious in its effects in Africa. In contrast to Asia, where most of the newly decolonized states had prior histories to fall

back upon and combine with the legacy of European colonial administration, most of the new African states had no such inheritance, being
largely the product of lines on a map drawn for the convenience of
European imperialists. Even in those rare cases where a state only
incorporated one ethnic group – Somalia is the only obvious example
– the lack of any kind of state tradition or clear borders doomed the
new state to a contest for power between competing clans.

To put the matter in sociological terms, many new states – probably
most new states in Africa – do not correspond to *social facts*, they
do not incorporate distinct groups, they are forced to engage in nation-
building as well as in state-building. This is very difficult, especially
for societies which are not rich enough to buy off all the potential
competing groups – hence the frequent breakdowns of such societies,
and hence also, fairly obviously the unwillingness of MNCs to invest
in quasi-states. No profit-seeking corporation is likely to invest in
societies where the safety of its workers cannot be guaranteed or
where the levels of pay-off officials will expect will eat into profits –
unless, of course, the corporation in question is obliged to operate in a
particular country because of its geology; as was noted in Chapter
9, oil companies go where the oil is – and they are often forced to
make unpleasant deals, or delve into local politics, or both, to do so.
By the same token, newer notions of self-rule, and institutions such
as producer cooperatives, will not be established in conditions of
general chaos.

Possibly the emergence of 'good governance' as a slogan suggests
that the era in which the norm of self- determination outweighed other
norms is coming to a close. Events in Somalia and Rwanda – as well as
closer to the North in Bosnia and Kosovo – in the 1990s suggest that
the international community may be in the process of developing a
doctrine of 'humanitarian intervention' which might change the fate of
many quasi-states. However, as against this possibility, the international community is also more sensitive to charges of cultural imperialism than it has been in the past, and societies with a different heritage
from the West – Muslim, Confucian, increasingly Hindu as well – are
beginning to challenge the right of the international community to
interfere in their affairs in the name of 'universal' values. A return of
the notion of standards of civilization will not take place without a
contest over the meaning of civilization and the Victorian view that
Europeans are in a position to referee this contest will no longer stand.
These are matters that will be returned to in the final chapter of this
book.

Conclusion: The International Politics of the New South

As we move into the twenty-first century there is evidence that some of the patterns of politics described above are being disrupted. The Washington Consensus is not as dominant in the IMF or the World Bank as it once was, and new approaches to poverty are emerging. Some Southern states are becoming effective players within bodies such as the WTO, while at the other end of the scale, significant 'anti-systemic' movements have begun to make their mark.

The Washington Consensus – broadly, the view that what developing countries needed was 'good governance', the end of price controls, low inflation, dramatic cuts in government spending, and an open attitude to the world economy – governed IMF conditionality and World Bank advice for much of the 1990s, but from the middle of that decade onwards many economists at those institutions – including Joseph Stiglitz, until 1999 Chief Economist at the World Bank, and Ravi Kanbur, until his resignation in 2000 the Editor-to-be of the *World Development Report 2000* – began to express doubts both about these policies, and about their actual effects on the citizens of the countries concerned. The basic point is that there were very few 'success stories' – examples of countries that had taken the advice from Washington to heart and improved their conditions thereby – and plenty of examples of increased suffering for ordinary people. Cuts in government spending were usually targeted on the poor, and the ending of price controls on basic foodstuffs added to the misery. Moreover, there were contradictions at the centre of the policy; it is one thing to advise a particular country to run a balance of payments surplus, but if the same advice is going to *all* developing countries then there had better be developed countries eager and willing to run a deficit to allow the former to expand. Again, part of the Consensus involved the encouragement of democratic forms of government, but democratically-elected leaders are likely to be less willing to lower the living standards of their constituents than unrepresentative elites – it is noteworthy that one of the few actual success stories for the neoliberal consensus can be found in Pinochet's Chile in the 1970s and 1980s, where democratic governance and a concern for human rights were spectacularly absent.

These points have been made by critics of neoliberalism throughout the period, but by the end of the 1990s they were being heard and to an extent acted upon in Washington itself – incidentally it should be noted that 'Washington' is shorthand here for the international agencies based in that city and not for the US Government, some elements of which have always been sceptical about the consensus. These criticism to some extent fit in with a wider critique of the very notion of 'development' that have been developed in the South, and in parts of the academy in the North. The governing assumption not just of neo-liberalism but of older notions of liberalism and of Marxism and socialism more generally, has been that development involves the spread of a money economy, high levels of growth of GDP, the growing of cash crops and the emergence of industry. Leaving aside for later consideration the thought that there might be environmental limits to this kind of growth, it is by no means clear that this economistic conception of development actually meets human needs. A great deal of new thinking on the eradication of poverty stresses instead self-management and self-reliance, the direct meeting of real needs rather than the growth of money income, and the importance of producer cooperatives. If a developed society is taken to be a society which has a degree of control over its environment, in the wide sense of that term, then strategies that stress markets and openness may be counter-productive. A number of 'anti-systemic' movements have developed along these lines, ranging from small-scale producer cooperatives in India, to the postmodern guerrilla movement based amongst the Chiapas in Mexico, with its anonymous, balaclava-helmeted leader SubComandante Marcos.

It is important not to be *too* impressed by these straws in the wind. In favour of traditional notions of development it can be noted that, as a broad generalization, the kind of indicators of human well-being set out in the UNDP *Human Development Report* are quite closely related to GDP – unsurprisingly, people tend to live longer healthier lives in 'rich' countries than they do in 'poor' countries. States such as India are only too well aware that feeding and clothing their growing populations require of them that they promote a vibrant industrial sector and as technically advanced an agriculture as they can sustain. The governments of India and other large Southern countries may not be enamoured of neoliberalism, but they have become quite effective players within organizations such as the WTO. It is noteworthy that an Indian delegate accused the demonstrators in Seattle in November 1999 of being in league with President Clinton to subvert the possibility of a trade deal that would open American markets to Southern goods! This was not, one suspects, altogether seriously meant, but it does underline the point that the common vision of the powerlessness of

Southern states within bodies such as the WTO owes as much to a patronizing attitude on the part of Western radicals as it does to the reality of those organizations. The US, the EU and Japan may be the main players in the WTO – along with the great corporations – but leading Southern states still have the capacity to make their voices heard, and are not ready to turn their backs on such bodies.

Further Reading

Once again, all of the textbooks and readers on international political economy listed at the end of Chapter 8 have extensive coverage of the political economy of the South. The annual *World Development Report* of the World Bank has been a major source of information on Southern economies, and of informed commentaries; nowadays the *Human Development Report* of the United Nations Development Programme is perhaps rather more useful. These documents, and the various *Annual Reports* of the International Monetary Fund are the best way of following official thinking in Washington, and the rise (and partial fall) of the 'Washington Consensus'.

Apart from the works by Frank and Wallerstein cited above, classic broadly 'structuralist' works would include Samir Amin, *Accumulation on a World Scale*, Vols I and II (1974), and *idem, Imperialism and Unequal Development* (1977); Fernando Cardoso and Enzo Faletto, *Dependency and Development in Latin America* (1979); Arghiri Emmanuel, *Unequal Exchange* (1972); Johan Galtung, 'A Structural Theory of Imperialism' (1971): Raúl Prebisch, *The Economic Development of Latin America and its Principal Problems* (1950); Walter Rodney, *How Europe Underdeveloped Africa* (1983); Immanuel Wallerstein, *Geopolitics and Geo-culture: Essays on the Changing World System* (1991a); and most recently André Gunder Frank and Barry Gills (eds), *The World System: Five Hundred Years or Five Thousand Years* (1993). See also 'Special Issue on Dependence and Dependency in the Global System', *International Organization* ed. James Caporaso (1978). Classic critiques of structuralism from the left include: Robert Brenner, 'The Origins of Capitalist Development' (1977); Ernesto Laclau, *Politics and Ideology in Marxist Theory* (1976); and Bill Warren, *Imperialism: Pioneer of Capitalism* (1980).

More orthodox development studies are represented by Ian M. D. Little, *Economic Development: Theory, Policy and International Relations* (1982). Powerful critics of structuralism from the position of neoclassical economics include Peter Bauer, *Equality, The Third World and Economic Delusion* (1981); and Deepak Lal, *The Poverty of 'Development Economics'* (1983). Stephen Krasner, *Structural Conflict: The Third World Against Global Liberalism* (1985) is an excellent work by a leading US International Relations theorist. On the 'debt crisis', see Miles Kaher (ed.), *The Political Economy of International Debt* (1986) and, for a different perspective, Susan George, *A Fate Worse than Debt* (1988).

The gap between 'structuralism' and new approaches to Southern poverty is partially bridged by works such as Immanuel Wallerstein, *Unthinking Social Science: The Limits of Nineteenth Century Paradigms* (1991b); and Caroline Thomas, *In Search of Security: The Third World in International Relations* (1987). Other works here would include Paul Ekins, *A New World Order: Grassroots Movements for Global Change* (1992); Amartya Sen, *Poverty and Famine* (1982); John Cavanagh, Daphne Wysham and Marcos Arruda, *Beyond Bretton Woods: Alternatives to the Global Economic Order* (1994); and Barry Gills *et al., Low Intensity Democracy: Political Power in the New World Order* (1993). Neil Harvey, *The Chiapas Rebellion* (1998) is the best account of that particular anti-systemic movement. Caroline Thomas and Peter Wilkin eds, *Globalization and the South* (1999) is a useful collection. The *Review of International Political Economy* is a useful source of heterodox work on Southern poverty.

The term 'Washington Consensus' was coined by John Williamson – 'What Washington Means by Policy Reform' (1990); for discussion, see Richard Higgott, 'Economic Globalization and Global Governance: Towards a Post Washington Consensus' (2000).

The evolution of offical thinking is traceable in quasi-official publications by the agencies, e.g. for the IMF, Jahangir Aziz and Robert F. Wescott, *Policy Complementarities and the Washington Consensus* (1997), and for the World Bank, Shahi Javed Burki and Guillermo E. Perry, *Beyond the Washington Consensus: Institutions Matter* (1998). Joseph Stiglitz has summarized his views in *More Instruments and Broader Goals: Moving Towards the Post-Washington Consensus* (1998).

G. C. Gong, *The Standard of 'Civilisation' in International Society* (1984) is the classic study of nineteenth-century theory and practice of the 'standards of civilization'. Robert Jackson, *Quasi-States: Sovereignty, International Relations and the Third World* (1990) is a modern classic.

Millennium has published a very valuable set of brief essays on the 'Battle for Seattle' at the WTO Conference in November 1999, with contributions from Steven Gill, Fred Halliday, Mary Kaldor and Jan Aart Scholte (2000). The WTO's web site <*http://www.wto.org*> is a useful source of information, and not to be confused with <*http://www.gatt.org*> which is a site run by opponents of the WTO, naughtily designed to look, at first glance, like the official site! The latter has links to the main anti-WTO organizations.

11

The Emerging Structure of International Politics in the Twenty-First Century

Introduction

The ending of the Cold War between 1988 and 1991 was an event of some significance in human history, and in international relations. As to the former, the fall of the Soviet Union has something important to say about the organization of social life, namely that the combination of some kind of market economy with some kind of representative democracy is the only effective way of running complex industrial and postindustrial societies. This should not be read as an endorsement of neoliberalism (which, unfortunately, is how the lessons of 1989 have sometimes been misunderstood in parts of East–Central Europe); rather, this combination leaves room for a great deal of variation in types of regime and in the level of planning that accompanies markets, from neoliberal systems, to welfare capitalism, traditional social democracy, the 'Third Way' and so on. But it does rule out some possibilities that have been taken very seriously in the past. Since the emergence of industrial society, the most persistent opponents of liberal capitalism from right and left have argued that it is both possible and desirable to replace the impersonal forces of the market by conscious human control. Even those who were repelled by the politics of the Soviet Union and the stupidities of Soviet central planning assumed that a better way of reaching the same goal could be devised. Part of this process would be the simultaneous replacement of 'bourgeois' democracy with a genuine people's democracy (as opposed to the fake version offered by 'really-existing socialism'). Recent experiences make it difficult to take either of these ideas seriously. The philosopher Richard Rorty has captured the significance of this with characteristic brio when he remarks that '[if] you still long for total revolution, for the Radical Other on a world historical scale, the events of 1989 show that you are out of luck' (Rorty 1998).

It seems quite likely that such a shift in political thinking will have some indirect influence on international relations, but a more obvious impact of these years on the international system has been the elimination of one of the two superpowers whose interactions had dominated most of the international politics of the previous half century. Russia is still a significant state with a Permanent Seat in the UN Security Council, and a large military force including an (ageing) nuclear arsenal, but it is no longer a direct competitor to US power in the way that it was for most of the twentieth-century. The purpose of this chapter is to tease out the implications of this shift in the distribution of power. This used to be called something like the 'emerging security architecture of the post-Cold War world', but, ten years after the fall of the Berlin Wall, this seems a little backward-looking. In the final chapter of this book the agenda of issues to be addressed will be much wider – including a wider definition of security – but here a fairly conventional account of international politics will be offered. The key question is what kind of international system is emerging, and to answer this some of the theories set out in earlier chapters will be employed and their approaches contrasted, beginning with the still-dominant neorealist model.

Neorealism, the Future and the Past

Given that, on a simple account of Waltz's rational choice approach to international relations it is axiomatic that states are concerned with self-preservation in a self-help system, that they are concerned with their position *vis-à-vis* other states ('relative gains') and that these concerns will lead them to attempt to form and/or preserve balances of power, explaining Soviet behaviour in the 1980s might seem to pose a problem, and cast doubts on the capacity of neorealism to offer much of a guide to the future. In a world in which the United States was, on some interpretations, actually attempting to enhance its power, or, at the very least, was not surrendering any positions, the leader of the USSR, Mikhail Gorbachov set out on a course which eventually involved giving up every key security achievement of the Soviet

Union since its foundation – the division of Germany, the Warsaw Pact, friendly governments in power in Eastern Europe, and, eventually, the continuation of Communist Party rule and the physical integrity of the Soviet Union itself. Of course, governments make mistakes and it is quite possible that had the Soviet leadership known in 1985 what we know now the course of events would have been very different. However, it must be remembered that the collapse took place, as it were, in slow motion; there were a number of points along the way at which the process could have been put in reverse, albeit at a high price. From a neorealist point of view this price would, surely, have been worth paying – virtually any price would have been worth paying to avoid the total collapse of the Soviet Empire. There are other anomalies in the 1980s – in particular the United States' unwillingness to cooperate in managing the system in the early years, and its unwillingness to exploit Soviet weakness in the later years, of the decade – but these are minor compared to Gorbachov's willingness to abandon empire for the sake of a new and better security relationship with the West.

In fact, Waltz and his followers have been unruffled by this charge. He is clear that he is not offering a theory of foreign policy. There is no assumption that states will always heed systemic imperatives – if they fail to do so they will suffer harm and experience loss, and since it is assumed that they do not want this to happen the presumption is that their conduct will adapt to the requirements of the system, but there is no guarantee that this will be possible. The distribution of power may be such that it simply is not possible to create a balance. William Wohlforth offers an interesting set of comments on this (1994/5). He makes two points, both pertinent; the first is that although neorealism is actually a rather 'weak' theory without a great deal of explanatory capacity, it survives largely because all the alternatives are even weaker, a sobering thought but not one to be lightly dismissed. More directly to the point, he suggests that the Waltzian emphasis on the balance of power is *not* actually required by neorealist assumptions, and that a model based on *hegemony* fits the facts of the case rather better. The United States has been the hegemonic power in the system since 1945, the Soviet Union was the challenger, and in the 1980s the challenge failed. Whereas, *ex hypothesi*, the hegemon will fight to preserve its hegemony, a challenger will not fight when its challenge is manifestly failing, hence the willingness of the Soviet Empire to allow itself to fade away. The interest of this argument is that it preserves the essence of neorealist thinking – the rational choice basis of state conduct – while abandoning what most had seen as an essential component of that thinking, the theory of the balance of power.

In any event, neorealists have not shut up shop after the end of the Cold War, and have quite clear thoughts on where the international system is going. The basic answer here, is that international relations in the future will be much as they were in the past. There is nothing essentially wrong with the neorealist model of state behaviour – the dynamics of international politics remain as they were. In an article published as early as 1990, that is before the collapse of the Soviet Union, albeit at a point when that collapse was clearly on the cards, John Mearsheimer set out the basic argument in an article entitled 'Back to the Future'. If we want to understand what the future structure of the international system is going to look like, we can get a rough idea by looking at the system as it operated in the past, before the emergence of the ideological contest between East and West, and before the emergence of the bipolar structure dominated by the two superpowers which has been a feature of the post-1945 era. The future will look much like the past – not the immediate past perhaps, but the past of the day before yesterday.

What does this mean in practice? In essence, a multipolar balance of power, but with the complication that in our age military 'power' is most importantly measured by the possession of nuclear weapons. Mearsheimer's most controversial stance is taken over the issue of nuclear proliferation. He regards it as highly likely – almost a forgone conclusion – that the major powers in the emerging balance will all wish to be nuclear powers; since these powers include Japan and Germany, this status would represent a potentially destabilizing break with one of the first principles of the old 'Cold War' order, which was that these two countries ought not to be nuclear armed. To avoid a situation in which these countries make a bid for nuclear weapon status in the face of international opposition, which, he believes, would be genuinely destabilizing, he suggests that they should actually be assisted to achieve this status by the existing nuclear powers as a conscious act of power management.

Mearsheimer assumes that it is more or less a matter of time before a new balance of power emerges, and similar thoughts have been expressed by Kenneth Waltz (1993). Indeed, Waltz is highly critical of US policy in the 1990s which he regards as being based on the wholly implausible proposition that it will be possible to maintain American dominance into the foreseeable future. This is a chimera; other countries are bound to try to balance US power, and the most sensible strategy for a status quo power such as the United States is to place no obstacles in their attempts to do this. Waltz is particularly critical of what he sees as American attempts to use their temporary dominance to attack the legitimacy of future rivals by, for example, promoting human rights in the People's Republic of China.

How is this position to be assessed? The underlying assumption of Mearsheimer's and Waltz's work is that states will act in such a way as to secure their survival in an anarchical society at minimum cost. In the case of the United States, under the new circumstances, this imperative dictates disengagement from European and Far Eastern affairs since, in the absence of a superpower enemy, it is no longer worthwhile for America to underwrite the security of its allies or become engaged in their conflicts. However, as Mearsheimer stresses, those allies may still feel threatened by the remnants of Soviet (now Russian) power, or by the United States, or, for that matter, by each other, and it follows therefore that they will wish to improve their capacity to protect themselves by re-alignment and by developing the most advanced weapon systems they can afford, which in the case of Japan and Germany means nuclear weapons. Neorealists are not, on the whole, much troubled by nuclear proliferation, and in this case the only real worry is not so much the effects of German and Japanese possession of nuclear weapons, but the instability likely while they are in the process of acquiring them – hence Mearsheimer's suggestion that they should be helped along the way.

Even in its own terms, this argument may be self-defeating. The assumption is that the US will be withdrawing from Europe and will therefore have to live with the consequences of this withdrawal, namely enhanced German power. However, it might be that one of the factors that will cause the United States to remain engaged in Europe – as it has over the last decade – is precisely that it does not want to have to live with these consequences. While it may be true that the US no longer needs to be 'in' Europe for Cold War reasons, it by no means follows that there are no other reasons for continued engagement.

But, in any event, this kind of reasoning rests upon the highly contestable assumption that systemic imperatives actually determine state outcomes. Is it actually the case that states work in this way – or, at least, that if they do not they will put themselves in harm's way and potentially suffer damage, conceivably severe damage? This is the neorealist position, but the events of the last few years do not seem to offer much support for it. United States foreign policy seems dominated by domestic political concerns; George Bush's main claim to re-election in 1992 rested on his assumed competence in foreign affairs. His defeat by Bill Clinton, a former state governor whose strategy was to stress the economy and downplay the importance of foreign policy, seemed to be sending a clear message to future American political leaders. The fact that, once his popularity began to decline, the victor in 1992 adopted a new strategy that stressed his international accomplishments does nothing to undermine this message. President Clinton became a foreign-policy-oriented president by default, because of the failure of his domestic programme. In the campaign for the presidency in 2000 neither candidate placed any stress on foreign policy issues.

A similarly anti-neorealist situation has emerged in Germany. Whatever imperative messages the international system is attempting to send to the German government, the general pacifism of the German people – and particularly their aversion to nuclear weapons – lays constraints on German leaders which are difficult to ignore. Even if German leaders wanted to turn the country into a nuclear power (and there is no evidence that they do) it is barely conceivable that they could carry through such a policy without destroying democratic structures in Germany. But, and this is the third point, why would Germany wish to take such a step? Germany already dominates the European Union via its industrial strength, and, especially, the financial power wielded by the *Bundesbank* and the influence of the latter in the new European Central Bank (ECB). The neorealist assumption that the only kind of power that matters in the last instance is military power is one of the reasons why neorealist thinking seems so often to be stuck in the past. The 'last instance' never – well, *hardly ever* – arises. One reason for thinking that we might not be about to go 'back to the future' is precisely that the global economy poses more of a constraint on state action now than it did pre-1914, and, equally, far more opportunities for states to exercise power in non-military forms.

Before moving on, it should be noted that there are ways of reading the contemporary state of power politics which remain true to the underlying methodological assumptions of neorealism but which abandon the focus on balances of power characteristic of Waltz and Mearsheimer. The work of William Wohlforth has been referred to above, and he has recently presented a very compelling counter-argument to Waltz's rejection of continued American hegemony (1999). Wohlforth's point is that US military superiority is now such that even quite moderate levels of investment in new technologies will make it very unlikely that any state or combination of states will be able to mount an effective challenge in the foreseeable future. Moreover, the potential challengers to US power – a revived Russia, and a German-led European Union, on the other side of the world, China, Japan – are all more afraid of each other than they are of the US, and for this reason are unlikely to be able to form effective coalitions directed against American power. The situation would only change if the US gave these countries good, specific, reasons to be afraid of its power, as opposed to the kind of generic opposition to hegemony touted by Waltz, and there is no reason to think this is going to happen.

The New Liberal Internationalism

If the US is likely to be dominant for the foreseeable future, what kind of world will emerge? One possibility was broached when, in the excitement generated by the end of the Cold War and the (apparently) successful rebuttal of Saddam Hussein's invasion of Kuwait, President George Bush announced the dawning of a New World Order. The reaction of most commentators was, perhaps predictably, somewhat jaundiced. 'The New World gives the Orders' was a characteristic jibe – and it did indeed seem that the New World Order was a slogan designed to give international legitimacy to US policy preferences. Moreover, when the outcome of the Gulf War proved to be much less conclusive than had, at first sight, seemed to be the case, it was a slogan that turned against its creator. After a year or two, or perhaps less, New World Order became a phrase that could only be used in a spirit of irony or bitterness, as in, for example, Bruce Springsteen's lyric: 'Hot soup in a campfire under the bridge, Shelter line stretching round the corner, Welcome to the New World Order, Families sleepin' in their cars in the South West, No jobs, no homes, no peace, no rest' (1995).

This political fate masked the fact that Bush and his advisers were actually offering a rather interesting and by no means entirely self-serving account of a possible future structure of the post-Cold War world. The essence of Bush's New World Order was to be: the sovereign state as the key unit of international relations; respect for the norms of non-aggression and non-intervention; support for international law and institutions, and, crucially, a willingness of the international community to act, forcefully if need be, in support of these positions. This is, in effect, the *liberal internationalist* position of the immediate post-First World War era, restated for the post-Cold War world, but, this time, with a promise that the leading world power, the United States, would not shirk its responsibilities. Unlike its failure to join the League after the First World War and its isolationism in the face of the dictators in the 1930s, this time the US would act – the war to reverse Iraq's aggression in the Gulf was intended as an illustration of this active internationalism, a demonstration that the disappointments of the inter-war years were not an inevitable outcome of these ideas.

Put another way, from a liberal internationalist perspective, in 1917–19 a set of essentially sound ideas were derailed by contingent factors. The unwillingness of Britain and France to display generosity in victory left Germany with a permanent sense of grievance; an inexperienced and short-sighted American political elite believed they could relieve the United States of the responsibilities of power by isolationism, and, most of all, the liberal constitutionalist ideology upon which the New World Order must rest was undermined by the disillusionments of war and the challenge of the Bolsheviks, and, later, Fascists and National Socialists. Now, in the 1990, things would be different. Liberal constitutionalism was resurgent and a wise American political elite, shaped by a half-century of conflict, realizing that isolationism is not a viable strategy, and willing to extend to the defeated regimes of Eastern Europe the sort of generosity not shown to Germany in 1919 would realize the promise of liberal internationalism. Such, at least, was the promise.

These ideas have been very heavily criticized from the Left as a cover for American imperialism, but it is worth noting that they have also been criticized from other points of the political compass, especially within the United States. Predictably enough, neoisolationist American conservatives rejected Bush's internationalism for much the same reasons that their spiritual grandfathers rejected Wilson's, and in this they were joined by traditional realists such as Robert Tucker and David Hendrikson, who applied strict 'national interest' criteria to American involvement in episodes such as the Gulf War (1992). Other opponents believed that Bush's internationalism was not 'liberal' enough. In 1919, a crucial element of Wilson's vision was that peace-loving states would be liberal-democratic. Bush, on the other hand, offered a New World Order in which all states of whatever political complexion would receive the protection of the norms of non-intervention and non-aggression – even if, as in the case of Kuwait, their internal political arrangements had been in no respect liberal. Reaganite 'liberals' who had been quite willing to countenance

US action in support of their friends – putative members of the 'Free World' – in Central America and the Caribbean, saw little reason to put US soldiers in harm's way on behalf of the Kuwaiti ruling house, whose stance had been anything but pro-American prior to August 1990.

These arguments very obviously recapitulate the debates of the 1930s, and the dilemmas of 'collective security' exposed in those years. One of the features of a collective security system is that it requires of its members that they set aside the usual considerations of state-interest, and adopt instead an impartial set of criteria for judging international acts. The fact that the Kuwaiti ruling family were despots – albeit relatively mild-mannered compared to the Iraqi leadership – or that they had previously acted contrary to United States interests – is neither here nor there; what matters is that they were victims of aggression and, as such, entitled to the support of the world community. Such a position loses contact with the more conventional international rule of thumb that suggests one should assist one's friends, and punish one's enemies.

In fact, in this particular case, the actions of the world community were overdetermined; not only did Saddam Hussein break the law, he also threatened the long-term security of the West's energy supplies, and was suspected, rightly as it turns out, of building up an arsenal of non-conventional weapons that would destabilize the region. Where the dilemmas of the New World Order are most clearly visible is in the aftermath of the war. The Coalition's refusal to overthrow Saddam Hussein was partly based on pragmatic considerations, but also reflected an unwillingness to break the norm of non-intervention even in the case of a regime which was clearly engaged in repressing its own people. The Kurds who rose against the Iraqi government in the spring of 1991 found themselves the victims of the logic of a conception of international order that, in effect, legitimizes the status quo, however oppressive that status quo may be. It was only with the greatest reluctance that the United States and its allies finally agreed to provide 'safe havens' for the Kurds within the territory of Iraq.

The fundamental point here is that for the leading powers of the world to offer a guarantee of all frontiers and all regimes regardless of their contestability or desirability would be to court disaster were it actually to be credible that these countries would in all circumstances deliver on their promises. During the Gulf War it was often noted that the West had not reacted similarly to previous acts of aggression in Tibet, East Timor, Nicaragua, Afghanistan, the Lebanon and so on.

What was less often noted was that to have so reacted would have involved the 'international community' in an endless series of wars against some of its most powerful members. The politics of liberal internationalism in the 1990s bears out these points. To the above list can be added the genocide in Rwanda, the war in Chechnya, and, until the end of the decade, the wars in former Yugoslavia. On each of these occasions liberal internationalists have either failed to act on their own stated principles, or have done so reluctantly and half-heartedly. It is possible that a norm of humanitarian intervention is emerging – this possibility will be investigated in Chapter 12 – but it can hardly be seen as emerging under the aegis of liberal internationalism.

The New World Order differed from previous notions of liberal internationalism in so far as it purported to offer security to all states, whatever their regimes. Post-1919 liberal internationalists were clear that states ought actually to be 'liberal' if its account of international relations was to work. Their point was that autocratic leaders took their countries into war without the support of the 'people' and that democracies, by way of contrast, would be peace-loving. In the 1930s this argument did not seem very convincing, but today a degree of support for the basic position can be drawn from another, different source, the so-called 'Democratic Peace' hypothesis, introduced in Chapter 4, above. To recapitulate, this hypothesis states that liberal-democratic states, while as war-prone in general as any other kind of state, do not fight each other, and emerged in the 1980s from two sources. A minor source is the 'Kantian' argument of Michael Doyle (1983). In 'Perpetual Peace', Kant constructs a model of a peaceful, international order in which only 'Republican' states are allowed to join; Doyle transforms 'republican' into 'liberal' – a suspect move – and argues that although liberal states often engage in war with non-liberal states, constitutionally stable liberal democracies never fight each other. He buttresses this point by reference to a simple statistical argument. He offers a list of 'liberal states' and a list of wars and participants and shows that, indeed, his theoretical proposition holds good. This latter argument rests on the fact-gathering of the 'Correlates of War' project and the 'Dimensions of Nations' project – authors from both operations published papers making the same point in the early 1980s.

It would be fair to say that this early work was not taken very seriously by most theorists. The notions of 'liberalism' and 'democracy' employed seemed thin and unconvincing, and the general view was that what we were seeing here was a statistical artefact rather than a real phenomenon. However, even then, one of Doyle's points was that the number of democracies – the size of the 'Pacific Union' as he termed it – was increasing. And, of course, in the post-Cold War era the spread of liberal democracies has become even more marked, a trend buttressed by the movement towards 'good governance' in the Third World. One side-effect of this was that a number of high-octane projects were launched to investigate this 'Democratic Peace' hypothesis. The result was that the basic hypothesis was found to be remarkably 'robust' – which is to say that whatever definition of democracy is employed, and however war is defined, the result comes out in much the same way. Constitutionally stable democracies do not fight each other, although they do engage in as much war as other states with non-democracies. Clearly, the more sophisticated and sensitive the indicators are, the more likely it is that there will be minor exceptions to the proposition, or 'near-misses' as Russett (1993) puts it, and it may be that the law-like statement that democracies never fight one another will not stand. Nonetheless, the research suggests that the general proposition is one of the best supported empirical hypothesis that contemporary International Relations can offer – although it must always be remembered that it is constitutionally stable liberal democracies that are the subject of this generalization, and as soon as the field is widened the generalization is much less compelling.

A statistically well-supported hypothesis is not the same thing as an explanation; how do we account for the democratic peace? Russett offers two possible explanations. First, there is the *cultural-normative* model. In stable democracies, decision-makers will expect to be able to resolve internal conflicts by compromise and without violence, and, hypothetically, they will carry over this expectation when dealing with decision-makers in other stable democracies which have similarly non-violent conflict-resolving mechanisms. Conversely, decision-makers in non-democratic systems are more likely to use and threaten violence in domestic conflict resolution, and this attitude is also likely to spill over internationally. Knowing this, and to avoid being exploited, democracies will adopt non-democratic norms in dealing with non-democracies. A second model stresses *structural-institutional* factors. Systems of checks and balances, and the need to generate public consent, will slow down decisions to use large-scale violence, and reduce the likelihood that such decisions will be taken. Recognizing this, leaders of other democratic states will not fear surprise attacks, and will allow peaceful conflict-resolution methods to operate. Leaders of non-democratic states, on the other hand, are less constrained, and can more easily initiate large-scale violence. Being aware that democratic leaders do not have this option they may be tempted to exploit what they see as a weakness – but being aware that this is so, leaders of democracies may set aside institutional constraints when dealing with non-democracies in order to avoid being exploited.

These two models are not the only explanations for the democratic peace that could be offered – although others, such as that of David Lake (1992), can be assimilated to one or the other – nor are they entirely separable; as Russett remarks, norms underlie and are buttressed by institutions. Probably a later account will merge the two. Moreover, the possibility that liberal democracy is not the independent variable cannot be disregarded – in spite of all the number crunching it may still be the case that it is some other feature of constitutionally secure liberal democracies which works against them going to war with each other (Brown 1992b). In any event, what is striking about the thesis is the support it gives to the idea that a liberal internationalist world order might now be possible, but *if, and only if*, constitutionally stable liberal democracies come to dominate world politics. President Bush's long discarded New World Order was designed to work in a pluralist world in which regime-type was irrelevant; the democratic peace hypothesis gives support to an older conception of liberal internationalism in which regime-type is quite crucial.

How likely is it that liberalism will come to be the dominant political form in the twenty-first century? At the moment most of the key actors in international relations are in some sense liberal states – the US, the EU, Japan – or at least aspire to be – Russia – and of the major powers only China rejects liberalism as a matter of principle. But is this simply an accidental conjuncture? Here it is necessary to return to the start of this chapter, and to the wider human consequences of the fall of communism.

The Liberal Moment?

Does the fall of the Soviet Union signpost the emergence of a world of relative ideological unity, based around an effective consensus as to how to organize industrial society? One of the most interesting arguments to this effect was set out in 1989 by Francis Fukuyama, a Washington-based policy analyst with quite close contacts in the US government, in a short paper entitled 'The End of History' – which attracted immense media interest and led to a rather portentous book, *The End of History and the Last Man* (1992). In essence, Fukuyama argues that in vanquishing Soviet communism, liberal democracy removed its last serious competitor as a conception of how an advanced industrial society might be governed. In the early nineteenth century, the shape of liberal democracy emerged as a combination of a market-based economy, representative institutions, the rule of law and constitutional government. Since then there have been a number of attempts to go beyond this formula, but each has failed. Traditional autocracy, authoritarian capitalism, national socialism and fascism each failed in wars against liberal societies. Liberalism's most powerful enemy (and also one of its earliest) was Marxian socialism, which held that the freedoms that liberalism offered were insufficient and could be transcended – specifically that political freedoms were undermined by economic inequality and that ways of running industrial society without the market and via party rather than representative government were viable. The events of the 1980s demonstrated the falsity of this claim. The societies of 'really-existing socialism' proved unable to keep up with liberal capitalist societies in the provision of consumer goods, and their citizens became increasingly unwilling to accept that party rule could substitute for genuine representative government. Eventually these regimes collapsed and have been replaced by political systems which are, at least in principle, liberal democratic.

It must be acknowledged that this account of events has much to be commend it. While there have indeed been a great many problems created for the West by the way the Cold War ended, it seems perverse to refuse to acknowledge that the destruction of the Soviet Empire and the adoption of Western forms of politics by its successor states constitutes a kind of victory for liberal ideas. What is interesting is why Fukuyama wishes to describe this victory as 'the End of History'. Here we encounter a particular form of Hegelian political and cultural criticism. The suggestion is that the triumph of 'liberalism' amounts to the firm establishment of the only kind of human freedom that is possible. Since 'History' was about the shaping and development of human freedom and since this task is now complete, History is over. There are not now (and, more importantly, will not be in the future) any systematic alternatives to liberalism: non-liberal regimes will persist on an ad hoc, contingent basis, but without being able to mount a coherent challenge to liberalism. It should be noted that the tone of Fukuyama's work is *not* triumphalist – he seems to rather regret the ending of diversity that he is predicting, and in his book, as opposed to his article, he makes a great deal of the Nietzschean figure of the 'last man', a soul-less being who faces no character-building problems in an age in which all the big issues have been settled.

Clearly this vision of the world tallies with the hegemonic role of neoliberalism described in Chapter 9; here, as there, the basic case is that 'there is no alternative'. There are things to be said about this, but first, we might ask what kind of international relations one might expect 'post-historical' politics to involve? Fukuyama's answer is that post-historical international relations would be not markedly dissimilar from historical international relations. The 'End of History' does not mean that there will be no more *events* taking place in the world – wars, conflicts and so on. It simply means that these events will no longer be charged with deep significance; conflicts will no longer be about ideology, but conflicts over interests will continue. In short, the End of History looks much like the 'Back to the Future' of neorealist writers – an international system of states competing with one another, concerned about their survival, perhaps fighting wars, but not engaging in the kind of ideological conflict characteristic of much of the twentieth century. At this point the theorists of the democratic peace have something interesting to say; if, indeed, it is the case that there are systematic reasons why we should expect the spread of liberalism, there are, equally, reasons why we should expect this diffusion to produce a new kind of international relations – 'post-historical' international relations may involve a Kantian 'pacific union' rather than a neorealist international system. Even if Fukuyama is right in his basic thesis, he may be wrong in the conclusions he draws from it.

Is Fukuyama right to think that the big issues have now been resolved, and that there is, in effect, only one way of organizing industrial society? He allows for the possible emergence of one-off autocratic, nationalist, regimes – his point is that there is no *systematic* alternative to liberal democracy available, at least for complex, modern societies. A good question is whether this position represents a particularly *Western* vision of the future of world politics; 1989 may have settled a contest between the heirs of the European Enlightenment, but does it necessarily follow that the result of this contest has the kind of global significance that the contestants believed it did? The final section of this chapter will examine this question, in the process asking what place there is in the emerging structure of world politics for those countries that are not in the top rank of industrial power.

International Politics and the 'Clash of Civilizations'

As (in)famous as Fukuyama's article on the end of history at the beginning of the 1990s was Samuel Huntington's influential account of the 'clash of civilizations' (1993a). The burden of Huntington's thesis is that, with the end of the Cold War, a new basis of division has emerged in the world; the ideological conflicts of the past will be replaced by conflicts between 'cultures' or civilizations. Huntington identifies as the major contemporary civilizations the Sinic, Japanese, Hindu, Islamic and Western, with Orthodox and Latin American civilizations as possible derivations of Western civilization with identities of their own, and Africa (perhaps) making up the list. In any event, on his account, there are three civilizations which are likely to generate serious potential problems in the near future – the declining West, the rising Sinic, and the unstable Islamic.

As this formulation might suggest, the first two components go together – economically, demographically and, ultimately, militarily, the West is losing power to the Asian civilizations and in particular to China (Huntington anticipates that China will come to dominate Japan and that the Japanese are likely to accept, tacitly, a subordinate status). This was, of course, written before the collapse of the Asian economic boom, but it is a moot point whether this would change the basic argument here. An increasingly successful and powerful China will not accept a world in which its values are regarded as inferior to those of the West and will not accept global socio–economic institutions which limit its possibilities – and Huntington acknowledges that the existing structure of international institutions is indeed a product of Western/American hegemony and reflects Western values. Only by the West adopting a policy of coexistence and recognizing the legitimacy of the Confucian way will violent conflict be avoided between these two civilizations. Chinese civilization will pose, indeed is posing, problems (particularly for the West but also for Japan) because of its success; the world of Islam will pose, indeed is posing, problems for all its neighbours because of its failure. Demographic pressures in Islam and the lack of any core Islamic state with the potential of China, or even the 'baby tigers' of Southeast Asia, will lead to frustrations; moreover, Islam is a proselytizing religion and Islamic civilization has borders with most of the other world civilizations. These borders ('fault-lines') will be, indeed already are, the site of many cross-civilizational conflicts, from Bosnia and Chechnya to Kashmir and the Sudan. Ending such conflicts may be virtually impossible, certainly far more difficult than the daunting enough task of promoting co-existence between Chinese and Western civilizations.

It is easy to pick holes in Huntington's work; right from the outset his account of 'civilization' is ad hoc and muddled; civilizations are systems of ideas, and, as such, it is difficult to see how they could clash, although individuals and groups claiming to represent these ideas certainly can. Moreover, these systems of ideas are not now, nor have they ever been, self-contained or impermeable, a fact that Huntington acknowledges, but the significance of which he, perhaps, underplays. On the other hand, he deserves considerable credit for attempting to break up what was becoming in the early 1990s a rather sterile debate about the post-Cold War world. In his response to critics 'If not Civilizations, What?', Huntington suggests that the only alternative models for what he is interested in are the old statist paradigm and a new 'un-real' vision of one world united by globalization (1993b). The issue of globalization will be addressed in Chapter 12, and the 'unreal vision' that is relevant here is, perhaps, better seen as Fukuyama's vision of the universal triumph of liberal ideas. In effect, Huntington is providing a non-statist, but nonetheless realist, account of the world, which is an interesting addition to the conceptual toolkit of contemporary international relations theory.

Part of the problem with Huntington's analysis, though, is that, although not statist, it remains spatial/territorial. His prevailing metaphor is of the physical 'fault-lines' between civilizations. There are two problems with this notion; first, the analysis underplays the extent to which key dividing lines are man-made and recent – in former Yugoslavia, for example, the recurrent crises of the 1990s owe more to the success of Slobodan Milosevic in mobilizing political support behind the nationalist cause of Greater Serbia than they do to, largely spurious, ethnic and religious differences, much less historical divides that go back to the middle ages or earlier. Such differences and divides certainly exist and have always existed, but their current political significance is the result of contingency rather than some inevitable process. Second, and rather more important, the 'tectonic' notion of civilizations does not recognize sufficiently the extent to which civilizations are already interpenetrated. The clash of civilizations, in so far as it exists at all, is more likely to take the form of the politics of multiculturalism and recognition in the major cities of the world than violent clashes on the so-called 'fault-lines'; policing problems in London are, thankfully, more characteristic of this politics than the violence of Kosovo or Chechnya, horrifying though the latter may be.

Perhaps the emergence of 'civilizational' world politics is implausible, but, nonetheless, there are reasons for doubting the applicability on a world scale of the kind of models set out in the first sections of this chapter. Liberal internationalism and the democratic peace clearly require a higher level of ideological uniformity on the part of the states that make up the system than seems plausible in the foreseeable future; it may be that most of the major powers are 'liberal' but the capacity of so-called minor powers to disrupt the system ought not to be underestimated. The agenda for much of the international politics of the 1990s was set by rulers of states that are in no sense major powers – most noticeably Saddam Hussein in Iraq and Slobodan Milosevic in Yugoslavia. An account of the world in which such figures feature only as anomalies, deviations from a supposed norm of democratic politics, owes more to rhetoric than to substantial analysis. On the other hand, neorealist analyses are also less helpful than one might have thought in under-standing such figures. An ultra-realist account of politics as simply a matter of the exercise of power may not be that far from the point, but the rather refined rational calculations of relative gains required by the more abstruse versions of neorealism seem to occupy a different world from the blood-soaked environment of, say, contemporary Iraqi politics.

Part of the problem here is that different parts of the world face different kinds of problems, and, as a result, produce different kinds of international relations. It has become quite common to speak of 'zones of peace' and 'zones of turmoil' or of 'arcs of crises' in, for example, the Middle East or Africa. The danger of this kind of language is that those who live in the zones of peace – and most books on international relations are written (and read) by such lucky beings – will come to think of what goes on outside of their world as alien to their experience and essentially incomprehensible. Theories of international relations concentrate on the interactions of those states whose basic motivations can be understood with the kind of reasoning we apply in other areas of contemporary modern social life. Other things take place beyond the pale, and different – or no – rules apply there.

Conclusion

It is a moot point whether such an attitude can be sustained into the twenty-first century. This chapter has focused on the emerging structure of international politics on the assumption that states will remain the key actors in international relations, and that, even if their influence is declining relative to other actors, the patterns of interactions the major states create will still be of central importance in the years to come. This seems a reasonable assumption, but in the final chapter of this book a wider agenda for international relations will be addressed, in which the traditonal concerns of power politics take second place, or, at the very least, are placed in a wider context.

Further Reading

Raymond Garthoff, *The Great Transition: American–Soviet Relations and the End of the Cold War* (1994) and Don Oberdorfer, *The Turn: How the Cold War Came to an End* (1991) are useful histories of the end of the Cold War. On the wider meaning of this event, see the essays in Michael Hogan (ed.), *The End of the Cold War: Its Meaning and Implications* (1992) and Alex Danchev (ed.), *Fin De Siècle: The Meaning of the Twentieth Century* (1995). Cynthia Enloe's *The Morning After: Sexual Politics at the End of the Cold War* (1993) also places these events in perspective.

   Richard Ned Lebow and Thomas Risse-Kappen (eds), *International Relations Theory and the End of the Cold War* (1995) – part of which appeared in *International Organization*, Vol. 48, Spring 1994 – is the best collection on its subject. Michael E. Brown *et al.*, *The Perils of Anarchy: Contemporary Realism and International Security* (1995) contains the essays by Mearsheimer and Wohlforth referred to above, as well as Kenneth Waltz's 'The Emerging Structure of International Politics' (1993). Scott D. Sagan and Kenneth Waltz, *The Spread of Nuclear Weapons* (1995) debate the implications of nuclear proliferation in a post-Cold War world. William C. Wohlforth, 'The Stability of a Unipolar World' (1999) appears in *International Security*, as does Kenneth Waltz, 'Structural Realism after the Cold War' (2000) a major restatement of his position.

   President George Bush announced the dawning of a new age in 'Toward a New World Order' (1990). Graham Allison and Gregory F. Treverton (eds), *Rethinking America's Security: Beyond Cold War to New World Order* (1992) is a very useful collection of essays. Robert W. Tucker and David C. Hendrickson, *The Imperial Temptation: The New World Order and American's Purpose* (1992) is a critique of the New World Order from an 'old realist' perspective. More predictable is

Noam Chomsky, *World Orders, Old and New* (1994) which presents a 'left' viewpoint. For the literature on the Democratic Peace, see Chapter 4 above. Daniel Deudeney and G. John Ikenberry, 'The Nature and Sources of Liberal International Order' (1999) is an excellent discussion of the contemporary liberal internationalism.

Fukuyama's works are cited in the text. For a very hostile liberal reaction, see Ralf Dahrendorf, *Reflections on the Revolution in Europe* (1990). Critical, but less outraged, are Fred Halliday, 'An Encounter with Fukuyama' (1992) and Chris Brown, 'The End of History?' in Danchev (1995). Huntington's essays are referenced in the text: his book *The Clash of Civilizations and the Remaking of World Order* (1996) is less convincing than the original shorter pieces. Kishore Mahbubani, 'The West and The Rest' (1992) and Eisuke Sakakiba, 'The End of Progressivism: A Search for New Goals' (1995) offer not dissimilar reflections on the same theme. Chris Brown, 'History Ends, World Collide' (1999) is a more extended discussion of some of the themes of this chapter.

12

Global Politics in the Twenty-First Century

Introduction

In Chapter 11, an attempt was made to restrict the focus to conventional great power politics, although, perhaps symptomatically, it turned out to be very difficult to talk about the emerging structure of international politics without all sorts of topics which previously would have been regarded as irrelevant creeping in. In this final chapter these topics take centre stage. The focus will be on global politics in a wide sense of the term; the state will no longer be at the centre of attention – but neither will it be marginalized, which is why the temptation to use the word 'globalization' in the chapter title has been resisted; perhaps wrongly, globalization suggests to many a tendency to marginalize the importance of the state. Rather the focus will be on new kinds of problems, new agendas in international relations, rather than directly on the actors who will have to deal with them, which will certainly includes the state. These new agendas include the international relations of environmental protection; the implications of the emerging human rights regime and associated issues; the increasing salience of cross-cultural relations, and, perhaps most general of all, the implications of the new information technologies for international relations. Many other issues could have been discussed – but for a fuller account of the new global politics readers are referred to the books listed below under 'further reading'.

There are at least two common features of these problems – which will be outlined in this introduction before the problems themselves are addressed – but the reader should be alerted that there is no intention to suggest that the new agendas the world will face in the twenty-first century can necessarily be made compatible with one another. In fact, the opposite may be the case – to anticipate somewhat, we may well find that the new concern for human rights is not compatible with steps that may need to be taken to protect the environment or the benefits of the information age, that social justice at home may involve imposing controls on borders that cannot be morally justified and that the rights of women internationally may, on occasion, clash with principles of respect for other cultures. Setting this issue aside for the moment, what are the common features of the new agendas?

The first common feature relates to one of the oldest and most traditional concerns of international studies – *security*. *Pace* the fears of some alarmists, the fall of the Soviet Union has materially improved the conventional security of the advanced, industrial, liberal-capitalist states. These states still have enemies, but they no longer have an enemy with the capacity, literally, to destroy them. But, as concern over military security becomes less pressing, so a wider conception of security has come to the fore, promoted by the 'Copenhagen School' whose leading members are Barry Buzan and Ole Waever, and the Critical Security Studies movement, many of whose most prominent members are to be found at the University of Wales, Aberystwyth. The basic thought for both groups is that, whether the referent object of security be an individual, group, state or nation, 'security' is an onto-logical status, that of feeling secure, which at any one time may be under threat from a number of different directions. Clearly one such is external military threat, but it is also the case that depletion of the ozone layer, mass unemployment, large-scale drug trafficking, crime and the arrival on its borders of large numbers of refugees can each threaten the security of a state. Moreover, the security of individuals is also bound up with these threats both in so far as individuals are members of communities, but also, and perhaps more importantly, in circumstances where the security of the individual may actually be threatened by the state itself. Denial of human rights, ill-treatment and persecution for reasons of gender or sexual orientation, the depri-vations of famine and poverty, these are all factors which threaten the security of individuals and fall within the purview of the new security studies.

As both Copenhagen and Aberystwyth are aware, there is clearly an issue here as to whether it is actually appropriate to 'securitize' these issue; it might well be held that securitization induces highly inap-propriate reactions to some of these problems – for example, the way in which asylum-seekers have been demonized as 'bogus' in a great deal of recent political discourse in Britain may reflect the view that these harmless individuals are represented as posing some kind of threat to the security of the nation. It might also be argued that in our modern 'risk society' too much emphasis on security is inappropriate; learning to live creatively with insecurity may be more to the point than excessive concern with the kind of stable identities that can no longer be sustained (Beck 1999). In any event, most of the problems and issues discussed below do relate to some extent to issues of security, widely defined, and so new conceptions of security may provide some pointers for relating these problems to each other.

A second common feature of the new agendas is the way in which most of them raise important questions about the relationship between the state and community on the one hand, and individuals and 'subnational' groups on the other: in particular, they raise questions that turn on moral aspects of the relationship between the community and the individual. The settled norms of the Westphalia System assume that the sovereign state is the mechanism through which the values and interests of individuals are protected and enhanced, and thus that the limits of moral obligation are defined by the state (Frost 1996); never very plausible, this assumption is clearly under more threat today than ever before. The question of the duties owed by individuals to the state and their fellow citizens as opposed to the duties they owe to humanity at large is posed in a very stark way by the differential treatment of 'insiders' and 'outsiders' in labour markets, by refugee crises, and by the images of starvation and poverty in far away places regularly transmitted by our television screens. Conversely, for probably the majority of the inhabitants of the planet, the state constitutes a bigger threat to their well-being than any external body, which, of course, raises the obvious question of why such states should be considered to be worthy of loyalty. Probably more than ever before, individuals in the advanced industrial world think of themselves as 'cosmopolitans', less tainted with nationalism than in the past. Yet the behaviour of the states of the advanced industrial world – with the apparent approval of their citizens – is still dominated by the maxim that charity begins at home. For all these reasons, *normative* concerns are a key part of the new agendas of international relations.

It is plausible to suggest that most people seek security, and, although less obviously part of 'common sense', it is also true that most people seek to live morally coherent lives. Even the amoralist beloved of a crude version of realism, usually confines his or her scepticism over morals to the public realm – the mid-century founders of American realism (Niebuhr, Morgenthau, Kennan) were all morally-upright figures whose opposition to moralism in foreign policy was based on a firm belief in the existence of a divide between public and private morality, and again between the morality of the state domestically and in its international dealings. In the twenty-first century it has to be doubted whether these distinctions can be sustained. Global politics presents us now with a range of questions which can no longer be compartmentalized into a box marked 'international relations – not for internal consumption'.

With these thoughts in mind we can now address the new agendas, beginning with one which is sufficiently well established to call in doubt the term 'new' – environmental protection – before moving to an examination of the new politics of human rights – and here 'new' is more appropriate – and then to international cultural politics and the politics of IT – where, in the latter case at least, 'new' hardly begins to express the novelty.

The New Politics of the International Environment

One of the first principles of traditional international law is that state sovereignty involves control over natural resources and local economic activity. Some such principle is implied by the nature of the modern state – unlike, for example, some medieval institutions, contemporary political forms have been territorial since at least the seventeenth century, and territoriality involves a claim of ownership over natural resources. Moreover, the nature of capitalist economies as they have developed over the same time period has been such that it was inevitable that in the advanced industrial countries 'ownership' would not be interpreted as 'stewardship' but as 'dominion'. Natural resources were there to be exploited for gain by landowners, the state, and perhaps, at least in modern welfare capitalist societies, the people. However, even in the latter case, 'the people' means 'citizens of the state in question' and not people generally: until comparatively recently, the idea that a state might be held accountable for economic activities conducted on its territory would have seemed incompatible with the first principles of the system.

This attitude began to change in the late 1960s and early 1970s. In the first place it became clear that certain kinds of economic activity could have quite dramatic effects beyond the borders of the state in question: the phenomenon of 'acid rain' is paradigmatic here, with deforestation in, for example, Scandinavia or Canada caused by industrial pollution originating in Britain, Germany or the United States. However, although these are serious issues, they pose no particularly interesting theoretical problems. In principle, cross-border pollution is much the same as intra-border pollution; cleaning up the Rhine is more complicated than cleaning up the Thames, but poses the same sort of problems – in particular, how to cost what economists call 'externalities', whether to regard pollution control as a general charge on taxation or something that can be handled on the basis that the polluter pays, and so on. Once the problem is recognized, capitalist economies have fewer problems dealing with this sort of question than one might expect. Private ownership cuts both ways – it can hinder collective action, but it also means that it is, in principle, possible to identify and hold accountable the agents of environmental degradation. An interesting contrast here is with the far greater difficulties in controlling direct pollution experienced by communist industrial powers, where 'public ownership' provided a reason for not tackling similar problems, as the post-communist states who have inherited dead rivers and urban industrial nightmares have reason to be aware.

Of greater long-term significance was the second reason for the increased salience of environmental issues in the early 1970s, namely a growing consciousness that there might be 'limits to growth' (Meadows *et al.* 1974). It was argued that industrial civilization depended on the ever-faster consumption of materials the supply of which was, by definition, finite. Hydrocarbon-based fuels that had been created over millions of years were being consumed in decades. Demand for resources that were, in principle, renewable – such as wood or agricultural products was growing faster than matching supplies, creating other potential shortages a little way down the line. The point about these rather doom-laden predictions was that, unlike phenomena such as acid rain, they challenged the prospects of continued and sustained economic growth, the central driving force and legitimating principle of contemporary industrial society. If sustained, such a challenge would bring about a dramatic reshaping of the politics of the advanced industrial countries, but it would pose far greater problems for the 'developing' world which was, if anything, even more reliant on the beneficial effects of general economic growth than the rich world.

In fact, these problems were put on hold for a few years. The downturn in economic activity in the 1970s reduced demand for raw materials and new technological advances such as the microchip revolution were less dependent on material input than the old technologies.

The 'limits to growth' predictions were, in any event, probably excessively pessimistic, and, moreover, self-defeating, since they concentrated minds to a far greater extent on energy conservation, recycling, and the development of new resources. In the sense in which the term was used then, we are, clearly, still a long way away from reaching the limits of growth. Nonetheless, the debates of the 1970s were a useful rehearsal for the actual problems that have emerged in the 1980s and 1990s. Climatological changes such as the depletion of the ozone layer and global warming, rising water levels, deforestation, loss of biodiversity and the desertification of large parts of Africa pose similar sorts of challenges to the civilization of productivity to those posed by the idea of limits to growth – with the significant difference that these challenges are rather better supported by scientific opinion, and rather less amenable to piecemeal responses. This time it really does seem possible that 'we', all of us, may have to change the way we live.

The case of chlorofluorocarbons (CFCs) which attack the ozone layer is instructive. The Vienna Convention for the Protection of the Ozone Layer in 1985, protocols on the same subject of Montreal 1987 and London 1990, and discussion at the United Nations Conference on Environment and Development (UNCED) in Rio in 1992 and in a number of subsequent forums – especially Kyoto 1998 – bear witness to the perceived importance of ozone depletion and the need to cut the emission of CFCs. An interesting question is: how did this perception arise? It is clear that there are quite good, albeit short-sighted, reasons why states might not want to take up this issue. CFCs are created by the employment of technologies which, although polluting, are undoubtedly cheaper than the alternatives. Developing states who wish to foster the increased use of refrigeration want to employ the cheapest technology available, which creates CFCs; developed countries are equally disinclined to cease using technologies on which they have come to depend. Everyone has a long-term interest in avoiding the stripping away of the earth's protective shield, but everyone has a short-term interest in not leading the way in this matter. This is a classic problem of collective action, notoriously difficult to address; however, while few would describe the response of the international community as wholly adequate, the issue is, at least, on the agenda – Why? How did it get there?

The answer seems to be that it got there because of the emergence of a consensus amongst scientists that it was a problem that could no longer be avoided; on the basis of this consensus, governments were lobbied and, often reluctantly, convinced that they had to act. This is an example of an interesting new phenomenon in international relations – the emergence of international 'pressure' groups the source of whose influence is the possession of highly specialized technical knowledge rather than more conventional political resources. Peter Haas has introduced the term *epistemic communities* into the literature to describe such groups (1989). It is clear that, in the right circumstances, they can be very effective; governments can be made to feel that they have no alternative other than to act in the way that the scientific consensus indicates. There may often be a scarcely concealed political threat here – act or we will reveal to the public your willingness to expose them to life-threatening risk – but the basic influence exerted by epistemic communities arises simply from their ability, or at least the public's belief in their ability, to provide a dominant interpretation of the nature of the problem.

Yet the significance of epistemic communities should not be overestimated. They require the right conditions to be effective; such conditions include a near-consensus amongst the relevant knowledge holders, and an issue that does not touch the core interests of states. An example of ineffective action is provided in the 1980s by the issue of the 'Nuclear Winter'; this hypothesis proposed that the explosion of only a small proportion of the nuclear arsenals of any one of the nuclear powers would create climactic effects such as would be devastating to at least the Northern hemisphere, if not the world as a whole. The weight of scientific opinion supported this hypothesis, but it had little influence on the nuclear powers; this was partly because there were significant scientific dissenters, but was more a matter of governments exhibiting what psychologists call 'denial'. Nuclear deterrence was simply so basic a component of national strategy for the nuclear powers that they were not prepared to listen to anything that would undermine it. In such circumstances, epistemic communities count for very little.

One interesting feature of epistemic communities, which cross-references to the normative issues raised in the introduction to this chapter, is their lack of democratic legitimacy. Greenpeace International is an interesting case here, because it is often seen as the paradigm of a pressure group which employs scientific expertise to make its case in global civil society. Greenpeace scientists are highly regarded and there opinions are taken very seriously by large parts of Western public opinion. They have been capable of scoring quite important political successes – the Brent Spar affair of 1995 is a case in point, when a

Greenpeace campaign involving a public relations blitz and consumer boycotts succeeded in reversing a decision by Shell and the British Government to scuttle the Brent Spar oil platform in the open sea. As it turns out, there were mistakes in Greenpeace's calculations, and it is still a matter of dispute whether disposal at sea might not have been the most environmentally sound strategy, but what is interesting, and might in some circumstances be rather sinister, is that the unelected, unaccountable Greenpeace scientists were able to manipulate public opinion and override the will of a democratically elected government and its scientific advisers. There is an added irony here – many of Greenpeace's supporters have a very sceptical view of the authority of science in general, and yet it is precisely the public's lack of scepticism on this issue that gives the organization its clout.

Moving away from epistemic communities, environmental politics have had a major impact on the normative issue of global justice, most importantly by highlighting the tensions between approaches to justice which focus on the rights of communities and those which focus on global concerns. A generation or so ago the issue of global inequality was relatively easy to comprehend and the remedy for world poverty appeared equally unproblematic – although, of course, action to relieve poverty was another matter. Poor states were 'underdeveloped' and thus needed to 'develop'; there were intense debates as to whether development was possible under the current world economic system but the goal itself was less at issue – the consensus in favour of 'development' ranged from free-market liberals to dependency theorists via old-style Marxists. We have seen in Chapter 10 that this consensus is under pressure today, and it is clear that in one crucial respect it was fundamentally wrong: the one thing we can be sure about the future is that it will *not* involve a global industrial civilization in which the developing nations become developed and possess advanced industrial economies on the model of the West in the 1950s and 1960s – or, at least, if such a future does come into existence the price paid will be intolerable unless some quite extraordinary technological advances change the calculations fundamentally.

If the dream of development has become a nightmare, where does this leave those countries whose current situation is such that even the scenario of a raped and pillaged environment might count as an improvement? The contrast between the needs and interests of the world as a whole and those of particular countries seems acute. It is clear that industrial development on the Western model, if generalized to China, the Indian sub-continent, Africa and Latin America, would be a disaster for everyone, including the peoples of those regions, but it is equally clear that the governments of the South will wish to go down this route unless they are presented with sufficient incentives to do otherwise. No such incentive scheme is likely to work if the end result is a world in which the peoples and governments of the North are allowed to preserve the undoubted benefits of an industrial civilization denied to the South. Although this situation reinforces the arguments of those who advocate a new, more self-reliant, approach to poverty nonetheless, providing a solution to poverty and malnutrition in the South has become a common project for the world as a whole – not just as a matter of rhetoric, but out of direct, albeit medium-term, self-interest.

This is an issue which strikes at the heart of the settled norms of the current international order. The ruling assumption of this order is that individual states have the right to pursue their own conception of the Good without external interference; the norms of the system are designed to promote coexistence rather than problem-solving. The challenge posed by the destruction of the environment is one of the ways in which this ruling assumption is under threat, one example of the way in which the emergence of a global industrial civilization has, apparently, outstripped the political forms available to us. Another concerns the emerging international human rights regime, to which we now turn.

Human Rights

If the threat of environmental degradation poses challenges to the norms of the Westphalia System, the same can be said with even greater force of the development of the notion that individuals have rights which they ought to be able to claim against their own governments. While this notion was first given expression by states in the Universal Declaration on Human Rights which was promulgated in the UN General Assembly in 1948, and most of the other major international instruments in this area are decades old, nonetheless, the 1990s saw more developments in the international human rights regime than the previous four decades put together. This is one area where the collapse of communism has had a clear demonstrable effect; during the Cold War questions of human rights were routinely treated as subjects for inter-bloc wrangling – after 1989 it became possible to put the West's declared adherence to human rights to the test in a way that simply was not possible previously. The result has been a flurry of new issues, and new life being breathed into some very old issues.

Some of these changes concern the legal side of the regime. In the past the basic legal remedies for human rights violations were to be found in national courts, except in those circumstances where states had specifically agreed to set up an external body, as in the case of the European Convention of 1950. The 1990s saw a number of shifts in this area. One such was the creation of International War Crimes Tribunals to deal with offences committed during the wars of former Yugoslavia and the genocide in Rwanda – unlike the post-1945 Nuremberg Tribunal, these Tribunals did not dispense the justice of victors, but were an expression of the will of a wider international community that the perpetrators of injustice should not go unpunished. These tribunals have had limited success, but establish an important precedent; indeed, it was partly to get beyond the ad hoc nature of these tribunals that a treaty to establish an International Criminal Court was signed in 1999. The United States is in opposition – partly because of fears that the Court will undermine the US legal system, partly for fear that US armed forces will be the subject of politically motivated prosecutions – but since its only supporters are such unlikely soul mates as Libya, Iraq and China, it is unlikely to be able to prevent the treaty coming into effect. Although the powers of the court are to be limited, and prosecutions subject to UN Security Council control, the very notion of an International Criminal Court represents a genuine break with the past. The same might be said of the Pinochet Case in Britain in 1999–2000; although Pinochet was allowed to return to Chile on health grounds, the British House of Lords in an important ruling held that former heads of state could not claim sovereign immunity in respect of acts such as torture which were international crimes, and could not be regarded as part of their regular duties. Whether this precedent will make human rights violations less likely in the future, or simply make autocratic rulers less likely to leave power voluntarily, is a matter for dispute, but the ruling itself constitutes another blow to older notions of sovereignty.

Perhaps more significant than these legal changes, is the putative emergence in the 1990s of an embryonic doctrine of 'humanitarian intervention' – the intervention (perhaps forcible) of one state, or group of states, in the internal affairs of another, conducted mainly, or substantially, in the interests of the inhabitants of the latter. This is something that gets to the heart of the issue of the international protection of human rights. The legal regime that has developed since 1945 has established that there are certain kinds of rights over their own citizens that states ought not to possess, certain activities that cannot be justified by reference to the principle of sovereignty; at the same time, and in apparent contradiction to this new regime, the UN Charter explicitly forbids intervention in the domestic jurisdiction of states (Article 2(7)) and virtually all states have stoutly resisted the idea that others ought to possess any kind of right to intervene in their internal affairs. Interestingly, prior to 1990, there have been a number of occasions when states might have been able to claim that they were acting for humanitarian reasons – such as the overthrow of Idi Amin in Uganda by Tanzanian forces in 1979, or the US intervention in Grenada after the murder of the elected Prime Minister during a coup in that country in 1983 – but they have preferred not to, citing instead general threats to the peace, or threats to their own nationals.

This has changed somewhat in the 1990s. After the Gulf War of 1990–91, the victorious coalition established a 'safe area' for the Kurdish population of Iraq into which Iraqi forces were not allowed to penetrate, and similar safe areas were established by NATO and the UN during the conflict in Bosnia. In neither case was the policy a success – the Bosnian 'safe area' of Srebrenica became one of the most dangerous places in Europe when it was allowed by the UN to fall to Serb forces in 1995 – but the very idea of justifying intervention in this way was innovative. Even more striking was the NATO action over Kosovo in the Spring of 1999. Here an external group of states intervened militarily to prevent Yugoslavia from exercising its sovereign rights over territory that everybody agreed was legally part of that country. The behaviour of the Yugoslav armed forces, police and paramilitaries was deemed to be such that armed external military observers were needed to prevent atrocities, and when Yugoslavia refused to accept such observers a military protectorate was established by force. By comparison, the insertion of an Australian-led UN force in East Timor in late 1999 was much less controversial – here Indonesia's right to the territory had never been accepted by the UN – but again involved an effective imposition of a humanitarian force against the will of the local government, even though, on this occasion, the government in question was 'persuaded' not to offer forcible resistance.

As each of these examples suggest, the notion of humanitarian intervention is highly controversial. In each case the humanitarian motives of the interveners have been questioned; this is hardly surprising since, whatever else is involved, forcible humanitarian action involves the domination of the weak by the strong, and it is not necessary to be an opponent of human rights to be concerned by this. It is not clear how humanitarian action can be legitimized. Is the, at least tacit, approval of the UN Security Council – missing in the case of NATO's action in Kosovo – necessary? If so, humanitarian action is at the mercy of Council politics and the veto of states who may not be motivated by humanitarianism, but if not, then how else can action be seen as anything other than arbitrary? Moreover, it is by no means clear that most humanitarian actions have actually produced the intended results; it may be that NATO's protectorate in Kosovo is a more desirable outcome than the alternative, the creation of nearly 2 million displaced ethnic Albanians, but it would be difficult to defend it in any other way.

On the other hand, the greatest humanitarian disasters of the 1990s occurred when the 'international community' *failed* to engage in humanitarian intervention – as in Rwanda in 1994 – or did so belatedly and ineffectively – as in Bosnia between 1990 and 1995. It would be difficult to argue that powerful states have been overenthusiastic interveners to prevent human rights abuses; on most counts the reluctance of the powerful to act is a far more noticeable tendency. Moreover, the relative lack of success, and high cost, of the interventions that have taken place, have put in question the willingness of states to act in the future. Far from constituting a precedent, the NATO action in Kosovo may actually act as a *deterrent* to future interventions. Still, for all these caveats, the steps that have been taken towards the emergence of at least the beginnings of a doctrine of humanitarian intervention may come to be seen as one of the most important trends to emerge in the 1990s.

Border Issues

Humanitarian interventions tend to be few and far between, dramatic events that affect the lives of large numbers of people. Other human rights issues are much less dramatic, and affect people one at a time – good examples here include migration, refugee status and asylum seeking, all those issues which emerge as a result of the mass movements of peoples across national borders. Few aspects of ordinary life have changed so dramatically over the last two centuries as this. New, relatively cheap and safe, transportation technologies (trains, ships and jet aircraft) have changed the meaning of distance, and political and economic changes provide reasons for mobility. The emergence of a global economy and global markets, including the market for labour, in a world characterized by extreme international economic inequality means that millions, indeed hundreds of millions, of people have very good reasons to think that they could better their life-chances by changing their country of residence. Migrant workers, who are 'pulled' by labour shortages in the host country and 'pushed' by poverty in their country of origin, are willing to work for wages that would be regarded as wholly unacceptable by the locals with whom they will be in competition. At the same time, the gap between the relatively benign modalities of rule in most of the advanced industrial countries and the more basic methods employed by elites in the periphery creates a powerful political motivation to relocate for those whose attempt to exercise rights and liberties denied them by authoritarian regimes can, accurately, claim a well-founded fear of persecution – the official definition of a 'political refugee'. The destructiveness of modern warfare means that people who find themselves in the path of the juggernaut and have the means to flee will do so. For all these reasons, the large-scale movement of peoples has become an important and unprecedented issue in late-twentieth-century international politics.

For one reason or another, millions of people desire to relocate in the modern world; the inhabitants of their potential destinations may have their own views about the consequences of this desire, and political authorities with the willingness and ability to act upon them. Until around a century and a half ago, very few states had effective census mechanisms, police forces or border controls; apart perhaps from levies on a few prominent individuals, taxation was indirect rather than personal and did not discriminate between outsiders and insiders; restrictions on who could work and on conditions of work were as likely to be guild-based as state-based; and few states had effective mechanisms for providing welfare to their citizens. All this has now changed in the advanced industrial world. States now have very effective regulatory and surveillance mechanisms which are tied into rather less effective but not inconsequential welfare systems. Determining who is or is not a citizen has become both possible and necessary; necessary because only citizens (or 'tax-payers', as the revealing locution sometimes has it) are entitled to the full range of benefits provided by the state – exactly who can claim such rights is a critical practical issue which, *in extremis*, can determine whether a particular individual lives or dies.

The combination of a mobile world population and an active state has shaped the international and national politics of border controls.

In this area – as in other areas of social life dramatically affected by global socio–economic change – political positions do not follow the lines established by class conflict and interest politics within late nineteenth- and early twentieth-century industrial societies. Nationalists who wish to preserve what they take to be the distinctive character of their nation oppose large scale influxes of 'aliens', but so do social democrats who are aware that a strong and effective welfare state is an impossibility in a society in which borders are open and entitlements unrestricted. Right-thinking liberal-minded folk resist immigration controls on human rights grounds; free-market liberals ('libertarians') agree, but on the basis of property rights – anyone ought to be able to buy or sell their property or labour without interference by the state. Revolutionary socialists claim that the worker has no country, but the state authorities of 'really-existing' socialism always prevented free movement because the alternative was that the majority of those who possessed transferable skills would have taken them to places where they would have been more highly rewarded. As in the case of environmental politics, what we are seeing here is an effect of the lack of fit between the political institutions of the current world order and realities which have emerged independently of those institutions.

There is, however, a significant difference between the environmental threat and the 'threat' (if such it is) of a breakdown of borders (it should be noted here that the way in which the language of security creeps into these discussions is not politically neutral). In the last resort, environmental degradation affects everyone, and there is no way the advanced industrial world can isolate itself from climate change or similar effects. Everyone must adapt. Such is not the case with population movements where it may, perhaps, be possible to throw the costs of change back on the dispossessed and needy. Faced with the possibility of even larger-scale population movements – refugees, 'economic' migrants or whatever – from the troubled lands to its South and East, the European Union could attempt to help these regions to solve their problems and thus reduce the pressures creating forced emigration, or it could strengthen border controls and develop a 'Fortress Europa' mentality. At the moment, it is attempting to do both in a half-hearted way. For example, programmes of assistance for Eastern Europe are combined with shifts in resources away from internal border controls to controls on the 'marches' of the Union.

However, there are two good reason why an attempt on the part of the advanced industrial world to isolate itself may be ineffective. The first concerns the demand for cheap labour – one of the reasons why, for example, US attempts to police its border with Mexico have been ineffective is because American agribusiness relies so heavily on migrant labour. The second is that it may simply be too late. Most of the great urban conglomerations of the advanced industrial world already have substantial populations of former migrants, legal or illegal. The human rights issues raised by migration and asylum seeking are not simply about the treatment of 'aliens' at the border; they also concern the rights of immigrants within the state, both as individuals and as communities. Moreover, these immigrant groups may well have political roles within their countries of origin. There is an important shift here from the early years of the last century and before; in those days immigrants from, say, Italy to the US would be obliged by reasons of distance to leave the old world behind – the first-generation immigrants characteristically could not afford to revisit their former homeland, and the second generation concentrated their efforts on becoming 'unhyphenated' Americans, and only with the third generation did an interest in the culture of the old world revive. The speed of modern communications technology has changed all this. Individuals, families and groups stay in touch with the homeland via global telephone networks, FAX, telex, the internet and satellite TV, and revisit regularly courtesy of cheap air travel (Appadurai 1996). They frequently remain actors within the politics of the country they have left; often supporting extremist movements, being safely removed from the adverse consequences of extremism – support for an independent 'Khalistan' by émigré Sikh communities in the UK and Canada is a case in point.

All this suggests that the question of the moral significance of borders is rather more complicated than might at first sight seem to be the case. Most of our thinking is cast in terms of 'insiders' and 'outsiders'; international political theory has both constituted and been buttressed by this distinction (Walker 1993). To this way of thought, *identity* requires *difference* – who we *are* is partly determined by who we are *not*, and the controlling of borders, literal and metaphorical, has been an important feature of identity formation. Most of the ideas we have about politics – certainly those developed over the last two centuries – rely on the proposition that we live in bounded communities. Democracy – rule by the people – requires that we know who the people are, that we can distinguish between fellow citizens and others; indeed democracy requires this capacity more than do authoritarian forms of rule where there is no presumption of self-government. The mutual inter-penetration of societies by the mass movements of population throws this requirement in doubt.

One response to this situation is to call for a redefinition of political community, a renegotiation of the boundaries between insiders and outsiders, and, perhaps for a global conception of democracy (Linklater 1998; Held 1995). Another response is to place even more emphasis on the *international* protection of human rights. The Westphalian norm was that individuals should look to 'their' state to protect their interests; this was never very plausible, since quite frequently the state itself was the oppressor, but the development of responsible and representative government made it at least possible that the state could perform this task. It is reasonable to speculate that the growth of an international human rights regime is not simply a response to the state as oppressor – it is also a response to a situation in which mass migration and everything that goes with it is in the process of breaking the link between 'the people' and 'their' state.

Universalism and its Critics

The foregoing discussion implies a kind of universal human identity that can profitably be set against particularistic identities, and advocates of the international human rights regime do often think about things in this way. Human rights adhere to individuals simply by virtue of their humanity, as opposed, for example, to the rights that individuals possess as citizens of the US or the EU. Universal rights come into play precisely when the rights associated with these identities are, for one reason or another, inoperative. An interesting question is whether it makes a great deal of sense to think of individuals in these universal terms? Perhaps something is lost thereby; the most general thought here would be that we are who we are by virtue of our embeddedness in particular social (and other) circumstances, and the things we possess in common with all others can form only the thinnest basis for an identity.

This argument has been made with some force by feminist critics of the universal human rights regime. The original language of the Universal Declaration of 1948 made it appear that the archetypical rights-holder was a man, the head of a family and the breadwinner. Subsequent international legislation has rectified this somewhat but it is still a matter of dispute whether the notion of universal rights can be genuinely gender neutral. No one doubts but that there are some human rights violations that bear down uniquely on women – the inferior legal status of women in some countries, and such local 'customs' as female genital mutilation – while others, although not exclusive to women, mainly concern them – rape as a weapon of war, and child prostitution. Moreover, there are other general sources of oppression which have more female victims than male – the conditions within sweatshops in some of the Newly Industrializing Countries, for example. What is still a matter of dispute is whether opposition to all of these practices can be mounted most effectively from the gender-neutral platform of universal human rights properly understood, or whether, by contrast, it is only by developing specifically feminist notions of rights that practices which degrade and devalue women can be resisted.

Feminist lawyers and social theorists can be found on both sides of this argument. For some, universalism properly understood – i.e. where the universal human being is not assumed to be male – must be the precondition for human emancipation. Others argue that the 'rights-holder' of Western liberal thought is not simply contingently male because of the history of the last few hundred years, but rather that the very idea of individuals as rights holders rests within a gendered account of humanity. The public/private distinction which has underpinned Western thinking about politics since the time of the Greeks represented the 'public' figure as a male soldier/statesman, while the 'private' female was confined to the domestic sphere. There is an interesting connection here – made explicit in Chapter 6 – between this way of thinking about politics and the role of war in conventional Western thought. This is an interesting debate, but it should be noted that in practical terms it matters little whether advocates of women's rights base their opposition to patriarchy on the human rights universalism or on some more particularist account of women's rights – mostly the campaigns are the same.

This discussion has highlighted the specifically Western origin of the international human rights regime – the drafters of the Universal Declaration in 1948 made much play with consulting representatives of other traditions, but the resulting document was clearly based on such obviously Western predecessors as the American 'Bill of Rights' and the French Revolutionary 'Declaration of the Rights of Man and the Citizen'. Some feminists may be concerned by the masculinist assumptions built into the Universal Declaration as a result of this heritage, but some non-Western leaders have been more directly concerned by the heritage itself. When the Declaration was promulgated there were very few non-Western members of the UN – even so Saudi Arabia abstained because it could not accept the clauses in the

Declaration on freedom of religion – but in the intervening half century, decolonization has changed this state of affairs, and the universal standing of the notion of human rights has come under attack from, for example, adherents of so-called 'Asian Values'. That Western states and NGOs have sometime taken it upon themselves to promote human rights has often been resented as hypocritical in the non-Western world where the memory of Western imperialism has not been forgotten, and this resentment has been expressed quite forcibly in some quarters in the 1990s.

A number of leaders of the quasi-authoritarian newly industrializing states of South-East Asia have been particularly vociferous in this respect, arguing that there are specifically 'Asian' values, centring on respect for the family, and an emphasis on religion and the community as opposed to the individualism of Western thinking. Some, especially the Malaysian Prime Minister, Mahathir Bin Mohammed, have described the West as morally decadent because of the growth of gay rights in the West and – ironically, in view of a sometimes shared critique of universalism – the relative progress made by the women's movement. The Bangkok Declaration of 1993 sets out some of these ideas, and the *Vienna Declaration on Human Rights* of that year gives expression to some of the concerns raised, by using language which stresses the point that 'the significance of national and regional particularities and various historical, cultural and religious backgrounds' should be taken into account when considering human rights. This formulation is often, and rightly, seen as undermining somewhat the universalism of the notion of human rights.

It is important not to take the arguments here too much in their own terms. 'Asia' is a continent with a great many different religions, peoples, customs and values, and the idea that there is one set of, mildly authoritarian, values that are 'authentic' is misleading. It has often been pointed out that while the interests of quasi-authoritarian leaders are served by accusing Western NGOs and governments of cultural imperialism, it is much less clear that the people profit thereby. On the other hand, if these arguments did not have some kind of popular resonance, leaders would not be able to use them, and there is a much more general issue at stake here, one that goes beyond the rhetorics of particular national figures. The modern international system – or, international society, if you prefer – is the product of a specifically European history, and the involvement of the rest of the world in that system is a by-product of European imperialism. The peoples of Africa and Asia, and the indigeneous peoples of the Americas and Oceania, are entitled to point out that they entered the modern international system more or less against their will – certainly those countries that had once been colonies wished for their independence, but as a result of several hundred years of imperialism the only form of independence that made sense was to join the system of states. As noted in Chapter 10, many of the 'nation-states' that resulted from this process did not, and do not, represent social facts, and this has been, and will be, a source of severe tension. In short, the 'clash of civilizations' identified by Huntington and discussed in Chapter 11 is likely to be a feature of global politics in the twenty-first century, although perhaps not in the form that he anticipated.

As with some other issues discussed in this chapter, what we are seeing here is a reflection in the international order of debates and problems that also are to be found within domestic societies. A feature of twenty-first-century life in many of the advanced industrial societies is the demand for respect and esteem made by groups of one kind or another who consider themselves to have been marginalized and undervalued by the dominant, patriarchal, heterosexualist, white culture. 'Multiculturalism' is one response to this situation, as is a politics based on uniting the fragments in a 'Rainbow Coalition' which would challenge the status quo on behalf of all oppressed groups. The problem with this strategy is clear, and is a mirror image of similar problems internationally. Although each of the fragments opposes the dominant culture, this does not mean that their demands are compatible with each other; Quebecois nationalists routinely deny that aboriginal Bands would have the right to secede from Quebec, while popular cultural representatives of African–American men, such as rap artists, routinely spread misogynist and homophobic attitudes. 'Multi-faith' education in schools attempts to instil respect for all religions, but while some liberal Christians may be happy with the thought that their faith is one among many valid possibilities, few other religions take such a relaxed attitude towards the truth of their basic tenets.

The general point is that an international order that has been based on an 'ethic of coexistence', in which political, social and cultural differences are preserved if not valued, faces the challenge of movements such as that supporting the growth of an international human rights regime which seek to impose common standards worldwide. As with the other issues discussed in this chapter, normative problems are central here. Do universalists have the right to impose common values on all peoples, however attractive those values may be to modern

Western liberals? On one argument this is simply not an interesting question, because global socio-economic forces and the new technologies are imposing certain patterns on all peoples, thereby legitimating common responses – thus while the notion of human rights may have a Western origin, the problem to which human rights are a solution, namely excessive state power, is now becoming a universal problem, and so universalist solutions make sense. In fact, as we have seen, global socio-economic forces may well take different forms in different places, and, more generally, globalization seems not to undermine local cultures – just the opposite, resistance to global forces actually seems to reinforce and re-legitimate local identities – but there is a real issue here nonetheless. In what ways do the dramatic changes in technology of recent years have an impact on global politics?

The New Technologies and Global Politics

The first edition of this book was written in 1996 on a 486 laptop, without internet access and with 4MB of memory; four years later the second edition is being completed on a full-multi-media Pentium III 650 Mhz desktop-replacement notebook, with 256 MB of SDRAM. This illustrates two points: first, and obvious, is the fact that the rate of change in the area of IT is staggering. 'Moore's Law' – named for the co-founder of Intel, Gordon Moore – states that the performance of processors will double every 18 to 24 months; physical limitations as to what can be done with silicon may end this process within the next decade, but the possibility of 'molecular electronics' could extend exponential growth into the 2050s (Overton 2000). Numbers of PCs and mobile phones, and use of e-mail and the internet has been increasing exponentially, and as saturation point is reached with one technology, another takes its place. At the time of writing (Summer 2000), 30 million mobile phones are in circulation in the UK; by the time this chapter is read they will be being replaced (or will have been replaced) by new mobiles connected to the internet. The 'runaway world' seems a reasonable sober characterization of this rate of change (Giddens 1999).

Second, it is clear that this progress is *not* being driven by need. For word-processing, e-mail and internet access, the use of spreadsheets and the playing of the vast majority of games – that is, for the things that most people buy PCs for – speeds of over 400 Mhz are more or less irrelevant, and large memories are only necessary because of the existence of complicated programmes which contain features that most people do not need, and because of continual upgrades of operating systems, the benefits of which for ordinary users are, again, doubtful. Nonetheless, by the time this chapter is read, the second set of specifications detailed above will probably seem as outdated as the first. It is not without significance that the single individual who is the most potent symbol of the new technology – Bill Gates of Microsoft – is at root a businessman rather than a scientist or technologist. It is international business that drives forward this technology, although, arguably, it has now reached the point where the dynamic is self-sustaining.

The new technologies have already revolutionized the way we live. Most of the readers of this book will be involved in education one way or another, and the majority will have first-hand experience of the way in which the internet can be used for the transmission of knowledge. Researchers exchange findings by e-mail and the World Wide Web, and international collaboration is easier than it has ever been. But it is not simply the intellectual proletariat whose lives have been transformed; the worker who reads your gas meter, or repairs your refrigerator will down-load the results via a laptop, modem and mobile phone, and order spares in the same way. Deskilling and re-skilling takes place in a great many professions and occupations; some things become easier, requiring fewer skills – shop assistants no longer actually have to work their cash registers and bank clerks no longer have to total-up manually at the end of the day – others more difficult – it is unlikely that fridge repairers ten years ago would have needed basic IT skills. And all this has taken place in less than ten years; even such basic technologies as the photocopier, FAX and the word-processor are less than 20 years old. Describing to today's students how mimeos were 'run off' in the early 1970s generates stares of blank incomprehension.

Sociologists have begun the process of studying and characterizing the 'information age' but students of international relations have been less interested in the subject – an extraordinary omission, given the obvious global significance of the new technologies. Some 'postmodern' writers have been fascinated by IT, and their interest in 'virtual reality' has sometimes led them to address specifically IR-oriented subjects, such as war, but on the whole the discipline of IR has been surprisingly uninterested in the subject. International political economists have noted the role of the new technology in making effective global markets possible, but the wider implications of IT have been less discussed. Partly there are generation issues at stake here; on the whole the people who follow the new technologies with avid interest tend to be under 40, while those who set the agendas for study both in the world and in the academy are not, and are frequently techno-phobic. Even the relentlessly modern British Prime Minister, Tony Blair, is well-known for not using or understanding the new technology – people in power have assistants who handle that side of the business, and are likely therefore to be the last people to recognize the scale of the changes that are taking place.

The neglect of IT is surprising because its impact on global politics has already been highly significant. On the whole, it has heightened differences between nations and continents. The rich world possesses three-quarters of the world's telephone lines – the single most import-ant indicator of the ability to use the new technologies – and is home to nearly 19 out of every 20 internet users. Even this underestimates the extent to which the poorest are being left behind; Thailand is not yet part of the rich world, but it is estimated to have more mobile tele-phones in use than the whole of sub-Saharan Africa. Even the com-paratively wealthy inhabitants of African cities cannot reliably access the internet via the unreliable telephone systems available to them, although this section of the population will benefit from the availabil-ity of inexpensive satellite phones in the near future. However, there have been some clear gainers in the periphery of the world economy. India's 'silicon valley' in and around Bangalore has benefited greatly from the presence of a well-educated, English-speaking population a convenient number of time-zones away from the United States; soft-ware problems can be passed at the end of the American working day from New York and Los Angeles to Indian programmers, in the hope that solutions can be found overnight – and many Indian programmers have made successful careers in the US as valued migrants.

This last example links migration to the new technologies, and wider social impacts of the new technologies on global politics ought not to be neglected. The involvement of immigrant populations in 'Diaspora' politics, made possible by the new technologies, was noted in Chapter 11. The most general impact has been to change the meaning of distance in the modern world even more radically than did the steamship or jet engine. Citizens of countries on the physical periphery of global society have the opportunity to participate in that society in ways their pre-decessors could not imagine, always assuming the countries in question are rich enough to run the necessary stable infrastructure. New Zealan-ders, for example, have taken to the internet like few others. By the same token, global trends in clothing, food and sporting heroes have become commonplace; McDonald's arches have become symbols of one world brand, and the Nike 'swoosh' is equally well-known – Michael Jordan, the basketball-playing symbol of Nike, has some claim to be the most recognizable man on the planet, except in the UK, where basketball has not yet become a mass TV sport (LaFeber 1999).

Does this move towards a world-wide culture of shopping based on global brands constitute a threat to local ways of life? Does the existence of a global 'infotainment' industry based on CNN and MTV and their competitors and imitators pose a threat to local cultures in the broad sense of that term? Here the issue of universalism vs. particularism discussed above in the context of human rights takes another form – although interestingly many of the strongest advocates of universal human rights are also the strongest opponents of 'McWorld', to use the term popularized by Benjamin Barber (1996). To a quite considerable extent the notion of a globalization of world culture has been tied up with the idea that the world is becoming 'Americanized'. Certainly most of the global brands are American in origin, as are most of the players in the infotainment business, and it has become customary for opponents of globalization to regard these forces as the instruments of American cultural imperialism. Trashing a McDonalds (or, more recently for the more politically sophisticated, a Starbucks or Seattle Coffee Company outlet) has become the twenty-first-century equivalent of the traditional protest of attacking the local American Embassy, and in France, in the Summer of 2000, a McDonalds worker fired by 'McDo' for distributing free burgers to passers-by as an act of protest has become a national hero. Meanwhile, the outsourcing of production by US clothing and leisure shoe companies to sweat-shops in South East Asia has become a major scandal, representing the dark side of the universal symbol of success that Michael Jordan has become.

Investigating these issues requires a degree of perspective. First, globalization is, if anything, more of a threat to American culture than to that of the rest of the world; French bistros and cafés will remain, but the American road-side diner is rapidly disappearing. Second, and rather more important, the extent to which global brands actually extend choice and improve quality ought not to be forgotten; the success of McDonalds in many parts of the world rests precisely on the standardization of quality disapproved of by gourmets – the certainty that the hamburgers they are eating are made of materials that pass stringent health tests is a major attraction for many consumers in parts of the world where this cannot always be guaranteed. Britons and Americans who enjoy good coffee have every reason to be grateful for the existence of chains such as Starbucks and the Seattle Coffee Company. There is a wider point here; the success of global brands rests ultimately on the consumer, and even when the consumer acts for reasons which are not as rational as that imputed to British coffee-lovers there is no justification for failing to respect their choices. To read the writings of some French intellectuals one would imagine that the streets of Paris are patrolled by American marines who kidnap innocent Frenchmen and women and force them to eat burgers, see Hollywood movies and, for that matter, talk about what they are going to do at le *'week-end'*; in fact such subversive activities are the result of free choices by the fashionable, and it is difficult to see why these choices should be pilloried in the way they sometimes are.

But the most significant feature of globalization in this sense of the term, is the way in which it has created its own anti-bodies. Benjamin Barber is wrong to counterpose 'Jihad' to 'McWorld' because not all of the resistance movements stimulated by globalization are Islamic, but the general idea is right (Barber 1996). Faced by the challenge of homogenizing external forces, many societies have responded by returning to their roots, or at least to the roots they imagine themselves to possess. Often these roots are preserved or propagated by the very technology that allegedly threatens them; the use of the Internet, satellite TV and other technologies by nationalist movements of one kind or another has been noted in Chapter 11.

Returning to the main theme of this section, contrary to some expectations, location in the world economy has not become irrelevant, even though the same consumption patterns can increasingly be found throughout the developed world. The vision of a world of IT home workers plugged into the internet from attractive rural locations and abandoning big cities has not come to pass, and if property values in global cities such as London are anything to go on is not likely to come to pass in the near future. The attractions of such cities seem to be as compelling as ever (Sassen 2000). This raises a wider point about globalization and the new politics of space and territory, comments on which can form the conclusion to this chapter.

Conclusion: Globalization, 'Supraterritorial Spaces' and the Study of International Relations

In a recent critical introduction to globalization, Jan Aart Scholte offers the following as the first of his core theses on the subject: 'globalization is a transformation of social geography marked by the growth of supra-territorial spaces *but* globalization does not entail the end of territorial geography; territoriality and supraterritoriality coexist in complex interrelations' (Scholte 2000: 8). This highlights a central feature of contemporary world politics, a feature the implications of which have been discussed in this chapter, and frequently throughout the rest of the book. We live in a world where the political organization of space is still based on territorial jurisdictions; whatever might be said about the institutions of global governance it remains the case that the state is still nominally, and much of the time actually, in control of the territories upon which people necessarily live their lives. From this control, states have the capacity to generate a great deal of power which they can use in ways in which they see fit. On the whole, the rulers of states are held accountable only to their own peoples for what they do with this power – and that is on an optimistic reading of the situation. In short, the state remains the key actor in international relations, and it is right that the academic study of IR should reflect this fact.

The complication comes from the existence of so many potent forces in our world which clearly cannot be understood within this framework. Many of these are rooted in the world economy, but others reflect the common concerns for security and a normative understanding of human existence discussed in this chapter. The growth of an international human rights regime, and of global concern for the environment cannot be explained within a state-centric view of the world, but neither is it possible to make sense of either phenomenon without reference to the important – crucial – roles played by particular states and the states-system itself. A complex relationship exists between these supraterritorial forces and the territorial state. Understanding this relationship is going to be a key task for twenty-first-century international relations – and a very difficult task, because the relationship is continually changing, and hitting a moving target is never easy. But it will also be a very rewarding task, especially if the discourse of international relations draws on its own history and is prepared to be as eclectic in the future as it has been in the past. The 'professionalization' of international relations, its establishment as an academic discipline in its own right, has brought advantages – the standards of rigour characteristic of modern rational-choice international relations, for example, represent real progress – but it has also sometimes brought a narrowing of sensibilities, an unwillingness to step beyond models which persist in conceptualizing the world in excessively statist terms. This simply will not do – an openness to other cultures, other discourses, other modes of reasoning is not simply desirable because it makes for a more interesting study, it is a necessity for the understanding of a world which is increasingly resistant to simplification. If scholars of 'International Relations' can manage to develop the right mind-set they can be at the forefront of the study of global society and politics in the new century; if not, the discipline will be one more casualty of the 'runaway world'.

Further Reading

On the economic dimensions of globalization, see the reading attached to Chapter 9; Held *et al.*, *Global Transformations* (1999) and *The Global Transformations Reader* (2000) and Scholte *Globalization* (2000) are as relevant for this chapter as that. On globalization as a social and cultural phenomenon, there is a vast amount of literature. Manuel Castells, *The Information Age: Economy, Society and Culture* 3 Vols (1996/7) is a monumental study, with Martin Albrow, *The Global Age: State and Society Beyond Modernity* (1996) equally ambitious, if on a smaller canvas. Zygmund Bauman, *Globalization: The Human Consequences* (1998), Ulrich Beck *World Risk Society* (1999), Saskia Sassen, *Globalization and its Discontents* (1998) and Leslie Sklair, *The Sociology of the Global System* (1995) offer further sociological perspectives. Anthony Giddens' Reith Lectures, *The Runaway World* (1999) is aimed at a wider non-academic market, but is highly thought-provoking nonetheless. John Tomlinson, *Globalization and Culture* (1999) pulls together a great deal of material on this subject. From within the world of IR theory, there have been a number of excellent contributions from different perspectives. Without relying on the term globalization, J. N Rosenau, *Along the Domestic-Foreign Frontier: Exploring Governance in a Turbulent World* (1997) is a valuable contribution to this literature. Richard Falk's *Predatory Globalization: A Critique* (1999) is a useful corrective to the over-enthusiasm of hyper-globalizers from the doyen of World Order Modelling; Ian Clark's *Globalization and International Relations Theory* (1999) represents the classical tradition at its best, and Martin Shaw (ed.), *Politics and Globalization: Knowledge, Ethics and Agency* (1999) is a very useful collection representing what may come to be known as the 'Sussex School'. It should be stressed that these references are only a small selection of the available material; David Held *et al.* (1999) and Jan Aart Scholte (2000) have excellent bibliographies.

The lack of material on IR and the new technologies is striking. For a broadly positive account of the future see Thomas Friedman, *The Lexus and the Olive Tree* (1999). For a more unsettling account of the possible impact of the new technologies, see Bill Joy, 'Why the Future Doesn't Need Us' (2000). The latter, which appears in the magazine *Wired* – which is an important source of ideas on the new world that is emerging – is particular disturbing because of Joy's position as co-founder and Chief Scientist at Sun Microsystems, and co-chair of the presidential commission on the future of IT research. The 1999 *Human Development Report* of the UNDP devotes a great deal of space to global inequalities in access to IT.

On new notions of security, for the Copenhagen School see Barry Buzan, *People, States and Fear* (1990), Buzan *et al.*, *The European Security Order Recast: Scenarios for the Post-Cold War Era* (1990), and, especially, *Security: A New Framework for Analysis* (1998): an informative debate on the Copenhagen School can be found in the pages of the *Review of International Studies* – Bill McSweeney, 'Identity and Security: Buzan and the Copenhagen School' (1996), Barry Buzan and Ole Waever, 'Slippery? Contradictory? Sociologically Untenable?: The Copenhagen School Replies' (1997) and McSweeney, 'Durkheim and the Copenhagen School' (1998). For Critical Security Studies see Ken Booth (ed.), *New Thinking about Strategy and International Security* (1991a); *idem*, 'Security and Emancipation' (1991c) and Keith Krause and Michael C. Williams (eds), *Critical Security Studies: Concepts and Cases* (1997). Steven Walt in 'The Renaissance of Security Studies' (1991) is, apparently, unconvinced by redefinitions. Sean M. Lynn Jones and Steven Miller (eds), *Global Dangers: Changing Dimensions of International Security* (1995) give the view from the pages of *International Security*. Terry Nardin and David Mapel (eds), *Traditions of International Ethics* (1992) present an overview of normative approaches; Mervyn Frost, *Ethics in International Relations* (1996) and Molly Cochran, *Normative Theory in International Relations* (2000) are important studies in this area.

Andrew Hurrell and Benedict Kingsbury (eds), *The International Politics of the Environment* (1992) is a very valuable collection with essays on institutions, standard-setting and conflicts of interest. Wolfgang Sachs (ed.), *Global Ecology: A New Arena of Political Conflict* (1993) and John Vogler and Mark Imber (eds), *The Environment and International Relations* (1995) are equally useful. Also see Garth Porter and Janet Welsh Brown, *Global Environmental Politics* (1991); and Caroline Thomas, *The Environment in International Relations* (1992).

Thomas (ed.), 'Rio: Unravelling the Consequences', special issue of *Environmental Politics* (1994) is the best single source on UNCED. Early warning of environmental problems ahead was given in Richard Falk, *This Endangered Planet* (1971). Peter Haas (ed.), 'Knowledge, Power and International Policy Coordination', special issue of *International Organisation* (1992) is the best source for epistemic communities. Oran Young *et al*, (eds) *Global Environmental Change and International Governance* (1996) is an important study. A new edition of John Vogler, *The Global Commons: A Regime Analysis* (1995) is due soon.

On human rights, Tim Dunne and N. J. Wheeler (eds), *Human Rights in Global Politics* (1999) is the best single-volume collection; R. J. Vincent, *Human Rights and International Relations: Issues and Responses* (1986) and Jack Donnelly, *International Human Rights* (1993) are useful studies. Karen Smith and Margot Light (eds), *Ethics and Foreign Policy* (2001) set out some of the difficulties involved in making human rights central to foreign policy. Brian Barry and Robert E. Goodin (eds), *Free Movement* (1992) is a good source for different perspectives on migration and refugees. Gil Loescher, *Beyond Charity: International Co-operation and the Global Refugee Crisis* (1993) is a standard work. See also on this subject Alan Dowty, *Closed Borders* (1987), and Chris Brown, 'On the Borders of (International) Political Theory' (2000b).

J. S. Peters and A. Wolper (eds), *Women's Rights, Human Rights: International Feminist Perspectives* (1995) is the best collection in its area. Joanne Bauer and Daniel A. Bell (eds), *The East Asian Challenge for Human Rights* (1999) judiciously presents the 'Asian Values' debate. Mahathir Bin Mohamed and Shintaro Ishihara's modestly titled *The Voice of Asia: Two Leaders Discuss the Coming Century* (1996) gives the case against the West. See also Chris Brown, 'Cultural Diversity and International Political Theory' (2000a). References to the 'clash of civilizations' in Chapter 11 are relevant here. Benjamin Barber, *Jihad vs. McWorld* (1996) is an interesting take on the global consumer culture.

On humanitarian intervention N. J. Wheeler, *Saving Strangers* (2000) is likely to come to be seen as a classic. William Shawcross, *Deliver Us From Evil: Warlords and Peacekeepers in a World of Endless Conflict* (2000) is a good popular survey of peacekeeping and intervention in the 1990s. Jonathon Moore (ed.), *Hard Choices: Moral Dilemmas in Humanitarian Intervention* (1998) is a valuable collection of papers by practitioners as well as academics. Thomas G. Weiss,

Military–Civil Interactions: Intervening in Humanitarian Crises (1999) is a good account of the technicalities of intervention. Oliver Ramsbotham and Tom Woodhouse, *Humanitarian Intervention in Contemporary Conflict* (1996) manages very effectively to move away from the traditional agenda. Noam Chomsky, *The New Military Humanism* (1999) attacks the motives of the interveners. The Journal *Ethics and International Affairs* published by the Carnegie Council for Ethics and International Affairs is a valuable source of material on this subject.

Bibliography

Adler, A. (1997) 'Seizing the Middle Ground', *European Journal of International Relations* (3) 319–64.

Albrow, M. (1996) *The Global Age: State and Society Beyond Modernity* (Cambridge: Polity Press).

Aldcroft, D. H. (1977) *From Versailles to Wall Street 1919–1929* (Harmondsworth: Penguin).

Allison, G. (1971) *Essence of Decision* (Boston: Little Brown).

Allison, G. and G. F. Treverton (eds) (1992) *Rethinking America's Security: Beyond Cold War to New World Order* (New York: W. W. Norton).

Allison, G. T. and P. Zelikow (1999) *Essence of Decision: Explaining the Cuban Missile Crisis*, 2nd ed. (New York: Longman).

American Political Science Review (1997) Forum on Neo-Realism (91) 899–936.

Amin, S. (1974) *Accumulation on a World Scale*, Vols I and II (New York: Monthly Review Press).

Amin, S. (1977) *Imperialism and Unequal Development* (New York: Monthly Review Press).

Angell, N. (1909) *The Great Illusion* (London: Weidenfeld & Nicolson).

Appadurai, A. (1996) *Modernity at Large: Cultural Dimensions of Globalization* (Minneapolis: Minnesota University Press).

Archibugi, D. and D. Held (eds) (1995) *Cosmopolitan Democracy* (Cambridge: Polity Press).

Aron, R. (1967) *Peace and War: A Theory of International Relations* (London: Weidenfeld & Nicolson).

Arrighi, G., T. Hopkins and I. Wallerstein (1989) *Anti-systemic Movements* (London: Verso).

Art, R. and K. Waltz (eds) (1993) *The Use of Force: Military Power and International Politics* (Lanham, MD: University Press of America).

Ashley, R. K. (1984) 'The Poverty of Neorealism', *International Organization* (38) 225–86.

Ashley, R. K. (1989a) 'Living on Borderlines: Man, Poststructuralism and War', in Der Derian and Shapiro, *International/Intertextual*.

Ashley, R. K. (1989b) 'Imposing International Purpose: Notes on a Problematic of Government', in Czempial and Rosenau, *Global Changes*.

Ashley, R. K. (1989c) 'Untying the Sovereign State: A Double Reading of the Anarchy Problematique', *Millennium* (17) 227–86.

Ashley, R. K. and R. B. J. Walker (eds) (1990) 'Speaking the Language of Exile: Dissidence in International Studies', Special Issue, *International Studies Quarterly* (34) 259–417.

Axelrod, R. (1984) *The Evolution of Cooperation* (New York: Basic Books).

Axelrod, R. and R. O. Keohane (1985) 'Achieving Cooperation under Anarchy: Strategies and Institutions', *World Politics* (38) 226–54.

Aziz, J., and R. F. Wescott (1997) *Policy Complementarities and the Washington Consensus* (Washington, DC: The International Monetary Fund).

Bachrach, P. and M. P. Baratz (1970) *Power and Poverty* (New York: Oxford University Press).

Balaam, D. and M. Veseth (1995) *Introduction to International Political Economy* (New York: Prentice-Hall).

Baldwin, D. A. (1985) *Economic Statecraft* (Princeton: Princeton University Press).

Baldwin, D. A. (1989) *Paradoxes of Power* (New York: Basic Books).

Baldwin, D. A. (ed.) (1993) *Neorealism and Neoliberalism: The Contemporary Debate* (New York: Columbia University Press).

Baldwin, D. A. (1997) 'The Concept of Security', *Review of International Studies* (23) 5–26.

Baldwin, D. A. (1998) 'Correspondence Evaluating Economic Sanctions', *International Security* (23) 189–98.

Baldwin, D. A. (1999/2000) 'The Sanctions Debate and the Logic of Choice', *International Security* (24) 80–107.

Baran, P. (1957) *The Political Economy of Growth* (New York: Monthly Review Press).

Barber, B. (1996) *Jihad vs. McWorld* (New York: Ballantine Books).

Barkawi, T and M. Laffey (1999) 'The Imperial Peace: Democracy, Force and Globalization', *European Journal of International Relations* (5) 403–434.

Barnard, F. M. (ed.) (1969) *J. G. Herder on Social and Political Culture* (Cambridge: Cambridge University Press).

Barnet, R. and J. Cavanagh (1994) *Global Dreams: Imperial Corporations and the New World Order* (New York: Simon & Schuster).

Barry, B. (1989) 'The Obscurities of Power', in *idem, Democracy, Power and Justice* (Oxford: Oxford University Press).

Barry, B. and R. E. Goodin (eds) (1992) *Free Movement* (Hemel Hempstead: Harvester Wheatsheaf).

Bauer, J. and D. A. Bell (eds) (1999) *The East Asian Challenge for Human Rights* (Cambridge: Cambridge University Press).

Bauer, P. (1981) *Equality, The Third World and Economic Delusion* (London: Weidenfeld & Nicolson).

Bauman, Z. (1998) *Globalization: the Human Consequences* (Cambridge: Polity Press).

Beck, U. (1999) *World Risk Society* (Cambridge: Polity Press).

Bender, J. and T. H. Hammond (1992) 'Rethinking Allison's Models', *American Political Science Review* (86) 301–22.

Bentham, J. (1789/1960) *Principles of Morals and Legislation* (Oxford: Basil Blackwell).

Berdal, M. (1996) 'The United Nations in International Relations', *International Affairs* (22) 95–106.

Bernstein, B. J. (2000) 'Understanding Decisionmaking, US Foreign Policy and the Cuban Missile Crisis: A Review Essay', *International Security* (25) 1, 134–64.

Berridge, G. R. (1995) *Diplomacy: Theory and Practice* (London: Harvester Wheatsheaf).

Best, G. (1994) *War and Law Since 1945* (Oxford: Oxford University Press).

Blainey, G. (1988) *The Causes of War* (New York: Free Press).

Blake, D. H. and R. S. Walters (1991) *The Politics of Global Economic Relations* (London: Prentice-Hall).

Block, F. (1977) *The Origins of International Economic Disorder* (Berkeley: University of California Press).

Bohman, J. and M. Lutz-Bachmann (eds) (1997) *Perpetual Peace: Essays on Kant's Cosmopolitan Ideal* (Cambridge, MA: MIT Press).

Booth, K. (ed.) (1991a) *New Thinking about Strategy and International Security* (London: HarperCollins).

Booth, K. (1991b) 'Security in Anarchy: Utopian Realism in Theory and Practice', *International Affairs* (67) 527–45.

Booth, K. (1991c) 'Security and Emancipation', *Review of International Studies* (17) 313–26.

Booth, K. (1997) 'A Reply to Wallace', *Review of International Studies* (23) 371–7.

Booth, K. and S. Smith (eds) (1994) *International Relations Theory Today* (Cambridge: Polity Press).

Boucher, D. (1998) *Political Theories of International Relations* (Oxford: Oxford University Press).

Boulding, K. (1962) *Conflict and Defense* (New York: Harper & Row).

Bozeman, A. B. (1960) *Politics and Culture in International History* (Princeton: Princeton University Press).

Brecher, M. (1993) *Crises in World Politics: Theory and Reality* (Oxford: Pergamon Press).

Brenner, R. (1977) 'The Origins of Capitalist Development', *New Left Review* (104) 25–92.

Brett, E. A. (1985) *The World Economy Since the War* (Brighton: Harvester Wheatsheaf).

Brewer, A. (1990) *Marxist Theories of Imperialism: A Critical Survey* (London: Routledge).

Brown, C. (1992a) *International Relations Theory: New Normative Approaches* (Hemel Hempstead: Harvester Wheatsheaf).

Brown, C. (1992b) ' "Really-Existing Liberalism", and International Order', *Millennium* (21) 313–28.

Brown, C. (1994a) 'Critical Theory and Postmodernism in International Relations', in Groom and Light, *Contemporary International Relations*.

Brown, C. (1994b) ' "Turtles All the Way Down": Antifoundationalism, Critical Theory, and International Relations', *Millennium* (23) 213–38.

Brown, C. (ed.) (1994c) *Political Restructuring in Europe: Ethical Perspectives* (London: Routledge).

Brown, C. (1995) 'The End of History?', in Danchev, *Fin de Siècle*.

Brown, C. (1999) 'History Ends, Worlds Collide', *Review of International Studies*: Special Issue *'The Interregnum'* (25) 45–57 (also M. Cox, K. Booth and T. Dunne (eds), *The Interregnum* (Cambridge: Cambridge University Press)).

Brown, C. (2000a) 'Cultural Diversity and International Political Theory', *Review of International Studies* (26) 199–213.

Brown, C. (2000b) 'On the Borders of (International) Political Theory', in O'Sullivan, N. (ed.) *Political Theory in Transition* (London: Routledge)

Brown, C., T. Nardin, and N. J. Rengger (eds) (2001) *Texts in International Relations* (Cambridge: Cambridge University Press)

Brown, M. E., S. M. Lynn-Jones and S. E. Miller (eds) (1995) *The Perils of Anarchy: Contemporary Realism and International Security* (Cambridge, MA.: MIT Press).

Brown, M. E., S. M. Lynn-Jones and S. E. Miller (eds) (1996) *Debating the Democratic Peace* (Cambridge, MA: MIT Press).

Bull, H. (1976) 'Martin Wight and the Theory of International Relations', *British Journal of International Studies* (2) 101–16.

Bull, H. (1977/1995) *The Anarchical Society* (London: Macmillan).

Bull, H. (1984) *Justice in International Relations: The Hagey Lectures* (Waterloo, Ontario: University of Waterloo).

Bull, H. and A. Watson (eds) (1984) *The Expansion of International Society* (Oxford: Clarendon Press).

Burchill, S. and A. Linklater (eds) (1996) *Theories of International Relations* (London: Macmillan).

Burkhi, S. J. and G. E. Perry (1998) *Beyond the Washington Consensus: Institutions Matter* (Washington, DC: The World Bank).

Burton, J. W. (1968) *Systems, States, Diplomacy and Rules* (Cambridge: Cambridge University Press).

Burton, J. W. (1972) *World Society* (Cambridge: Cambridge University Press).

Bush, President G. (1990) 'Towards a New World Order', Address before a joint session of Congress, September 11, *US Department of State Dispatch* 17.9.90, 91–4.

Butterfield, H. (1953) *Christianity, Diplomacy and War* (London: Epworth).

Butterfield, H. and M. Wight (eds) (1966) *Diplomatic Investigations* (London: George Allen & Unwin).

Buzan, B. (1990) *People, States and Fear*, 2nd edn (London: Harvester Wheatsheaf).

Buzan, B. (1993) 'From International System to International Society: Structural Realism and Regime Theory Meet the English School', *International Organization* (47), 327–52.

Buzan, B. (1999) 'The English School as a Research Programme' BISA Conference, Manchester, and at *http://www.ukc.ac.uk/politics/englishschool/*.

Buzan, B. *et al.* (eds) (1990) *The European Security Order Recast: Scenarios for the Post-Cold War Era* (London: Pinter Publishers).

Buzan, B., C. Jones and R. Little (1993) *The Logic of Anarchy: Neorealism to Structural Realism* (New York: Columbia University Press).

Buzan, B. and O. Waever (1997) 'Slippery? Contradictory? Sociologically Untenable? The Copenhagen School Replies' [to McSweeney 1996] *Review of International Studies* (23) 241–50.

Buzan, B., O. Waever and J. de Wilde (1998) *Security: A New Framework for Analysis* (Boulder, CO: Lynne Rienner).

Byman, D. A. and M. C. Waxman (2000) 'Kosovo and the Great Air Power Debate', *International Security* (24) 5–38.

Campbell, D. (1993) *Politics without Principle: Sovereignty, Ethics, and the Narratives of the Gulf War* (Boulder, CO, Lynne Reinner).

Campbell, D. (1998) *National Deconstruction: Violence, Identity and Justice in Bosnia* (Minneapolis, University of Minnesota Press).

Caporaso, J. (ed.) (1978) 'Dependence and Dependency in the Global System', Special Issue *International Organization* (32) 1–300.

Cardoso, F. and E. Faletto (1979) *Dependency and Development in Latin America* (Berkeley: University of California Press).

Carr, E. H. (1939) *The Twenty Years Crisis* (London: Macmillan).

Carver, T., M. Cochran and J. Squires (1998) 'Gendering Jones', *Review of International Studies* (24) 283–97.

Castells, M. (1996/7) *The Information Age: Economy, Society and Culture*, 3 Vols (Oxford: Basil Blackwell)

Cavanagh, J., D. Wysham and M. Arruda (1994) *Beyond Bretton Woods: Alternatives to the Global Economic Order* (London: Pluto Press).

Cerny, P. (1990) *The Changing Architecture of Politics* (London: Sage Publications).

Chalmers, A. F. (1982) *What is This Thing Called Science?*, 2nd edn (Milton Keynes: Open University Press).

Chase-Dunn, C. (1989) *Global Formation: Structures of the World Economy* (Oxford: Basil Blackwell).

Chomsky, N. (1994) *World Orders, Old and New* (London: Pluto Press).

Chomsky, N. (1999) *The New Military Humanism* (London: Pluto Press).

Clark, G. and L. B. Sohn (1966) *World Peace through World Law* (Cambridge, MA: Harvard University Press).

Clark, I. (1999) *Globalization and International Relations Theory* (Oxford: Oxford University Press).

Clarke, M. and B. White (eds) (1989) *Understanding Foreign Policy: The Foreign Policy Systems Approach* (Aldershot: Edward Elgar).

Claude, I. L. (1962) *Power and International Relations* (New York: Random House).

Claude, I. L. (1971) *Swords into Plowshares* (New York: Random House).

Clausewitz, C. (1976) *On War* (trans. and ed. by Michael Howard and Peter Paret) (Princeton: Princeton University Press).

Cochran, M. (2000) *Normative Theory in International Relations* (Cambridge: Cambridge University Press).

Cohen, B. (1990) 'Review Article: The Political Economy of International Trade', *International Organization* (44) 261–78.

Cohen, R. (1994) 'Pacific Unions: A Reappraisal of the Theory that " Democracies Do Not Go To War With Each Other"', *Review of International Studies* (20) 207–23.

Coker, C. (1994) *War in the Twentieth Century* (London: Brassey's).

Coker, C. (1998) *War and the Illiberal Conscience* (Boulder, CO: Westview Press).

Connolly, W. E (1983) *The Terms of Political Discourse* (Oxford: Martin Robertson).

Connolly, W. E. (1991) *Identity/Difference: Democratic Negotiations of Political Paradox* (Ithaca: Cornell University Press).

Connolly, W.E. (1995) *The Ethos of Pluralization* (Minneapolis, MN: University of Minnesota Press).

Constantinou, C. (1994) 'Diplomatic Representation, or, Who Framed the Ambassadors?', *Millennium* (23) 1–23.

Constantinou, C. (1996) *On the Way to Diplomacy* (Minneapolis, MN: University of Minnesota Press).

Cottam, M. (1986) *Foreign Policy Decision-Making: The Influence of Cognition* (Boulder, CO: Westview Press).

Cox, R. (1981) 'Social Forces, States, and World Orders: Beyond International Relations Theory', *Millennium* (10) 126–55.

Cox, R. (1987) *Production, Power and World Order: Social Forces in the Making of History* (New York: Columbia University Press).

Cox, R. and H. K. Jacobson (eds) (1973) *The Anatomy of Influence* (New Haven: Yale University Press).

Cox, R. (with T. Sinclair) (1996) *Approaches to World Order* (Cambridge: Cambridge University Press).

Craig, G. C. and A. L. George (eds) (1983) *Force and Statecraft* (New York: Oxford University Press).

Crane, G. T. and A. M. Amawi (eds) (1999) *The Theoretical Evolution of International Political Economy: A Reader* (New York: Oxford University Press).

Creasy, E. (1902) *Fifteen Decisive Battles* (London: Macmillan).

Czempial E.-O. and J. N. Rosenau (eds) (1989) *Global Changes and Theoretical Challenges* (Lexington: Lexington Books).

Dahl, R. (1961) *Who Governs?* (New Haven: Yale University Press).

Dahl, R. (1970) *Modern Political Analysis* (New York: Prentice-Hall).

Dahrendorf, R. (1990) *Reflections on the Revolution in Europe* (London: Chatto and Windus).

Danchev, A. (ed.) (1995) *Fin de Siècle: The Meaning of the Twentieth Century* (London: I. B. Tauris).

Dehio, L. (1965) *The Precarious Balance* (New York: Knopf).

Der Derian, J. (1987) *On Diplomacy: A Genealogy of Western Estrangement* (Oxford: Basil Blackwell).

Der Derian, J. (1992) *Antidiplomacy: Spies, Terror, Speed and War* (Oxford: Basil Blackwell).

Der Derian, J. (1998) *The Virilio Reader* (Oxford: Basil Blackwell).

Der Derian, J. and M. Shapiro (eds) (1989) *International/Intertextual: Postmodern Readings in World Politics* (Lexington: Lexington Books).

Deudeny, D. (2000) 'Geopolitics as Theory: Historical Security Materialism', *European Journal of International Relations* (6) 77–108.

Deudeney, D. and G. J. Ikenberry, (1999) 'The Nature and Sources of Liberal International Order', *Review of International Studies* (25) 179–96.

Devetak, R. (1996) 'Critical Theory', and 'Postmodernism', in Burchill and Linklater, *Theories of International Relations*.

Dicken, P. (1992) *Global Shift: The Internationalization of Economic Activity* (London: Chapman & Hall).

Donnelley, J. (1993) *International Human Rights* (Boulder, CO: Westview Press).

Donnelly, J. (2000) *Realism and International Relations* (Cambridge: Cambridge University Press).

Dowty, A. (1987) *Closed Borders* (New Haven: Yale University Press).

Doyle, M. (1983) 'Kant, Liberal Legacies and Foreign Policy', Parts I and II, *Philosophy and Public Affairs* (12) 205–35 and 323–53.

Doyle, M. (1986) 'Liberalism and World Politics', *American Political Science Review* (80) 1151–70.

Doyle, M. (1997) *Ways of War and Peace: Realism, Liberalism and Socialism* (New York: Norton).

Dunne, T. (1995) 'The Social Construction of International Society', *European Journal of International Relations* (1) 367–89.

Dunne, T. (1998) *Inventing International Society* (London: Macmillan).

Dunne, T. and N. Wheeler (1996) 'Hedley Bull's Pluralism of the Intellect and Solidarism of the Will', *International Affairs* (72) 91–107.

Dunne, T. and N. Wheeler (eds) (1999) *Human Rights in Global Politics* (Cambridge: Cambridge University Press).

Edkins, J. (1999) *Poststructuralism and International Relations: Bringing the Political Back In* (Boulder, CO: Lynne Rienner).

Edkins, J., N. Persram, and V. Pin-Fat (eds) (1999) *Sovereignty and Subjectivity* (Boulder, CO: Lynne Rienner).

Ekins, P. (1992) *A New World Order: Grassroots Movements for Global Change* (London: Routledge).

Elshtain, J. B. (ed.) (1981) *Public Man, Private Woman* (Oxford: Martin Robertson).

Elshtain, J. B. (1987) *Women and War* (Brighton: Harvester Wheatsheaf).

Elshtain, J. B. (1998) '*Women and War* Ten Years After', *Review of International Studies* (24) 447–60.

Emmanuel, A. (1972) *Unequal Exchange* (London: New Left Books).

Enloe, C. (1989) *Bananas, Beaches and Bases* (London: Pandora Books).

Enloe, C. (1993) *The Morning After: Sexual Politics at the End of the Cold War* (Berkeley: University of California Press).

Evans, G. (1975) 'E. H. Carr and International Relations', *British Journal of International Studies* (1) 77–97.

Evans, P., D. Rueschemeyer and T. Skocpol (eds) (1985) *Bringing the State Back In* (Cambridge: Cambridge University Press).

Evans, P. B., H. K. Jacobson and R. D. Putnam (eds) (1993) *Double-Edged Diplomacy: International Diplomacy and Domestic Politics* (Berkeley: University of California Press).

Falk, R. (1971) *This Endangered Planet* (New York: Vintage).

Falk, R. (1999) *Predatory Globalization: A Critique* (Cambridge: Polity Press).

Forsyth, M. G., H. M. A. Keens-Soper and P. Savigear (eds) (1970) *The Theory of International Relations* (London: Allen & Unwin).

Fox, W. R. T (1985) 'E. H. Carr and Political Realism: Vision and Revision', *Review of International Studies* (11) 1–16.

Frank, A. G. (1971) *Capitalism and Underdevelopment in Latin America* (Harmondsworth: Penguin).

Frank, A. G. and B. Gills (eds) (1993) *The World System: Five Hundred Years or Five Thousand Years* (London: Routledge).

Freedman, L. (ed.) (1994) *War* (Oxford: Oxford University Press).

Freedman, L. (2000) 'Victims and victors: reflections on the Kosovo war' *Review of International Studies* (26) 335–58.

Freud, S. (1985) *Civilisation, Society and Religion* (Harmondsworth: Penguin).
Frieden, J. A. and D. A. Lake (eds) (2000) *International Political Economy: Perspectives on Global Power and Wealth* (London: Routledge).
Friedman, M. (1966) *Essays in Positive Economics* (Chicago: Chicago University Press).
Friedman, T. (1999) *The Lexus and the Olive Tree* (New York: Harper Collins).
Frost, M. (1996) *Ethics in International Relations* (Cambridge: Cambridge University Press).
Fukuyama, F. (1989) 'The End Of History', *The National Interest* (16) 3–16.
Fukuyama, F. (1992) *The End of History and the Last Man* (New York: Free Press).
Galtung, J. (1971) 'A Structural Theory of Imperialism', *Journal of Peace Research* (13) 81–94.
Gardner, R. N. (1980) *Sterling–Dollar Diplomacy in Current Perspective: The Origins and Prospects of our International Economic Order* (New York: Columbia University Press).
Garthoff, R. (1994) *The Great Transition: American–Soviet Relations and the End of the Cold War* (Washington, DC: Brookings Institute).
Gellman, P. (1988) 'Hans Morgenthau and the Legacy of Political Realism', *Review of International Studies* (14) 247–66.
Gellner, E. (1988) *Plough, Sword and Book: The Structure of Human History* (London: Collins Harvill).
George, A. L. (1971) *The Limits of Coercive Diplomacy* (Boston: Little Brown).
George, J. (1994) *Discourses of Global Politics: A Critical (Re) Introduction to International Relations* (Boulder, CO: Lynne Reinner).
George, S. (1988) *A Fate Worse than Debt* (Harmondsworth: Penguin).
Germain, R. and M. Kenny (1998) 'Engaging Gramsci: International Relations Theory and the New Gramscians', *Review of International Studies* (24) 3–21.
Gerner, D. J. (1991) 'Foreign Policy Analysis: Exhilarating Eclecticism, Intriguing Enigmas', in Howell, 'International Studies'.
Giddens, A. (1985) *The Nation-State and Violence* (Cambridge: Polity Press).
Giddens, A. (1999) *The Runaway World* (Cambridge: Polity Press).
Gill, S. (ed.) (1993) *Gramsci, Historical Materialism and International Relations* (Cambridge: Cambridge University Press).
Gill, S. and D. Law (1988) *The Global Economy: Prospects, Problems and Policies* (London: Harvester).
Gills, B. *et al.* (1993) *Low Intensity Democracy: Political Power in the New World Order* (London: Pluto Press).
Gilpin, R. (1975) *US Power and the Multinational Corporation* (New York: Basic Books).
Gilpin, R. (1981) *War and Change in World Politics* (New York: Cambridge University Press).
Gilpin, R. (1984) 'The Richness of the Tradition of Political Realism', *International Organization* (38) 287–304.
Gilpin, R. (1987) *The Political Economy of International Relations* (Princeton: Princeton University Press).
Gilpin, R. (2000) *The Challenge of Global Capitalism: The World Economy in the 21st Century* (Princeton: Princeton University Press).

Gleditsch, N. P. and T. Risse-Kappen (eds) (1995) 'Democracy and Peace', Special Issue, *European Journal of International Relations* (1) 429–574.

Goldstein, J. and R. O. Keohane (eds) (1993) *Ideas and Foreign Policy* (Ithaca: Cornell University Press).

Gong, G. C. (1984) *The Standard of 'Civilisation', in International Society* (Oxford: Oxford University Press).

Gowa, J. (1983) *Closing the Gold Window: Domestic Politics and the End of Bretton Woods* (Ithaca: Cornell University Press).

Gowa, J. (1999) *Ballots and Bullets: The Elusive Democratic Peace* (Princeton: Princeton University Press).

Grant, R. and K. Newland (eds) (1991) *Gender and International Relations* (Milton Keynes: Open University Press).

Gray, C. (1999) 'Clausewitz Rules OK! The Future is the Past with GPS', *Review of International Studies* Special Issue *'The Interregnum'* (25) 161–82 (also M. Cox, K. Booth and T. Dunne (eds), *The Interregnum* (Cambridge: Cambridge University Press)).

Grieco, J. M. (1988) 'Anarchy and the Limits of Cooperation: A Realist Critique of the Newest Liberal Institutionalism', *International Organization* (42) 485–508.

Griffiths, M. (1992) *Realism, Idealism and International Politics: A Reinterpretation* (London: Routledge).

Groom, A. J. R. and M. Light (eds) (1994) *Contemporary International Relations: A Guide to Theory* (London: Pinter Publishers).

Groom, A. J. R. and P. Taylor (eds) (1975) *Functionalism: Theory and Practice in World Politics* (London: University of London Press).

Groom, A. J. R. and P. Taylor (eds) (1984) *The Commonwealth in the 1980s* (London: Macmillan).

Groom, A. J. R. and P. Taylor (eds) (1994) *Frameworks for International Cooperation* (London: Pinter).

Gulick, E. V. (1955) *Europe's Classical Balance of Power* (Ithaca: Cornell University Press).

Guzzini, S. (2000) 'A Reconstruction of Constructivism in International Relations', *European Journal of International Relations* (6) 147–82.

Haas, E. B. (1964) *Beyond the Nation State* (Stanford: Stanford University Press).

Haas, P. (1989) 'Do Regimes Matter: Epistemic Communities and Mediterranean Pollution Control', *International Organization* (43) 377–403.

Haas, P. (ed.) (1992) 'Knowledge, Power and International Policy Coordination', Special Issue, *International Organization* (46) 1–390.

Habermas, J. (1994) *The Past as Future* (Cambridge: Polity Press).

Habermas, J. (1997) 'Kant's Idea of Perpetual Peace, with the Benefit of Two Hundred Years' Hindsight' in Bohman and Lutz-Bachmann (eds) *Perpetual Peace*.

Habermas, J. (1999) 'Bestialität und Humanität: Ein Krieg an der Grenze zwischen Recht and Moral' *Die Zeit* 18, 29 April.

Hall, R. B. (1999) *National Collective Identity: Social Constructs and International System* (New York: Columbia University Press).

Halliday, F. (1992) 'An Encounter with Fukuyama', *New Left Review* (193) 89–95.

Halliday, F. (1994) *Rethinking International Relations* (London: Macmillan).
Hamilton K. and R. T. B. Langhorne (1995) *The Practice of Diplomacy* (London: Routledge).
Hanson, V. D. (1989) *The Western Way of War: Infantry Battle in Classical Greece* (New York: Knopf).
Harding, S. (1986) *The Science Question in Feminism* (Milton Keynes: Open University Press).
Harris, N. (1986) *The End of the Third World* (Harmondsworth: Penguin).
Harvey, N. (1998) *The Chiapas Rebellion* (Durham, NC: Duke University Press).
Hasenclever, A., P. Mayer, and V. Rittberger (1997) *Theories of International Regimes* (Cambridge: Cambridge University Press).
Hasenclever, A., P. Mayer, and V. Rittberger (2000) 'Integrating Theories of International Regimes', *Review of International Studies* (26) 3–33.
Hegel, G. F. W. (1821/1991) *Elements of the Philosophy of Right* (Cambridge: Cambridge University Press).
Held, D. (1995) *Democracy and the Global Order* (Cambridge: Polity Press).
Held, D. *et al.* (1999) *Global Transformations* (Cambridge: Polity Press).
Held, D. *et al.* (eds.) (2000) *The Global Transformations Reader* (Cambridge: Polity Press).
Hermann, C. F., C. W. Kegley and J. N. Rosenau (eds) (1987) *New Directions in the Study of Foreign Policy* (London: Allen & Unwin).
Higgott, R. (1994) 'International Political Economy', in Groom and Light, *Contemporary International Relations*.
Higgott, R. (2000) 'Economic Globalization and Global Governance: Towards a Post Washington Consensus', in Rittberger and Schnabel (eds) *The UN Global Governance System in the Twenty-First Century*.
Hill, C. (1989) '1939: The Origins of Liberal Realism', *Review of International Studies* (15) 319–28.
Hill, C. (2001) *The New Politics of Foreign Policy* (London, Macmillan).
Hinsley, F. H. (1963) *Power and the Pursuit of Peace* (Cambridge: Cambridge University Press).
Hinsley, F. H. (1966) *Sovereignty* (London: Hutchinson).
Hirst, P. and G. Thompson (1999) *Globalization in Question: The International Economy and the Possibilities of Governance* (Cambridge: Polity Press).
Hobbes, T. (1946) *Leviathan* (ed. with an introduction by M. Oakeshott) (Oxford: Basil Blackwell).
Hobson, J. A. (1902/1938) *Imperialism: A Study* (London: A. Constable).
Hobson, J. M. (2000) *The State and International Relations* (Cambridge: Cambridge University Press).
Hodges, M. (ed.) (1972) *European Integration* (Harmondsworth: Penguin).
Hoffmann, S. (1977) 'An American Social Science: International Relations', *Daedalus* (106) 41–61.
Hogan, M. (ed.) (1992) *The End of the Cold War: Its Meaning and Implications* (Cambridge: Cambridge University Press).
Holbraad, C. (1970) *Concert of Europe* (London: Longman).
Hollis, M. (1995) *The Philosophy of the Social Sciences* (Cambridge: Cambridge University Press).

276 *Bibliography*

Hollis, M. and S. Smith (1991) *Explaining and Understanding International Relations* (Oxford: Clarendon Press).
Howard, M. (1983) *Clausewitz* (Oxford: Oxford University Press).
Howell, L. D. (ed.) (1991/2) 'International Studies: The State of the Discipline', Special Issue, *International Studies Notes* (16/17) 1–68.
Hume, D. (1987) *Essays: Moral, Political and Literacy* (Indianapolis: Liberty Classics).
Huntington, S. (1993a) 'The Clash of Civilizations', *Foreign Affairs* (72) 22–49.
Huntington, S. (1993b) 'Response: If not Civilizations, What?', *Foreign Affairs* (72) 186–94.
Huntington, S. (1996) *The Clash of Civilizations and the Remaking of World Order* (New York: Simon & Schuster).
Hurrell, A. and B. Kingsbury (eds) (1992) *The International Politics of the Environment* (Oxford: Oxford University Press).
Ignatief, M. (2000) *Virtual War* (New York: Metropolitan Books).
Ikenberry, G. J. (1998) 'Constitutional Politics in International Relations', *European Journal of International Relations* (4) 147–77.
Ikenberry, G. J. (1998/1999) 'Institutions, Strategic Restraint and the Persistence of American Post-War Order', *International Security* (23) 43–78.
International Organization (1998) Special Issue: *'International Organization' at Fifty.*, P. Katzenstein, R. O. Keohane, and S. Krasner (eds) (52) 645–1012.
Jackson, R. (1990) *Quasi-States: Sovereignty, International Relations and the Third World* (Cambridge: Cambridge University Press).
Jackson, R and G. Sorenson (1999) *Introduction to International Relations* (Oxford: Oxford University Press).
Janis, I. (1972) *Victims of Groupthink* (Boston: Houghton Mifflin).
Jarvis, A. (1989) 'Societies, States and Geopolitics', *Review of International Studies* (15) 281–93.
Jervis, R. (1976) *Perception and Misperception in World Politics* (Princeton: Princeton University Press).
Jervis, R. (1999) 'Realism, Neoliberalism and Co-operation: Understanding the Debate', *International Security* (24) 42–63.
Joll, J. (1984) *The Origins of the First World War* (London: Longman).
Jones, A. (1996) 'Gendering International Relations', *Review of International Studies* (22) 405–29.
Jones, A. (1998) 'Engendering Debate', *Review of International Studies* (24) 299–303.
Jones, R. W. (1999) *Security, Strategy and Critical Theory* (Boulder, CO: Lynne Rienner).
Joy, B. (2000) 'Why the Future Doesn't Need Us', *Wired* (8.04) 238–62
Kaher, M. (ed.) (1986) *The Political Economy of International Debt* (Ithaca: Cornell University Press).
Kaplan, M. (1957) *System and Process in International Politics* (New York: Wiley).
Keegan, J. (1978) *The Face of Battle* (London: Jonathan Cape).
Kegley, C. W. (ed.) (1995) *Controversies in International Relations Theory: Realism and the Neoliberal Challenge* (New York: St Martin's Press).
Kegley, C. W. and E. Wittkopf (1999) *World Politics: Trend and Transformation*, 7th edn (New York: St Martin's Press).

Kennan, G. (1952) *American Diplomacy* (New York: New American Library).

Kennedy, P. (1981) *The Realities Behind Diplomacy* (London: Allen & Unwin).

Kennedy, P. (1988) *The Rise and Fall of the Great Powers* (London: Unwin, Hyman).

Kennedy, P. (1993) *Preparing for the Twenty-First Century* (New York: Random House).

Keohane, R. O. (1980) 'The Theory of Hegemonic Stability and Changes in International Economic Regimes 1967–1977', in O. Holsti *et al.*, *Change in the International System* (Boulder, CO: Westview Press) 132–62 (also in Keohane 1989).

Keohane, R. O. (1984) *After Hegemony* (Princeton: Princeton University Press).

Keohane, R. O. (ed.) (1986) *Neorealism and its Critics* (New York: Columbia University Press).

Keohane, R. O. (1988) 'International Institutions: Two Approaches', *International Studies Quarterly* (32) 379–96 (also in Keohane 1989).

Keohane, R. O. (1989) *International Institutions and State Power* (Boulder, CO: Westview Press).

Keohane, R. O. and S. Hoffmann (eds) (1991) *The New European Community* (Boulder, CO: Westview Press).

Keohane R. O. and J. S. Nye (eds) (1971) *Transnational Relations and World Politics* (Cambridge, MA: Harvard University Press).

Keohane, R. O. and J. S. Nye (1989) *Power and Interdependence* (Boston: Little Brown).

Keylor, W. (1992) *The Twentieth Century World: An International History* (New York: Oxford University Press).

Keynes, J. M. (1919) *The Economic Consequences of the Peace* (London: Macmillan).

Kindleberger, C. (1973) *The World in Depression 1929–1939* (Harmondsworth: Penguin).

Kissinger, H. (1994) *Diplomacy* (London: Simon & Schuster).

Knorr, K. and J. N. Rosenau (eds) (1969) *Contending Approaches to International Politics* (Princeton: Princeton University Press).

Koch, H. (ed.) (1972) *The Origins of the First World War* (London: Longman).

Krasner, S. D. (ed.) (1983) *International Regimes* (Ithaca: Cornell University Press).

Krasner, S. D. (1985) *Structural Conflict: The Third World Against Global Liberalism* (Berkeley: University of California Press).

Krasner, S. D. (1994) 'International Political Economy: Abiding Discord', *Review of International Political Economy* (1) 13–19.

Krasner, S. D. (1999) *Sovereignty: Organized Hypocrisy* (Princeton: Princeton University Press).

Kratochwil, F. (1989) *Rules, Norms and Decisions* (Cambridge: Cambridge University Press).

Kratochwil, F. (1995) 'Sovereignty as *Dominium*': Is there a Right of Humanitarian Intervention?', in Lyons and Mastanduno, *Beyond Westphalia?*

Kratochwil, F. (2000) 'Constructing a New Orthodoxy? Wendt's *Social Theory of International Politics* and the Constructivist Challenge', *Millennium: Journal of International Studies* (29) 73–101.

Kratochwil, F. and Y. Lapid (eds) (1996) *The Return of Culture and Identity in International Relations Theory* (Boulder, CO: Lynne Rienner).

Kratochwil, F. and E. Mansfield (eds) (1994) *International Organization: A Reader* (New York: HarperCollins).

Kratochwil, F. and J. G. Ruggie (1986) 'International Organisation: A State of the Art on the Art of the State', *International Organisation* (40) 753–75.

Krause, K. and M. C. Williams (eds) (1997) *Critical Security Studies: Concepts and Cases* (Minneapolis, MN: University of Minnesota Press).

Krugman, P. (1994) *Rethinking International Trade* (Cambridge, MA: MIT Press).

Krugman, P. (1996) *Pop Internationalism* (Cambridge, MA: MIT Press).

Krugman, P. (1998) *The Accidental Theorist and Other Despatches from the Dismal Science* (Cambridge, MA: MIT Press).

Krugman, P. and M. Obstfeld (2000) *International Economics: Theory and Policy* (New York: HarperCollins).

Kubálkova, V., N. Onuf, and P. Kowert (1998) *International Relations in a Constructed World* (Armonk, NY: M. E. Sharpe).

Laclau, E. (1976) *Politics and Ideology in Marxist Theory* (London: New Left Books).

LaFeber, W. (1999) *Michael Jordan and the New Global Capitalism* (New York: Norton).

Lakatos, I. and A. Musgrave (eds) (1970) *Criticism and the Growth of Knowledge* (Cambridge: Cambridge University Press).

Lake, D. (1988) *Power, Protection and Free Trade: International Sources of US Commercial Strategy, 1887–1939* (Ithaca: Cornell University Press).

Lake, D. (1992) 'Powerful Pacifists: Democratic States and War', *American Political Science Review* (86) 24–37.

Lake, D. (1993) 'Leadership, Hegemony and the International Economy: Naked Emperor or Tattered Monarch with Potential', *International Studies Quarterly* (33) 459–89.

Lal, D. (1983) *The Poverty of 'Development Economics'* (London: Institute of Economic Affairs).

Lapid, Y. (1989) 'The Third Debate: On the Prospects of International Theory in a Post-Positivist Era', *International Studies Quarterly* (33) 235–54.

Layne, C. (1994) 'Kant or Cant: the Myth of the Democratic Peace' *International Security* (19) 2, 5–49.

Lebow, R. N. (1981) *Between Peace and War: The Nature of International Crisis* (Baltimore, MD: Johns Hopkins University Press).

Lebow, R. N. and T. Risse-Kappen (eds) (1995) *International Relations Theory and the End of the Cold War* (New York: Columbia University Press).

Lebow, R. N. and J. Stein (1994) *We All Lost the Cold War* (Princeton: Princeton University Press).

Legro, J. W. and A. Moravcsik (1999) 'Is Anybody Still a Realist'? *International Security* (24) 25–55.

Levi-Faur, D. (1997) 'Economic Nationalism: From Friedrich List to Robert Reich', *Review of International Studies* (23) 359–70.

Levy, M. A., O. R. Young and M. Zürn (1995) 'The Study of International Regimes', *European Journal of International Relations* (1) 267–330.

Light, M. and A. J. R. Groom (eds) (1985) *International Relations: A Handbook in Current Theory* (London: Pinter Publishers).

Linklater, A. (1990) *Beyond Realism and Marxism* (London: Macmillan).

Linklater, A. (1992) 'The Question of the Next Stage in International Relations Theory: A Critical-Theoretic Approach', *Millennium* (21) 77–98.

Linklater, A. (1998) *The Transformation of Political Community* (Cambridge: Polity Press).

Liska, G. (1990) *The Ways of Power: Patterns and Meanings in World Politics* (Oxford: Basil Blackwell).

List, F. (1966) *The National System of Political Economy* (London: Frank Cass).

Little, I. M. D. (1982) *Economic Development: Theory, Policy, and International Relations* (New York: Basic Books).

Little, R. (1994) 'International Relations and Large Scale Historical Change', in Groom and Light, *Contemporary International Relations*.

Little, R. and M. Smith (eds) (1991) *Perspectives on World Politics: A Reader* (London: Routledge).

Loescher, G. (1993) *Beyond Charity: International Co-operation and the Global Refugee Crisis* (New York: Oxford University Press).

Long, D. and P. Wilson (eds) (1995) *Thinkers of the Twenty Years Crisis: Interwar Idealism Reassessed* (Oxford: Clarendon Press).

Lukes, S. (1974) *Power: A Radical View* (London: Macmillan).

Lynn-Jones, S. M. and S. Miller (eds) (1995) *Global Dangers: Changing Dimensions of International Security* (Cambridge, MA: MIT Press).

Lyons, G.M. and M. Mastanduno (eds) (1995) *Beyond Westphalia?* (Baltimore, MD: Johns Hopkins Press).

MacMillan, J. (1996) 'Democracies Don't Fight: A Case of the Wrong Research Agenda', *Review of International Studies* (22) 275–99.

MacMillan, J. and A. Linklater (eds) (1995) *Boundaries in Question* (London: Pinter Publishers).

Macridis, R. C. (ed.) (1992) *Foreign Policy in World Politics* (London: Prentice-Hall).

Mahbubani, K. (1992) 'The West and The Rest', *The National Interest* (28) 3–13.

Mann, M. (1986/1993) *The Sources of Social Power*, Vols I and II (Cambridge: Cambridge University Press).

Mannheim, K. (1936/1960) *Ideology and Utopia* (London: Routledge & Kegan Paul).

Martel, G. (ed.) (1986) *The Origins of the Second World War Reconsidered: The A. J. P. Taylor Debate after Twenty-Five Years* (Boston: Allen & Unwin).

Mayall, J. (ed.) (1996) *The New Interventionism: 1991–1994* (Cambridge: Cambridge University Press).

McGrew, A. *et al.* (1992) *Global Politics: Globalisation and the Nation State* (Milton Keynes: Open University Press).

McSweeney, B. (1996) 'Identity and Security: Buzan and the Copenhagen School', *Review of International Studies* (22) 81–94.

McSweeney, B. (1998) 'Durkheim and the Copenhagen School', *Review of International Studies* (24) 137–40.

Meadows, Donnella *et al.* (1974) *Limits to Growth* (London: Pan).

Mearsheimer, J. (1990) 'Back to the Future: Instability in Europe after the Cold War', *International Security* (15) 5–56 (and collected in M. E. Brown (1995)).

Mearsheimer, J. (1994/5) 'The False Promise of International Institutions', *International Security* (19) 5–49 (and collected in M. E. Brown *et al.* (1995)).

Meinecke, F. (1957) *Machiavellism: The Doctrine of Raison D'Etat and its Place in Modern History* (London: Routledge & Kegan Paul).

Millennium (1991) 'Sovereignty at Bay, 20 Years After', Special Issue (20) 198–307.

Millennium (1995) 'The Globalization of Liberalism', Special Issue (24) 377–576.

Millennium (2000) 'Seattle December 1999' (29) 103–40.

Mitrany, D. (1966) *A Working Peace System* (Chicago: Quadrangle Books).

Mitrany, D. (1975) *The Functional Theory of Politics* (London: Martin Robertson).

Modelski, G. (1987) *Long Cycles in World Politics* (London: Macmillan).

Mohamed, M. Bin and S. Ishihara (1996) *The Voice of Asia: Two Leaders Discuss the Coming Century* (Tokyo: Kodansha International Ltd).

Moore, J. (ed.) (1998) *Hard Choices: Moral Dilemmas in Humanitarian Intervention* (Lanham, MD: Rowman & Littlefield).

Moravcsik, A. (1997) 'Taking Preferences Seriously: The Liberal Theory of International Politics', *International Organization* (51) 513–53.

Moravcsik, A. (1998) *The Choice for Europe: Social Purpose and State Power from Messina to Maastricht* (Ithaca: Cornell University Press).

Morgenthau, H. J. (1948) *Politics Among Nations: The Struggle for Power and Peace* (New York: Alfred P. Knopf) (5th edn 1978).

Murphy, C. (1994) *International Organization and Industrial Change: Global Governance Since 1850* (Cambridge: Polity Press).

Murphy, C. and R. Tooze (eds) (1991) *The New International Political Economy* (Boulder, CO: Lynne Reinner).

Murray, A. J. (1996a) 'The Moral Politics of Hans Morgenthau', *The Review of Politics* (58) 81–107.

Murray, Alastair (1996b) *Reconstructing Realism* (Edinburgh: Keele University Press).

Nardin, T. (1983) *Law, Morality and the Relations of States* (Princeton: Princeton University Press).

Nardin, T. (ed.) (1996) *The Ethics of War and Peace* (Princeton: Princeton University Press).

Nardin, T. and D. Mapel (eds) (1992) *Traditions of International Ethics* (Cambridge: Cambridge University Press).

Neufeld, M. (1995) *The Restructuring of International Relations Theory* (Cambridge: Cambridge University Press).

Nicholas, H. G. (1985) *The United Nations as a Political System* (Oxford: Oxford University Press).

Nicholson, M. (1996) *Causes and Consequences in International Relations: A Conceptual Survey* (London: Pinter Publishers).

Niebuhr, R. (1932) *Moral Man and Immoral Society* (New York: Charles Scribner's Sons).

Nye, J. (1971) *Peace in Parts* (Boston: Little Brown).

Nye, J. S. (1988) 'Neorealism and Neoliberalism', *World Politics* (40) 235–51.

Nye, J. S. (1990) *Bound to Lead: The Changing Nature of American Power* (New York: Basic Books).

Oberdorfer, D. (1991) *The Turn: How the Cold War Came to an End* (London: Cape).

Ohmae, K. (1990) *The Borderless World* (London: Collins).

Olson, W. C. and A. J. R. Groom (1992) *International Relations Then and Now* (London: Pinter Publishers).

Onuf, N. (1989) *World of Our Making* (Columbia, SC: University of South Carolina Press).

Onuf, N. (1995) 'Levels', *European Journal of International Relations* (1) 35–58.

Overton, R. (2000) 'Molecular electronics will change everything', *Wired* (8.07) 240–51.

Palan, R. and J. Abbott (1996) *State Strategies in the Global Political Economy* (London: Pinter Press).

Pape, R. A. (1997) 'Why Economic Sanctions Do Not Work', *International Security* (22) 90–136.

Pape, R. A. (1998) 'Why Economic Sanctions *Still* Do Not Work', *International Security* (23) 66–77.

Paret, P. (ed.) (1986) *Makers of Modern Strategy from Machiavelli to the Nuclear Age* (Princeton: Princeton University Press).

Peters, J. S. and A. Wolper (eds) (1995) *Women's Rights, Human Rights: International Feminist Perspectives* (New York: Routledge).

Peterson, V. S. (ed.) (1992) *Gendered States: Feminist (Re) Visions of International Relations Theory* (Boulder, CO: Lynne Reinner).

Pijl, K Van der (1998) *Transnational Classes and International Relations* (London: Routledge).

Polanyi, K. (1975) *The Great Transformation* (Boston: Beacon Books).

Porter, B. (ed.) (1969) *The Aberystwyth Papers* (Oxford: Oxford University Press).

Porter, G. and J. Welsh Brown (1991) *Global Environmental Politics* (Boulder, CO: Westview Press).

Posen, B. (2000) 'The War for Kosovo: Serbia's Political Military Strategy,' *International Security* (24) 39–84.

Powell, R. (1991) 'Absolute and Relative Gains in International Relations Theory', *American Political Science Review* (85) 1303–20.

Powell, R. (1994) 'Anarchy in International Relations: The Neoliberal–Neorealist Debate', *International Organization* (48) 313–34.

Prebisch, R. (1950) *The Economic Development of Latin America and its Principal Problems* (New York: United Nations).

Price, R. and C. Reus-Smit (1998) 'Dangerous Liaisons: Critical International Theory and Constructivism', *European Journal of International Relations* (4) 259–94.

Ramsbotham, O. and T. Woodhouse (1996) *Humanitarian Intervention in Contemporary Conflict* (Cambridge: Polity Press).

Reich, R. (1992) *The Work of Nations* (New York: Vintage).

Reiss, H. (ed.) (1970) *Kant's Political Writings* (Cambridge: Cambridge University Press).

Review of International Studies (1999a) Special Issue: *The Interregnum* (25) (also published as M. Cox, K. Booth and T. Dunne (eds) (1999) *The Interregnum* (Cambridge: Cambridge University Press).

Review of International Studies (1999b) Forum on Andrew Linklater's *The Transformation of Political Community* (25) 139–75.

Review of International Studies (2000) Forum on Alexander Wendt's *Social Theory of International Politics* (26) 123–80.

Ricardo, D. (1971) *Principles of Political Economy and Taxation* (Harmondsworth: Penguin).

Richardson, J. L. (1994) *Crisis Diplomacy* (Cambridge: Cambridge University Press).

Risse-Kappen, T. (ed.) (1995) *Bringing Transnational Relations Back In: Non-State Actors, Domestic Structures and International Institutions* (Cambridge: Cambridge University Press).

Rittberger, V. (ed.) (1993) *Regime Theory and International Relations* (Oxford: Oxford University Press).

Rittberger, V. and A. Schnabel. (eds) (2000) *The UN Global Governance System in the Twenty-First Century* (Tokyo: United Nations University Press).

Roberts, A. and R. Guelff (eds) (2000) *Documents on the Laws of War* (Oxford: Oxford University Press).

Roberts, A. and B. Kingsbury (eds) (1993) *United Nations, Divided World: The UN's Role in International Relations* (Oxford: Oxford University Press).

Robertson, E. M. (ed.) (1971) *The Origins of the Second World War: Historical Interpretations* (London: Macmillan).

Rodney, W. (1983) *How Europe Underdeveloped Africa* (London: Bogle-Louverture). Rorty, R. (1998) 'The End of Leninism, Havel, and Social Hope', in *Truth and Progress: Philosophical Papers Vol. 3* (Cambridge: Cambridge University Press).

Rosenau, J. N. (ed.) (1967) *Domestic Sources of Foreign Policy* (New York: Free Press).

Rosenau, J. N. (ed.) (1969) *International Politics and Foreign Policy: A Reader* (New York: Free Press).

Rosenau, J. N. (1997) *Along the Domestic-Foreign Frontier: Exploring Governance in a Turbulent World* (Cambridge: Cambridge University Press).

Rosenau, J. N. and E.-O. Czempiel (eds) (1992) *Governance without Government: Order and Change in World Politics* (Cambridge: Cambridge University Press).

Rosenberg, J. (1994) *The Empire of Civil Society* (London: Verso).

Rosenthal, J. (1991) *Righteous Realists* (Baton Rouge, LA: University of Louisiana Press).

Ruggie, J. G. (1982) 'International Regimes, Transactions and Change: Embedded Liberalism in the Postwar Economic Order', *International Organization* (36) 379–415.

Ruggie, J. G. (1983) 'Continuity and Transformation in the World Polity: Towards a NeoRealist Synthesis', *World Politics* (35) 261–85.

Ruggie, J. G. (1998) *Constructing the World Polity* (London: Routledge).

Russett, B. (1993) *Grasping the Democratic Peace: Principles for a Post-Cold War World* (Princeton: Princeton University Press).

Russett, B., J. L. Ray and R. Cohen (1995) 'Raymond Cohen on Pacific Unions: A Response and a Reply', *Review of International Studies* (21) 319–25.

Sachs, W. (ed.) (1993) *Global Ecology: A New Arena of Political Conflict* (London: Zed Books).

Sagan, S. D. and K. Waltz (1995) *The Spread of Nuclear Weapons* (New York: W. W. Norton).

Sakakiba, E. (1995) 'The End of Progressivism: A Search for New Goals', *Foreign Affairs* (74) 8–15.

Sassen, S. (1998) *Globalization and its Discontents* (New York: New Press).

Sassen, S. (2000) *Cities in a World Economy* (Thousand Oaks CA: Pine Forge Press).

Schelling, T. (1960) *The Strategy of Conflict* (Cambridge, MA: Harvard University Press).

Schmidt, B. (1998) *The Political Discourse of Anarchy: A Disciplinary History of International Relations* (Albany, NY: State University of New York Press).

Schmitt, C. (1932/1996) *The Concept of the Political* (Chicago: University of Chicago Press).

Scholte, J. A. (2000) *Globalization* (London: Macmillan).

Schroeder, P. (1994) 'Historical Reality vs. Neo-Realist Theory', *International Security* (19) 108–48 (and collected in M. E. Brown 1995).

Searle, J. (1995) *The Construction of Social Reality* (London: Allen Lane).

Sen, A. (1982) *Poverty and Famine* (Oxford: Clarendon Press).

Sen, A. (2000) *Development and Freedom* (Cambridge: Cambridge University Press).

Sewell, J. P. (1966) *Functionalism and World Politics* (Princeton: Princeton University Press).

Shapiro, M. and H. R. Alker (eds) (1996) *Challenging Boundaries: Global Flows, Territorial Identities* (Minneapolis, MN: University of Minnesota Press).

Shaw, M. (ed.) (1999) *Politics and Globalization: Knowledge, Ethics and Agency* (London: Routledge).

Shawcross, W. (2000) *Deliver Us From Evil: Warlords and Peacekeepers in a World of Endless Conflict* (London: Bloomsbury).

Shonfield, A. (ed.) (1976) *International Economic Relations of the Western World 1959–1971*, Vol. I, *Politics and Trade* (Shonfield *et al.*), Vol. II, *International Monetary Relations* (Susan Strange) (Oxford: Oxford University Press).

Singer, J. D. *et al.* (1979) *Explaining War* (London: Sage Publications).

Sklair, L. (1995) *The Sociology of the Global System* (Hemel Hempstead: Harvester Wheatsheaf).

Smith, H. (1994) 'Marxism and International Relations', in Groom and Light, *Contemporary International Relations*.

Smith, K. E. and M. M. Light (eds) (2001) *Ethics and Foreign Policy* (Cambridge: Cambridge University Press).

Smith, M. J. (1986) *Realist Thought from Weber to Kissinger* (Baton Rouge, LA: University of Louisiana Press).

Smith, S. (1986) 'Theories of Foreign Policy: An Historical Overview', *Review of International Studies* (12) 13–29.

Smith, S. (1997) 'Power and Truth: A Reply to William Wallace', *Review of International Studies* (23) 507–16.

Smith, S., K. Booth and M. Zalewski (eds) (1996) *International Theory: Post-Positivist Perspectives* (Cambridge: Cambridge University Press).

Smith, S. and M. Clarke (eds) (1985) *Foreign Policy Implementation* (London: Allen & Unwin).

Spero, J. (1997) *The Politics of International Economic Relations* (London: Allen & Unwin).

Springsteen, B. (1995) 'The Ghost of Tom Joad', Sony Records.

Spykman, N. (1942) *America's Strategy in World Politics* (New York: Harcourt Brace).

Steans, J. (1998) *Gender and International Relations: An Introduction* (Cambridge: Polity Press).

Stein, A. (1982) 'Coordination and Collaboration: Regimes in an Anarchic World', *International Organization* (36) 294–324.

Stiglitz, J. (1998) *More Instruments and Broader Goals: Moving Towards the Post-Washington Consensus* (Helsinki: UN University Press).

Stoessinger, J. G. (1990) *Why Nations Go to War* (New York: St Martin's Press).

Stopford, J. and S. Strange (1991) *Rival States, Rival Firms: Competition for World Market Shares* (Cambridge: Cambridge University Press).

Strange, S. (1970) 'International Economics and International Relations: A Case of Mutual Neglect, *International Affairs* (46) 304–15.

Strange, S. (1971) *Sterling and British Policy* (Oxford: Oxford University Press).

Strange, S. (1985) 'Protectionism and World Politics', *International Organization* (39) 233–59.

Strange, S. (1986) *Casino Capitalism* (Oxford: Basil Blackwell).

Strange, S. (1987) 'The Persistent Myth of Lost Hegemony', *International Organization*, (41) 551–74.

Strange, S. (1988) *States and Markets* (London: Pinter Publishers).

Strange, S. (1992) 'States, Firms and Diplomacy', *International Affairs* (68) 1–15.

Strange, S. (1994) 'Wake up Krasner! The World *Has* Changed', *Review of International Political Economy* (1) 209–219.

Strange, S. (1996) *The Retreat of the State* (Cambridge: Cambridge University Press).

Strange, S. (1998a) 'Globaloney', *Review of International Political Economy* (5) 704–711.

Strange, S. (1998b) *Mad Money* (Manchester: Manchester University Press).

Strange, S. (1999) 'The Westfailure System', *Review of International Studies* (25) 345–354.

Stubbs, R. and G. Underhill (eds) (1999) *Political Economy and the Changing Global Order* (London: Macmillan).

Suganami, H. (1990) 'Bringing Order to the Causes of War Debate', *Millennium* (19) 19–35.

Suganami, H. (1996) *On the Causes of War* (Oxford: Clarendon Press).

Sylvester, C (1994) *Feminist Theory and International Relations in a Post-Modern Era* (Cambridge: Cambridge University Press).

Taylor, A. J. P. (1961) *The Origins of the Second World War* (London: Hamish Hamilton).

Taylor, C. (1971) 'Interpretation and the Sciences of Man', *Review of Metaphysics* (25) 3–51.

Taylor, P. (1993) *International Organization in the Modern World* (London: Pinter Publishers).

Taylor, P. and A. J. R. Groom (eds) (1978) *International Organization: A Conceptual Approach* (London: Pinter Publishers).

Taylor, P. and A. J. R. Groom (eds) (1989) *Global Issues in the United Nations Framework* (London: Macmillan).

Taylor, P. and A. J. R. Groom (1992) *The UN and the Gulf War, 1990–1991: Back to the Future* (London: Royal Institute of International Affairs).

Thomas, C. (1987) *In Search of Security: The Third World in International Relations* (Brighton: Wheatsheaf Books).

Thomas, C. (1992) *The Environment in International Relations* (London: RIIA).

Thomas, C. (ed.) (1994) 'Rio: Unravelling the Consequences', Special Issue, *Environmental Politics* (2) 1–241.

Thomas, C. and P. Wilkin (eds) (1999) *Globalization and the South* (London: Macmillan).

Tickner, J. A. (1989) 'Hans Morgenthau's Principles of Political Realism: A Feminist Reformulation', *Millennium* (17) 429–40.

Tickner, J. A. (1992) *Gender in International Relations* (New York: Columbia University Press).

Tilly, C. (ed.) (1975) *The Formation of National States in Western Europe* (Princeton: Princeton University Press).

Tilly, C. (1990) *Coercion, Capital and European States AD 990–1990* (Oxford: Basil Blackwell).

Toffler, A. and H. Toffler (1993) *War and Anti-War* (Boston: Little, Brown).

Tomlinson, J. (1999) *Globalization and Culture* (Cambridge: Polity Press).

Treitschke, H. von (1916/1963) *Politics* (abridged and ed. by Hans Kohn) (New York: Harcourt, Brace and World).

Tucker, R. W. and D. C. Hendrickson (1992) *The Imperial Temptation: The New World Order and America's Purpose* (New York: Council on Foreign Relations).

Turner, L. and M. Hodges (1992) *Global Shakeout* (London: Century Business).

United Nations (1995) *Our Global Neighborhood: Report of the Commission on Global Governance.* (New York: United Nations).

Van Evera, S. (1998) 'Offence, Defence and the Causes of War', *International Security* (22) 5–43.

Van Evera, S. (1999) *Causes of War: Power and the Roots of Conflict* (Ithaca, NY: Cornell University Press).

Vernon, R. (1971) *Sovereignty at Bay* (New York: Basic Books).

Veseth, M. (1998) *Selling Globalization: The Myth of the Global Economy* (Border, CO: Lynne Rienner).

Vincent, R. J. (1986) *Human Rights and International Relations: Issues and Responses* (Cambridge: Cambridge University Press).

Viotti, P. and M. Kauppi (1993) *International Relations Theory* (New York: Macmillan).

Vogler, J. (1995) *The Global Commons: A Regime Analysis* (New York: Wiley & Sons).

Vogler, J. and M. Imber (eds) (1995) *The Environment and International Relations* (London: Routledge).

Waever, O. (1996) 'The Rise and Fall of the Inter-paradigm Debate', in Smith, Booth and Zalewski, *International Theory.*

Walker, R. B. J. (1993) *Inside/Outside: International Relations as Political Theory* (Cambridge: Cambridge University Press).

Wallace, W. (1994) *Regional Integration: The West European Experience* (Washington, DC: Brookings Institute).

Wallace, W. (1996) 'Truth and Power, Monks and Technocrats: Theory and Practice in International Relations', *Review of International Studies* (22) 301–21.

Wallace, W. (1999a) 'The Sharing of Sovereignty: The European Paradox', *Political Studies* (47) 503–21.

Wallace, W. (1999b) 'Europe after the Cold War: Interstate Order or Post-Sovereign Regional System', *Review of International Studies* (25) 201–33.

Wallerstein, I. (1974/1980/1989) *The Modern World System*, Vols I, II and III (London: Academic Press).

Wallerstein, I. (1991a) *Geopolitics and Geoculture: Essays on the Changing World System* (Cambridge: Cambridge University Press).

Wallerstein, I. (1991b) *Unthinking Social Science: The Limits of Nineteenth Century Paradigms* (Cambridge: Polity Press).

Walt, S. (1985) 'Alliance Formation and the Balance of World Power', *International Security* (9) 3–43 (and collected in M. E. Brown (1995)).

Walt, S. (1987) *The Origin of Alliances* (Ithaca, NY: Cornell University Press).

Walt, S. (1991) 'The Renaissance of Security Studies', *International Studies Quarterly* (35) 211–39.

Waltz, K. (1959) *Man, the State and War* (New York: Columbia University Press).

Waltz, K. (1979) *Theory of International Politics* (Reading, MA: Addison-Wesley).

Waltz, K. (1990) 'Realist Thought and Neorealist Theory', *Journal of International Affairs*, (44) 21–37.

Waltz, K. (1993) 'The Emerging Structure of International Politics', *International Security* (18) 44–79 (and collected in M. E. Brown (1995)).

Waltz, K. (1997) 'Evaluating Theories', *American Political Science Review* (91) 913–18.

Waltz, K. (1998) 'An Interview with Kenneth Waltz' (conducted by Fred Halliday and Justin Rosenberg), *Review of International Studies* (24) 371–86.

Waltz, K. (2000) 'Structural Realism after the Cold War', *International Security* (25)(1) 5–41.

Walzer, M. (1992) *Just and Unjust Wars*, 2nd edn (New York: Basic Books).

Warren, B. (1980) *Imperialism: Pioneer of Capitalism* (London: New Left Books).

Watson, A. (1982) *Diplomacy: The Dialogue of States* (London: Methuen).

Watson, A. (1992) *The Evolution of International Society: A Comparative Historical Analysis* (London: Routledge).

Watt, D. C. (1989) *How War Came* (London: Heinemann).

Weber, C. (1999) *Faking It: US Hegemony in a 'Post-Phallic' Era* (Minneapolis, MN: University of Minnesota Press).

Wee, H. Van der (1986) *Prosperity and Upheaval 1945–1980* (Harmondsworth: Penguin).

Weinberg, G. L. (1994) *A World at Arms: A Global History of World War II* (Cambridge: Cambridge University Press).

Weiss, T. G. (1999) *Military–Civil Interactions: Intervening in Humanitarian Crises* (Lanham, MD: Rowman & Littlefield).

Welch, D. A. (1992) 'The Organizational Process and Bureaucratic Politics Paradigm', *International Security* (17) 112–46.

Wendt, A. (1987) 'The Agent/Structure Problem in International Relations Theory', *International Organization* (41) 335–70.

Wendt, A. (1992) 'Anarchy is What States Make of It: The Social Construction of Power Politics', *International Organization* (46) 391–426.

Wendt, A. (1999) *Social Theory of International Politics* (Cambridge: Cambridge University Press).

Wheeler, N. J. (1992) 'Pluralist and Solidarist Conceptions of International Society: Bull and Vincent on Humanitarian Intervention', *Millennium* (21) 463–87.

Wheeler, N. J. (2000) *Saving Strangers* (Oxford: Oxford University Press).

White, B. (1999) 'The European Challenge to Foreign Policy Analysis', *European Journal of International Relations* (5) 37–66.

Wiener, J. (1995) 'Hegemonic Leadership: Naked Emperor or the Worship of False Gods', *European Journal of International Relations* (1) 219–43.

Wight, M. (1946/1978) *Power Politics*, 2nd edn (Leicester: Leicester University Press).

Wight, M. (1977) *Systems of States* (Leicester: Leicester University Press).

Willetts, P. (ed.) (1983) *Pressure Groups in the International System* (London: Pinter).

Williamson, J. (1990) 'What Washington Means by Policy Reform' in Williamson (ed.) *Latin American Adjustment: How Much Has Changed* (Washington: Institute for International Economics).

Williamson, J. and C. Milner (1991) *The World Economy* (Hemel Hempstead: Harvester Wheatsheaf).

Wohlforth, W. (1994/5) 'Realism and the End of the Cold War', *International Security* (19) 91–129.

Wohlforth, W. C. (1999) 'The Stability of a Unipolar World', *International Security* (24) 5–41.

Wright, M. (ed.) (1989) 'The Balance of Power', Special Issue, *Review of International Studies* (15) 77–214.

Young, O. *et al.* (1996) *Global Environmental Change and International Governance* (Hanover, NH: University Press of New England).

Zacher, M. with B. A. Sutton (1996) *Governing Global Networks: International Regimes for Transport and Communication* (Cambridge: Cambridge University Press).

Zakaria, F. (1992) 'Realism and Domestic Politics: A Review Essay', *International Security* (17) 177–98.

Zakaria, F. (1999) *From Wealth to Power* (Princeton: Princeton University Press).

Zalewski, M. and J. Papart (eds) (1997) *The 'Man' Question in International Relations* (Boulder, CO: Westview Press)

Index